Holistic London

The London Guide to Mind, Body & Spirit

Kate Brady
Mike Considine

Brainwave • London

Acknowledgements

Book reviews
Brian Wade of Changes Bookshop for reviews in the Psychotherapy Section
David Redstone and staff at Watkins Bookshop for reviews in Body and Spirit section

Writers
Will Parfitt for the section on Qabalah
Richard Mowbray for the section on Primal Integration

Anecdote writers
Gill Stow, Karin Grey, Malcolm Stern, Sabine Kurjo McNeil, Alex Read, Anne Turner, David Templar, Christine Davidson, Sue Anne Deakin, Andy Hilton, Sue Woen, Imogen Fox, Mary Fee, Maureen Kennedy.

Production team
Danielle Juving, Gill Stow, Karin Grey, Ofra Anker, Sarah Giles, Ralph Manning

Other help
Thanks also to: The Institute of Complementary Medicine, Malcolm Stern, William Bloom, Stephanie Collins and Guy Dauncey for information; Tony Day for emergency computer counselling.

Further copies of this book
These can be obtained from Brainwave, BCM Raft, London WC1N 3XX. Please send £9.95 plus £1.50 post and packing (UK only).

Published by Brainwave
BCM Raft
London WC1N 3XX

© Brainwave November 1991

Printed in Great Britain by BPCC Wheatons Ltd, Exeter.

Cover illustration by Bodel Rikys

ISBN 0 9513347 4 3

Published November 1991

Line illustrations from a selection of Dover Publications Inc. New York, copyright free books.

Like to write about your experience?

We are looking for anecdotes and stories about readers' experiences of psychotherapy, alternative medicine, spiritual approaches and aspects of holistic health and growth, for the next edition.

If you would like to contribute, send your stories to us at **Brainwave BCM Raft, London WC1N 3XX**. Stories should be a maximum of 350 words long, and names of real people or organisations should be omitted or changed. You will be credited in the book (though you may retain anonymity if you wish) and receive a free copy of the edition in which your story is published.

Looking forward to hearing from you!

Like to be listed in the next edition?

Inclusion in the listings of Holistic London is *free*. If you would like your centre or organisation to be included in the next edition of Holistic London, or know of a centre or organisation which you think would like to be included, please fill in the form below (alternatively put us on your mailing list so that we receive you brochure) and send to **Brainwave, BCM Raft, London WC1N 3XX.**

- -

Please include me in the next edition of Holistic London.

Name of contact in organisation_____

Organisation_____

Address_____

_____

_____

Telephone number_____

Type of organisation (e.g. psychotherapy or natural therapies centre, spiritual group etc)

_____

Any other comments_____

_____

PSYCHOTHERAPY

Introduction

Training in Psychotherapy

The Psychotherapies

Other Psychotherapies

Eclectic or Special Trainings 85

BODY THERAPIES

Introduction
Alternative and Complementary Medicine 90 • The Holistic Approach 91 • Diagnosis 92 • Choosing a Particular Therapy 94 • Finding the Right Practitioner 96 • Length and cost of treatment 97 • What the Centres are Like 97 • Finding Practitioners Outside the Centres 98

Training in Body Therapies 98
Why Train? 98 • Finding the Right Course 99 • Entry Requirements 100 • Getting Clients 101 • Future Legislation Governing Practitioners - 1992 101 • Useful Contacts 102

The Body Therapies

Other Body Therapies 168
Active Birth 168 • Aston Patterning 168 • Cranial Osteopathy 168 • Hellerwork 168 • Laser Therapy 168 • Magnetic Therapy 168 • Nutritional Counselling/diet Therapy 168 • Postural Integration 169 • Rebalancing 169 • Reiki 169 • Tibetan Medicine 169

Other Trainings 169
Active Birth 169 • Diet Therapy/nutritional Counselling 169 • Macrobiotics 170

Eclectic/Special Trainings 170

SPIRIT

Introduction
The Difference between Religion and Spirituality 172 • The Search for a New Spirituality 172 • East meets West 173 • Gurus and spiritual teachers 174 • Cults 175 • What they do 177 • Spiritual Groups in London 178 • Spirituality versus Psychology 178 • The 'New Age' 179

Meditation 180

The Traditions 182
Buddhism 182 • Christianity 184 • Paganism 188 • Qabalah 189 • Shamanism 190 • Spiritualism 191 • Sufism 193

Modern Teachers 194

Other Groups 199

RESOURCES

Communication 203
Bookshops 203 • New Age Shops 208 • Libraries 208 • Publishers and Distributors 208 • Films 211 • Magazines & Publications 211 • Networks 214

Products 216
Air Purifiers 216 • Aromatherapy Oils 216 • Back Products 218 • Biofeedback Machines 219 • Biorythm Charts 220 • Birthing Pools 220 • Books 220 • Clothes And Shoes 221 • Cruelty Free Products 221 • Crystals 221 • Daylight Bulbs 223 • Diy Acupuncture 223 • Ethically Sound Investments 223 • Float Tanks 223 • Food Products 224 • Futons 224 • Games 224 • Herbs And Herbal Remedies 224 • Homoeopathic Pharmacies 225 • Ionisers 226 • Jewellery 227 • Juicers 227 • Martial Arts Suppliers 228 • Massage Aids 228 • Miscellaneous 229 • Natural Birth Control Equipment 229 • Nutritional Supplements 229 • Organic Wine 229 • Pollution Control 230 • Posters And Prints 230 • Tapes - Personal Development 230 • Tapes (music) 231 • Tapes (relaxation) 233 • Treatment Couches 233 • Videos 233 • Water Purifiers 233

Education 235
Adult Education 235 • Recognised Academic Courses 235

Services 236
Ethically Sound Investments 236 • dating agencies 238 • Rooms For Hire 238 • Practitioners Services 239

Food 241
Macrobiotics 241 • Vegetarianism and Veganism 242 • Vegetarian Restaurants 243

London Getaway 246
Residential Communities 246 • Residential Health Centres 247 • Residential Workshops 247 • Retreats 251 • Holidays 252

Events 254
Lectures 254 • Festivals 255 • Galleries And Museums 255 • Other Events 256

Help 257
Organisations For 257 • Specific Problems 257 • Useful Organisations 258

LIST OF CENTRES 263

Whole Person Catalogue

psychotherapy • complementary medicine • spiritual groups • metaphysical groups • s e r v i c e s • p r oducts education • holidays • networks • bookshops resources • list of centres • residentials • new age shops • contacts • books • events • courses

The UK Guide to Mind Body & Spirit

Survivors London

the capital's foremost alternative guide

HOUSING • SEX • GREEN ISSUES • LAW BARGAINS • MEDIA • SELF DISCOVERY • DRUGS • COMMUNICATIONS • DIY • WOMEN • COMPUTERS • PUBLISHING KIDS • ALTERNATIVE MEDICINE • ARTS TRAVEL • ETHNIC MINORITIES • BENEFITS BUSINESS • LESBIANS & GAYS • JOBS • CONTACTS • NETWORKS • FOOD • EMERGENCY • HELP • AND MUCH MORE

304pp p/b Illustrated 0 951486306
£6.95 + £1 p/p

— not just for Londoners

Mailing Lists

If you need to send your brochure/leaflet to individuals or organisations in the holistic health/ New Age field, we have a range of mailing lists on offer. Our laser printed address labels are high quality at a very affordable price.

BCM Raft, London WC1N 3XX
(071) 733 7883 or (071) 978 9062
serving holistic business

Who are we?

Brainwave is a publisher and marketing specialist serving the Holistic health/New Age field. We serve publishers of books, audio and visual tapes, product suppliers and holistic health centres.

Trade Directory (USA)

Brainwave are agents for 'First Editions' a publishing company in the USA that produces a trade directory for the holistic health/New Age field. Our own trade directory is based on their excellent guide to the USA New Age marketplace. We have both volumes of this directory for sale.

Guidebooks

We publish two guidebooks aimed at the public who are interested in the holistic health/New Age field. This book *Holistic London*, now in it's third edition is packed with information on psychotherapy, alternative medicine and spiritual centres in the capital, as well as a list of resources including bookshops, products etc. It's an easy to use guidebook which has stood the test of time and is the only book of its kind for London. *The Whole Person Catalogue* is new and is destined to be the definitive nationwide guide to this growing field.

Co-operative Mailings

We mail out on a regular basis to individuals and businesses in the holistic health/New Age field. If you wish to reach this specialist market we can include your brochure/leaflet in our mailings. This is a cost effective way to promote yourself. You simply supply the leaflets and we take care of the rest. We have regular mailouts to *retailers, centres, core advertisers and the general public.*

Marketing Packages

We supply marketing packages. Each package enables you to easily reach your chosen target group. It contains a set of labels and a description of each organisation on the label. Simply read the information we supply on an organisation, and if they are someone you wish to reach, then stick the appropriate label on to the envelope containing your book/product/press release/brochure etc and post. Some packages we offer are *Reviewers Package, Press Release Package, Exhibitions Package, Core Advertisers Package, Publications Package,* and *Submissions Package.* The *Reviewers Package* is handy for publishers, audio and visual producers, and product suppliers who wish to promote their new book, product etc. The *Press Release Package* is useful for anyone wishes to mail off their press release, (we supply details of specialist and national press). The *Exhibitions Package* consists of details of holistic exhibitions so that you can plan ahead. The *Core Advertisers Package* consists of advertisers that advertise regularly in the MBS/New Age press; useful for those who wish to get advertising for their publication. The *Submissions Package* is for authors wishing to get their work published.

realise your business potential

At last! Everything

you ever wanted to know about marketing in the field of Mind/Body/Spirit collected together in one great book. Sell more products, attract more clients, expand your business with our new **Brainwave Marketing Book**. We provide comprehensive lists of contacts who can help you promote and market your centre, business or product, from journalists and radio to specialist magazines and networks, from exhibitions and reviewers to New Age shops and distributors.

We publish the **Brainwave Marketing Book**, an A4 size, 304 page business guide to the holistic health / new age field.

BCM Raft, London WC1N 3XX
(071) 733 7883 or (071) 978 9062
serving holistic business

Over 5,000 questionnaires were sent out to organisations to compile this trade directory. Not only are there comprehensive listings, but the book is packed with information and tips on how to promote and market your business more effectively. Save yourself years of research - we've done it all for you.

Essential Marketing Topics

Topics covered in parts 2 and 3 of the Brainwave Marketing Book are:

Market research techniques
Researching your market
Pricing
Planning
Discovering your customer
Writing good copy
Selling face to face
Designing a successful advert
Designing a successful leaflet
Getting the most out of exhibitions
Effective presentation
How to market a New Age book/ tapes
Marketing for Practitioners
Using marketing consultants
Marketing through Video
And much much more!

detailed listings

publishers	conferences
magazines	radio stations
consultants	festivals
exhibitions	retailers
bookshops	new age shops
journalists	reviewers
directories	resources
networks	wholesalers
mailing lists	holistic health
associations	centres
joint mailing	services

Over 2,700 connections and opportunities are listed! We provide full details of each contact.

Money back guarantee!

If you are not delighted with it, return it to us within 21 days of delivery and we will refund your money in full.

How to Order

To order your copy of **The Brainwave Marketing Book** post a cheque (made out to Brainwave) for £35 + £2 p/p to Brainwave, BCM Raft, London WC1N 3XX`z. or phone Mike Considine on (071) 733 7883 to find out more. Credit cards also welcome. Please supply your name and address of your business together with phone number.

Introduction to this book

Most people don't read the preface, so I omitted that heading here in order to catch the maximum number of readers.

The previous edition of Holistic London was praised as one of the most useful guidebooks in the Mind/Body/Spirit field; notably because we did not use enigmatic codes, nor did we have a section on 'How to Use this Book', as no such section was needed. In all of our publications we have endeavoured to keep it simple, research the material and provide as much information as is necessary.

Like any guidebook Holistic London grows old and needs updating, hence this new revised edition appears a year and a half after the last edition. We have kept to a similar layout and style, believing that the formula has worked well, and so made only small adjustments where necessary. However, considerable revision and changes in the material have taken place. Not only has information been updated, new organisations have been added and defunct ones deleted.

Having sung its praises I want also to state my misgivings. What is badly needed is a section on how to go about choosing a particular therapy: how to point someone in a particular direction if they have questions or problems such as 'How do I cure my persistent tiredness?' or 'I don't feel my life has any meaning now my children have grown up'. I do not believe that such questions about life are best answered by a GP. Nor do I believe a GP will necessarily offer what is needed. At present we do not have the equivalent of a GP in the alternative health field i.e. someone who can advise you, and refer you to a specialist who can deal with your query. It's 95% certain that if you go to an acupuncturist in order to cure your headache, you will get acupuncture. If you go to a gestalt therapist for those same headaches you will get gestalt therapy. Neither one of these therapies may be the best for you. Trial and error is a costly way of determining which path works. At present you have to make up your own mind from the myriad choices available. Perhaps in the next edition of this book we will address this thorny issue.

It upsets me knowing that many people train in therapy and end up not practising as therapists. To this end and to help other businesses in the holistic field, **Brainwave** have produced a book called *The Brainwave Marketing Book*. The book contains essential listings of information to help holistic businesses deal with marketing and promotion. Many therapists leave their training organisation ill equipped to deal with the practical aspects of running a business. The trainings help them become effective professionals, but do not attend to the everyday currency of running a business. Nor are therapists the only people in this field that need specialist information. Publishers need a specialist directory of outlets and mailing lists. Someone who produces an audio or visual tape on hypnosis, for instance, needs to know the outlets where the product can be marketed. To this end The *Brainwave Marketing Book* provides the information that holistic businesses need to do business. This is in line with the aims of **Brainwave** who wish to help holistic business grow and prosper.

If you are a centre offering therapy then please put us on your mailing list so that we can list you in our directories. There is no charge to be listed, all our listings are free.

We welcome feedback. If you have any suggestions about how Holistic London could be improved please let us know. Only by feedback can we know where change is needed. Share it. There is room for Holistic London to grow. If you have an anecdote related to a holistic therapy or product please write it down and send it to us. We may publish it in the next Holistic London and you will receive a free copy.

Mike Considine
London, October 1991.

INTRODUCTION TO PSYCHOTHERAPY

What is Psychotherapy?

Psychotherapy is a term used to denote a variety of methods in dealing with emotional problems. There are many different types of psychotherapy, and each of these therapies may differ considerably from one another. What they all have in common is they all try to help the client in changing. In each of their own ways they will enable the client to better understand his or her self, feelings and relationships with others and help to explore new ways of behaving. It may involve the client re-enacting old conflicts within the therapy but with a resulting different outcome so that the client finds new ways of dealing with, and resolving those conflicts. Most of the therapies can be seen as a teaching in the art of therapy so that when the client leaves the therapy he or she will be able to continue his or her own analysis.

In general usage the word psychotherapy is confined to what goes on between a therapist and a client, though this limited definition leaves out self-help and help that can be offered by lay people - and the magnitude of this help should not be underestimated. The advantage of seeing a therapist is that the client will have the space to deal with his or her concerns with someone who has an armoury of strategies in helping.

The Difference between Psychotherapy and Counselling

Counselling used within this book refers to psychotherapeutic counselling rather than other types of counselling such as career or financial counselling. A caption on an Oxfam billboard advertisement many years ago read 'Give a man a fish and you feed him for a day. Teach a man to fish and you feed him for a lifetime'. Analogously counselling is usually an approach which helps the client with a problem, whereas psychotherapy is aimed at helping the client to help himself with his own problems. After receiving psychotherapy the client should be able to manage the daily tasks of living without getting tied up in destructive or mundane patterns of behaviour or negative feelings. Counselling is usually much shorter and involves less personal change on the part of the client. Counselling usually revolves around a specific problem while psychotherapy may not do so. However, having said that, there is still a great overlap between counselling and psychotherapy.

1

PSYCHOTHERAPY

The Difference between Psychology and Psychotherapy

Psychology is the study of human behaviour. It is primarily a science. The domain of psychology is large and covers such things as perception, intelligence, conditioning, the nervous system, and the behaviour of people in groups, to name but a few. Psychotherapy is only one aspect of psychology. Psychologists enter the jobs market within a specialised field, either as industrial psychologists, educational psychologists, experimental psychologists, social psychologists or clinical psychologists. Clinical psychologists have more experience of psychotherapy than their fellows as they apply their knowledge of psychology to dealing with emotional and behavioural problems. They work in different settings throughout the National Health Service, especially in mental hospitals and institutions for people with a mental handicap. Psychotherapists, on the whole, have much more varied backgrounds. Whilst some are clinical psychologists, others are psychiatrists and social workers, and there are many who have a teaching and management background.

Approaches to Psychotherapy

There are four main approaches to psychotherapy: psychoanalytic, humanistic, cognitive and behavioural. The psychoanalytic approach developed by Sigmund Freud explains behaviour in terms of the interplay between the conscious and unconscious mind of an individual. Freud believed that innate instincts, especially the sex and aggressive instincts, are often disapproved of in our society and are driven out of the individual's awareness, but remain in the unconscious affecting behaviour. Glimpses of the unconscious are to be had from dreams, slips of the tongue, mannerisms, some symptoms of mental illness and some artistic endeavours. Most psychoanalysts prefer to speak in terms of levels of awareness rather than a conscious-unconscious divide.

The second approach is humanistic or phenomenological. The ideas of the humanistic psychologists are similar to, and draw upon, the writings of the existentialists. Emphasis is placed on how individuals subjectively experience the world, and what sense they make of it. The humanistic psychologists are concerned with the inner life of individuals and how they experience themselves and others. They are interested in concepts of self-esteem, feelings, authenticity, self awareness and consciousness.

Thirdly there is the cognitive approach. This approach argues that we are constantly processing information in selective and organised ways, such as when planning and solving problems. We make sense of the world using particular views and assumptions which have been conditioned by our previous experience. By consciously adopting another point of view, we can change our behaviour.

Fourthly there is the behavioural approach, sometimes known as Stimulus/ Response Psychology. This approach is based on 'learning theory' which grew from experiments with animals. Behaviourists emphasise how the environment 'conditions' people to behave in certain ways and that people modify their behaviour to suit the surroundings. Punishment and reward are the stick and the carrot for this process. For instance if a child is punished for succeeding and rewarded for failing then the child will learn to fail; or we might say the child has been conditioned to fail. Since behaviour was learned, behaviourists argue that undesirable behaviour could be unlearned and be replaced by more desirable forms of behaviour.

The Varieties of Psychotherapy

Most therapists practise one of the four approaches (or a combination of these approaches) described above. There are, however, literally hundreds of different types or 'schools' of psychotherapy which come under the four basic approaches. Each of these schools has its own theories about why people behave the way they do and on how to treat emotional problems. These different types of psychotherapy may differ dramatically from one another, even though the desired aims of the therapies may well be the same.

In this book we describe the major schools of psychotherapy, enabling the reader to steer through the minefield. The less well known psychotherapies are catalogued at the end of this section.

Does Psychotherapy Work?

Nobody knows if any one psychotherapy is better than another. This is partly because a great deal of research has yet to be carried out before any satisfactory conclusions can be drawn, and partly because the effectiveness of psychotherapy depends on the particular circumstances of the client and upon the unique quality of any therapeutic relationship. This is one reason why therapists tend to draw upon other psychotherapeutic approaches in their work. A transactional analysis therapist, for instance, may at times use a psychoanalytic approach, or some technique he or she has borrowed from another school of psychotherapy.

Styles of the Therapist

Any label the therapist gives herself may not accurately describe what she does. Two gestalt therapists, for instance, may operate in completely different ways. One may tend to ask the group to try out lots of exercises, whereas the other may not do this at all. One therapist may be very warm and protective of the group members whereas the other may be cold and reserved. This is partly due to the character of the therapist, but it is also because no psychotherapeutic approach can ever fully determine a therapist's behaviour.

Who Should have Psychotherapy?

Most people can benefit from psychotherapy. Some people are put off therapy because they think it is just for people who are mad, or that it is an admission of weakness and of not being able to cope, or that it is something that New Yorkers spend a great deal of time and money having without ever really getting anywhere. Therapy is usually intended both as a way of healing and a method of personal growth. It is meant to help those with conflicts and problems, as well as those who are simply dissatisfied with themselves and their lives, who feel blank, bored or want more out of themselves and their relationships. Sometimes people in this last category feel drawn to psychotherapy, but worry that if they go to see a therapist, he or she will think they are 'malingering' because they are not desperate or in crisis. In fact many therapies concentrate a great deal on the idea of growth, and that therapy is too good to be limited just to those whose problems severely restrict their lives.

The most important thing is perhaps that you make the choice to do it. While this is not irrevocable, and leaves room for experimentation, it is important that you do not feel pushed into doing it by someone else, or that you know it would be a good idea but do not really feel very enthusiastic. If you do not feel it is your decision then you may just feel resentful so that the whole process may not work for you. Sometimes people who are doing therapy may try and push partners, friends or relatives into therapy because they want them to change. Unfortunately this kind of pressure can turn the decision into a kind of power struggle, and make it very difficult for the person considering therapy to feel that they can make the decision of their own free will.

How to Choose a Particular Psychotherapy

This book explains many of the different psychotherapies on offer. If any particular approach appeals to you, further reading will give you more information, though this will be theoretical. To get an experience of therapy, many of the centres listed run weekend workshops which will enable you to get a taste of the therapy in action in a group setting. If you want to get an idea of what a particular approach is like in one to one sessions, then introductory sessions with a psychotherapist who uses the approach might be indicated.

How to Choose a Therapist

The title 'psychotherapist' is not regulated by law and at present in this country there is no licensing procedure. This means that anyone can set themselves up as a psychotherapist, even if they have no formal training in psychotherapy. So it is possible that you might choose a therapist who has not undergone adequate training. However, having said that, in our experience those therapists who are poor at their job don't last long in the marketplace, and soon retire.

If you have decided that a particular therapy appeals to you then there are a number of ways of finding a psychotherapist. Look up that therapy in this book and you will find the organisations that practise them listed, together with training organisations. It is suggested that you contact one of the training organisations if one is listed. They usually keep a register of practitioners they have trained and will be able to refer you to one. Training organisations are a reliable way of finding a therapist because they are likely to recommend only those who they think have reached a certain standard, and who and subscribe to their code of ethics. If no training organisation is listed, then choose one of the centres which practice the therapy and contact them. They are listed under the description of the therapy. It's worth asking either the training organisation or centre to send you a brochure of what they offer. This will enable you to browse through their literature before making any commitment.

If you do not know which type of therapy you want and you do not feel you can make that decision then you can contact an umbrella organisation, such as the *Association for Humanistic Psychology Practitioners (AHPP), the British Psychoanalytic Society (BPS)* or the *British Association for Counselling (BAC)*. All are listed at the back of this book with some details about them. A new independent organisation who will refer you to a therapist is Neal's Yard Agency in Covent Garden. You can browse round their shop, look at the leaflets on display and at biographies of practitioners they have on their records.

Having found a psychotherapist, it is advisable to have a few introductory sessions before embarking on a long-term commitment. It is important to find a therapist with whom you can have a good working relationship. Carl Rogers, a well-known figure in the field of counselling and psychotherapy, suggests that clients gain positive benefits from psychotherapy if the therapist is perceived by the client to be warm and caring, authentic and honest, and understanding of the way the client sees the world. If you perceive your therapist to have these qualities, and if you are learning about yourself in the therapy, then he or she may be the right therapist for you.

Individual Therapy Versus Group Therapy

Individual psychotherapy is the most common form of psychotherapy. The advantage of this type of approach is that the client and the therapist can focus on the client's particular problems for the entire session. Individual therapy also has the advantage that confidential information can be discussed without fear of public criticism. It is also useful in that the client has the opportunity to develop a close relationship with one person. This might be useful if the client has had difficulty in forming close relationships and finds the idea of groups frightening.

In individual therapy the client and therapist usually meet at least once a week for one hour. Some therapists prefer to work to the golden 50 minute hour, others may work for up to two hours. Often therapists insist on meeting for more than once a week and for psychoanalysis five times a week is the norm. Many therapists work outside of normal office hours to accommodate their clients.

The advantage of group therapy is that it allows others to give feedback on one person's behaviour, rather than the solitary feedback offered by the therapist in individual therapy. The therapist sees how you are interacting with other members of the group rather than simply listening to your reports. It may be that the therapist and the group members can offer some observations on your behaviour with others of which you may have been unaware. A further advantage of group therapy is that it enables you to understand how others may have similar problems and difficulties as yourself and so feel less alone.

Group therapy is usually conducted in small groups of between four and fourteen members with one psychotherapist present, though there are a number of exceptions to this. There may be more than one therapist; for instance in couple therapy the norm is two therapists. Sometimes the groups can be larger, and 'large group therapy' as it is called can involve over one hundred people in one group (the Introductory Course at the The Institute of Group Analysis runs a group of one hundred and forty members) though such large groups in therapy are rare.

The timeframe for the group may vary considerably between different groups and different therapies. The two most frequent formats are weekend workshops or once weekly evening workshops. Some of the other variations include meeting throughout the day for one, two, three or four weeks (these are usually residential and are sometimes known as intensives); 24 and 48 hour marathons (the members stay together for all of this period and get little sleep); meeting in the early morning before normal working hours; twice weekly evening groups; a combination of the aforementioned. Some people prefer to live in therapeutic communities where the boundary between therapy and everyday life can be blurred.

Does the Sex of the Therapist Matter?

Generally the sex of the therapist does not matter. Many people have difficulty in communicating with people of one or other gender. In this case they may find it too difficult to develop a relationship of trust with a therapist of this gender, and it might be best to choose a therapist of the sex with which they feel more comfortable. For example if a woman is scared of men it might be best if she chooses a female therapist, or if a man is angry at women he might do better choosing a male therapist. However it may not necessarily be the opposite sex which the client finds difficult. The individual might, after some therapy, switch to a therapist of the more problematic sex to work through any unresolved issues to do with that gender.

Too Old for Therapy?

Undergoing therapy requires that you be open to change and open to new feelings

and experiences. This openness to what is new and novel in understanding oneself is not related to chronological age.

Cost

Psychotherapy is expensive, but the rates may vary enormously from practitioner to practitioner. Usually the more experienced a practitioner is the more he or she will charge. But don't think that if you pay more you will automatically get a better practitioner. It is best to hunt around for value for money. Some therapists offer discounts for the low waged.

What the Different Centres are Like

Psychotherapy centres can vary from a therapist working from a room at his or her own house to a bevy of practitioners and associated administrative staff accommodated in a six storey purpose-built block. The usual set-up is a handful of practitioners who have banded together to form a practice, and use a room in one of their houses, or hire rooms in a building in which to practise. It is therefore advisable if you are not familiar with the centre to ring beforehand to make an appointment rather than turn up on the doorstep. Do not be disconcerted if the centre does not turn out to be a prestigious building. The cost of running a prestigious building may well be reflected in the fees that are charged. What is important is the quality and training of the therapist.

TRAINING IN PSYCHOTHERAPY

Why Train in Psychotherapy?

Helping other people can be very rewarding. Training as a psychotherapist means that you will have the opportunity to work on your own growth and use what you have learnt to help others undergoing the same process. Some practical advantages of working as a therapist are that you are your own boss, you can earn a decent living, and, having trained, you may also be able to apply your skills in some other setting, such as education or social work. However, the work of a psychotherapist can also be very stressful. Sometimes it is hard to cut off emotionally from clients outside working hours. It may well not turn out to pay as well as you think it will. You may even end up finding that you cannot get enough clients to support yourself. You may need to work outside of the normal nine to five office hours, and this may well bite into your social life. Are you sure you want to do it?

Which School of Psychotherapy to Train In?

Before you apply for training in any psychotherapy you should have some experience of that psychotherapy yourself. In fact many training organisations make this a requirement. Rather than embark on a training programme for a therapy

PSYCHOTHERAPY

you have been involved in, it might be best to sample different psychotherapies before training, just to be sure that you are making the right decision.

The Training Programmes

A training programme should include (1) opportunity for the trainee to work on own personal material (2) observation of practitioners at work with their clients/groups (3) adequate supervision when a trainee begins to see clients/groups (4) personal experience of being a participant in a group if training is in group work, or of being a client in one to one sessions if the training is in individual therapy. A training programme in psychotherapy is usually at least three years long. Most are conducted on a part-time basis, utilising evenings and weekends, so that it is possible to hold a full-time job at the same time. It is best to be wary of trainings that are only short in duration. Whilst they may be called a 'training' they will not be able to offer you a full programme which will equip you for this profession. Trainings in counselling are usually shorter than therapy training.

However, bear in mind that these training programmes have not been independently assessed. This means that any graduation certificates or diplomas they award on completion of the training may, in the end, be recognised only by the institute itself. The value of the training rests upon whether or not the therapeutic community as a whole finds the institute to be reputable. If you know someone who is a psychologist, therapist, psychiatrist, social worker, counsellor or psychiatric nurse, they may be able to advise you about the reputation of the training institute.

Accreditation and 1992

At present there is no licencing procedure for counsellors or psychotherapists in this country. Many therapists have invested a lot of money in training, in the knowledge and fear that future legislation may exclude them from practising. Many potential trainees are wondering whether to invest their money in training for similar reasons. What is the story so far, and what advice can be offered, bearing in mind that the European Economic Community will be dropping its internal trade barriers in 1992?

In Holland and Italy only psychiatrists and clinical psychologists are allowed to practise psychotherapy. After 1992 this will mean that psychotherapists from Italy and Holland will be able to come to the UK to practise but many British psychotherapists will not be able to practise there, as many British psychotherapists are not clinical psychologists or psychiatrists. If more EEC countries adopt Holland's and Italy's approach this will eventually mean British psychotherapists will be at a disadvantage and the UK will be forced into opting to go the way of allowing only graduates with relevant degrees to practise psychotherapy. It may take five to ten years for this to happen, though it could be sooner.

In Britain a move towards some form of regulation for psychotherapy began with the formation of a federation of psychotherapy training organisations, the *Rugby Conference*, to talk about this issue. It has recently changed its name to the *U.K.*

Standing Conference on Psychotherapy (UKSCP - address at the back of the book). Their aim is to accredit trainings in psychotherapy by a process of self-regulatory monitoring of each other's training programmes, and to accredit the therapists who have trained with those organisations. It looks as if they are still a couple of years away from being able to answer potential trainees' questions about whether particular training organisations are accredited by them. If you are a psychotherapist and are worried about your future status you might keep in touch with and support the *UKSCP.*

The situation for counselling is different from that of therapy. The *British Association for Counselling (BAC* - an independent charity, address at the back of the book) has recently started accrediting organisations which offer a training in counselling. They are able to tell potential trainee counsellors which organisations they accredit, but they are still some way off from processing all the trainings in the UK. The *British Psychological Society* has recently introduced a Diploma in Counselling Psychology which is likely to become a standard in the field of counselling.

Can I get Work When Trained?

Few psychotherapists are employed within the NHS, though there are many health service professionals who practice psychotherapy. The majority of psychotherapists work in the private sector and are thus self employed. Working for oneself can be perilous as one is at the mercy of market forces. Should the market be saturated with psychotherapists at any one time then there are less clients to go round and psychotherapists trying to set up a practice will find it especially difficult. Before you embark on a training programme you should be thinking about how you will get your clients when you have finished. Will the training institute supply you with clients? Will they supply you with enough clients? It is important that they will support you when you are initially setting up a practice, as this is a most difficult time. You should discuss these points with them. There are quite a few therapists now barely scratching out a living from the few clients they have on their books. Very few training institutes equip their trainees with knowledge of business practices, something every successful psychotherapist operating in the private sector must know.

Entry Requirements

Most centres do not require that you hold a degree to be accepted for training. Many of the centre organisers believe that a degree is not a good indicator of what makes a good therapist. There is no general agreement as to what makes a good therapist. Different institutes have their own criteria, based on their own idea of what qualities are needed in a therapist. Some prefer you to be medically trained, other centres think this might work against you. Some prefer you to be somewhat crazy (so that you will have some idea of mental suffering), others want the opposite. We indicate wherever possible the basic entry requirements of each training centre.

Cost of Training

Training is expensive and in some cases may run into five figures. There are not only fees for the course, but there may also be hidden costs, such as supervision fees and own required psychotherapy, which may be considerable and far in excess of the training fees. For instance if you are required to undergo personal therapy three times a week then this could amount to £3000 per year alone. We have tried to include all of these costs wherever possible. Do not forget to include VAT at 17.5% in your calculations when determining the total cost of training.

THE PSYCHOTHERAPIES

Art Therapy

People know intuitively that self expression is a way of healing oneself, whether it is through drawing, dancing, sculpting or building. Art therapy is one such means of seeking release and of understanding oneself. Its usefulness is not only for emotional release. An art therapist, through interpreting the meaning of the symbols produced, hopes to come to some understanding of the client, and to enable the client to make fresh discoveries about life and self.

The process of drawing, painting or modelling can help the client to objectify or detach themselves from feelings or problems that may seem otherwise too overwhelming to deal with. The contents of the unconscious can become visible in a very immediate way, and this method often by-passes the censoring process with which we obscure feelings and thoughts which disturb us.

Therapists of different persuasions use the medium of art. Their approach will differ depending on their school of thought. Art therapy is widely used in the humanistic psychologies, where there is more emphasis on interpretation by the client of his or her own productions. They may be interpreted in a Freudian or Jungian way if the art therapist subscribes to either of these frameworks.

Within the health service it is used mainly in psychiatric hospitals and day centres. It is especially effective with severely disturbed people who find it difficult to express their feelings verbally.

It may be used by psychotherapists practising within the NHS, or by specifically trained Art Therapists.

READING

Art As Therapy *by Dalley, T. (eds) RKP £5.95.* Subtitled 'An Introduction to the Use of Art as a Therapeutic Technique', this is a collection of articles by practitioners of various backgrounds showing the many ways art therapy is used. It covers work both inside institutions and outside in growth oriented situations. **The Inward Journey; Art as Therapy** *by Keyes, M. Open Court 1984, £9.50.* Based around Jungian and Gestalt approaches, this is a practical handbook, full of strategies using sculpture, painting, mandalas, music and myth, providing a useful insight into how art therapy can work for the individual.

CENTRES OFFERING ART THERAPY

Art from Within N5, British Association for Social Psychiatry, Circle of Creative Arts Therapy N8, Highbury Centre N5, Imprint SW19, Institute For Arts In Therapy & Education N16, London Lighthouse W11, Person-Centred Art Therapy Centre NW11, Playspace NW1, Resonance SW17, St James Centre for Health and Healing W1, Studio 8, Tobias School of Art, Universitas Associates, Women's Therapy Centre N7.

TRAININGS IN ART THERAPY

Goldsmiths' College *Title of Training* (1) Diploma in Art Therapy (2) M.A. in Art Therapy (3) Diploma in Group Therapy. *Duration* (1) Two years part-time or one year full-time (2) Two years part-time (3) Three years part-time. *Entry requirements* For the art therapy courses, non art graduates need to demonstrate a long standing commitment to practise in the visual arts. (1) Degree in Art or Design or other approved subject (2) Should be a qualified art therapist or other professional with a commitment to the theoretical development of art therapy (3) Degree or professional qualification. *Fees* (1) For a unsponsored student £304 p.a. part-time, £607 p.a. full

DRAWING FROM WITHIN

Unusual ways to bypass that 'inner critic' which interferes with drawing, painting and vitality!
Including
SEEING/DRAWING, a meditative seeking of the inner essence of what we see.

ART AND PSYCHOSYNTHESIS

A fascinating journey through your inner world of image, sensation and feeling.
Lack of technical ability could be an advantage!
Contact Avril Wigham, qualified art therapist and psychosynthesis counsellor on 071 354 1603

PERSON-CENTRED ART THERAPY CENTRE offers

<u>Courses:</u> a part-time course in **Person Centred Art Therapy**; a course bringing the person-centred approach originated by Carl Rogers to Art Therapy, leading to a certificate from Crawley College of Technology. Three terms 2 hours per week, 50 weeks in all. Previous art training <u>not</u> required

<u>Art therapy days</u>	with **Liesl Silverstone**, Dip. Art
<u>Counselling</u>	Therapy, Dip. Counselling,
<u>Supervision</u>	Dip. Social Services, Cert.
	Transpersonal Psychology

Person Centred Art Therapy Centre,
17 Cranbourne Gdns, London NW11 0HN.
Tel. 081-455 8570

time (2) For a unsponsored student £595 p.a. part-time, £1890 p.a. full time (3) £750 p.a. part-time.

Tobias School of Art *Title of Training* Artistic Therapy. *Duration* Three years. *Fees* £2,500 per year tuition + room fees. *Comments* An exciting course on an international campus (students from all five continents attend).

Person-Centred Art Therapy Centre *Title of Training* Person-centred art therapy. *Duration* One year, two hours per week for thirty weeks. *Fees* £330. *Comments* The certificate is based on self/peer assessment and the learning is mainly experiential.

Institute For Arts In Therapy & Education *Title of Training* Integrative Arts Therapy. *Duration* One year part-time. *Entry requirements* Experience in the helping professions. Must agree to undergo psychotherapy during the training. *Fees* £1,650 per year.

Assertion Training

Assertion training, which is sometimes known as assertiveness training, aims to help the client gain specific social skills in expressing feelings, thoughts, wishes and behaviours which allow her or him to stand up for their rights in particular situations. Because the focus is on particular change in behaviours, behaviour therapy has contributed much to this field, although humanistic psychology has also had its part to play.

The procedure of assertion training can be mapped under three headings. Firstly there is skills training, where verbal and non-verbal behaviours are taught and practised. This is mostly done in role play, where a situation requiring assertion is rehearsed and acted out. For example, a situation of returning faulty goods to a store may be enacted. The client is instructed on how to go about getting satisfaction, and the stage is set for the client to act as the irate customer with other members of the group playing the part of shopkeeper, manager and so on. Emphasis is placed on the difference between acting assertively and appearing aggressive. Homework may also be given and clients may be asked to keep a journal. Clients may be asked to assert themselves in situations outside the group and to report back on their endeavours.

Secondly, methods of reducing anxiety are taught. This may take the form of relaxation exercises, or of desensitisation. Desensitisation as used in assertion training is the process of learning to handle one's anxiety by taking the assertive role in easy stages, perhaps initially by fantasising about it and then taking on an easy assertiveness task, so that in this way the anxiety does not overwhelm. To some extent anxiety is reduced when a role play is satisfactorily completed.

Thirdly, values and beliefs about the rights of the individual in society are examined. This is particularly the case for groups within society such as women, children and ethnic minorities. The effects of social conditioning and the part it plays in people's perceptions of their own rights is considered.

In London there is a wealth of adult education classes on this subject. Consult *Floodlight* for a list of venues.

READING

A Woman in Your Own Right *by Dickson, A. Quartet 1982 £4.95*. Assertion is often confused with aggression. In this book the author dispels this myth and presents a full programme for developing a more fulfilling life by standing up for yourself. She deals with assertive approaches to sexuality, the workplace, money, personal criticism and more. Although aimed at women, the ideas are usable by men and she has applied the techniques in mixed sex situations. **Your Perfect Right; A Guide to Assertive Living** *by Alberti, R & Emmons, I. Impact Publications 1970 (revised 1989) £6.95*. The original book on assertion training and still one of the most comprehensive. It's written as a workbook to read and work through, using the exercises and practice situations. These are related to how one can incorporate the ideas into one's life.

CENTRES OFFERING ASSERTION TRAINING

Centre for Stress Management SE3, Life Directions W1, Lilly Stuart Resource Development Consultants SE7, Minster Centre NW2, Psychotherapy for Individuals, Couples & Groups, Redwood Women's Training Association, South Camden Women's Centre, Spiral W12, UK Training College of Hypnotherapy and Counselling W2, Women Unlimited SW16, Women's Therapy Centre N7.

TRAINING IN ASSERTION

Redwood Women's Training Association *Title of Training* Training in training others to be Assertion Trainers. *Duration* Seven to nine months. *Entry requirements* Nothing formal, places allocated by interview. *Fees* £950 - £1250.

Astrological Counselling

In astrological counselling the positions of the planets are believed to indicate the character and functioning of the individual's psyche.

The astrological counsellor will draw up the client's 'birth chart', which is a symbolic diagram of the positions of the planets at the time of birth. Through the interpretations of the chart the counsellor hopes to provide the client with insights into his or her own psychology. Events in the client's life may also be assessed by comparison between the position of planets at birth and their present position or at a time of major life events. Through interpretation of the symbolism of these, the counsellor aims to determine what psychological forces are at work and may suggest what action, if any, the client should take. The birthchart of the client may also be compared with a birthchart of a partner, to throw light on the workings of the relationship.

Astrological counselling can be distinguished from other forms of astrological birth chart interpretation because it focuses on issues broached by psychotherapy (such as how the 'shadow' of mother affects present relationships with men) rather than on character traits (such as being overgenerous). It attempts to find meaning and reveal patterns in life events rather than attempting to predict future events. The astrological counsellor will not only interpret, but also allow the client's own response to the material to emerge and become part of the counselling relationship.

Much astrological counselling has been influenced by the psychology of C G Jung (see Jungian Analysis in this section), who was interested in astrology, stating that it was 'the summation of all the psychological knowledge of antiquity'.

All but one of the research studies undertaken to confirm a connection between the planets and an individual's psyche have failed. This does not mean that astrological counselling does not work, but suggests the factors for therapeutic change lie outside that explained by its theory - though the same could be said for some other therapies.

CENTRES OFFERING ASTROLOGICAL COUNSELLING

Astro-Psychotherapeutic Practice W3, Centre for Psychological Astrology NW3, Cheirological Society W6, Healing Fields Practice N7, Reiki Centre NW3.

Autogenic Training

Autogenic training is a procedure which has many elements in common with biofeedback, relaxation training, hypnotherapy and some types of stress management, but at the same time adds some new elements of its own. It helps to induce a particular hypnotic state which is somewhere between full consciousness and sleep, and in which one has greater access to the unconscious. In this state repressed material can be accessed and then used for creative problem solving, or positive affirmations can be implanted in the unconscious. Once the technique is learned from the therapist it can be practised on one's own.

At the turn of the century Oscar Vokt found that his patients could hypnotise themselves once they had been initially hypnotised by him, and were then able to use this new-found method to relieve stress and induce relaxation. A few years later H. Schultz developed a series of formulaes to help patients to enter this state quickly.

The particular hypnotic state is induced by passive concentration. The client is asked to concentrate either on the breathing process, on differences between the right and left side of the body or on tensions within the body and to repeat such statements as 'I am calm and quiet'. The client is then given exercises inducing warmth and heaviness in various parts of the body. Once the client has reached a particular stage in the training, which may take many months and which may require practice several times a day, he is then given visual exercises, such as recalling incidents from the past, or recalling the face of someone known in vivid detail. If a pleasant incident is recalled it can be 'anchored' by crossing finger and thumb, so that in the future crossing finger and thumb can induce the pleasant feelings associated with the incident.

Unwanted behaviour patterns are changed when the client is open, in the hypnotic state, to ways of being and acting which are different from his or her normal stereotyped responses. The origins of the feelings associated with the behaviour pattern may also be explored. Self affirmations such as 'I am a loving and valuable person' are often used, especially to finish the session.

Autogenic training would seem best suited to those who have difficulty relaxing and who suffer from physical ailments induced by tension, such as headaches, ulcers, high blood pressure and colitis.

READING

Autogenic Therapy *by Luthe, W & Schultz, J. (Gruer & Stratton 1969).* These are the original manuals produced by the originators of the method, unfortunately out of print (and extremely expensive when they were available). There are no easily available books on the subject, but is is worth checking out **The Silva Mind Control Method** *by Silva, H. (Grafton £3.99)* as he incorporated much autogenics into his work.

CENTRES OFFERING AUTOGENIC TRAINING

All Hallows House EC3, Centre for Autogenic Training, Hampton Healing Centre, Hampton Holistic Centre for Homoeopathy and Autogenic Training, Homoeopathic Centre W13, Neal's Yard Therapy Rooms WC2.

Bioenergetics

Bioenergetics is a body-oriented psychotherapy. The term was introduced by Alexander Lowen who evolved this particular therapy based on the initial insights and theories of Wilhelm Reich. Lowen, an American, was analysed by Reich, and he developed Reich's work in two ways. He modified and evolved Reich's approach into his own particular school of therapy. He also wrote lucidly on the mind/body relationship, avoiding the psychoanalytic jargon which abounded in Reich's writings, and made it accessible to a larger number of people.

Much of the theory is based on Reich's original formulation that the body, mind and feelings are interrelated. The body reflects the person's character. A particular configuration of tensions within the body reflects the psychological make-up of the person. It is possible to diagnose someone's emotional constraints from looking at the tensions in their body, how they hold themselves and how they move.

By working on areas of tension within the body it is possible to contact some underlying feelings. For example, if a client grinds his or her teeth at night and complains about difficulty expressing anger, the therapist may massage or knead the jaw muscles and surrounding area which is likely to provoke this underlying rage.

Much of the therapy is taken up by doing exercises which release chronically tense muscles. Lowen was creative in inventing such exercises. Attention is paid to respiration, frozen chests, locked pelvises, tensions in the throat, feeling sick (clients are often asked to vomit rather than suppress this feeling). Lowen paid particular attention to the legs which he saw as important in terms of balance and contact with the ground and introduced the concept of grounding. Unlike Reich who worked from the head down, Lowen believed in working from the feet up. Both stressed the central role of breathing.

Bioenergetics is best done as individual therapy, where the therapist can give the client individual attention. When it is practised in groups it usually follows one of the following formats or a mixture of each: the therapist works with one individual at a time, the rest of the group learn by observing; participants pair up and help each other with a bioenergetic exercise; each participant does an exercise on his or her own with the therapist doing rounds to make sure they are getting the most from the exercise.

Many people find bioenergetics bewildering at first because they are not used to the connections between bodily tensions and feelings.

You may be asked to remove much of your clothing. Clients are often asked to wear swimwear or leotards.

READING

Bioenergetics *by Lowen. A. Penguin 1975 £4.95.* Lowen developed his approach out of his work with Wilhelm Reich, and this book is his attempt to put his theories into a usable form for the interested lay reader. Bioenergetics is a study of the human personality through the energy processes of the body, and this book is a good place to start. You may also look for his book of exercises **Way to Vibrant Health** *Harper & Row, 1977, £7.95.* **Lifestreams; An Introduction to Biosynthesis** *by Boadella,*

A. Routledge and Kegan Paul 1987, £6.50. Boadella, an English therapist, also worked with Reich and has developed a different approach to bodywork, bringing insights from Lowen and other Reichian influenced therapists, such as Stanley Keleman, whose books **Your Body Speaks Its Mind** and **Living Your Dying** both b*y Center Press* are also worth reading.

CENTRES OFFERING BIOENERGETICS
Abshot Holistic Centre, Bioenergetic Partnership, Bodyspace, British Association of Analytical Body Psychotherapists., Chiron W5, Healing Fields Practice N7, Human Potential Resource Group , Open Centre EC1, Spectrum N4, Women's Therapy Centre N7.

TRAINING IN BIOENERGETICS
British Association of Analytical Body Psychotherapists. *Title of Training* Body Oriented Psychotherapy in an Analytical Setting: Training for Practitioners. *Duration* Five years; four training blocks of four days per annum plus seminars, group process workshops, supervision and individual therapy. *Entry requirements* Previous experience in individual and group psychotherapy; current client load; references from therapist and/or supervisor. *Fees* £1,000 per annum payable in instalments plus residential costs, individual therapy and individual supervision.

Biofeedback

Biofeedback training uses electronic gadgetry to feed back information about specific internal physiological states to the person using it. It is claimed that specific physiological states correspond to certain types of mental activity. For instance, a change in skin resistance from low to high and an increase in finger temperature corresponds to the person feeling more relaxed. These changes are signalled to the user by changes in sound tone or lights from the machine. Thus by using a small electronic box a person is able to monitor his or her particular level of relaxation. Further, from being able to monitor one's level of relaxation, it can be used to learn how to change one's own physiological responses and hence change how one feels.

Learning how to relax is one of the uses of biofeedback training, though it is not confined to this. It can be used to prevent and control stress related diseases, or to monitor changes in states of consciousness. After much research, Maxwell Cade, who pioneered biofeedback training in this country, was able to plot the significance of brainwave activity against states of consciousness. Alpha, beta and theta brainwave patterns correspond respectively to the state of consciousness one enters when meditating, to normal everyday consciousness and to the state of consciousness one enters when hypnotised.

The purpose of feedback training is to accelerate the process of learning how to relax, or how to meditate, or to know when one is in a hypnotic state. It is not intended that people should become hooked on the use of the machine to enter any particular mental state. The idea is that after training one becomes independent of the machine. It thus makes sense to take a course and use a machine rather than purchasing one for oneself, though it is possible to buy one. They range from under £100 for a relaxation meter to over £2500 for the 'Mind Mirror' (a brainwave monitor) developed by Maxwell Cade and Geoffrey Blundell.

READING

The Awakened Mind *by Cade, M. and Coxhead, N., Element 1987.* Subtitled *Biofeedback and the Development of Higher States of Awareness,* this book combines an outline of the principles of biofeedback regulation with the authors' exploration of its combination with meditation techniques to achieve a 'maximal mind-body awareness' leading to higher levels of consciousness. Another book worth seeking out is **Beyond Biofeedback** *by E and A. Green, Knoll 1989,* two of the originators of biofeedback techniques.

CENTRES OFFERING BIOFEEDBACK

Acumedic Centre, Audio Limited, Belgravia Beauty SW1, Centre for Stress Management SE3, Mental Development Ltd E5, Neal's Yard Therapy Rooms WC2.

Client-centred therapy

This is sometimes called Rogerian counselling or therapy after its founder Carl Rogers. His theory, method, and research has had a profound effect on the world of counselling.

Client-centered therapy is both an attitude on the part of the therapist which affects the style of intervention, and a particular way of behaving with the client. The therapist is trained to listen in an empathetic way and respond to the client by reflecting back to the client his or her own thoughts and feelings.

Client-centered therapy is phenomenological in its orientation. This means that the way the client perceives the world is seen as valid. The therapist will not impose any interpretations on the client's behaviour or invalidate the way the client sees himself or herself.

Rogers states that if a therapist possesses three qualities then the client will benefit. Firstly if the therapist has the quality of empathy and the client perceives this then the client will find the therapy beneficial. Empathy is the ability to put oneself in the shoes of the client, to understand the way the client sees the world and to be able to see it through his or her eyes. It is not enough that the therapist is empathetic but this quality must be perceived by the client. An essential skill for an empathetic counsellor is listening.

Secondly the therapist must be real. He or she must be genuine. It is essential that the client does not receive 'double messages' such as the therapist saying 'Yes of course I don't mind you talking about homosexuality' whilst crossing legs and going red in the face. This requires that the therapist must have undergone therapy, as being real requires understanding oneself. It means an ability to listen and be open to oneself.

Thirdly if the therapist can show a non-possessive warmth towards the client, prizing the client in a non-threatening way, then the client will feel valued and supported.

Client-centered therapy is practised on a one to one basis and in groups. Most trainings in counselling study the Rogerian approach. See 'Counselling' section.

READING

The Carl Rogers Reader *by Rogers, C. Constable 1990, £8.95*. This is a recent title, a sort of 'portable Carl Rogers'. It covers all the main areas and ideas in his work. For a more in-depth view, read **Client Centred Therapy** *£8.95* or his more popular **On Becoming a Person** *£7.95* both published by *Constable*.. **Person Centred Counselling in Action** *Mearns, D. & Thorne, B. PBK 1988, £8.95*. Part of an excellent series, this book gives the background theory of Rogers' ideas and gives guidelines as to how these are used in therapy. The major themes, Empathy, Unconditional Positive Regard and others are explored in depth.

CENTRES OFFERING CLIENT-CENTRED THERAPY

Eigenwelt London NW3, Healing Fields Practice N7, Lifespace Associates SW7.

Co-counselling

Co-counselling does not involve a professionally trained therapist. Two lay people meet to counsel each other for a set time. One assumes the role of client and talks to the other person, whose role is as a counsellor. When the allotted time is up they then switch roles and continue in a similar way.

This is a very simple idea, which was initially formulated by Harvey Jackins under the banner Re-evaluation Counselling. Courses were set up by him for people to receive guidance and training in these techniques. An emphasis was placed on learning how to practice the therapy without hurting or damaging one another.

The client is in charge and determines what he or she wants to talk about, for how long and how much he or she wants the counsellor to intervene. The counsellor's job is mainly to listen and pay attention to the client. Validation of the client's experience by the counsellor is seen as crucial, and this is imparted by the counsellor paying attention to the client and sticking with the material the client produces.

Repeating key phrases the client uses, and contradicting self-deprecatory statements are two of the few intervention techniques the counsellor uses.

Harvey Jackins set up the main organisation in America, and one of the main organisations in this country is Co-counselling International which is a break-away from the former.

Intending co-counsellors participate in a 40 hour training course, and after the training join a network where they can meet prospective partners, and practise co-counselling. They usually meet once a week with the same partner for two hours, until they both decide to terminate the arrangement. They can then choose another partner.

This method has two advantages. Firstly it is cheap. After paying for the initial training course only a small fee is required to be on the network list. Secondly the two people remain on an equal level, and much of what seems mysterious in therapy intervention becomes obvious when playing the part of the counsellor.

There are many adult education classes in this subject. Refer to *Floodlight* .

READING
Fundamentals of Co-counselling Manual *by Jackins, H. National Island Publications1982, £4.50.* This is the basic 'textbook' of Re-evaluation Co-counselling as used in training workshops. It is an explicit guide to the method. **How To Change Yourself and Your World** *by Evison, R. Co-counselling Phoenix1985, £4.95.* An English produced manual by people who broke away from the Jackins' Re-evaluation Counselling Network. Brings in many more (acknowledged) ideas from other therapies for use in the co-counselling situation.

CENTRES OFFERING CO-COUNSELLING
Co-Counselling NW3, Human Potential Resource Group, London Co-counselling Community W6, London Co-counselling Community W6.

TRAINING ON CO-COUNSELLING
London Co-counselling Community *Title of Training* Co-counselling Training. *Duration* 40 hours (either once a week or over weekends). *Entry requirements* None. *Fees* Payment is always based on ability to pay (£40-£80). *Comments* Training courses are run periodically. Contact the centre for information. The course is run by Co-counselling International (London). They do a further skills course for those wishing to progress further. Once trained on this course all two-way and group counselling sessions are free and you are free as a member to attend various workshops (day or residential) very cheaply. Must be able to give another person full attention without own distress disrupting the session.

Counselling

Counselling is not a particular form of therapy. We have included it in this section because of the many centres which offer counselling. The term covers a wide area of approaches, ranging from simple advice-giving to something which is indistinguishable from psychotherapy.

Counselling can be used to denote consultation and advice giving on a particular subject, as in Careers Guidance Counselling. Someone like a student counsellor may deal with practical problems like the late arrival of a grant cheque, or may give full blown psychotherapy. The Samaritans give telephone counselling to people who are in acute distress, and it is intended not so much to be an in depth exploration of someone's problems, but to provide whatever support, comfort and advice is needed to get someone through a crisis.

Counselling as a therapy is often associated with the client-centred therapy of Carl Rogers (see client-centred therapy section). The reflective technique evolved by Rogers, where the client's statements are not analysed but simply reflected back or rephrased, is often used by counsellors to help the client clarify issues. The focus of the counselling usually revolves around a specific issue or problem, such as sexual behaviour, financial situation or family crisis.

A few practitioners of alternative and complementary medicine also incorporate counselling into their approach. Many of the natural health centres offer counselling as well as body therapies. Because the term is so broad, it is as well to ask what kind of approach you will actually be getting, and what kind of training the counsellor has had.

The **British Association for Counselling** situated in Rugby is a large body which may help you with any questions about counselling and provide you with a practitioner in your area.

READING

The Counselling Handbook *by Quilliam, S & Grove-Stephenson, I., Thorsons 1989 £5.95.* A relatively recent book (Mar '90) aimed at clients and potential clients of counselling. It is a well researched, easy to read guide to most of the different styles/approaches available and where to find them. One of its strengths is the discussions included with both therapists and clients, which may ease one's apprehensions before taking the plunge. **Handbook of Counselling in Great Britain** *by Dryden, W. et al (Eds), Routledge 1989 £15.* A large and expensive book produced in conjunction with the British Association for Counselling. Gives an outline of the major situations where counselling is used and the major themes that can be covered. Less expensive if you are considering being counselled is the pamphlet **Counselling and Psychotherapy... Is it for me?** *by Hetty Einzig* for the British Association for Counselling, a brief 30 page introduction to what to expect.

CENTRES OFFERING COUNSELLING
All Hallows House EC3, Barnes Physiotherapy Clinic SW13, Bennet and Luck Natural Health Centre N1, Bodywise E2, Brackenbury Natural Health Centre W6, British Association for Counselling (North London Branch) N2, British Association for Counselling (South London Branch) SE6, British Association for Counselling, Cental School of Counselling and Therapy NW7, Centre for Counselling and Psychotherapy Education W11, Centre for Health and Healing W1, Centre for Stress Management SE3, Chelsea Pastoral Foundation SW3, City Health Centre EC1, Clapham Common Clinic SW4, Clissold Park Natural Health Centre N16, Counselling in North London N11, Dancing on the Path, Demigod SW10, Edgware Centre for Natural Health, Eigenwelt London NW3, Equilibrium Therapy Centre SW18, Hampstead Healing Centre NW3, Hampton Holistic Centre for Homoeopath and Autogenic Training, Healing Workshops NW5, Highbury Centre N5, Hillside Practice, Homoeopathic Centre W13, Homoeopathic Health Clinic, Human Potential Resource Group, Hypnotherapy/Psychotherapy Practice SW6, Identity Counselling Service W2, Isis Centre for Holistic Health N17, Isis SW9, Kensington Consultation Centre SW8, Living Centre, London Lighthouse W11, London Natural Health Clinic W8, Lotus Healing Centre, Mill Hill Health Care NW7, Moving Line Counselling and Therapy, Natural Healing Centre E7, Natural Healing Centre, Natureworks, North London Counselling Practice NW11, Nutribiotics , Primrose Healing Centre NW1, Refuah Shelaymah Natural Health Centre N16, Resonance SW17, School of the Dancing Dragon N16, Serpent Institute W12, Shirley Goldstein, Silver Birch Centre NW10, Skills with People N5, South London Natural Health Centre SW4, Spiral W12, St James Centre for Health and Healing W1, St. Marylebone Healing and Counselling Centre NW1, Sunra SW12, UK Training College of Hypnotherapy and Counselling W2, Welbeck Counselling Service W1, Wellspring Clinic SW6, Westminster Natural Health Centre SW1, Westminster Pastoral Foundation W8, Wimbledon Clinic of Natural Medicine SW19, Women and Health NW1, Women's Natural Health Centre NW5, Wood Street Clinic EN5.

TRAINING IN COUNSELLING
CAER (Centre For Alternative Education And Research) *Title of Training* Royal Society of Arts Counselling Skills In The Development of Learning. *Duration* Five x 3-day residentials and an introductory weekend. *Entry requirements* Previous experience of guidance or counselling. *Fees* Organisations £750, Individuals £660, YTS/ET £520.

Centre for Counselling and Psychotherapy Education *Title of Training* (1) Fundamentals of Counselling and Psychotherapy (2) Diploma in Counselling and Psychotherapy. *Duration* (1) One year part-time (Certificate course) (2) Four years part-time (Diploma course). *Entry requirements* (1) By Interview (2) Must have been in therapy for at least one year, plus one year part-time counselling training.

Fees (2) £950 per year excluding personal psychotherapy. *Comments* Holistic approach to counselling and psychotherapy which includes the spiritual dimension. Weekend workshops and short-term groups open to the public.

Spectrum *Title of Training* (1) Foundation course in counselling skills. *Duration* Foundation course is half a day per week for 1 year, plus 2 three-day groups. *Fees* £375 per term.

Westminster Pastoral Foundation *Title of Training* Diploma Course in Advanced Psychodynamic Counselling. Refer to organisers for details.

School of Psychotherapy and Counselling *Title of Training* (1) Certificate in Counselling (2) Diploma in Counselling (3) Master Degree (see heading under 'Education' in this book) (4) Post Graduate Course (see heading under 'Education' in this book). *Duration* (1) One year part-time (2) Two years part-time. *Entry Requirements* (1) No previous counselling experience required (2) Applicants will need to give evidence of preliminary study relevent to counselling, and of appropriate life experience and motivation for learning in its practical as well as its theoretical aspects. *Fees* (2) £400 per term. *Comments* (1) The course consists of a series of lectures with discussion, counselling skills training, and small group work (2) The course is largely based on experental learning and on practice. There is no written work in the first term, but two essays are required in later terms.

Couple Therapy

Couple therapy is applicable to all couples, married or unmarried, homosexual or heterosexual, however long the partners have been together.

The couple are seen together so that both sides of any relationship conflict can be appreciated. However if it is impossible for both partners to be present, either because one partner does not want to be involved in therapy, or because the partner seeking therapy does not feel they can discuss their feelings with their partner at first, then one partner can go along independently. The therapist will then discuss

---

Paul Allsop & Oriel Methuen

We work with individuals, couples and groups. In our practice, we deal with very specific problems involving relationship issues, family conflicts, infertility, sexual abuse, obsessional behaviour such as substance abuse, anxiety attacks and phobias. We also work with people who don't identify themselves as having a particular problem, but who feel the need to learn new personal skills and develop their potential as people.

Gestalt therapy forms the basis of our approach to therapy. We also use other aspects of our training, such as guided fantasy, psychodrama, family therapy and sensitivity training.

Our time is divided between working with Spectrum - a centre for Humanistic Psychology - and our own private practice.

101 The Avenue, London N10.
Telephone (081) 365 3951

with the client whether he or she wants to include the other partner at any stage. Different areas will be covered in the course of therapy depending on what the problems are. Often conflict may be caused because the partners do not know how to communicate with each other, and misunderstandings may have escalated. The therapist can help the couple to develop ways of expressing their feelings without blaming each other. Sometimes there may be more specific problems, such as an unsatisfactory sex life, and in this case if the difficulties are not just due to a more general difficulty in communicating, these can be dealt with (see Sex Therapy section). Sometimes there may be a need for individual work if one or both partners have personal issues which need to be explored. Sometimes the issues may involve quite a practical solution, for instance if one partner needs to find a means of self-expression outside the relationship such as study or work, the therapy can be used to explore the possibilities.

In some cases it may be that the couple discover that they do not want to stay together. The therapist can then help them to negotiate a separation which is satisfactory in emotional terms. If there are children involved, the therapist may suggest that they become included in the sessions so that they can participate in this process. RELATE (formerly Marriage Guidance) gives free counselling to couples.

READING

Couples in Counselling *by Gough, T. (Dartman, Longman & Todd 1989)* *£6.95.* Most therapy approaches can be, and are used when working with couples. What is useful about this book is its down to earth appraisal of the issues that may be causing problems in a relationship, to either or both partners, and the techniques that may be applied to help resolve such difficulties.

CENTRES OFFERING COUPLE THERAPY

Association for Analytic and Bodymind Therapy and Training N10, Association for Marriage Enrichment W8, Brackenbury Natural Health Centre W6, Centre for Counselling and Psychotherapy Education W11, Chiron W5, Ealing Psychotherapy Centre W3, Equilibrium Therapy Centre SW18, Gestalt Therapy in West London W3, Hampstead Healing Centre NW3, Hillside Practice, Holistic Yoga Centre MK19, Institute of Group Analysis NW3, Kensington Consultation Centre SW8, London Institute for the Study of Human Sexuality SW5, Metanoia, Minster Centre NW2, North London Centre for Group Therapy N14, North London Counselling Practice NW11, North London Counselling Service N5, Pellin Centre SW8, Resonance SW17, Spectrum N4.

Dance Therapy

Dance therapy aims to release the natural flow of bodily expression which is unique to each individual. Movement is a way of communicating from direct physical experience which children use quite naturally. In growing up, we are often taught to restrict this joyful and expressive movement. Dance therapy concentrates on spontaneous, individual movements which proceed from the dancer's experience rather than on learning formal dance patterns.

Tribal societies have long used dance as a way of expressing feelings, of accomplishing the transition to other states of consciousness (for instance the trance state), and for connecting to their community and environment in a way which has meaning, often through the mythic significance of the dance. In Europe over the centuries since medieval times, dance has become more and more formalised, until the appearance of Isadora Duncan at the turn of the century with her free form, emotive dancing which shocked many of her straight-laced contemporaries.

Rudolph Laban, a German psychotherapist was the first to incorporate dance into his treatment of patients between the wars. Marian Chace, an American dance therapist, developed another form of dance therapy when she was asked to work with patients in a mental hospital, after psychiatrists there had been impressed by the improvements in patients who attended her dance classes privately.

Dance therapists differ widely in their approach. Usually therapy takes place in a group. First the participants are asked to do warming up exercises, and some material to be developed in the course of the class may emerge at this stage. Music may be played, but this is not necessarily the case. The therapist may reflect the dancer by mirroring his or her movements, drawing attention to particular gestures, or inviting the dancer to find words for the emerging feelings or connect more fully to them. Interaction between the group as a whole may also be encouraged. In some dance therapy classes the emphasis may be less on 'therapy' and more on 'creativity'

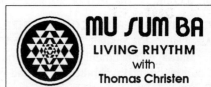

where the dancers are encouraged to find their own style of dance to express their uniqueness.

Dance therapy can also be used in a Jungian framework. Here movement functions as a bridge to the unconscious mind. The movements, once developed and repeated, may come to embody symbols or mythological themes, which will then be discussed by therapist and client.

Dance therapy can be used in a wide variety of situations. It is useful for people who are unable to speak about their feelings, such as autistic children or psychotics. Those who suffer from physical symptoms related to stress or other emotional difficulties can also benefit, as well as those who are suffering from immobilising organic complaints such as Parkinson's disease or a stroke. It is also useful for people who tend to intellectualise too much.

READING

The Mastery of Movement *by Laban, R. Northcote House 1980, £8.95.* This is Laban's classic book on human movement, as we follow his methods of exploring the inner motivation of movement and its expression in emotion, intellect and values/meanings. Another book worth looking at is **Personality Assessment Through Movement** *by North, M. Northcote Press 1989.*

CENTRES OFFERING DANCE THERAPY

5 to Midnight (some workshops in London), Creative Arts and Therapy Consultants N16, Dancing on the Path SE22, Open Gate (various locations in London), Playspace NW1.

Encounter

Social convention dictates that we restrain ourselves. There are many times when we have to suppress certain feelings for social reasons, but we are also imprisoned by our own neurotic constraints. Whether the suppression is due to real external constraints or whether it is due to a neurotic withholding is something an encounter group tries to find out.

Will Schutz pioneered the 'open encounter', the version of the encounter group which was the most successful in this country, and which grew at a phenomenal rate in the late sixties and reached the height of its popularity in the early seventies.

Schutz would follow the energy in the group at any one moment. For instance if a member was tapping his foot he would ask him to exaggerate it and get in touch with what this impulse was about. If the person were to say he felt impatient with someone in the group and would like to kick him into action, Schutz would have him kick a cushion and get more in touch with this feeling and to express this pent up emotion. Where this would lead to would depend on many factors. It might be that many of the group also have this feeling towards the same person, but held back from saying so for one reason or another. It might be that the impulse was a frustration at his own feeling of getting nowhere, which would be further therapeutic grist for the mill. As more physical movement is required than in most other therapy groups, participants sit on cushions rather than on chairs so that they are not in any way obstructed.

Encounter groups give people permission to cut through social convention and politeness and openly encourage the expression of feeling and honesty. Rather than talking about feelings the encounter group encourages their physical expression. If you were to say you would like to hug a particular person in the group, you might be asked to go ahead and do it.

66 Johnny (name changed) was a central character in an encounter/gestalt group that I participated in over six months. The group was held in 1973 at Quaesitor, a large 'growth' centre in leafy Willesden. Johnny was from Glasgow and was fond of recounting stories of his violent background. One such story was that when he felt depressed he would go out on to the street and beat up the first person he came across. Apparently this eased his own internal pain. Over a period of a few months he had punched me twice in the group and I was outraged that he had got away with this. He was not banned from the group, but instead gained a lot of support from other group members who felt sorry for him because of his troubled upbringing. I figured that the group members supported him mainly from fear, lest their own noses got punched, rather than for any altruistic reasons. Johnny loved to be in the limelight in the group, which was much resented by the other members who felt cast into the shadows. One day the group decided to cope with Johnny's 'attention seeking' by ignoring him. After about an hour Johnny could cope with this no more. He let out a big 'Ahhhhh', picked up a stool (used for bioenergetic work) by its legs, and threw it through the closed windows. They were large bay windows which had been specially double-glazed so that the sounds made in the group room would not percolate out into the street. It made an thunderous crash, and a small crowd appeared to view the spectacle. After this incident Johnny was still not banned, but instead was given the attention he sought.

I must add that this particular group was untypical of therapy groups in general. Since then I have participated in many encounter/gestalt groups and consider this one to be an isolated yet disturbing experience. **99**

Mike Considine

There are two other types of encounter groups, neither of which are as common as the 'open encounter'. Carl Rogers pioneered a form of encounter where he encouraged a more honest engagement between members and tried to induce an atmosphere of empathy, regard for the other members and genuineness in relating. It is called 'basic encounter'. Chuck Dederick pioneered the 'Synanon encounter' specifically for drug abusers. Members were asked to focus on one person and verbally attack him or her. Members would take it in turn to be target. The aim of this 'shock therapy' was to wake them up from an habitual lifestyle.

Encounter is practised in groups. Often the setting is residential. It may be a two, three or five day workshop. They have been known to go on for a month. If it is described as a 'marathon encounter', this means you are likely to get little sleep for the duration of the workshop. In this country the 'marathon encounter' usually lasts between twenty four and forty eight hours.

READING
Joy... 20 Years Later *by Schutz, W. Ten Speed Press, 1989, £7.95.* This is a revised edition of Schutz's original text on the principles and practice of his ideas. Although not so specific to the actual workings of an encounter group as his other book **Elements of Encounter** (long out of print, and never widely available in the UK), it nevertheless gives a good grounding in the encounter approach and what to expect. **Theories and Practise of Group Psychotherapy** *by Yalom, I. Harper and Row, 1987, hardback £17.95.* The chapters on Encounter and T-Groups (the origins of Encounter) in this book are excellent introductions to the method. The whole book is recommended to anyone who wants to look at the many and various 'human potential' approaches to group work.

CENTRES OFFERING ENCOUNTER
Human Potential Resource Group , Open Centre EC1, Spectrum N4.

Existential Psychotherapy

Existential psychotherapy can be considered more an approach than a therapy in the normal sense of the term, as it is against techniques and weak on a classification of intervention strategies on the part of the therapist. Indeed, the training of an existential therapist is quite different from that followed by trainees in many other psychotherapies. The trainee existential psychotherapist is expected to become steeped not only in psychological theory, but in the philosophy of existentialism. Most of all, she is encouraged in taking a particular attitude towards herself, towards others and towards life itself. To this end the trainee undergoes a form of apprenticeship with a supervisor who acts as a guide. The training therefore bears more resemblance to the guru/student relationship found in oriental religions than it does to western psychotherapy.

To understand existential psychotherapy it is necessary to know something about its philosophical underpinning. The work of the existentialists such as Heidegger, Boss, Sartre, Kierkegaard, Nietzsche and Husserl provided the philosophical movement upon which existential psychotherapy is based. Existentialism focuses on the 'givens of existence', such as being, death, alienation, authenticity, suffering, responsibility in choosing and meaning. These themes were also echoed by clients in psychotherapy and soon the the philosophy of existentialism filtered through into the psychotherapeutic arena. Existential psychotherapy grew to occupy a place of its own, with its own style of expression.

In this country, the psychiatrist Ronald Laing became famous in the 1960s for his existentialist approach in working with schizophrenics. He placed importance on understanding the subjective world of the client and attacked the swiftness of psychiatry in objectively labelling the so-called psychotic. He saw madness as an authentic experience which is in itself a healing process, through which one could journey and emerge on the other side. Laing set up the Philadelphia Association in London from which the break-away organisation, the Arbours Association was formed. This organisation turned private houses into therapeutic communities where the previously labelled schizophrenics were allowed to express their madness.

READING
Existential Counselling in Practice *by Van Deurzen-Smith, E., Sage 1988.* The first practical book written in the UK on this form of therapy. Quite readable for a book on a subject which many find intellectually difficult. She weaves the philosophy, and practice of the approach into an interesting framework. A heavier tome is *Yalom's Existential Psychotherapy, Harper and Rowe £17.95*, but for anyone interested in the flavour of the existential approach, try reading any of R.D. Laing's works, all published by Penguin.

CENTRES OFFERING EXISTENTIAL PSYCHOTHERAPY
Eigenwelt London NW3, Philadelphia Association NW3, South London Network for Counselling and Psychotherapy, Society of Existential Analysis.

TRAININGS IN EXISTENTIAL ANALYSIS PSYCHOTHERAPY
Society for Existential Analysis Plans for a one-year course in existential psychotherapy. Are also associated with a post-qualifying diploma in existential psychotherapy (a two year training for those in this field). When phoning you will get through to Regent's College.

Family Therapy

There are a number of different schools of family therapy, but most follow a systems theory approach whilst drawing on different therapeutic models such as psychoanalytic psychotherapy, gestalt, transactional analysis, client-centred therapy, behavioural methods and psychodrama for some of their intervention tactics.

The focus is not on the individual family member. If any one individual suffers symptoms within the family, such as a child suffering from 'school phobia', this is considered a symptom of the family, and the family must be treated as a whole. It may be that the child will not go to school because of the distant relationship that has developed between the parents, and consequently the child feels a need to support the mother.

The aim is to discover how the behaviour of members within the family perpetuates the symptom, and to change the relationship between the members so that the symptom disappears. Emphasis is placed not on why the family is behaving the way it is, but on what present behaviour is causing the symptom.

Therapy may be carried out with one or two therapists working with the family. It is usually brief because of the difficulty often involved in bringing the whole family together at one time. Sessions are usually at least six in number.

Usually the family will go the therapist/s place of work, but sometimes the therapist/s will go to the family's home to undertake therapy or will make at least one attempt to go to the home of the family to see how they behave in their surroundings.

Family therapy is often suggested to families where one of the children has a problem, for instance an unruly teenager or a young child experiencing difficulties at school.

READING

Peoplemaking *by Satir, V. Science & Behaviour 1972, £6.95.* This was the first book to bring the benefits of the insights gained from family therapy to the general public. It's an easy read that brings many of the problems of family life into sharp focus, and has been generally hailed for its healing potential. Another similar title that is worth looking at is **Families and How to Survive Them** *by Cleese, J. & Skynner, R.*, the latter being one of the principal developers of Family Therapy in the UK. **Family Therapy in Britain** *by Street, E & Dryden, W. Open University Press 1988, £12.50.* Another manual containing articles on the major approaches to Family Therapy in use in the UK, by many of the leading practitioners in their fields.

CENTRES OFFERING FAMILY THERAPY

British Association for Social Psychiatry, Camden Psychotherapy Unit WC1, Gale Centre for Creative Therapy, Institute of Family Therapy W1, Institute of Group Analysis NW3, Kensington Consultation Centre SW8, Metanoia, North London

Centre for Group Therapy N14, Tavistock Clinic NW3, Westminster Pastoral Foundation W8.

TRAINING IN FAMILY THERAPY

Institute of Family Therapy *Title of Training* (1) Introductory course in Family and Marital Therapy (2) Part I, Training in Family Therapy (3) M. Sc in Family Therapy (4) Advanced Clinical Training in Family Therapy (5) Introductory Course in Alcohol and Substance Abuse and the Family. *Duration* (1) One year part-time (2) One year part-time (3) Two years part-time (4) Two years part-time (5) Twenty weeks part-time. *Entry requirements* See training prospectus available from the Training Dept at above address. *Fees* (1) £495 per annum payable in termly instalments (2) £575 per annum payable in termly instalments (3) £1,950 per annum (4) £1,750 per annum 5) £265 per course, payable in two instalments.

Tavistock Clinic *Title of Training* Programme of Training in Child and Family and Adolescent Psychiatry. *Duration* Four years full time. *Fees* £1450 per annum if UK or EEC. £3350 for others. *Comments* trainees are required to have personal psychotherapy at least three times a week at their own expense.

Feminist Therapy

Feminist therapy is an attitudinal approach to the practice of therapy. It was founded by women who observed sexism and patriarchal values on the part of therapist and client which became reinforced within the therapy. Women found they were being undermined in their determination to grow when confronted with a sexist male therapist. They also found that some of the assumptions of traditional psychotherapy were based on social values which subtly affected the therapeutic encounter, whether the therapist was male or female.

Feminist therapy began at a grass roots level, and through consciousness raising groups, rape crisis work and work with battered women there has emerged a therapy with a clear philosophy.

Three common issues emerge in the therapy of women: anger, self-nurturance and autonomy or power. Women tend to turn their anger inwards rather than outwards. In feminist therapy the client is helped to be more expressive and to direct the anger to where it belongs. Women tend to have devoted themselves to others at the expense of themselves, and a consequence of this can be depression. In feminist therapy they are asked to take care of their own needs too. To gain autonomy women are asked to expand the options they allow themselves and are helped to confront the role restrictions society places on them, at home and at work.

Susie Orbach and Luise Eichenbaum founded the Women's Therapy Centre in London.

While feminist therapy is not exclusive to women, men have not opted for it. Virtually all the clients are women, and all of the therapists are. However, some male

❝ Barry told me he used gestalt and another psychotherapy (I forget now which one). There was a mattress and cushion in the room, but - no other furniture. He stated categorically that 'ANYTHING goes in this room, except violence towards me'. My thoughts drifted immediately to sex - he was quite attractive. However the first session consisted of me sitting on the mattress (shoes off), and him sitting on the floor (shoes off). We talked about my childhood and I wanted to cry with frustration and anger, aimed primarily against my brother. Barry then picked up a large cushion and invited me to punch it as if it were my brother. At this point I toppled over and dissolved into helpless laughter. Barry looked extremely hurt. He got his own back in the next session by us sitting in silence for a whole hour, me waiting for him to 'begin' and him waiting for me to start. I didn't begin and didn't go back. ❞

Gill Stow

therapists have begun to explore the theme of men's socialisation and are reaching for new definitions of masculinity.

A feminist therapist may incorporate gestalt, client-centred therapy or T.A. into the therapy, but the essential ingredient is the emphasis that is placed on the individual worth of the client, and on her socialisation. Issues frequently dealt with are body image, eating problems, self-care and sexuality.

READING
What Do Women Want *by Eichenbaum, L. & Orbach, S. Fontana 1983, £3.50.* The authors are pioneers of the Feminist Therapy approach, and are co-founders of the Women's Therapy Centre. This book explores the many issues that women have to come to terms with to fulful their own emotional needs. A book for men as well. **Feminist Counselling in Action** *by Chaplin, J. Sage 1988, £8.95.* Written for counsellors and therapists to understand a feminist approach, it is also useful for people who may be drawn to the approach. Further readings can be found in **In Our Experience; Workshops at the Women's Therapy Centre** *by Krzowski, S. & Land, P. (Eds) Womens Press £6.95.*

CENTRES OFFERING FEMINIST THERAPY
CAER (Centre For Alternative Education And Research), Communication and Counselling Foundation, Gestalt Studio, Hidden Strengths, Human Potential Resource Group, Isis SW9, London Institute for the Study of Human Sexuality SW5, Minster Centre NW2, Pellin Centre SW8, Psychotherapy Workshops for Women, Redwood Women's Training Association, Serpent Institute W12, Spectrum N4, Women Unlimited SW16, Women's Therapy Centre N7.

TRAININGS IN FEMINIST THERAPY
Women's Therapy Centre *Title of Training* Working with women - a psychodynamic approach. *Duration* 1 year, 1 evening per week. *Entry requirements* For women who have some professional training, and have some psychodynamic input into their work with women. *Fees* Apply to organisers. *Comments* Training workshops for people working as social workers, health care services workers, psychotherapists and those in the voluntary sector. Includes working with women with eating problems, incest survivors, including the black experience, groupwork etc.

Gestalt Therapy

Fritz Perls was a Freudian trained psychoanalyst who became disenchanted with the practice of psychoanalysis. He was analysed by Reich for whom he expresses much affection and by whom gestalt thinking was heavily influenced. He set up the South African Institute of Psychoanalysis and then later went to America where, with his wife Laura Perls, he evolved gestalt therapy. In the sixties he introduced gestalt therapy to Esalen, California, the first growth centre. Rather than paying attention to why clients behaved the way they did as was common in psychoanalysis, he paid attention to what they did and how they behaved. He helped them become more aware of what their behaviour meant to them and what it signified to others. Thus gestalt therapy pays attention to the non-verbal more than the verbal. This does not mean that people talk less in gestalt groups, but that the focus of concern of the therapist is much more on the bodily messages than in more orthodox psychotherapies.

Another theme that Perls stressed was responsibility. He insisted clients take responsibility for themselves. If someone would say 'It feels good when you say that' he would ask them to rephrase it as 'I feel good when you say that', thus enabling them to become more in touch with their own feelings.

Talking to the 'empty chair' is the hallmark of gestalt therapy. If for instance you had not expressed your feelings to someone close to you, such as your mother, you may be asked to imagine her sitting in an empty chair, and to say the things you wished you had said to her. You may be then asked to switch chairs and to sit in the chair you imagined her sitting in, and pretend to be her responding to you. Thus a dialogue might ensue between yourself and what you imagine your mother would say to you. This unrehearsed dramatisation of how you see your relationship with your mother is likely to provide the group members and the therapist with a detailed and revealing story. The use of the 'empty chair' is not limited to being filled with persons. Parts of oneself can be placed there as well. For example, if you are the type of person who constantly criticises yourself, you may be asked to put the critical side of yourself in the empty chair and to have a dialogue with that side of yourself. Such a public display of the contents of one's own psyche engenders strong emotional bonds between the group members and can produce an intense emotional atmosphere.

People who could most benefit from this type of therapy are those who feel they have difficulty expressing their feelings, those who feel stuck, those who feel cut off from others and those who would like feedback on how people see them.

READING
Gestalt Therapy *by Perls, F, Goodman, P and Hefferline, R. Souvenir Press, 1974,* £7.95. The original work describing the theory of Gestalt therapy. Good to explore its basis thoroughly, but many people find it a difficult 'read'. Probably more accessible is his later book **The Gestalt Approach & Eye-Witness to Therapy** *(S &B, £8.95).* This was originally published as two books, the first being a last revision of his theoretical ideas, the second, transcripts of some of his films giving an insight into Perls 'live'. **The Red Book of Gestalt** by *Houston G. Rochester Foundation 1982 £3.50.* A delightful little book, self published and illustrated by line drawings, giving a simple, but not simplistic, introduction to how Gestalt Therapy works, both in group and individual settings.

Qualified, experienced, caring,
counselling psychologist, hypnotherapist/
hypno-analyst.
*Help given with smoking, slimming,
anxiety, panic attacks, phobias and
other stress related problems.*

For further information telephone:
C O Murray, BA (Hons), MA, PhD (Psychology), DHP, MYAH on 081-767 9006.

Consultation hours: 10am-7.30pm weekdays,
10am-2.30pm Saturdays.
(Answerphone, reply assured)

GESTALT THERAPY
in
WEST LONDON
■■■■■■■

A group of fully qualifed Gestalt
therapists offering individual,
couple and group work.
Ring for details (081) 993 0868

GESTALT CENTRE
LONDON
*Member of the UK Standing Conference
for Psychotherapy*

OPEN PROGRAMME
Programme includes gestalt, encounter, marathons, weekend workshops and ongoing groups.
PERSONAL DEVELOPMENT GROUP
An intensive ongoing therapy group of 10 evenings and 2 weekends per term. Termly intake.
BASIC TRAINING
To incorporate Gestalt into your life and work. A 3-4 year course of 11 evenings and 2 weekends per term plus individual therapy. Termly entry and evaluation allows each trainee to progress through the training at their own pace. Emphasis is on experiencial learning so that skills emerge from personal experience rather than taught as techniques.
ADVANCED TRAINING
This practitioner level leads to a Diploma and membership of the Centre Associates who provide an extensive open programme.

**For prospectus and details contact
Thelma Breed Tel: (0727) 864806**

Individuals   Groups

OLIVIA THORNE
Pellin Trained Gestalt Therapist

Make important changes through practical and in-depth work
in a safe & supportive environment. Lewisham area.

Tel. 081-852 4647

66 I came to London at 19 to study for a degree in Electronics. My life was in front of me and the thought of moving to the big capital thrilled me. I had not anticipated being lonely when I came to London as I thought of it as the big city where I was certain to make some friends amongst the millions of people living there. I knew that I had difficulty relating to people. I was shy but wanted so much to enjoy my life with other people. After three years I realised that something was wrong. I had few friends and I related to them in superficial ways. I found it especially difficult to make friends with women. I became very distressed at the thought of the rest of my life continuing in the same way. I decided I needed some help. The thought of seeing a psychiatrist appalled me as I did not consider myself to be mentally ill. Nevertheless I went to my GP and insisted on seeing a psychiatrist. After a six week wait I had an appointment to visit one at a hospital in Mile End. I climbed the stairs to the top floor where the psychiatrist shook my hand and led me into a room where there were a group of about fifteen students with clip boards sitting in a semi-circle facing two empty chairs, one of which he beckoned me to be seated in. He seated himself in the other chair and asked me if I minded the students observing the session. Can you imagine how I felt! I had come to get help with difficulty in being open and expressing who I was, and here I was being asked to talk about my life and problems in front of a group of strangers. I was enraged though I kept my feelings to myself (I sat on my feelings in those days). I told him there was nothing wrong with me (I wanted to get out of that situation as soon as possible, I could not bear being watched by those others). He said I had been wasting his time and I agreed with him. He then escorted me out. I remember we were on the top floor and I looked for a window to jump out of. I had a delicious fantasy of how foolish he would look in front of his students if someone he had just diagnosed as a timewaster took a suicide leap from his hospital window. Fortunately I realised it was a too high a price to pay and found my way home.

After several months of depression I saw a classified ad in *Time Out* for a Gestalt group and signed myself up. This was 1972 and it was the first Gestalt workshop in England. It proved to be the answer I had been looking for. I learned how my shyness was an expression of fear of the hostility towards me I imagined I saw in other peoples eyes. I learned how to make contact. It was not easy. In fact it was often painful. But it was also wonderful. It was such a release to be able to talk in a genuine way to others and not to feel so anxious. I remember writing then that 'it blew my mind into outer space and that I wanted to become a therapist and blow other peoples' minds into outer space'. I did later become a gestalt therapist. 99

Mike Considine

CENTRES OFFERING GESTALT THERAPY

Arcadia Creative Therapy Centre SE6, Association for Analytic and Bodymind Therapy and Training N10, CAER (Centre For Alternative Education And Research), Chiron W5, Gestalt Centre London, Gestalt Studio, Gestalt Therapy & Contribution Training SE13, Gestalt Therapy in West London W3, Hillside Practice, Jeyrani Health Centre E18, Lifespace Associates SW7, Metanoia, Minster Centre NW2, Natural Medicine Centre, New Cross Natural Therapy Centre, Pellin Centre SW8, Pellin Training Courses SW8, Person-Centred Art Therapy Centre NW11, Psychotherapy for Individuals, Couples & Groups, Resonance, Resonance SW17, South London Network for Counselling and Psychotherapy, Spectrum N4.

TRAININGS IN GESTALT THERAPY

Gestalt Centre London *Title of Training* (1) Basic gestalt Training (2) Practitioner Training. *Duration* (1) Three to four years. Twelve weekly evenings plus two weekends per term. (2) Additional two years to the above, usually full-time. *Entry requirements* Experience of gestalt necessary. Other than that the course can take a trainee from scratch to psychotherapy practitioner. *Fees* Course fees are £390 per term plus individual therapy fees. *Comments* The course operates a unique termly system that allows each person to progress at his/her own work rate. Since it is both a personal and professional training, the therapy, theory and practice are interlinked.

Metanoia *Title of Training* Gestalt Psychotherapy Diploma Training. *Duration* Three years. Modular basis of between one to eight five day workshops per year. *Entry requirements* Completion of introduction course on the fundamentals of gestalt (held three times a year) or its equivalent. *Fees* £160 per workshop. *Comments* requires personal psychotherapy for the duration of the training. Some bursaries available.

Pellin Training Courses *Title of Training* Pellin counselling/Gestalt Training Course. *Duration* Three years part-time, one year basic, two years advanced. *Entry requirements* Should be in helping professions or wishing to find work with people. *Fees* £950 per year (incl. VAT). *Comments* They do in-depth interviews and ask for a reference.

Gestalt Studio *Title of Training* Gestalt Studio Training. *Duration* Three years plus two years` supervision. *Fees* Arranged on interview.

Group-oriented Therapy

By group-oriented therapy we mean therapy where the group process is deemed to be important and worthy of analysis, and where the dynamics of the group compose part of the therapy, so that it becomes therapy *of* the group and *by* the group. Although no firm line can be drawn here, because many psychotherapies would argue that the dynamics of the group are important, the crucial thing is that the dynamics of the group take up a central role in the therapy and that historically the origins of the therapy evolved around group processes. In London the three major schools have different theoretical origins.

The 'group analytic' approach was developed by S.H. Foulkes. It was developed not only as a way of applying psychoanalytic knowledge to group practice, but takes into account factors specific to groups. In this type of group the therapist, or 'conductor' as they prefer to be called, may remain in the background much of the time, but can at times be much more active. The free floating group discussion is to group analytic therapy what free association is to psychoanalysis. Eight people (four men and four women) is seen as the optimum number for this type of group. Therapy is usually twice a week, one and half hours for each session.

The Tavistock approach to group work was developed by W. Bion. Bion (a Kleinian analyst) saw much of what went on in groups as issues over leadership. The therapist or 'consultant' usually stays in the background and offers interpretations about what is going on in the group. Groups can go on intensively for a week and are affectionately known as 'Tavi' groups.

The humanistic approach offers 'T-groups', sometimes referred to as sensitivity training groups. These groups meet residentially, often for a week. The focus is on the 'here and now' activity of the group and feedback and self-expression are a prime concern. The leader reflects, for instance, on how the group conducts itself, and the leader will focus not on 'what' decisions the group took but 'how' it went about deciding and which roles people took up in this decision making.

All of the above approaches are useful in learning both about how groups function and about your contribution to the group process. For those who feel they would like to know more about groups or for those who work in groups and need to understand more of group processes, all can be recommended, but remember that the style of each of the above schools are quite different from each other.

READING

Group Therapy in Britain by Aveline, M. & Dryden, W. (Eds). Open University Press 1988, £12.50. A manual, giving theoretical background and practical usage of the major approaches to group therapy. Another book worth looking at is by Yalom, reviewed in the 'Encounter' section. **Once Upon A Group** by Kindred, M. Self published 1987, £3.00 A light- hearted look at what can be quite a heavy subject. The author draws out, in basic lay language, the themes and issues that can be dealt with in any of the group therapies practised today.

CENTRES OFFERING GROUP-ORIENTED PSYCHOTHERAPY

Association for Analytic and Bodymind Therapy and Training N10, Association for Group and Individual Psychotherapy N19, Gale Centre for Creative Therapy, Group Relations Training Association , Human Potential Resource Group, Institute of Group Analysis NW3, Minster Centre NW2, North London Centre for Group

66 I participated on an 'intensive' psychotherapy group in the seventies, which comprised a series of weekend workshops over six months with visiting groups leaders. The group was dominated by the women. They did most of the talking and took most of the decisions about what we should do as a group. My perception was that the women partly maintained control by putting the men down and I resented this. So when we had a visiting male group-oriented leader, I complained to him about this and I explained how I felt impotent in the group. He suggested the following exercise: he would go to the toilet and wait there for me to fetch him; he would *only* leave the toilet if I personally came to bring him back. The theory behind this, he said, was that he was giving me his power; it was up to the group to persuade me to bring him back so that the weekend workshop could continue; I therefore would be able to regain my potency and hold my head high once more. Upon that he disappeared from the room and went down to the basement where the toilet was located (in retrospect I think that he needed to go to the toilet anyway and was killing two birds with one stone with this exercise). To my surprise the women sat and talked to themselves and completely ignored me. I maintained my composure knowing full well that sooner or later one of them would crack and would have to ask the favour of me. I felt gleeful of this opportunity to be in command. After about half an hour one woman turned to me and asked me to fetch our group leader to which I said 'No'. The women again resumed chatting to each other and ignoring me. After another half hour my thoughts turned to our beloved leader pent up in the loo, so I decided to go down and tell him what had transpired since he had left. No sooner had I tapped on the loo door than he shot out, but I pushed him back inside saying that the women had not even tried to persuade me to let him out, and I explained to him that I was paying him a visit rather than arranging his release. He was downcast at this, and told me to tell the women to hurry up. I went back to the group and sat there another half hour before giving up and rescuing him. **99**

Mike Considine

Therapy N14, Playspace NW1, Skills with People N5, Tavistock Clinic NW3, Will (Workshop Institute for Living Learning) .

TRAININGS IN GROUP-ORIENTED PSYCHOTHERAPY
Goldsmiths' College *Title of Training* Diploma in Group Therapy. *Duration* Three years part-time. *Entry requirements* Degree or professional qualification. *Fees* £750 p.a. part-time.

Human Potential Resource Group *Title of Training* Facilitator Styles Course. *Duration* Two years part-time. Approx 60 days each year including regular meetings, one day per week & 3 weekend workshops each term, plus 2 x 5 day workshops per year. *Entry requirements* For those in the teaching/training professions. The course is a balance of theoretical with experiential and practical work. *Fees* Approx £400 per term.

Institute of Group Analysis *Title of Training* (1) Introductory General Course in Group Work. (2) Qualifying Course in Group Work. *Duration* (1) One academic year, Thurs 4.30-7.30. (2) At least three years. *Entry requirements* (1) None specified. (2) Must have completed the General Course in Group Work. Degree with some knowledge of the field. *Fees* (1) £485 (2) Selection procedure fee: £65 . Twice weekly group analysis: £1464 per annum. Theoretical and supervision seminars: £1,095 per annum. Professional indemnity insurance: £45. *Comments* (1) Small and large group experience. (2) Training takes the form of twice weekly personal group analysis (each session lasts one and half hour). Theory and supervision.

Tavistock Clinic *Title of Training* Training in Group Work. For details of training apply to the Clinic.

Westminster Pastoral Foundation *Title of Training* (1) Certificate in Groupwork in Community and Organisational Settings. (2) Diploma in Group Counselling. *Comments* Refer to organisers for details.

Hypnotherapy

There are as many types of hypnotherapy as there are practitioners. They may have different aims, but they do share one characteristic. All begin with the therapist guiding the client into an hypnotic state. The client is simply required to respond positively to the direction of the therapist. Once in this state, what happens next will depend on the aims of the therapy and the background and training of the therapist.

Hypnotherapy tends to be symptom oriented. It offers help for tension, smoking, pain relief, obesity, psychosomatic ailments and phobias - the list is extensive. Some hypnotherapists claim to be able to uncover repressed material from the unconscious. Indeed, Freud gave hypnosis respectability when he got results from using it on his early clients, but later abandoned it when he found it induced idealisation of the analyst and when its effects proved to be transient. He replaced it with *free association* within psychoanalysis which would seem to have been the kiss of death

❝ Several years ago I visited a hypnotherapist because I was severely depressed, tense and my general health was suffering. I went down to 7 stone in weight. Things had been brought to a head by an unfortunate incident at work. I could see no meaning in life and had no interests. The hypnotherapist told me that he was a Jungian psychologist and thought he could help me. He said that he took the whole person into consideration.

He recommended that I take vitamin B12 and have a tonic consisting of 1/4 pint of sherry, 1/4 pint of evaporated milk and an egg, all beaten up together. I soon put on weight and felt stronger.

Through hypnosis he helped me to relax, I found his voice very soothing and calming. He taught me self hypnosis for relaxation which I find very useful.

Through auto suggestion he used the word 'metaphysical', a word which I was not familiar with. Since treatment, a whole new world has opened up for me. Through studying metaphysical subjects such as philosophy, yoga, the after-life, psychology, spiritual healing, the works of Jung, Fromm and Laing, I have found a completely new outlook on life, something which has helped me greatly. I found that as I studied one subject, it led to another.

I feel that this was really the root of my depression, not something that could have been dealt with by antidepressants alone. I consider that I have benefited greatly from this treatment and I feel that it has expanded my mind considerably. ❞

Christine Davidson

to hypnosis as a treatment tool. Nevertheless the use of hypnosis it seems has grown unabated, but the type of therapy that it is offered within, as was mentioned earlier, varies a great deal from practitioner to practitioner. It may be the therapist will simply impose a counter suggestion upon the client such as 'when you leave here you will want to smoke less', or he or she may want to explore some of the client's unwanted feelings and will perhaps encourage the client to explore the physical manifestations of the feelings.

Usually a contract is agreed between therapist and client before hypnosis begins about what the aims of the therapy are and what suggestions will be given to the client. The therapist cannot make you do anything against your will in hypnosis, or make you do anything that is outside your normal code of ethics.

READING

Hypnosis *by Waxman, D. Unwin 1981, £3.95*. Subtitled 'A Guide for Patients', this is a thorough introduction to the history, development, and practice of classical hypnosis. One flaw however : the heavy bias against non-medical practitioners. Another introductory book is **Hypnotherapy, is it for you?** *by Sleet, R., Element 1989*. **Hypnotherapy; A Modern Approach** *by Golden, W. et al. Pergamon 1988, £7.50*. Another book for practitioners, which can be of use to interested or potential clients. The authors use many of the 'newer' approaches to hypnosis, for example the non-directive approach developed from the work of Milton Erikson, who is now acknowledged as the greatest hypnotherapist of our time.

CENTRES OFFERING HYPNOTHERAPY

Acupuncture and Osteopathy Clinic SW1, Alternative Medicine Clinic NW1, Association for Analytic and Bodymind Therapy and Training N10, Association of Natural Medicines, Barbican Natural Health Centre EC1, Bexleyheath Natural Health Clinic , Body Clinic NW11, Body-Mind Health Private Clinic, Brackenbury Natural Health Centre W6, British Foundation for Past Life Therapy and Research, British Hypnosis Research, British Hypnotherapy Association W1, British Society of Hypnotherapists SW6, Capital Hypnotherapy Centre W6, Care-Healing Centre W9, Centre for Stress Management SE3, Chessington Hypnotherapy Clinic, Community Health Foundation EC1, Edgware Centre for Natural Health, Equilibrium Therapy Centre SW18, Homoeopathic Centre W13, Kingston Natural Healing Centre, Pearl Healing Centre, Sheila Revell Centre SW16, South London Hypnotherapy, UK Training College of Hypnotherapy and Counselling W2, Wholeness E18.

TRAININGS IN HYPNOTHERAPY

Hypnotherapy Training Centre *Title of Training* Hypnotherapy Training Centre Training Course. *Duration* 6-12 months + one year supervision part-time. *Fees* £220 + £10 per tutorial. *Comments* At least 190 hours of written and taped tuition and 8 days of workshops and seminars.

National School of Hypnosis and Advanced Psychotherapy *Title of Training* Dip.THP (diploma in therapeutic hypnosis and psychotherapy). *Duration* 144 hours spread over 12/18 months, followed by one year's clinical supervision via the professional society. *Entry requirements* Usual university entrance requirements; mature candidates without formal qualification and background in the caring professions will need to demonstrate their ability and commitment to undertake the courses. *Fees* Approx £600 incl. VAT for each half of the course. *Comments* No classes held at address, for enquiries only in writing or by telephone. Interviews by appointment.

UK Training College of Hypnotherapy and Counselling *Title of Training* (1) Foundation Course in Hypnotherapy and Counselling. (2) Diploma Course in Hypnotherapy and Counselling. *Duration* (1) On year part-time (120 classroom training hours). (2) A further 240 classroom training hours part-time weekends or evenings. *Entry requirements* (1) Applicants must be at least 23 years of age. Good general standard of education. Interview given. For (2), applicants must have successfully completed (1).

Jungian Analysis

Analytical psychology is the more common name given to the psychotherapeutic approach founded by Carl Jung. Although Jung initially agreed with Freud's formulation of the unconscious he later came to view the unconscious in wider and more transpersonal terms. For Freud, the patient's history was detailed in the unconscious mind, and through the process of free association would yield up its secrets, secrets which had been buried during childhood, when natural desires and social demands came into conflict. Thus for Freud the unconscious was a chronicle of traumatic events and a repository of repressed infantile fantasies. Jung, however, came to a quite different view. He saw the content of the unconscious not just in Freud's terms, but also as something which reflected the history of the human species and the cosmic order. He called this particular unconscious the 'collective unconscious'.

The conscious and unconscious mind are seen as complementing and interacting with one another. The individual is seen as striving towards integration of these two aspects, and he called this process 'individuation'. Manifestations of the collective unconscious are to be found in dreams, symbolic language and fantasies. By exploring the meaning of these manifestations one can come to a deeper understanding of oneself. For instance, the 'archetypes' (such as the 'wise old man') which according to Jung, are part of the collective unconscious, could be known through understanding the symbols of one's dreams. Another central theme of Jung is the relationship between the 'masculine' ('animus') and 'feminine' ('anima') abilities within each of us. In this sense he was a pioneer of present day understanding of sexuality.

Jung advocated the 'eyeball to eyeball' encounter, where both analyst and client sit upright facing each other. Rather than focussing on the past he was more inclined to focus on the present and the future.

Two schools predominate in London. Firstly there is the classical school which has stuck closely to Jung's original writings. Then there is the Society of Analytical

Psychology which while still working within a Jungian framework has assimilated the work of others on early childhood development.

READING

Memories, Dreams and Reflections *by Jung, C. Fontana 1963, £6.99*. Jung's autobiography, full of insights into his life and the development of his ideas. A good place to start to explore Jungian analysis. **Practical Jung** *by Wilmer, H. Chiron 1987, £9.95*. Subtitled 'The Nuts and Bolts of Jungian Psychotherapy', this is a fun, but seriously researched look at how Jungian Therapy works. Illustrated with cartoon-type line drawings. A more classical approach can be found in *Fordhams, M.* **Jungian Psychotherapy** *(Wiley 1978, £9.95)*.

CENTRES OFFERING JUNGIAN ANALYSIS

Abraxas W2, Association of Independent Psychotherapists N6, Association of Jungian Analysts, Astro-Psychotherapeutic Practice, Biodynamic Psychotherapy and Teaching W3, Float Experience, Guild of Pastoral Psychology SW20, Hillside Practice, Human Potential Resource Group, Imprint SW19, Society of Analytical Psychology NW3.

TRAININGS IN JUNGIAN ANALYSIS

British Association of Psychotherapists They offer brief external courses. Jungian section: 'Working with Analytical Concepts'; 10 three hour seminars for each of three terms, £185 per term. Freudian section: 'Psychoanalytic Aspects of Work with Individuals'; 10 one and half hour sessions for each of two terms £195 per term.

Association of Jungian Analysts Refer to organisers for details of training programme.

Society of Analytical Psychology *Title of Training* Training in Adult Analysis. *Duration* Three years part-time. Two evenings per week and own analysis 4 times a week. *Entry requirements* Candidates must have a degree or professional qualification (e.g. Social Work or Counselling). If the degree held has not included substantial study of psychology evidence of own study in this area required. Some clinical experience of patients also required. Candidates must be under 50 years of age. *Fees* Refer to organisers.

Kleinian Analysis

The work of Melanie Klein has had a major influence on the British Psychoanalytical school of thought. She lived and worked in London from 1926 onwards evolving theories of personality development which were to lead her to the creation of a variation of the style of treatment advocated by Freud. Though she accepted the common themes of psychoanalytic theory, such as the importance of the unconscious and the influence of early childhood upbringing on the later life of the individual, she also focused on some hithero unexplored areas of early development. She is most well known for her contributions towards understanding psychic development in the first two years of life and the emphasis she placed on aggression. Her focus was on the oral stage of development whereas Freud had devoted more attention to later stages of development.

She believed that the child in the first few months of life cannot make a clear distinction between himself as a separate entity and the world he inhabits. The child at this stage experiences the world in terms of what is pleasurable and what is unpleasurable. For instance he experiences the mothers breast, a warm cot, being picked up and held as good, and feeling hungry or cold as bad. The two prime emotions that the baby feels as a response to these good and bad experiences are warmth and anger respectively (Klein uses the terms love and hate). The infant may fluctuate between these two prime emotions rapidly as he does not have a developed sense of time or sequence of events. This rapidity of fluctuation can be observed when an infant in rage through hunger suddenly changes to feeling warmth and love towards the mother when fed. The mother is not only the object of these warm feelings but is also, in the child's mind, the object of rage when the child has unpleasurable experiences, and to the child she is then the bad mother. After a few months the child comes to realise that it is experiencing both rage and love towards his mother whom he can then see as a separate person from himself. The interplay between these two powerful emotions towards the same person sets up conflicts in the child which he has to deal with. Klein believed that the resolution of this conflict and the primitive way in which the child perceives the world lay the foundations for defences and for transference.

So how does the theory affect the practice of Kleinian analysis? Transference interpretations are likely early on in the therapy whereas in Freudian analysis they are usually allowed to develop before being interpreted. This transference tends to be focused on interpreting good or bad feelings that are directed towards the analyst to help the client realise that these feelings may be repetitions of earlier feelings towards the good and bad mother.

The couch is used. There may be a chair so that the client can have a choice of seating, though he may prefer not to sit facing as this may impede fantasy life.

The Kleinian approach would seem best suited to those who have a sympathy with the above ideas, who feel pent up with negative feelings, have difficulty making contact with others, who may feel anxious or who find it difficult to love others and be loved.

READING
Selected Melanie Klein *by Mitchell, J. (Ed). Penguin 1986, £5.99.* An excellent

❝ It wasn't the idea of walking along a narrow pole 45 feet up in the pine trees with no visible means of support. Or even spending two nights out alone in the wilderness. What was bothering me about this six day training programme was the *running*. A two mile run was not my idea of how to begin the day, especially a day of intensive emotional and spiritual angst and inner turmoil. The whole idea took me back to school, aged 11, slithering through muddy country lanes while Mr Wrench, the games master, ran backwards in front of me shouting 'Look at me, I can run faster than you, and I'm going backwards!'

After twenty minutes of gentle meditation in the misty morning light, things didn't look so bad. The start of the run was almost ethereal. Then, about two thirds of the way up the mountain, I met Bruce Surely on his way down.

Bruce is a tall, wiry Texan who looks as though he runs up and down mountains every day before cleaning his teeth. The moment he flashed past, I felt my legs turn to lead.

I walked along, listening to the inner dialogue 'what a competitive, macho, creepy, driven character...that is the kind of man who just can't stop proving himself...boy, am I glad I'm not like that'.

Until I heard the voice of one of my teachers 'And what, David, does it cost you to think this way?'

I decided to go through the steps of the forgiveness exercise we practised the previous day. I was definitely getting off on hating Bruce Surely. And the cost to me was - the very thing I was hating him for! All my energy was being consumed in a competition that went on all the time, with any man who I thought was doing 'better' than me.

I resolved to ask for his forgiveness. 'Forgive me, Bruce!' And the strength came back into my body, as if someone had turned the lights back on.

They say you become what you hate. I just never realised that it could happen so quickly! ❞

David Templar

collection of Klein's work with analysis and comment by Juliet Mitchell. Shows the development of her ideas and how her therapy works. **My Kleinian Home** *by Herman, N. Free Association Books 1988, £9.95.* An account of the author's journey through four therapies, ending with a full Kleinian analysis. Moving and enlightening.

CENTRES OFFERING KLEINIAN ANALYSIS

Tavistock Clinic NW3.

Men's Therapy

Historically, men only therapy groups evolved initially as a response to the Women's Movement in the early 1970s. Groups such as *Achilles' Heel* and *Red Therapy* attempted to link left wing and feminist politics with therapy.

PSYCHOTHERAPY

The rationale behind men's therapy is that men may find it easier to talk about issues such as misogeny or sexuality honestly in an all men group. Exponents of these groups see men as relying largely on women for their emotional support. In a men's therapy group they may be able to become less competitive with other men, and develop deeper friendships with them. Through this process they may become less dependent on women for emotional support, and more able to give them emotional support when necessary. The aim is to develop less polarisation in relationships into 'opposite sex' roles and characteristics. This is seen as not only benefitting the men involved by releasing them from a narrow 'masculine' role, but also their relationships with partners, children and others.

Men leading men's groups may employ a variety of methods and approaches. Some may explicitly explore the theme of masculinity. In some groups, the political or social effects of men's therapy may be seen as the most important effects of the work, while in others are more focused on individual, psychological change, though these two aspects are seen as inseparable in practice.

The voice and the psychological make-up of an individual mutually influence each other. Psychological factors often inhibit the voice and in turn restriction of the voice has a negative influence on the psyche. By developing the sound of the human voice through singing for health, the whole personality is influenced in a favourable manner. This, simply, is the meaning of psychophonology; based upon the philosophy of C.G. Jung, it combines singing, massage and movement to liberate the voice from restriction and develop the whole person towards fruition.

Performance
The extensive vocal liberation , range and flexibility resulting from Psychophonic training is shown in live demonstrations performed by Paul Newham and his students internationally and about which the Guardian recently said: "vocalisations which were magical in themselves-the human voice throbbing, coaxing, ringing like a bell, breathing, sighing, moaning in infinite and hypnotising variety a triumph."

Voice therapy
Individual consultations and small group practice

Singing lessons

Singing for Health **The Paul Newham voice centre**
Founded for the development of Psychophonology

For further information, telephone

VOICE CENTRE

(071) 226 8370

Training
Programmes of weekend and one week courses in:
Voice & Massage
Voice & Movement
Psychophonology

The Voice Centre publishes Vox Humana, a regular Booklet of articles and information for subscribers, Cassette Tapes of psychophonic music, demonstrations and lectures are also available.

CENTRES OFFERING MEN'S THERAPY

Astro-Psychotherapeutic Practice, Brothers SE14, CAER (Centre For Alternative Education And Research) TR19, Man To Man NW3, Working With Men SE5.

Music Therapy and Voice Therapy

Music has been used for healing purposes for many centuries. Culturally it is used to unify groups, for relaxation, stimulation or to evoke a particular mood or response. It evokes feelings, and is also a powerful means of expressing feelings and communicating non-verbally. It can promote a feeling of bonding and closeness in a one to one therapeutic relationship or within a group. Music can provide a safe context through which feelings which otherwise might seem unacceptable can be expressed, acknowledged and subsequently understood. Like the other creative arts, it can provide an objective framework through which the individual can bring to light perhaps hitherto hidden aspects of his or her experience, and reflect on them objectively within this framework.

Though the use of music in a therapeutic way is usually expressive - it involves playing an instrument or singing (voice therapy), it may also involve listening to music.

Music therapy has wide applications. It can be used to help those with mental or physical handicaps develop skills and satisfying means of expression. It is also useful in developing self-confidence and concentration, releasing feelings and increasing vitality.

CENTRES OFFERING MUSIC THERAPY

Centre for Health and Healing W1, Institute For Arts In Therapy & Education N16, London Lighthouse W11, Mu Sum Ba - Living Rhythm W12, Nordoff-Robbins Music Therapy Centre W11.

PSYCHOTHERAPY

CENTRES OFFERING VOICE THERAPY
Augenblick Centre, Creative Journey, Healing Voice N4, Highbury Centre N5, IBISS, Little Grove Education, Paul Newham Voice Centre, Playspace NW1, Primrose Healing Centre NW1, Redwood Women's Training Association, Silver Birch Centre NW10, Sound Health SE8, Sound Moves SE20.

TRAINING
Nordoff-Robbins Music Therapy Centre *Title of Training* Diploma Course in Nordoff-Robbins Music Therapy. *Duration* Apply to organisers for details.

Neuro-linguistic Programming

In the early seventies Neuro-Linguistic Programming (NLP) was developed by Richard Bandler, John Grinder, Leslie Cameron-Bandler, Judith DeLozier and Robert Dilts. In 1975 and 1976 Richard Bandler and John Grinder were the co-authors of *The Structure of Magic I* and *The Structure of Magic II*, which are still considered to be the definitive books on NLP. They claimed to have isolated important factors which underlie the work of well-known therapists. These factors were seen to be common to the three therapists they studied. The three therapists were Fritz Perls, Virginia Satir and Milton Erikson.

Rather than pay attention to the therapists' notion of how therapeutic change occurred Grinder and Bandler noted patterns in the communication in these different therapist/client relationships and from these drew the conclusion that these patterns were the 'magic' ingredient that elevated these practitioners above the rest. In this sense a parallel can be drawn with Carl Rogers' thesis that it is not so much the particular technique or theory the therapist uses that brings about psychotherapeutic change, but the underlying attitudes of the therapist, even if he or she is unaware of having these attitudes.

❝Most of my therapy has been a rather haphazard process over several years, through various workshops and series of individual sessions. Through this I have gradually lowered my anxiety level by giving up the search for 'what I should be doing' (the internalised parental demand for success) and learnt to accept the ordinary person that I am.

Along the way I discovered some fascinating ways through primal work, in which my langauge reflected by birth trauma, e.g. "I feel under pressure", "I don't know which way to go", "I'm going round and round in circles", "I can't make any headway". This knowledge has made my tendency to struggle in life less frightening and more predictable without altering the underlying pattern.

My major breakthrough was unexpected and inexplicable. At the time I was stuck in a mediocre job, having decided to give up the search for a better job or retraining. I had been married for three years after a longer period of living together, and had been unable to conceive sucessfully, having had one miscarriage at three months. My situation could aptly be described by any of the phases above.

I attended a workshop given by a lady from California specialising in Artistic Counselling, called Margret Elson. However, as I was administrator and host of the event, I did not go with much anticipation of personal gain. My usual pattern in workshops was to avoid the limelight by giving way to more assertive types, but Margret insisted that each participant have a fair turn. The workshop topic was 'Overcoming blocks in creativity'. Margret had an uncanny ability to discover the problem in a few moments of conversation. Participants wanted to lose their stage fright in singing or playing, or to lose their writer's block etc. In each case Margret devised an exercise in performance, using the group as a sympathetic audience.

I too had had these kind of difficulties and spoke about the tension which had prevented me playing the violin well, and the rigid way in which I had been taught the piano, each year replacing one set of pieces with the ones for the next exam, all learnt by rote, never developing the ability to sight read from new pieces. The exercise Margret devised for me was a pretend performance, crashing about the keyboard at will, with no regard for the actual notes being played. This I did with due ceremony. The lack of prohibition struck a deep chord in me, the tears flowed, the audience applauded and my performance ended. I never bothered much about the piano or violin afterwards, but nine months later my daughter was born. ❞

Mary Fee

PSYCHOTHERAPY

They believed that each client should be approached differently. Therefore, they gave microscopic attention to how the client acted and looked, and from these signs could identify mechanisms of perceptions for each person. For example they were able to deduce whether or not a person was using visual recall rather than auditory recall from noting shifts in pupil size, breathing, direction of gaze and head movements. The therapist can then communicate to the other person in the appropriate mode, thus inducing rapport.

NLP is a technique based therapy used mainly in a group setting. As a client you will not only be the recipient of these techniques but will, by participation, learn some of these skills for yourself. Some of the techniques are mirroring and matching, and reframing, pacing, V/K disassociation and anchoring. An emphasis is on 'accessing' an 'anchor', that is, recalling good experiences and using them as resources for the future. This is done by superimposing good feelings from a past event onto a situation that has unpleasant feelings, so that the unpleasant feelings become less potent.

READING

Frogs into Princes *by Bandler, R. & Grinder, J. Real People Press 1978, £6.95.* This was one of the first books on NLP and in a burgeoning literature, it stands as probably the nearest one can come to 'experiencing' NLP in a book. It contains edited transcripts of weekend workshops and covers all the basics of the subject with live interaction between the authors (as workshop leaders) and the participants. **What is NLP?** *Eric Robbie, Self-Published 1989, £2.95.* A small pamphlet, actually an extended version of the author's article in *Innovative Therapies in Britain* (Eds. Dryden & Rowan, Open Univ. Press), which gives a concise history of NLP, a good exposition of its theoretical background, and examples of how it works in practice. It is also written in 'English', rather than 'American'. Available from specialist bookshops.

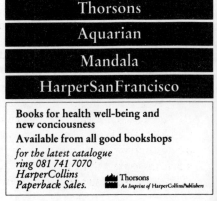

CENTRES OFFERING NEURO-LINGUISTIC PROGRAMMING
Association for Neuro-Linguistic Programming N16, British Hypnosis Research BN2, Care-Healing Centre W9, City Health Centre EC1, Community Health Foundation EC1, Human Potential Resource Group, International NLP Training N4, Natureworks, New Cross Natural Therapy Centre, Pace Personal Development NW3, Raphael Clinic NW6, Wholeness E18.

TRAININGS IN NEURO-LINGUISTIC PROGRAMMING
John Seymour Associates *Title of Training* NLP Diploma. *Duration* Eight weekends (one a month). *Entry requirements* Must have completed their introductory weekend. *Fees* £85 + VAT. 10% discount if total course fee is paid in advance. Concs. *Comments* All courses are held in Bristol. There will be opportunities for further training.
NLP Training Program *Title of Training* Neuro-linguistic Programming Practitioner Certification Training. *Duration* One year part time (7 weekends) + one evening per week for 20 weeks. *Fees* £900 (including VAT) + £75 testing and certification fee.

Personal Construct Therapy

George Kelly proposed this theory of personality and a method of treatment in 1955. Though it has gained a major foothold in academic circles and now ranks as a major theory of personality, it has not been widely used as a form of treatment.

According to Kelly we all have a personal construct system. 'Construct' because we construe people, events and situations. 'Personal' because we construe in a highly personal way, and 'system' because the constructs are related to each other in a particular order or system.

Whilst PCT draws on a number of other therapies for techniques it also claims a number of techniques of its own, namely enactment, self-characterisation, fixed role therapy and repertory grid analysis.

Enactment is used on a one-to-one basis, and is an informal role-play technique. A situation is elaborated and the therapist and client act out the situation. The aim of this is to allow the client a fresh and detached view of a familiar situation.

The client may be asked to write a biography of him or herself as if written by a good friend. This is analysed by the therapist and is used as an evaluation technique in establishing the client's self image. This technique is known as self-characterisation.

The fixed-role technique is rather novel. Once the therapist has a picture of how the client sees him or herself and the world, a fictional character is created by the therapist. This fictional character views the world in a way which is quite different, though not opposite, from the way the client does. The client is then presented with a description of this fictional character and is asked to pretend to be this person for at least a week. The aim of this is for the client to note how others react to the new character, and from this the client will review his or her own construct system.

The repertory grid technique may involve filling out a questionnaire that asks for ways the client pictures his or her world. It is then used for further analysis.

Personal Construct Therapy can also be practised in a group. George Kelly saw a group as a vehicle for its members to elaborate their construct system. By being a member of a group one has the opportunity of seeing how others see you and one can gain a new perspective on how people relate to each other.

Fay Fransella has pioneered work in PCT with stutterers at the Royal Free Hospital.

READING

Theory of Personality *by Kelly, G. Norton 1955 (63), £5.95.* This book consists of the first three chapters of Kelly's major work **The Psychology of Personal Constructs**, and gives the basic background and theory to Personal Construct Psychology. Another book to look for is **Inquiring Man** *by Bannister, D. & Fransella, F. (Croom-Helm 1986).*

CENTRES OFFERING PERSONAL CONTRUCT THERAPY
Centre for Personal Construct Psychology SW1.

TRAININGS IN PERSONAL CONSTRUCT THERAPY
Centre for Personal Construct Psychology Refer to Organisers for details.

Postural Integration

Similar to Rolfing (see the section on 'Body Approaches') from which it is derived, but rather than just physical manipulation of the body, as in Rolfing, postural integration delves into the emotional issues connected with body tensions. It takes the form of a manipulation of deep tissue combined with Reichian analysis and awareness of the body through movement.

The format of the session is similar to Rolfing, ten sessions of up to two hours. The client is encouraged to focus on breathing and feelings whilst the practitioner works on the body. New physical movements are encouraged with a focus on their meaning to the client.

CENTRES OFFERING POSTURAL INTEGRATION
Centre for Release and Integration, New Cross Natural Therapy Centre, Open Centre EC1.

Primal Integration

Primal Integration is a term coined by Bill Swartley to describe the very free-form type of primal work he developed (independently of Arthur Janov - see 'Primal Therapy' below) within a growth model.

Primal Integration works with very early preverbal experiences from the womb, birth and infancy, as well as with later experiences, in an eclectic way. The emphasis is on self-direction and self-regulation and allowing spontaneous growth processes to unfold rather than employing a highly structured or directed programme. The work is frequently undertaken in groups with a minimal leader-determined structure but with appropriate ground rules for safe working. Thus primal material is allowed to emerge under its own dynamic but is not directly aimed for.

There is not usually an individual intensive when commencing the work as is the case with Primal Therapy. Intensives are usually on a group basis and undertaken at a later stage in the work.

Primal material is worked with through bodywork, through transference (see Psychoanalysis for a definition of 'transference'), through face to face work and a variety of other ways.

CENTRES OFFERING PRIMAL INTEGRATION
International Primal Association, Open Centre EC1, Primal Integration Programme N8.

Primal Therapy

Arthur Janov, the founder of primal therapy, holds that the seat of neurosis lies in the past and that the maltreatment of children, some of society's child-rearing practices, pain and lack of love in upbringing all contribute to this. Neurosis consists of pain that is warded off, and which lies deep within the person, profoundly affecting feelings towards self and others. By re-experiencing this pain and hurt and expressing it, neurosis will dissolve.

The process of therapy is sequential. First the client is asked to submit an autobiography and history. There then follow two interviews. If the client is accepted for treatment a three week intensive process begins. During the three weeks the client is seen daily for up to three hours. After the three weeks the client enters individual or group therapy for up to a year.

The therapy usually takes place in a room that is sound protected, with cushions and mattresses. The lighting is usually dim.

During the therapy the focus is on the client's hurt. Time is spent going over incidents of neglect or abuse. Freedom is given to physical expression of these feelings, whether it is curling up into a foetal position, screaming abuse, or sobbing with pain, while the therapist acts supportively to enable this healing of past pain.

READING
The Primal Scream *by Janov, A. Shere 1973, £4.99*. Some people find the claims made by Janov in this book somewhat extravagant, but it makes compulsive reading and there can be no denying that Primal regressive therapy can be a powerful therapeutic tool. **The Primal Issue Revisited** *by S&S (Eds) in Self & Society 1987, £1.50* . A special issue of the *Journal of Humanistic Psychology* devoted to developments in primal type work. Worth seeking out to look at the wide range of practitioners working and their different approaches.

CENTRES OFFERING PRIMAL THERAPY
Association for Analytic and Bodymind Therapy and Training N10, Hillside Practice, London Association of Primal Psychotherapists NW5.

TRAININGS IN PRIMAL THERAPY
London Association of Primal Psychotherapists *Title of Training* Primal Psychotherapy Training. *Duration* Three years part-time, two to three evenings per week. *Entry requirements* Must have been in primal therapy at least one year and have a good academic degree. *Fees* £750 per annum payable in three instalments, plus cost of personal therapy.

Psychoanalysis

Classical full scale Freudian psychoanalysis requires the client, referred to as patient or analysand, to attend a fifty minute session with an analyst four or five times a week, for at least three years. It thus means a huge investment in time and money which is one of the reasons it is not as widely practised as psychoanalytic psychotherapy (see below).

The reasons for such prolonged and regular contact are to be found in the theory initially formulated by Freud. Two cornerstones of the theory are transference and resistance. Such prolonged contact revives feelings and impulses one originally had towards significant figures from the past (usually one's parents) which become directed towards the analyst. This is transference. Time is needed for resistances to emerge too. Resistance is the withholding from oneself and the analyst of one's psychic interior. By helping the patient to become more aware of the workings of the unconscious in transference and resistance, he or she can become free of neurotic symptoms.

The basic rule is that the analysand 'free associates', in other words says whatever comes to mind. The analyst pays attention to the emergence of transference and resistance and tries to tease them out further.

The analyst may intervene in various ways, but usually by confrontation or interpretation, for example 'you're really angry at me and you express this by being continually late', or 'you seem to feel you have been mistreated by fate and dealt an unfair hand'.

Classically, the analysand lies on the couch with the analyst sitting behind, out of sight. Usually the analysand does most of the talking.

Analysts often work early in the morning or early evening, to accommodate their clients' employment schedules.

READING
What Freud Really Said by *Stafford-Clark, D. Peng 1967, £4.50* . As its title suggests, this book explains in down to earth terms the major ideas of the father of psychoanalysis. He also examines the context in which Freud developed those ideas.

CENTRES OFFERING PSYCHOANALYSIS
British Psycho-Analytical Society and The Institute of Psycho-analysis .

TRAININGS IN PSYCHOANALYSIS
British Psycho-Analytical Society and The Institute of Psycho-analysis
Title of Training Training in the Psycho-analysis of Adults. *Duration* Minimum of four years. *Entry requirements* (1) Medically qualified or undergoing medical training, or (2) a good university degree or its equivalent. *Fees* £60 per term approximately for the seminars. Personal psychoanalysis fees £20 per session on average. Supervision fees are the same as personal psychoanalysis fees. *Comments* Trainees must undergo personal psychoanalysis (five sessions per week). Seminars and supervision are provided. If the trainee does not have sufficient experience of working with psychiatric patients he/she may be required to get more experience. Loans may be provided if the student does not have sufficient funds.

Psychoanalytic Psychotherapy

Psychoanalytic psychotherapy takes its lead from psychoanalysis. It upholds the basic psychoanalytic theory but takes into account some the realities of commitment of time and money. Unlike psychoanalysis, sessions are usually only once or twice, though sometimes three times a week with a fifty minute hour.

Also, unlike psychoanalysis, patient and analyst sit upright facing each other, and the engulfing intensity of the relationship which distinguishes psychoanalysis is tempered as the patient's everyday life becomes more the currency of the transactions.

Psychoanalytic psychotherapy is a name that covers a wide range of psychotherapies that either hold to the basic Freudian theory or to one of the neo-Freudian theories. When one thinks of visiting a psychotherapist this is what most people expect to get.

PSYCHOANALYTIC PSYCHOTHERAPY

❝ I had wanted to go into therapy to 'sort out my life' for several years before I actually took the plunge and did something about it. One evening, flicking through the first edition of this book, I came across the listings for psychotherapy centres and picked one that seemed the right place for me to approach. I also obtained a letter of referral from my very unsympathetic doctor who told me that 'life is not a bowl of cherries', who dashed off a quick letter to get me out of her surgery.

I contacted the centre which set up an initial assessment interview with a therapist. When I got there I felt fine - or so I thought. The first question put to me was 'tell me about yourself', so I rattled off factual information from my curriculum vitae. The therapist gently suggested that this was not very helpful and asked me to talk about how I felt about my life. It was like the opening of a dam. I spoke about each area in which I experienced difficulty - work, friends, family, boyfriends i.e. everything - and to my surprise could not stop sobbing. I left fifty minutes later feeling completely drained, but with a promise that a suitable therapist would be found for me, convenient for either my office or home. I specified that I would prefer to see a female.

About six weeks later I received notification of my allotted therapist and I duly went along. The first few sessions were very difficult in that I did not know what to expect, what I should talk about, or how to deal with her. I also found it hard to keep to the appointments even though she was very flexible as to the times she would see me. I wanted either early mornings or late evenings so as not to take time off from work.

Gradually I felt I was beginning to get the hang of it and was persuaded to lie down on the couch rather than sit bolt upright in the chair opposite. Lying down means you don't have to make eye contact all the time and it is less like a social occasion. You feel more relaxed and are able to stare at the ceiling, close your eyes or say nothing for a while.

Having fixed an appoinment, one is expected to keep it, if not you are charged, unless there is a very good reason why you haven't turned up. My therapist also allows payment on a sliding scale according to how much you think you can afford - from £16 to £20 per session. I have been in therapy for nearly a year now and expect to keep going for another year or two. It's a long process and often not easy or fun, but for anyone who thinks they could benefit from it, do it! ❞

Sue Owen

READING
Introduction to Psychotherapy *by Brown, D. & Pedder, J. RKP 1979, £8.95.* Although not only on the psychoanalytic approach, this book provides a good background introduction to how psychotherapy is practised.

CENTRES OFFERING PSYCHOANALYTIC PSYCHOTHERAPY
Arbours Consultation Service, Association for Group and Individual Psychotherapy

N19, Association of Independent Psychotherapists N6, British Association of Psychotherapists, British Psycho-Analytical Society and The Institute of Psychoanalysis, Camden Psychotherapy Unit WC1, Centre for Psychoanalytical Psychotherapy NW4, Centre of Integral Psychoanalysis W11, Ealing Psychotherapy Centre W3, Institute of Psychotherapy and Social Studies, London Centre for Psychotherapy NW3, New Cross Natural Therapy Centre, Philadelphia Association NW3, Sheila Revell Centre SW16, Tavistock Clinic NW3, Women's Therapy Centre N7.

TRAININGS IN PSYCHOANALYTIC PSYCHOTHERAPY

Arbours Association *Title of Training* Training Programme In Psychotherapy. *Duration* Three years. *Entry requirements* Personal maturity and academic competence. *Fees* £1,050 per year exclusive of fees for individual therapy and personal supervision. *Comments* Trainees are required to be in individual psychoanalytic psychotherapy at least three times a week for the duration of the training. Training is individual psychotherapy. Trainees are expected to complete a six month placement in one of the Arbours therapeutic communities. All prospective students must complete at least two terms on the Associates programme before beginning the full training.

British Association of Psychotherapists *Title of Training* Training In Adult Individual Psychotherapy. *Entry requirements* University degree in medicine, psychology or social science or an equivalent professional qualification and some experience of working with disturbed people. The age limit for the Freudian section is 45 years and for the Jungian section it is 50 years. Only in exceptional circumstances will these criteria be waived. *Fees* Apply to secretary for details. *Comments* They also do brief external courses. Jungian section: 'Working with Analytical Concepts'; 10 three hour seminars for each of three terms, £185 per term. Freudian section: Psychoanalytic Aspects of Work with Individuals'; 10 one and a half hour sessions for each of two terms, £195 per term.

Tavistock Clinic *Title of Training* An Interdisciplinary Programme of Training in Adult Psychotherapy for Experienced Professional Workers in the Health and Social Services. *Duration* Four years full time. *Entry requirements* Must be a clinical psychologist *Fees* £1,450 per annum if UK or EEC. £3,350 for others. *Comments* Trainees are required to have personal psychotherapy.

London Centre for Psychotherapy *Title of Training* (1) One year introductory course in Analytical Psychotherapy (2) Three year qualifying course in Analytical Psychotherapy. *Duration* (1) One year part-time (2) Three years part-time. *Entry requirements* (1) Applicants should be graduates or professional in the health field. *Fees* (1) £775 exclusive of personal psychotherapy (2) £800 at present for first year but may be raised. Enrolment fee £40.

Association for Group and Individual Psychotherapy *Title of Training* Psychotherapy Training. *Duration* Three years part-time. Seminars and analytic groups twice weekly. Weekly evening and weekend day groups. Personal therapy, twice weekly required. *Entry requirements* Applicants should have at least one year's personal psychotherapy with an approved psychotherapist before starting the course. *Fees* £800 per annum.

Outreach Counselling *Title of Training* Introductory Diploma Course in Counselling and Community Skills. *Duration* One to three years. *Fees* £300-£600 according to course.

Centre for Psychoanalytical Psychotherapy *Title of Training* (1) Introductory Course (2) Clinical course *Duration* (1) One year. (2) Three years. *Entry requirements* Professional qualification in psychology, medicine or social work or appropriate experience in caring capacity. *Fees* £85 selection fee £300 per term, three terms. *Comments* Consultation and supervision, individual or group.

Psychodrama

Jacob Moreno created psychodrama. He began experimenting with the use of role playing with children as early as 1908 and evolved his method in the intervening years before his death in 1974.

Moreno felt that 'all the world's a stage'. He believed that we adopt rigid roles and act them out and so focused his work on freeing spontaneous expression through make-believe situations.

Psychodrama is psychotherapy married to the theatre. The therapist is called the director, and the client the protagonist. The client produces a scene from his or her life that is loaded with feeling - it may be getting a salary rise at work, leaving home, or whatever, and this becomes the drama that the protagonist and the other members of the group enact. The director tries to recreate the scene in all its vividness with a here and now quality.

As in the theatre the director encourages members to visualise what the surroundings are, and may point out where the imaginary door or window is and ask members to keep these in mind when dramatising the incident. The director may also use props as in theatre improvisation.

The group members do not learn lines for the characters they are playing, but feed on the descriptions given by the protagonist of how they are likely to respond in certain situations. Thus they slowly build up a picture of their assumed character, and modify it by a process of improvisation and rehearsal. The protagonist may switch roles to gain insight into another character's position. Such insight is often a revelation to the client.

If a group member does not appear to be acting out the character as the protagonist remembers him or her, the director may ask another group member to play the character.

If the group members feel the protagonist is not saying what he or she really feels in the situation, they are allowed to go up behind that person and say what they think he or she really feels. The protagonist has the option of rejecting or adopting this new thought.

Eventually a climax is reached and catharsis occurs. The cast then sit down and assimilate what transpired. Members may relate how they felt playing their particular character.

Another client may then choose to relate another incident, and so the process goes on.

READING

The Essential Moreno *by Fox, J. (Ed) Springer 1987, £14.95* . Moreno was, of course, the father of Psychodrama and the editor here has made an excellent selection from his work, showing the development of his ideas and how they work in practice. **Acting In** *by Blatner, H. Springer 1976, £15.95*. Blatner worked with Moreno towards the end of his life and this book has long been thought of as *the* basic textbook of psychodramatic methods. **Psychodrama: Inspiration and Technique** *by Holmes, P. & Karp, M. (Routledge £14.99)*, a collection of articles by twelve psychodramatists who have developed beyond the ideas of Moreno.

CENTRES OFFERING PSYCHODRAMA

Bodyspace, Eigenwelt London NW3, Gale Centre for Creative Therapy, Holwell Centre for Psychodrama and Sociodrama, Minster Centre NW2, Open Centre EC1, Playspace NW1, Spectrum N4.

Psychosynthesis

Psychosynthesis is sometimes called a 'transpersonal' psychology. It is one of the psychologies which emphasise the importance of the spiritual dimension, and of developing higher levels of consciousness and self actualisation.

Its founder, Roberto Assagioli, was trained in psychoanalysis but became dissatisfied with Freud's preoccupation with the 'basement' of the psyche, and with the existing concepts of repressed feelings and neurosis. While acknowledging the importance of bringing to light these feelings for psychological health, Assagioli felt that there was also a 'higher' unconscious as well as the 'lower' unconscious. The 'higher' unconscious is the source of inspiration, imagination and 'peak' experiences - experiences of unity or joy which transcend the individual's sense of existing as a separate, isolated unit. Assagioli studied Indian philosophy and religion and sought to marry western psychology which emphasises the importance of the individual and the personality, with eastern mysticism's concern with higher levels of consciousness.

In psychosynthesis the psyche is seen as being made up of many different parts

: our body, feelings and mind; the different roles we play in life which are all part of our overall personality but which may seem in conflict; and our experience of the depths and heights of the psyche. The process of psychosynthesis is to synthesise these often seemingly different and even contradictory parts. What unites all these elements is the self, a conscious experience of ourselves which is not identified with any one part, but which can observe and direct awareness of them.

Assagioli also emphasised the importance of what he called the 'will'. By this he did not mean will in the sense of will power, but the ability to make choices and to mould our selves and lives which is based on a deep experience of our own individuality.

Psychosynthesis therapists may use a variety of techniques. They may ask you to engage in an inner dialogue with particular parts of yourself, or lead you through a guided fantasy to clarify your feelings about a particular issue. They may encourage you to draw or paint from material which arises in the course of therapy. Therapists also draw on techniques used in other therapies such as gestalt and psychodrama. While the basic theory has been applied as a kind of psychotherapy, it also has applications in education, medicine and religion.

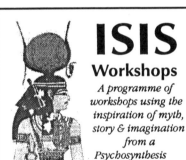

READING
Psychosynthesis; A Collection of Basic Writings *by Assagioli, R, Thorsons 1976*. In this book, Assagioli outlines his theory, and its difference to the other psychotherapies. He then describes the techniques that are used. A very full explanation but some people find it quite a difficult read. **What We May Be** *by Ferruci, P., Thorsons 1982*. Ferruci was originally a student of Assagioli, and later his collaborator. This book is a manual of self help exercises in psychosynthesis. Well laid out and easy to read and use.

CENTRES OFFERING PSYCHOSYNTHESIS
Art from Within N5, Brothers SE14, Communication and Counselling Foundation , Cortijo Romero UK W3, Healing Fields Practice N7, Highbury Centre N5, Institute of Psychosynthesis NW7, Isis SW9, Living Qabalah SE22, Moving Line Counselling and Therapy, North London Counselling Service N5, Psychosynthesis and Education Trust SW8, Re-Vision NW2..

TRAININGS IN PSYCHOSYNTHESIS
Communication and Counselling Foundation *Title of Training* (1) Professional Training in Psychosynthesis and Counselling Skills and Attitudes (2) Psychosynthesis and counselling Skills and Attitudes for Professionals. *Duration* (1) Three years part-time (2) Two years part-time. *Entry requirements* (1) Completion of The Psychology of Transition programme and substantial personal growth work (2) Suitable for those who are currently working in a chosen field who want to enhance their own skills through this course. Substantial personal growth work is also a prerequisite. Applicants may be required to complete The Psychology of Transition course. *Fees* Apply to organisers.

Institute of Psychosynthesis *Title of Training* Diploma in Psychosynthesis Psychotherapy. *Duration* 4 years part-time : 9 weekends, 1 week residential, plus some evenings, plus personal therapy, each year. *Entry requirements* Completion

Using the tools of psychosynthesis in creative painting and writing

66 I have a painting before me, conceived from an emotional side of me. It allows me to see how a part of me is and can be. This 'can be' is often held in shadow but when revealed shows new possibilities and passions.

I permit myself to see my thoughts of design, of making something which gives shape, form, and rhythm; allows colour and shade of how I feel. I am mindful that I have accepted to draw, to move my hand across the page, quite freely. My body willingly accepts and holds itself steady, a receptacle, but it allows the intent of my purpose to spill out as milk from the jug.

And as I look someone fights to shut my eyes. It is my mind furtively searching his cold cabinets to reject this change in my body. He is vain and arrogant, greedy for success and control of his making. Here he is forced to be a silent observer of these new characters who have for long stood in his shadow.

In the painting these characters appear exuberant, excited, engaged and passionate. They are modestly arrayed and I experience them in my body. It is not difficult for me to gladden as they rise from the paper for here they lend hope. I would lift the twists of colour, the volumes of shape, and dance to their music.

He, my mind, is tempted to join in to take rest from his high throne. To lay off his judge's ermine and jewels and welcome these modest strangers into his palace. The king is saddened at his years of self-imposed exile, remembers the scars he bore in battles never won, and sees now these new friends could help him to be a kinder, wiser king. 99

Maureen Kennedy

of prerequisite course, Fundamentals of Psychosynthesis. *Fees* £1,500 per annum.
Psychosynthesis and Education Trust *Title of Training* Professional Training Programme: Counselling and Psychotherapy Diploma Course. *Duration* 3 Years part-time (evenings and weekends). *Entry requirements* Relevant degree or sufficient life experience. *Fees* Apply to organisers for details. *Comments* Professional training is recognised by the British Association for Counselling.
Re-Vision *Title of Training* (1) Psychosynthesis Counselling Training. (2) Advanced training in psychosynthesis therapy and group leadership. *Duration* (1) Two and a half years part-time. First year and a half courses held over weekends plus some intensive residential courses. Final year one weekday over three 10-week terms plus some extra requirements. (2) Two years part time, one day a week (total 30 weeks), plus 3-4 day intensive. Courses may also be taken individually. *Entry requirements* (1) Preference is given to applicants in the caring professions. Those who have successfully qualified will be eligible for the Advanced Training Programme. (2) Must be professionally qualified counsellor or therapist. *Fees* (1) Details on request (2) Approximately £800 per annum plus VAT. Individual courses vary from £75-120 plus VAT. *Comments* Also offer training courses for professionals who want to broaden their field of work without making a training commitment.

Rebirthing

Rebirthing is the process of reliving one's own birth and of coming to terms with the original experience. It is therefore a regression technique. Frederick Le Boyer, a leading exponent of natural birth, has suggested that birth can be painful for the baby and that this might affect the baby's outlook on the world. If it was harsh then the person might grow up to view the world in a negative way. Rebirthers argue that if one can regress to the initial birth and live it through, one can change negative thoughts and attitudes.

There are two different types of rebirthing in this country. One was founded by Leonard Orr on the West Coast of America in the 1970s and the other was developed by Frank Lake.

Orr rebirthing involves using a breathing exercise. The therapist and client occupy a quiet room and pillow and blankets may be used to cover the client if necessary. The client is asked to lie down and breathe in and out in a regular way without pausing. A contract is made beforehand about how long this will continue. Usually it is for an hour or until the client experiences a breathing release, which is the eventual aim of rebirthing.

An Orr rebirther also employs 'affirmations'. These are sentences which are repeated by the client such as 'Every breath I take, increases my aliveness' or 'I feel much love for people'. They affirm how the client would like to feel or be, and are intended to counteract negative attitudes.

Sometimes clients are asked to be reborn in water, as this is closer to the original experience of birth. A bath is usually used for this, and so that the client can remain submerged. He or she may be asked to use a snorkel.

The other type of rebirthing is usually done in a group. One member chooses to be reborn. The other members physically assemble themselves into a simulated womb around the member who lies on the floor in a foetal position. Cushions are liberally employed and are used as buffers between the group 'womb' and the 'foetus'. Gradually the members apply increasing pressure (usually by sitting on or pressing against the 'foetus') which simulates the growth of the foetus in the contained environment. The 'foetus' decides (usually when overcome with claustrophobia) to get out from the enclosing walls and makes its way out of an opening. This is a physically demanding exercise.

Both of these techniques are quite different so make sure you know which one you have signed up for.

READING

Rebirthing: The Science of Enjoying All of Your Life, *Laut, P., Trinity 1983*. An excellent manual of rebirthing techniques as originated by Leonard Orr. It shows how it works, how sessions may proceed and gives affirmations to further the growth process. **Clinical Theology** *by Lake, F., (Dartman, Longman & Todd). 1980*. This is Lake's major work on his approach, a fusion of theological, analytical/ psychodynamic, and existential ideas. It doesn't give a clear outline of how his approach is used. His ideas are usually defined as being 'Primal Integration'. There have been two special issues of *Self & Society* which cover this approach, 'Birth and Rebirth' and 'Voices from the Past', both of which may be available from specialist shops or direct from *Self & Society*.

CENTRES OFFERING REBIRTHING

CAER (Centre For Alternative Education And Research), Centre For Healing Through Forgiveness N15, Man To Man NW3, Primrose Healing Centre NW1, Rebirthing Centre SW18, Refuah Shelaymah Natural Health Centre N16, Sunra SW12.

❝ One of my flatmates who was a new age junkie was constantly trying out his latest new found therapy. He had recently discovered rebirthing and would practise it in the bath. He would lock himself in for at least an hour in the bathroom and submerge himself in the bath water and use a snorkel to aid his breathing. My other flatmate was an architect who worked at home. He hated his work though and would drop his work to visit the toilet where he spent much of his time there reading. I remember how I resented each of them enjoying their 'therapy' while I waited to use the shared facilities. **❞**

Anon

❝ When I did rebirthing I did not regress to my actual birth. I initially found the breathing very difficult to get into, but when I did grasp it, I had some amazing physical experiences - tingling in my chest, arms and hands - the vibration was so strong that I felt I was purring! On my second attempt sorrows welled up. I actually felt acute physical pain in my left arm and it seemed immobile.

Rebirthing was an interesting experience (I thought it would be terrifying) and coupled as it was with affirmation work, was also a positive one. **❞**

Karin Grey

Relaxation Training

Relaxation training is a method of inducing in the client the relaxation response. The relaxation response was identified by Wallace and Benson as a decrease in blood pressure, respiratory and heart rate and an increase in alpha and theta brainwaves and skin resistance. These physiological changes correspond to a state of calm and well being. There are a variety of approaches which bring about the relaxation response, such as biofeedback, autogenic training, hypnosis, tai chi, yoga and some forms of meditation, all of which are covered elsewhere in this book. There is another method, however, which is to systematically tense and let go of various muscles in the body to achieve a state of reduced tension, which is the main focus here. This method of progressive relaxation was developed by Jacobson.

Relaxation training takes place in quiet surroundings with the client in a rested position. The client is asked to focus on relaxing the muscles one by one, usually starting from the feet. First the client is asked to tense a foot and then relax it, and to notice the difference between the foot when it is tense and when it is relaxed. This tensing and relaxing is done systematically throughout the muscles of the body. At times the client will be directed to focus on parts that have been tensed and relaxed, such as the right hand side of the body and asked how this compares with the left hand side of the body which has not yet undergone the process. By comparing differences the client is helped to gain awareness of muscular tension and how to relax all of the muscles throughout the body. The client may be asked to practise at home and supplied with an instruction led audio tape as an aid.

Relaxation training was incorporated into behaviour therapy when Joseph Wolpe adopted it to help hypertense people relax. It has also been used for helping people suffering from anxiety. On its own, the relaxation response will help reduce anxiety, but will not effectively help in situations which provoke anxiety unless it is used within a programme of desensitisation or another psychotherapy.

Relaxation training is something that can be learned quite quickly so that one can practise it on one's own. It is possible to learn from audio tapes alone and there are an abundance of such tapes on the market.

As mentioned above, there are many techniques for inducing the relaxation response, relaxation training being only one of them. It does not suit everyone and there are a significant number of people who find, for one reason or another, that they cannot learn the relaxation response. Some people even have an aversion to it, and are therefore advised to try a different approach entirely.

Courses offering relaxation may provide one of the approaches listed above or the one focused on here, or a combination of these.

READING
The Relaxation Response *by Benson, H., Fontana 1977 £2.95.* A description of relaxation response discovered by the author, and an outline of techniques and

exercises to develop it for oneself. **You Must Relax** *by Jacobson, E., Unwin 1975, £3.95.* A popular introduction to his work, outlining the dangers of tension and its effects on oneself and society, followed by a 'manual' of techniques in Progressive Relaxation.

CENTRES OFFERING RELAXATION TRAINING
Audio Limited, Belgravia Beauty SW1, Equilibrium Therapy Centre SW18, Green Wood college W6, Natureworks, St James Centre for Health and Healing W1.

Sex Therapy

This is a short term therapy designed to help couples who are suffering from a range of sexual difficulties including premature ejaculation, impotency, vaginismus (an involuntary spasm of the vaginal muscles which makes penetration impossible), non-ejaculation and orgasmic problems. As it is a therapy for couples it could be considered part of family or couple therapy with a specific issue in focus, though due to the work of Masters and Johnson it has grown into a therapy in its own right.

Usually, though not always, a male and female therapist work with the couple. The couple are asked to give their medical history so that any organic reasons for the sexual problem can be eliminated. After some discussion about the nature of the problem the couple are asked to follow homework assignments. The first stage is often an exercise called 'sensate focus' where the couple are asked to touch each other and to communicate to each other how it feels and what is, or is not, pleasurable. They are asked to abstain from sexual intercourse and genital and breast touching is usually forbidden. In the second stage breast and genital touching is allowed but intercourse and orgasm are not. The path of the third stage depends on the presenting problem. For instance, if the couple is a heterosexual one and impotence is the problem, the woman is taught how to manipulate the penis in specific ways and she is instructed to insert the penis into the vagina, thus relieving the man of the responsibility. However, many sex therapists nowadays do not adhere any more to such a 'performance orientated' programme, and find it more important to help couples relieve the pressures that are caused by the performance orientation in their sex lives.

It is not necessary to go along with a partner at first to receive sex therapy. Some people prefer to go on their own to build up confidence before they talk with their partner.

For sex therapy to be effective the couple should still be able to communicate with each other and it works best if there is a specific behavioural problem with sex, such as one of those listed above. In fact there can be a great deal of overlap between sex, couple and family therapy. There may be other attitudes, problems or conflicts at the root of the difficulties and in this case couple or family therapy might be more suitable. If there is still love between the couple and a mutual desire to work on the problem then sex therapy has a good success rate.

READING

Sex Therapy in Britain *by Cole M. and Dryden, W. (Eds)*. Another textbook giving articles by leading practitioners on various approaches to, and themes in, sex therapy. Quite a heavy read. Before taking the plunge into therapy, you may want to look at the many self-help books on the market, for instance, **Treat Youself to Sex** *by Brown and Faulder, Penguin 1977* or **Sex Problems; Questions and Answers** *by Cole and Dryden, Optima 1989*.

CENTRES OFFERING SEX THERAPY

London Institute for the Study of Human Sexuality SW5, Neal's Yard Therapy Rooms WC2, North London Counselling Practice NW11, Redwood Women's Training Association, Spectrum N4, Welbeck Counselling Service W1, Women's Therapy Centre N7.

TRAININGS IN SEX THERAPY

London Institute for the Study of Human Sexuality *Title of Training* Training to Certificate and Diploma Level. Course takes the form of 5 modules: (1) Basic counselling skills (2) Human sexuality (3) AIDS counselling (4) Sex education (5) Sex therapy. Certificate is awarded on satisfactory completion of (1). *Fees* Basic counselling skills £600. Human sexuality £600. Integrative sex therapy £900. Sex education - composite fee AIDS counselling £200.

Stress Management

Two researchers, Rosenman and Friedman, found that people could be divided into two categories which they called 'A' and 'B'. 'Type A' people tend to suffer from hurry-up sickness; they are aggressive, have difficulty relaxing, have few friends and tend to be workaholics. 'Type B' have opposite characteristics. 'Type A' people have a tendency to develop hypertension, heart problems, stomach aches, ulcers, diabetes and alcoholism. It is the 'Type A' person who may want to consider participating in a stress management programme.

The treatment programme is holistic and many techniques such as hypnosis, biofeedback, behaviour therapy and massage are combined with information on diet and exercise. It also employs 'cognitive restructuring' which is a means of teaching clients new ways of interpreting what they themselves and others do or say. These individual and often habitual interpretations are an important aspect of the 'stress response' in that they determine a person's stress related behaviour.

Practitioners vary in the emphasis they place on the above treatments. Some put physical exercise above all else and some see cognitive restructuring as more important, so it is worth seeing details of the programme before opting for this type of therapy to see if it suits your needs.

Many stress management consultants teach clients to hypnotise themselves. Some practitioners use relaxation audio tapes and will sell these to you. If biofeedback is taught then technical equipment to monitor physiological activity may to be used to help clients relax more (see Biofeedback).

Stress management is practised in group settings. Programmes tend to be short and deliver a package of treatments for managing stress. For those who wish to delve more deeply into their own psyche and their relationships with others, some of the other therapies mentioned in this book might be preferable.

READING
Stress Management *by Charlesworth, E., Cogi 1989.* Of the many stress books available, this is one of the most comprehensive. The authors look at what stress is physiologically and gives exercises using most relaxation techniques, including progressive relaxation, imagery and visualisation, autogenics and diet. **Guide to Stress Reduction** *by Mason, L.J., Cel. Arts 1985.* A nicely presented collection of stress reduction techniques. Less comprehensive than the above but probably easier to use.

CENTRES OFFERING STRESS MANAGEMENT
Acumedic Centre, All Hallows House EC3, Alternative Medicine Clinic NW15, Brackenbury Natural Health Centre W6, Brunel Management Programme, C.H.I Clinic SW6, CAER (Centre For Alternative Education And Research) , Centre for Stress Management SE3, Falcons SW11, Green Wood college W6, Hampton Healing Centre, Health Management NW3, Human Potential Resource Group, IBISS , Jeyrani Health Centre E18, Kingston Natural Healing Centre, Life Directions W1, Lilly Stuart Resource Development Consultants SE7, McCarthy Westwood Consultants SW11, Minster Centre NW2, Natureworks, Primrose Healing Centre NW1, Silver Birch Centre NW10, Skills with People N5, Spiral W12, St James Centre for Health and

Healing W1, UK Training College of Hypnotherapy and Counselling W2, Universitas Associates, Welbeck Counselling Service W1, Women Unlimited SW16, Women's Therapy Centre N7.

Transactional Analysis

Eric Berne, a Canadian psychoanalyst was the founder of transactional analysis or T.A. as it is also known. As its name indicates, transactional analysis concerns itself with the analysis of transactions, a transaction being a unit of communication. In 1964 Berne wrote the bestseller *Games People Play*, which describes particular ways in which people relate to each other, which he calls 'games'. These are habitual and often destructive with titles like 'Kick Me', 'Wooden Leg' and 'Yes - But'. In his follow-on book, *What Do You Say After You Say Hello?* he develops his original ideas and posits that we live our lives in terms of a 'script'. A script is a life plan which we live out from decisions made in childhood, decisions which we still act upon although we have forgotten about them.

Through learning about the theory of games and scripts it then becomes possible to use these as a map to understand one's own history and one's present way of relating to others.

Part of the initial sessions of most T.A. groups is educational. Clients are taught the language and theory, which is subsequently put to use when analysing a member's behaviour in a group. For example a client may be provoking others in the group to become angry, whilst denying any responsibility for this. The therapist may interpret this behaviour as a game of 'Kick Me', a masochistic game of manipulating others into a persecutory role, so that the 'victim' can cry 'why does it always happen to me'. Further analysis might follow as to why certain people chose to take on the persecutory role.

T.A. provides a set of theories with which clients can see life and relational patterns more clearly. Once understood, the original decisions upon which these patterns are based can be changed, and as a result of this, the client's behaviour can then become more appropriate.

T.A. provides a palatable and often amusing jargon. Unlike most therapies which keep the theoretical jargon out of the consulting room, T.A. employs it as part of the process of understanding.

READING
What Do You Say After You Say Hello? *by Berne, E., Corgi 1975.* Probably a better place to start looking at Berne's ideas than **Games People Play**. It oulines the principles of TA and covers many of the developments of his ideas including the 'script theory'. **TA Today** *by Stewart, I. and Joines, V., Lifespace 1986.* Subtitled *A New Introduction to T.A.*, this is a comprehensive textbook of the theory and

practice of T.A. Widely recommended to clients by most TA practitioners and the obvious work to refer to understand how T.A. could work for you.

CENTRES OFFERING TRANSACTIONAL ANALYSIS
Heron Training Workshops, Lifespace Associates SW7, Lilly Stuart Resource Development Consultants SE7, Metanoia, Minster Centre NW2, Open Centre EC1.

TRAININGS IN TRANSACTIONAL ANALYSIS
Metanoia *Title of Training* Training in Transactional Analysis and Integrated Psychotherapy. *Duration* Four years. Ten weekends per year. *Fees* £600 per annum. *Comments* Require personal psychotherapy for the duration of the training. Some bursaries available.

metanoia offers training courses towards a Diploma in General **counselling** for people who want to train as counsellors, TRANSACTIONAL ANALYSIS, **Gestalt Psychotherapy** and **Integrative Psychotherapy** for professionals in medicine, psychology, social work, counselling, psychotherapy and other 'helping professions'. Also available, an **Advanced Integrative Psychotherapy** programme intended for experienced psychotherapists, trainers and supervisors and a **Supervision Skills** course suitable for supervisors of counsellors and psychotherapists. We also offer workshops of general interest such as Health & Healing, Bereavement, Assertion Training and Stress Management.

A full range of psychological services is provided from corporate, team and individual assessment, counselling and individual, family or group psychotherapy, as well as training and service provision in organisational development and consultation through our **metanoia** divisions.

For further information, please contact:

metanoia Psychotherapy Training Institute,
13 North Common Road, London W5 2QB,
Tel: 081-579 2505

Transpersonal Psychotherapy

The term 'transpersonal psychotherapy' covers a wide area, and can be used to describe Jung's analytical psychology and psychosynthesis (qv). It emphasises the spiritual aspect of people's experience, and the search for meaning. It has its roots in both eastern and western religious traditions on the one hand, and in Abraham Maslow's work on peak experience and the psychology of what he called 'self actualising' people on the other.

A key concept in transpersonal psychology is the belief that the central organising principle of the individual's life is the 'self'. The 'self' goes beyond the personal sense of I or ego, and is seen to include this personal sense with an awareness of the collective and universal. This self is also sometimes called 'soul' in transpersonal therapy. The self is seen to unit the different parts of the personality in an experience of wholeness.

Myth and archetypes are used to connect the individual with the collective and historical search of the human race for meaning. Crises are not seen as 'illness' or even 'problems' but rather as part of the process of the individual becoming more aware. Dreamwork, symbols, guided imagery, fantasy and meditation are used in sessions, as well as more extroverted methods of gestalt dialoguing with empty chairs, dialogue between the client and a part of themselves. The therapist may also make use of the 'Chakras' model. The chakras are the eight energy centres of the body according to Indian philosophy, which are situated at various points from the base of the spine to the top of the head. Work here may include for instance visualising an energy blockage at a particular chakra, and exploring what it means in terms of the client's life. Astrology may also be used to clarify the life events of the client.

CENTRES OFFERING TRANSPERSONAL PSYCHOLOGY
Association of Independent Psychotherapists N6, Centre for Counselling and Psychotherapy Education W11, Centre for Transpersonal Psychology W2, Dancing on the Path, Studio E NW6.

OTHER PSYCHOTHERAPIES

ADLERIAN PSYCHOTHERAPY
Adlerian Society for Individual Psychology SE7.

ANTI-SMOKING THERAPY
Capital Hypnotherapy Centre W6, Redwood Women's Training Association.

BEREAVEMENT COUNSELLING
Bereavement and Loss Workshops N15, British Association for Social Psychiatry,

TRANSPERSONAL/OTHER PSYCHOTHERAPIES

Elizabeth Kubler Ross Foundation NW6, London Lighthouse W11, Natural Death Centre NW2, North London Counselling Practice NW11, Psychotherapy for Individuals, Couples & Groups, Trinity Hospice SW4, Westminster Pastoral Foundation W8.

BIOSYNTHESIS
Minster Centre NW2.

CHILD PSYCHOTHERAPY
Anna Freud Centre NW3, British Association of Psychotherapists, Children's Hours Trust N7, Institute of Group Analysis NW3.

CREATIVITY COUNSELLING
Circle of Creative Arts Therapy N8, Cortijo Romero UK W3, DMA UK Technologies for Creating N19, Human Potential Resource Group, Institute for Social Inventions NW2, Open Gate, Resonance SW17, Skills with People N5, Tobias School of Art, Universitas Associates SM2.

DREAM THERAPY
Abraxas W2, Art of Dream Fulfilment N16, Highbury Centre N5, Imprint SW19, Playspace NW1.

EATING PROBLEM COUNSELLING
Equilibrium Therapy Centre SW18, Women's Therapy Centre N7.

ENLIGHTENMENT INTENSIVES
Holistic Yoga Centre (Milton Keynes).

HAKOMI METHOD
Hakomi Institute W4, Iris E3.

INTER-CULTURAL THERAPY
Nafsiyat Inter-Cultural Therapy Centre N4.

JOURNAL KEEPING
Humanistic Psychology at LSE.

LIFE IMPROVEMENT WORKSHOPS
Life Training Centre.

MANAGEMENT TRAINING
Brunel Management Programme, Heron Training Workshops, Human Potential Resource Group, Life Directions W1.

MIND CLEARING
Holistic Yoga Centre (Milton Keynes), Sunra SW12.

REGRESSION THERAPY
Bexleyheath Natural Health Clinic, Bumblebees Natural Remedies N7.

RESONANCE THERAPY
Abshot Holistic Centre, CAER (Centre For Alternative Education And Research), Open Gate.

VIDEO THERAPY
Video Therapy WC1.

OTHER TRAININGS

The following list of trainings are included here because either the range of therapies they draw upon for the training is very broad and therefore will not fit into any one particular category, or because the training is one which we have not covered in the list of major therapies explained.

ADLERIAN
Adlerian Society for Individual Psychology *Title of Training* Certificate and diploma in Adlerian counselling. *Duration* Certificate 2 years part-time (evenings and weekends). Diploma one year part-time under supervision. *Entry requirements* None for the certificate. For diploma, must have certificate. *Fees* £85 per term. *Comments* Courses based in London and Cambridge.

ARTS/CREATIVITY
Creative Arts and Therapy Consultants *Title of Training* Diploma in the Therapeutic and Educational Application of the Arts. *Duration* One year part-time.

One day a week plus six weekends (300 hours). *Entry requirements* 2 'A' Levels; agreement to undergo personal therapy throughout the course; have worked or are presently working within education, a helping profession or the arts; have sufficient maturity and life experience to cope with course material. *Fees* £1200 pa. Comments The course is ideally suited to those already working in a counselling, therapy or education, who wish to work with the arts in ways which enhance personal growth. The course is run at Regent's College, London.

Living Art Training *Title of Training* The Living Art Training. *Duration* One year part-time of twelve weekends and a week in the country. *Entry requirements* Application can only be made after taking a living art seminar weekend, and having a private interview. *Fees* £1,950 + VAT. Payment in three equal instalments of £650 + VAT. *Comments* No art experience necessary.

BIODYNAMIC PSYCHOLOGY
Institute of Biodynamic Psychology and Psychotherapy *Title of Training* (1) Certificate in Biodynamic Massage Methods and Biodynamic Physiatry (Basic Methods). (2) Certificate in Biodynamic Psychotherapy (Advanced Course). (3) Certificate in Biodynamic Psychology and Psychotherapy. *Duration* (1) Two years part-time, one weekend per month, one full day per weeek, five day seminars in spring and summer holidays. One year post-graduate clinical practice and supervision leading to Practicing Certificate and Register of Practitioners. (2) Two years part-time. One weekend per month, one day per week during three ten week terms. Five day seminars in spring and summer holidays.(3) Three years part-time, one weekend a month, one full day per week. Five day seminars in spring and summer holidays each year. *Entry requirements* (1) All professional and academic qualifications acknowledged. Good general basic education and/or life experience essential. Experience of biodynamic therapy and/or other therapeutic approaches an advantage. All applicants interviewed and considered. (2) Certificate in Biodynamic Massage Methods and Biodynamic Physiatry. (3) All professional and academic qualifications acknowledged. Good general basic education and/or life experience essential. Experience of biodynamic therapy and/or other therapeutic approaches an advantage. All applicants interviewed and considered. *Fees* (1) £2100 per annum. If paid in advance £2000, or each term £700 or monthly standing orders of £210 x 10 months. (2) £2100 per annum. If paid in advance £2000, or each term £700, or monthly standing orders of £210 x 10 months. (3) £2100 per annum. If paid in advance £2000, or each term £700, or monthly standing orders of £210 x 10 months. *Comments* (1, 2 & 3) Regular Biodynamic Psychotherapy sessions during training compulsory (exclusive of fees).

CHILD PSYCHOTHERAPY
Anna Freud Centre *Title of Training* Training in the Psychoanalysis and psychotherapy of children and young people. *Duration* 4-5 years, first three years

full-time. *Entry requirements* One of: Degree in psychology or equivalent (e.g. sociology, social anthropology); post-graduate diploma or higher degree in psychology, social work etc. *and* previous experience of working with children, and preferably some experience of residential care of children. Applicants of 40 or over accepted only in exceptional circumstances. *Fees* Tuition fees are waived because students contribute to services of the centre. Personal analysis five times a week at minimum of £15 per session, and supervision of one session weekly in second year rising to 4 or 5 sessions weekly in latter three years of training (£12 per session). *Comments* Admission is by written application and two interviews.

British Association of Psychotherapists *Title of Training* (1) Training In Adult Individual Psychotherapy (2) Training in Adult Psychotherapy for Child Psychotherpists. (3) Training in Child Psychotherapy. *Duration* Approximately three years part-time (details of above trainings available from secretary) *Entry requirements* (1) University degree in medicine, psychology or social science or an equivalent professional qualification and some experience of working with disturbed people. The age limit for the Freudian section is 45 years and for the Jungian section it is 50 years. Only in exceptional will these criteria be waived. (2) Apply to secretary. (3) Honours degree in Medicine, psychology or Social Science or an honours degree plus a higher degree or diploma in a relevant subject. To have some professional experience of working with children. To be of a suitable personality for psychotherapeutic work with children. *Fees* Different for each course, apply to secretary for details. *Comments* They also do brief external courses : Jungian section, 'Working with Analytical Concepts' ; 10 three hour seminars for each of three terms, £185 per term. Freudian section, 'Psychoanalytic Aspects of Work with Individuals'; 10 one and half hour sessions for each of two terms, £195 per term.

ENLIGHTENMENT INTENSIVES

Holistic Yoga Centre *Title of Training* Enlightenment Intensive Masters Training. *Duration* 10 days residential (plus previous participation in Enlightenment Intensives). *Entry requirements* At least one 3-day Enlightenment Intensive, preferably a 14-day EI. *Fees* £325 (£75 deposit, balance payable at start of course). *Comments* Study of two 250 page manuals has to be completed prior to the course.

MIND CLEARING

Holistic Yoga Centre 1) Basic Mindclearing Training (2) Advanced Mindclearing Training. *Duration* (1) and (2) 2-3 months weekday evening and 3-5 day residential. *Entry requirements* (1) at least 30 hours of mindclearing in one to one sessions (2) At least 50 hours of mindclearing in one to one sessions. *Fees* (1) £475 all inclusive (2) £425 all inclusive. *Comments* (1) and (2) Study of three substantial manuals must be completed by end of course.

OTHER TRAININGS

ECLECTIC OR SPECIAL TRAININGS
Association for Analytic and Bodymind Therapy and Training *Title of Training* Diploma Training in Modern Therapeutic Methods. *Duration* 2 years: one evening per week, weekend larger group training, six-day intensive training, residential in Cornwall. *Entry requirements* Must have completed 2-year (minimum) therapy to satisfaction of both therapist and client, or be in ongoing therapy, or be willing to run therapy concurrently with course. Degree and advantage, but not essential. *Fees* £320 per term, payable before each term begins. *Comments* Training groups are kept small and intimate (maximum 10). Includes interpretation of group dynamics, gestalt therapy, hypnotherapy, relaxation techniques, therapeutic holding, regression therapy etc.

Association of Independent Psychotherapists *Title of Training* (1) Foundation Certificate Course (2) Training in Psychotherapy. *Duration* (1) One Year (2) Three years *Entry requirements* (2) Completion of the Foundation course. Some experience of working with people in distress. Personal therapy twice a week. Minimum age 30. *Fees* (1) £750. *Comments* (2) Begins in 1992.

CAER (Centre For Alternative Education And Research) *Title of Training* (1) Royal Society of Arts Counselling Skills In The Development of Learning (2) Royal Society of Arts Certificate in Groupwork Skills (3) Institute for the Development of Human Potential Diploma in Humanistic Psychology. *Duration* (1) Five x 3-day residentials and an introductory weekend (2) 9 months course, 1 weekend per month (3) 2 years, part-time. *Entry requirements* (1) Previous experience of guidance or counselling (2) Preference given to those with previous experience of counselling or personal development. Participants should be actively engaged in working in a group context (3) Apply for details. *Fees* (1) Organisations £750, Individuals £660, YTS/ET £520 (2) Organisations £1,459, Individuals £850 (3) £1,400 per annum.

Chiron *Title of Training* Training in Holistic Psychotherapy. *Duration* Three years part-time, approx eleven hours per week. *Entry requirements* None specified. *Fees* Refer to organisers. *Comments* Programme consists of body-centred psychotherapy, biodynamic massage, gestalt and 'charge therapy'.

Institute of Psychotherapy and Social Studies *Title of Training* Diploma in Psychotherapy (Analytic and Humanistic). *Duration* Three years, two days a week and individual therapy twice a week. *Entry requirements* Degree or equivalent. Some professional experience. Two hundred hours of growth work. Emotional stability and maturity. Ethical life. Reading of literature. *Fees* £1300 pa. (payable in instalments) plus individual therapy fees. *Comments* Special interest in social context.

Minster Centre *Title of Training* Psychotherapy and Counselling. *Duration* Four years part-time. *Entry requirements* None specified. *Fees* Apply to organisers for details of fees. *Comments* Training includes a wide variety of approaches, both traditional and humanistic.

Monkton Wyld Court *Title of Training* Art of Loving *Duration* One year. Nine weekends and one five day workshop. *Fees* £800 fully inclusive *Comments* Held in a community based centre in Dorset. Possible to commute from London to this retreat in the country.

Philadelphia Association *Title of Training* (1) Study programme in Social Phenomenology (2) Training in Individual Psychotherapy and Community Therapy. *Duration* (1) Minimum of one term (one night/week). Three terms per year (2) Min three years, open ended. (one night per week plus therapy plus supervision). *Entry requirements* (a) None (b) Completed three terms of study programme; must have been in own therapy for at least a year; relevant experience of working with disturbed/distressed people. *Fees* (1) £120 per term (2) £150 per term plus therapy plus supervision fees.

Serpent Institute *Title of Training* (1) Diploma course in counselling (2) Diploma course in psychotherapy. *Duration* (1) Two years (2) Three years. *Entry requirements* Acceptance for the course is based on the applicant's readiness and own self development as well as ability and commitment. *Fees* £1,000 per year. *Comments* Theoretical framework is Goddess spirituality - the valuing of the feminine principle within everyone. Training is for both sexes, with some single sex opportunities within it.

Spectrum *Title of Training* (1) Foundation course in counselling skills (2) 1st and 2nd year psychotherapy course. *Duration* (1) Foundation course is half a day per week for 1 year, plus 2 three-day groups (2) Two residentials, one day per fortnight plus 3 weekends over a year. *Entry requirements* Individual. *Fees* (1) £375 per term, (2) £600 per term.

S U N R A

YOGA & HOLISTIC HEALTH CENTRE

• YOGA •

classes every day, for beginners, intermediate and advanced, pregnancy and children.

• COUNSELLING •

for compulsive eaters, relationship problems, decision making, self confidence, self-assertion, AIDS.

• WORKSHOPS •

on self image, eating problems, rebirthing, reflexology, dream interpretation, 'Women who love too much', relationships, massage to professional standard.

• WEEKEND RETREATS •

Two yoga classes a day, plus meditation, indoor heated swimming pool, sauna and jacuzzi. Held at a stunning Manor House on the edge of Dartmoor, and at a Tudor stately home in Dorset.

• FLOTATION TANK •

Let your tension float away and experience enhanced relaxation by floating in our large tank of body temperature salt-water that supports your body as if floating on air! The tank is fully equipped with an internal light and underwater sound speakers.

- Acupuncture
- Aromatherapy
- Art Therapy
- Astrological Charts
- Chi - Kung
- Counselling
- Cystitus clinic
- Homoeopathy
- Hypnotherapy
- Meditation
- Mind clearing
- Oriental medicine
- Osteopathy
- Psychotherapy
- Reflexology
- Reiki healing
- Shiatsu
- Tai - Chi
- Tarot counselling

For more information please telephone 081 675 9224

26 BALHAM HILL CLAPHAM SOUTH LONDON SW12 9EB

Chlorella Health

SUN POWDERED SUPERNUTRIENT
The most nutritionally potent wholefood available

- 65% PROTEIN
- HIGH IRON/CALCIUM
- OVER 20 VITAMINS &MINERALS
- 19 AMINO ACIDS (NATURALLY OCCURRING)
- ZINC & SELENIUM
- B COMPLEX (INCLUDING PLANT SOURCE B 12)
- HIGHEST SOURCE OF CHLOROPHYLL AND RNA/DNA
- EFA'S – ESSENTIAL FATTY ACIDS – OMEGA 3 & OMEGA 6

These substances in their correct balance are thought by nutritionists to aid in blood oxygenation and production of red blood cells, maintenance, metabolism, fat mobilisation, maintain healthy cholesterol levels, regeneration of tissues & cells, restoration of health and as protectors against disease.

Chlorella is a sun-powered micro-alga, packed with micro-nutrients. Cultivated in pure mineral water, utilising the vital force of the sun for its nutrition. As a pure organic wholefood (nothing added or taken away) it is an ideal natural, alternative way to obtain those micronutrients often missing from today's diet. These deficiencies can lead to the body becoming depressed and unable to function at optimum health. In the long term this can be responsible for a variety of chronic conditions; allergies and viral illness, despite the apparent consumption of a healthy diet. As a natural multi-nutrient Chlorella health is more likely to be assimilated than a synthetic multi-pill and as the nutrients are naturally occurring they are perfectly balanced by nature to have a synergistic effect.

Chlorella has been researched by NASA as a food for astronauts and as a solution to world hunger. It is eminently suitable for vegetarians and vegans and renowned as a toxin absorber.

No heat or chemicals are used to break down the cell wall, which is mechanically crushed to aid assimilation. Digestibility is 70-78% and the cultivation is monitored by micro-biologists to ensure nutritional levels of the highest quality.

"LET YOUR FOOD BE YOUR MEDICINE, LET YOUR MEDICINE BE YOUR FOOD"

Hippocrates–father of medicine

* special discounts for clinics & practitioners.

To obtain direct or for FREE information pack contact:–
Chlorella Health Ltd, 28 Nottingham Place, London W1M 3FD
Tel: 071 487 5665

INTRODUCTION TO BODY THERAPIES

It could be said that in the twentieth century western world we have a curious and often paradoxical relationship with our bodies. While many are no longer dependent on hard manual labour to earn their living, most of us spend our working lives sitting in offices using only our heads or performing repetitive manual tasks which impose a strain on the body, while the rest of our way of life also offers little in the way of creative physical expression. Cars and public transport, while greatly convenient have obviated the need to walk anywhere. In the big cities, especially London, we usually live crammed together and have little more than the prospect of a Sunday afternoon walk in the park with the hundreds of other people looking for a dose of nature in the urban jungle.

Though a modern city lifestyle seems to offer little opportunity for us to express natural physical energy, paradoxically our culture also seems to be very concerned with the body in some ways. We are surrounded with images of fitness and beauty on billboards, TV and in films giving impressions of how our bodies ought to look. The 99% of us whose bodies don't measure up to this fantasy ideal may end up feeling self-conscious or dissatisfied with our physique. This pressure to focus on how the body looks from the outside can also leave us out of touch with how it feels from inside and from an immediate experience of our physical self expressing itself in its own unique way.

Western philosophy has tended to see mind and body as separate and science too has played its part in fostering the idea that our bodies are somehow different from our real selves. Modern medicine tends to treat the body in this way and on the whole deals with it as a machine, replacing defective parts if they malfunction, or readjusting the body with drugs and other chemicals, sometimes without much sense that the physical level might be connected with other levels of experience - emotional, mental or spiritual.

We have a long life expectancy now in the modern west, due largely to improved sanitation and nutrition. But we still fear the spectre of disease as much as ever. Perhaps more because most people living in this secular, semi-atheistic culture have little belief in the prospect of an after-life. So with little prospect of a hereafter, most people are even more anxious to conserve the life they have in the here now. Modern medicine has made advances particularly in the areas of surgery, vaccination and medicines. However, we are becoming increasingly dependant on modern medicine and drugs to cure quite common or relatively minor complaints. Modern drug therapy can be like using a hammer to crack a nut. By continual increasing reliance on this powerful method of disease control, we are in danger of upsetting the natural powers which the body has to cure itself. The more we rely on intervention from outside, the more we are in danger of losing our own innate power to heal ourselves, and others.

Alternative and Complementary Medicine

Not all the therapies and practices dealt with in the 'Body' section of this book come under the banner of 'Alternative Medicine'. For instance, the Alexander technique is an educational method which seeks to teach people to use their bodies in a more natural way, and to regain a freedom of movement which may have been lost. Similarly tai chi, which is a system of physical movements, is very much part of a wider philosophical and spiritual system and outlook. The title 'Body' is intended as very broad, and we have used it to include all approaches - therapeutic, educational and inspirational - which encompass the whole person through the medium of the body.

In the ever-growing field of holistic health there is still a lot of debate about what these much used words such as 'holistic', 'alternative medicine', 'complementary medicine' and 'natural therapies' mean, and different people define them in different ways. Most practitioners feel that their therapy is not 'alternative' to conventional medicine in the sense that it is a case of 'either/or' - either you go for traditional treatment or you go to a homoeopath - but rather that it broadens the patient's choice about how to get treatment.

The term 'complementary' is now being used more to stress that these natural therapies can be used alongside conventional medicine. 'Complementary' can also be used in the sense that different natural therapies may be needed to treat one patient and therefore complement each other. Sometimes these complementary therapies are referred to as 'natural' therapies because on the whole they aim to work by co-operating with natural processes, rather than trying to override them as conventional medicine often does.

'Holistic' too seems to be a word which has as many meanings as there are different people using it. One possible definition is that it is an approach which takes into account the whole person, and the whole range of their experience; physical, mental, emotional and spiritual within their whole environment; physical, social and personal.

The Holistic Approach

The holistic approach to health does not just treat symptoms in order to 'get rid' of them. It tries to treat the underlying causes of the symptoms, which may be found in considering the patient's history, lifestyle, relationships, temperament and his or her whole outlook on life. Within the holistic framework, disease is not seen as a matter of chance, or as an affliction which comes purely from outside the body, but more as the whole organism's attempt to reach once again a state of harmony and equilibrium with itself and its environment. An illness, especially a chronic one, can be the body's way of drawing attention to the fact that something needs to change in the sufferer's lifestyle, that he or she may need something they are not getting, that some part of him or her self which was previously unacknowledged is seeking recognition, or it can even be part of an overall point of spiritual crisis or growth, part of a reorientation of life purpose.

An experienced holistic practitioner will look at particular symptoms in any of these contexts as appropriate. The holistic approach stresses the responsibility the individual has for his or her own health and well-being. This may mean taking active steps to change the things which cause illness where possible. This is not to say that the patient is in some way to blame for his or her malaise, but that we have the power to cure ourselves, or at least to change our attitude to our disease. Alternative medicine offers the opportunity to co-operate with the processes by which the body heals itself.

The core of the holistic approach is that it sees all aspects of the human being as connected and interrelated: body, mind, emotions and spirit.

Diagnosis

Most people turn to complementary medicine when conventional medicine has failed to cure them, or offers no treatment. It is often stubborn, chronic conditions such as backache, migraines, asthma, menstrual problems, insomnia, arthritis or chronic indigestion with which the practitioner is presented.

Alternative therapies have their own methods of diagnosis - an acupuncturist will

take your pulses, an osteopath will examine your spine, and a shiatsu practitioner will feel your abdomen. There are also specific forms of alternative diagnosis which you may want to try if you want more information. Iridology examines the eyes for signs of physical weakness and Kirlian photography shows the electrical field round the body and in this way detects early signs of illness. These alternative diagnostic methods can be most useful in helping people to develop a more positive and balanced attitude towards their bodies, thus preventing illnesses.

Most forms of diagnosis in complementary therapies are non-invasive; they do not probe into the body but are carried out by observing the signs given by the body.

Choosing a Particular Therapy

So how to choose the approach which will be most effective for you? It is easy to feel bemused by all the therapies on offer. Most people choose either by having a particular therapy recommended to them by a friend, or by reading something about a therapy and feeling attracted to that particular approach. With the descriptions of the therapies in this book, we offer some guidelines about the kinds of ailment they may deal with best. However, it is by no means obvious that if you have a bad back you should visit an osteopath, although this may be a good start. The pain in your back could also be due to other physical or psychological problems.

Reading about the different therapies can give you a good lead. Then, follow your instincts. If you feel interested in a particular therapy or don't like the sound of another you probably do have a real sense of what might or might not be helpful for you. It must also be stressed that if you have not already done so, you should always consult your doctor if you have any troublesome symptoms, just to be sure that your complaint is not one which would be better treated by modern medicine. You may also think of discussing any alternative treatment with your doctor, who is hopefully understanding and not totally dismissive of alternative medicine. There are some contra-indications for particular natural therapies. For instance, shiatsu is not recommended for people with cancer, because the stimulation of the metabolism can spread the cancer cells throughout the body. In pregnancy care should be taken with some of the therapies listed here. Once again, your doctor can give advice, and the complementary therapy practitioner needs to be informed of the full details of your condition.

Some of the centres listed in this book which offer more than one therapy give advice on which one would be most effective. Practitioners should tell you if they think that their form of therapy is not appropriate for your symptoms, or may even suggest another form. However, it must be stressed that what works for one person will not necessarily work for another, even if they have the same complaint. Some are now offering consultations specifically to help people choose.

Finding the Right Practitioner

At present there is no law in the U.K. which stipulates that a practitioner of alternative therapies must have reached an agreed standard and must be registered. Complete quackery is not so much the problem - there are probably few people with no qualifications who set themselves up to treat people. However, although a practitioner may seem to be qualified, there is little way of knowing whether their qualification has demanded that they undertake the necessary study and experience to make them effective. In this sense, letters after the name are no guarantee of good service!

For osteopaths, medical herbalists and chiropractors there are registers compiled by governing bodies, and you can write off for registers of members to be sure of getting a well-qualified practitioner. If in doubt about practitioners of other therapies it may be as well to ask about their training - how long it was, how intensive, how much experience they had and also if they are insured, so that if anything does go wrong, at least you have the chance of a successful comeback.

There is of course also the question of rapport. It is important that you trust the practitioner and feel able to talk to him or her. If you feel uncomfortable with a therapist and this fails to change, it might be best to try another one who you feel more able to get on with. You might also like to consider whether the sex of the practitioner matters to you. Some people find it easier to talk about their health problems with someone of the same sex, and some with members of the opposite sex. Again, follow your gut feeling in this, and don't be afraid to ask for the practitioner you want.

Length and cost of treatment

There is no way of saying how long you may have to persevere with any particular treatment. This all depends on the kind of illness you have, the seriousness of the condition, how long you have had it, whether and how well you may be able to change any of the conditions which may be contributing to it and many other factors. If you are worried about how long it make take (and consequently how much you may have to pay) ask the practitioner after the initial session if they can give you any idea of how many sessions you will need. Few practitioners are so hard up for patients that they will string out a treatment longer than necessary. Similarly, if at any time you feel you are getting nowhere and want to try another therapy, talk with the practitioner about it. They may also be able to throw some light on a new approach, or be able to explain why the treatment does not seem to be having the desired effect.

Cost too is variable, depending on the experience of the practitioner, and sometimes where he or she practises. Initial consultations usually cost more and last longer for homoeopathy, acupuncture and osteopathy because the practitioner will have to take some time to make the diagnosis. A few practitioners will give discounts for the unwaged. Some training institutes of body therapies such as massage and Alexander technique offer sessions given by trainees at a cheap rate. Homoeopathy is available on the National Health Service at the Royal Homoeopathic Hospital, and there are some homoeopathic GPs, though many of these work in the private sector and therefore charge for treatment. While finding the money for the cost of these treatments may be quite a problem for the low waged, we include details of centres which do offer lower rates for cases of hardship.

What the Centres are Like

Centres vary enormously. Some are really people's homes where perhaps a couple of people practice. Others may be rented rooms, and some are large, permanent buildings which may include restaurants and bookshops. Appointments are always necessary, although some centres run an emergency service or acute clinic. Even if they do, it is advisable to ring beforehand. Some centres have secretaries or receptionists who are always by the telephone to take your call, others make do with an answerphone.

Finding Practitioners Outside the Centres

If for any reason you want to find a practitioner who does not work in a centre there are several ways in which this can be done. Some training institutes or governing bodies provide registers of qualified practitioners. We list these after each therapy with 'register' after their name, rather than a postcode. In this way you can at least be sure that the therapist is qualified. You can telephone the training institute in question and ask them about the length and thoroughness of their training before you ask for the register. Some practitioners are listed in the local Yellow Pages. Local health food shops, community centres, specialist bookshops or wholefood restaurants sometimes have practitioners' cards on noticeboards, though you may have to check their qualifications for yourself in this case. There are also some directories available which list practitioners who advertise in them.

Another way of finding a practitioner is to apply to the Institute of Complementary Medicine, who run a referral service for the general public and the British Register of Complementary Practitioners, which is now recognised by the government. They can give you the names of practitioners of a particular therapy in your area. However they are not allowed to recommend a particular therapy for a particular complaint.

TRAINING IN BODY THERAPIES

Why Train?

Alternative and Complementary Medicine is a growing concern. The number of people who are consulting practitioners of the natural therapies is increasing every year. At the moment, there are hardly enough practitioners to meet this demand, and most good practitioners are extremely busy. Healing people in this way can of course be tremendously satisfying, and it is also a great responsibility. The training can be long and expensive, but most people who really feel motivated to undertake a course find the time and money in some way.

Before you start training, it is helpful to decide what level of skill you want in your chosen therapy. There are three different levels of expertise.

(1) Awareness of the principles, and to a certain extent the practice of a particular therapy, to a level where one can practice it on oneself. The degree to which one can do this depends very much on the therapy in question. For instance, Bach flower remedies can be self-applied very successfully, but osteopathy is not suitable for self-treatment.

(2) Application of the principles and practice to friends and relatives. This requires more skill and training, and though it may give a great deal of satisfaction, will probably not involve any financial reward.

(3) Treatment of members of the public. To do this, a practitioner needs insurance and preferably the protection of a governing body, if there is one for their particular therapy.

It is a good idea to ask yourself what level of training you really want. You may decide that (1) is a good place to start, and to that end you may then choose a less intensive, introductory course. If you want to train to treat the general public, then this is a much more serious undertaking. It is certainly makes sense to find out as much as you possibly can about the therapy you are thinking of training in. It is not unknown for people to discover at the end of a three year course that they do not want to practice that therapy.

Finding the Right Course

There are many different courses around, and they vary a great deal in terms of time commitment, teaching methods and cost. What constitutes a satisfactory course varies enormously from therapy to therapy. Before enrolling for any course, it is advisable to shop around and this will give you an idea of what the norm is for training in your chosen therapy. A shorter, cheaper course may seem more attractive in some ways than a lengthy intensive course, but it may not provide you with the skills and experience you need to practice successfully and well. Though it is difficult to make hard and fast rules because different therapies require different levels of knowledge and experience, there are some guidelines when looking at trainings.

(1) How long has the training institute been established? What kind of experience do the teachers have?

(2) On completion of training, will you be eligible for membership of a professional association which has its own register, code of ethics and disciplinary procedures? Homoeopathy, acupuncture, chiropractic, osteopathy, naturopathy, medical herbalism, reflexology, Alexander technique, polarity therapy and aromatherapy all have professional bodies to which qualified practitioners may belong. With other therapies this is not the case however, and so this criterion cannot be applied.

(3) How much home study is required? How much clinical training will you get? Will you receive thorough tuition in the philosophy and theory of the discipline? There should be a good deal of all of these elements.

(4) What kind of teaching facilities does the training institute have?

(5) Is the personal development of the trainee taken into account? To be able to help other people some measure of self knowledge and stability is necessary.

(6) For courses in homoeopathy, chiropractic, acupuncture and medical herbalism there should be a great deal of time devoted to the study of anatomy and physiology.

(7) Look carefully at the amount of tuition time given. It may seem that the course is long and takes place over a year or two, but if it is taught over weekends at six monthly intervals the actual time you are going to get being taught may be very little.

The Institute of Complementary Medicine offers a list of courses which they think provide a satisfactory training to those thinking of studying a particular therapy. Of course, if you simply want to learn about a therapy out of interest, or to practise on your family and friends in a modest way, the correspondence course or low time commitment course may be just what you want. However, if you are intending to treat the public the above are important considerations.

Entry Requirements

Once again, entry requirements vary enormously from college to college and therapy to therapy. For some courses, notably some of those in homoeopathy and acupuncture, training in orthodox medicine is required. Some require that applicants are medical doctors, or at least that they have been trained in nursing, or in one of the paramedical professions. For courses in reflexology, aromatherapy, massage and Alexander technique there are often no formal educational requirements, and the personal qualities and suitability of the applicant will form the basis for selection.

In general to become an effective practitioner in a natural therapy, you will need a genuine desire to help people, a certain amount of sensitivity and a lot of stamina to cope with the physical and emotional demands of healing.

Getting Clients

Some professional bodies place the same restrictions on advertising as those which govern medical doctors. However, to offset this these bodies will usually have a register of qualified practitioners which is sent out to enquirers. Many people starting out choose to work at a centre through which they can get clients more easily. However, practitioners of natural therapies are in great demand, especially those where the training is long and intensive.

Future Legislation Governing Practitioners - 1992

In some countries, practitioners of alternative and complementary medicine must be medical doctors. In some, such as France, even such things as herbal medicines and some dietry supplements can only be obtained on prescription. In Britain at the moment there are no such laws which means that we have been able to benefit from the proliferation of these therapies. However, an EEC directive has been issued to get Britain more in line with the rest of Europe when the 'single market' comes into force in 1992. This may not mean that our legislation has to be the same, but there is a possibility that the very restrictive standards which apply in some European countries could also be adopted here. Those who oppose such standards in Britain point out that most training courses in homoeopathy for doctors consist of a few weekends, whereas a lay practitioner usually has to study for three or four years. Thus though a medical doctor may know a great deal about orthodox medicine, the lay practitioner has by far the greater knowledge of homoeopathy.

On the positive side, the next ten years may see more standardisation in training courses, and a system of accreditation developing. As yet there is some doubt about who is going to be doing the accreditation, and whether it will be a government body or a body formed of those within the Alternative and Complementary medical professions. The latter would of course be more acceptable to practitioners.

It is difficult to predict how this will affect things. However, in the light of the reorganisation of these professions, it certainly makes sense for the intending trainee to be especially careful about the kind of training course he or she opts for.

Useful Contacts

Institute for Complementary Medicine, *21 Portland Place, London W1N 3AF. (071) 636 9543.* Referral service for the public to complementary pracitioners, and network of public information points around the country. Advice on trainings to those thinking of training.

British Holistic Medical Association, *179 Gloucester Place, London NW1 6DX (071) 262 5299.* Membership/networking organisation for those interested in promoting holistic approaches to health care. Produce quarterly newsletter and professional journal, organise conferences and workshops. Produce self-help books and tapes and general information about holistic medicine, available mail order. Send SAE for full details. Members receive the qrtly 36-page newsletter *Holistic Health*, get discounts on self-help tapes, books and events and details of regional group activities. Membership for different categories: health care professional, health care student, and open membership for the public. Sliding scale from £15-£45 depending on income.

POPULAR HEALTH BOOKS from PIATKUS

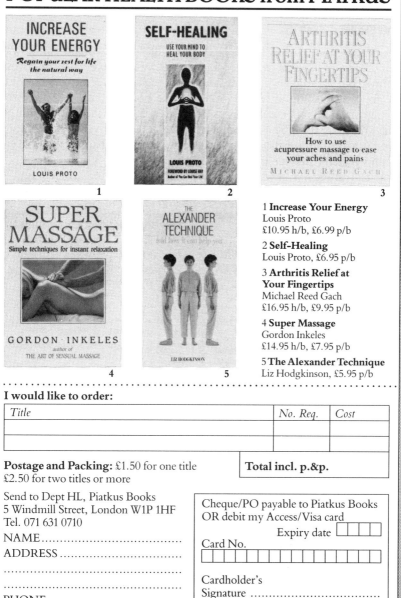

INCREASE YOUR ENERGY
Regain your zest for life the natural way
LOUIS PROTO

1

SELF-HEALING
USE YOUR MIND TO HEAL YOUR BODY
LOUIS PROTO
FOREWORD BY LOUISE HAY
Author of 'You Can Heal Your Life'

2

ARTHRITIS RELIEF AT YOUR FINGERTIPS
How to use acupressure massage to ease your aches and pains
MICHAEL REED GACH

3

SUPER MASSAGE
Simple techniques for instant relaxation
GORDON INKELES
author of THE ART OF SENSUAL MASSAGE

4

THE ALEXANDER TECHNIQUE
and how it can help you
LIZ HODGKINSON

5

1 **Increase Your Energy**
Louis Proto
£10.95 h/b, £6.99 p/b

2 **Self-Healing**
Louis Proto, £6.95 p/b

3 **Arthritis Relief at Your Fingertips**
Michael Reed Gach
£16.95 h/b, £9.95 p/b

4 **Super Massage**
Gordon Inkeles
£14.95 h/b, £7.95 p/b

5 **The Alexander Technique**
Liz Hodgkinson, £5.95 p/b

I would like to order:

Title	No. Req.	Cost

Postage and Packing: £1.50 for one title £2.50 for two titles or more

Total incl. p.&p.

Send to Dept HL, Piatkus Books
5 Windmill Street, London W1P 1HF
Tel. 071 631 0710
NAME......................................
ADDRESS.............................
....
PHONE................................

Cheque/PO payable to Piatkus Books
OR debit my Access/Visa card
Expiry date ⬚⬚⬚⬚
Card No.
⬚⬚⬚⬚⬚⬚⬚⬚⬚⬚⬚⬚⬚⬚⬚⬚
Cardholder's
Signature ....

THE BODY APPROACHES

Acupuncture

Acupuncture is the ancient Chinese healing art which, at least until recently, was the standard form of medical treatment in China. How the system was discovered is unknown, but one theory is that as far back as the stone age healers noticed that small areas of the skin at certain points on the body became sensitive when a particular organ was affected by illness. These areas indicate the acupuncture points of which there are about 800. The points are linked together by their association with a particular organ or function and form pathways or meridians as they are called, through which the life energy or ch'i flows.

The ch'i energy is made up of two forces, *Yang* and *Yin* energy. Yang corresponds to the masculine, positive, active principle and Yin to the feminine,

&& I had never had any experience of alternative medicine before, but several of my friends were visiting this acupuncturist and reporting fantastic results. I had had a chronic problem with inflamed gums for years, so I thought this would give me something to go along with.

I felt quite excited about my foray into the esoteric world of Chinese medicine, though I was worried that the needles would hurt. The visit certainly lived up to expectations. The acupuncturist worked from home and led me into a dark room with a massage table in it. Then she asked me some questions about my complaint, and some more about how I reacted to certain situations, which didn't seem to me to have anything at all to do with my gums. The she asked me when my birthday was and worked out something in her head which she wrote down in a kind of diagram. She told me that I was mostly wood and not much metal - or was it the other way round? - at any rate it didn't make much sense.

Then she told me to lie on the couch, and she held my wrists and seemed to be tapping them very slowly and gently with her fingers. I wondered if this was some sort of massage; it was very soothing anyway. When she eventually got out the needles, she stuck one in my knee and another in my foot, and this certainly seemed like a long way from my gums.

After lying there for what seemed like half an hour she took the needles out. To my surprise I felt incredibly relaxed, so much so that I could hardly get up. This was most unusual since I tend to be rather hyperactive. My acupuncturist solemnly instructed me to eat miso (a Japanese food made out of matured soyabeans). I walked out feeling dazed but calm.

Despite the evident after-treatment effects, after a course of treatments my gums weren't that much better. But two things did change dramatically. I always used to be picky about food, and I never ate breakfast. However, during my treatment I started to develop a much better appetite, and starting eating much more, though I didn't put on any weight. Another effect was that my periods became much heavier. Though my gums didn't get any better, I felt like I became a heartier person, and these effects have lasted in the years subsequently &&

Alex Read.

negative, receptive principle. Good health is maintained while these two forces are balanced, and while the energy is flowing freely through the meridians.

The art of the acupuncturist is to restore any imbalances in energy and to unblock the pathways by stimulating the points along them where there may be a blockage. This is done in one of three ways. Usually very fine needles made of silver or stainless steel are inserted a little way into the skin. The needles may be just left there to have their effect, or they may be stimulated by the acupuncturist who may twirl them or push them gently in and out of the point. Sometimes moxa (dried mugwort, a pleasantly aromatic plant) may be burnt over the point, and this is a popular form of self-treatment practised in some countries. Thirdly the points may be massaged or gently scratched with the fingers.

When you visit an acupuncturist for a treatment, he or she will first take a case history of your complaint and will try to build up a picture of any imbalances in energy by asking you about such things as your food preferences, your reactions to heat and cold, and your emotional reactions in certain circumstances. Then they will take your pulses. Although these are taken at the wrist as they are by any ordinary doctor, the acupuncture pulses are a more complex and subtle aid to diagnosis than the one recognised by western medicine. There are six pulses on each wrist, and these are felt with three fingers by the acupuncturist, who will note the quality and relative strength of each one. Having made the diagnosis in this way, the needles will be inserted.

The idea of having needles stuck into your skin may be very alarming, especially if it brings back memories of injections and innoculations! But there is usually no pain involved in the treatment because the needles are very fine and inserted very lightly, usually only a little way into the skin. The needles are sterilised, but since the advent of AIDS many acupuncturists are making extra sure of hygiene by using disposable needles.

The treatment may last from 20 minutes to an hour. After a treatment some people feel relaxed, some elated or as if they are walking on air. Occasionally you may feel worse before you feel better. You will probably need to go for treatment once or twice a week for chronic ailments, and more often for an acute illness. Acupuncture is also very effective if used preventatively. Traditionally, a treatment at the turn of the season will keep your energy balanced and maintain good health.

The effectiveness of acupuncture in relieving pain has been shown rather dramatically by stories of major operations carried out in China using only skilfully applied needles for anaesthesia. These are rather special cases, but acupuncture can be used effectively for relief of less acute pain. While acupuncture can theoretically cure any reversible disease it is best when there is no actual damage to organs or tissues, and especially for chronic conditions which conventional medicine cannot deal with. Complaints such as headaches, toothache and inflamed gums, colds and asthma, digestive disorders, menstrual disorders, obesity, rheumatism and 'nervous' problems can all benefit from treatment.

READING
Alternative Health - Acupuncture *by Dr Michael Nightingale, MacDonald £3.95.* This consumer's guide to acupuncture concentrates on the actual treatment itself seen from the patient's viewpoint. It answers practical questions about acupuncture as well as providing background information about this popular therapy. The author tries to dispel the concerns of first time patients. **Traditional Acupuncture - the Law of the Five Elements** *by Diane Connelly, Centre for Traditional Acupuncture £9.99.* Diane Connelly is a qualified acupuncturist and author. This book is primarily intended for students of the discipline. It is also useful for the interested lay person. This book has been popular for the depth and seriousness with which it approaches its subject.

CENTRES OFFERING ACUPUNCTURE

Academy of Systematic Kinesiology, Acumedic Centre, Acupuncture and Osteopathy Clinic SW1, Acupuncture Clinic NW10, Acupuncture Clinic of North London, All Hallows House EC3, Association of Natural Medicines, Barbican Natural Health Centre EC1, Bennet and Luck Natural Health Centre N1, Bexleyheath Natural Health Clinic, Body Clinic NW11, Body-Mind Health Private Clinic, Bodywise E2, Brackenbury Natural Health Centre W6, British Acupuncture Association and Register SW1, British College of Acupuncture WC1, British School of Oriental Therapy and Movement, Bumblebees Natural Remedies N7, Camden Osteopathic and Natural Health Practice NW5, Chinese Clinic W1, Chung San Acupuncture School W2, City Health Centre EC1, Clapham Common Clinic SW4, Clinic of Alternative Therapies E18, Clissold Park Natural Health Centre N16, College of Nutribiotics NW3, East-West Clinic of Natural Healing, Edgware Centre for Natural Health HA6, Edmonton Acupuncture Clinic N9, Equilibrium Therapy Centre SW18, Faculty of Traditional Chinese Medicine of the UK, Fook Sang Acupuncture and Chinese Herbal Practitioners Training College UK NW11, Forty Hill Natural Therapy Centre, Haelen Centre, Hale Clinic W1, Hampton Healing Centre, Healthy Living TW9, Hong Tao Acupuncture and Natural Health Clinic, Insight Care N1, Institute of Botanic Medicine E17, Isis Centre for Holistic Health N17, Jeyrani Health Centre E18, Kingston Natural Healing Centre, Lavender Hill Homoeopathic Centre SW11, Lever Clinic, Lever Clinic EN1, Lifeworks, London College of Shiatsu W1P, London Lighthouse W11, London Natural Health Clinic W8, London School of Acupuncture and Traditional Chinese Medicine EC1, Lotus Healing Centre, Meridians Clinic W1, Natural Healing Centre E7, Natural Healing Centre, Natural Medicine Centre, Nature Cure Clinic W1, Natureworks, Neal's Yard Therapy Rooms WC2, New Cross Natural Therapy Centre, Nine Needles Health Care Centre, Portobello Green Fitness Centre W10, Primrose Healing Centre NW1, Private Health Centre E7, Private Polyclinic, Putney Natural Therapy Clinic, Raphael Clinic NW6, Sayer Clinic, School of Complementary Medicine NW1, South Camden Women's Centre, South London Natural Health Centre SW4, St James Centre for Health and Healing W1, Sunnyholt Natural Health Centre W3, Sunra SW12, Traditional Chinese Medicine Clinic , Tyers St. Centre SE11, Wellspring Clinic SW6, Westminster Natural Health Centre SW1, Wholistic Health Centre, Wimbledon Clinic of Natural Medicine SW19, Women and Health NW1, Women's Natural Health Centre NW5, Wood Street Clinic EN5.

TRAINING IN ACUPUNCTURE

British College of Acupuncture *Title of Training* Postgraduate Training in Acupuncture. *Duration* Three years. *Entry requirements* Applicants should be registered members of one of a number of professions, e.g. doctor, osteopath, naturopath, chiropractor, dental surgeon, vetinary surgeon, physiotherapist, nurse. *Fees* First year £600, second year £900, third year £1,000.

BODY THERAPIES

Chung San Acupuncture School *Title of Training* (1) Training in acupuncture. (2) Training in Chinese herbal medicine. *Duration* (1) Three years part time, weekends. (2) 2 years part time. *Entry requirements* (1) Must have 'A' levels in science subjects. (2) Must have Chinese medical background (e.g. qualification in acupuncture). *Fees* (1) £100 enrolment, £1,900 study fee for whole course. (2) £100 plus £1,300 for whole course.

College of Traditional Chinese Acupuncture *Title of Training* Training in Acupuncture. *Duration* Three years part-time. Fourteen weekend sessions per year in the first two years. You work under supervision in the final year. *Fees* £1516 per annum.

Faculty of Traditional Chinese Medicine of the UK Refer to organisers for details of training.

Fook Sang Acupuncture and Chinese Herbal Practitioners Training College UK *Title of Training* Acupuncture and Chinese Herbal Practitioners Training (including training in traditional diagnosis). *Duration* Three years. Weekend attendance. October start. *Entry requirements* Preferably degree level or vocational training. Minimum 'A' level standard. Mature students must show enthusiasm and desire to learn. *Fees* Year 1 £1,500, year 2 £1,200, year 3 £1,200. Payable in instalments. *Comments* Successful graduates eligible for membership of Acupuncture Practitioners Association and Hong Kong Chinese Acupuncture Association. They offer their graduands the opportunity to join their clinical practice in order to further their skills.

International College of Oriental Medicine *Title of Training* Acupuncture and Massage Course *Duration* Three years full-time, fourth year part-time. *Entry requirements* Minimum of 2 'A' levels preferred, but will consider serious applicants individually. *Fees* £3,60000 per annum approximately. *Comments* As a full time course, this attracts local authority grants.

London School of Acupuncture and Traditional Chinese Medicine *Title of Training* Diploma Course in Traditional Chinese Medicine *Duration* Three years part-time, 27 weekends per year. *Entry requirements* 2 'A' levels or equivalent in experience. Applicants should be aged 21 years or over. *Fees* £2,000 per annum, payable quarterly. *Comments* Course requires 12-15 hours of home study per week. Basics of western medicine taught to those without a background in it.

Nine Needles Health Care Centre *Title of Training* (1) One year evening course in Shiatsu (2) 3 year course in Oriental Medicine including acupuncture, shiatsu, moxibustion, etc. *Fees* (1) £1,410 or £1,100 on lump payment. (2) First and third years as above, second year £2,800 or £2,500 on lump payment.

Aikido

Aikido is a Japanese martial art developed by Morihei Uyeshiba who popularised the art after the Second World War. He felt that the object of a martial art should not be to win, but to promote harmony and co-operation, a message which was as sorely needed in the post war world as it is today.

The word comes from 'ai' which means 'union', 'ki' which is 'life force' and 'do' which means road or way. The object of aikido is to achieve harmony and union with the life energy which is in and around all of us. Power is not a matter of physical strength, but comes from strengthening and deepening the connection with this life force. As with tai chi chuan, the expert does not exert his or her strength over the opponent, but uses the attacker's own force for defence. The student must learn that winning itself is not important, and a contest between two practitioners is not so much a fight to the death as a dance in which there is a high degree of co-operation.

Although aikido can be an effective method of self-defence, responsibility is taken for not inflicting unnecessary harm on the attacker. The method should have given the practitioner sufficient skill and awareness to make it unnecessary for them to use the same kind of brute tactics as the aggressor. Strength comes from concentration and awareness, and for this reason aikido is a spiritual discipline as well as a form of self defence. In becoming more in tune with the 'ki' or life energy, one also becomes more centred or rooted in the 'hara'. The 'hara' is the physical centre of gravity in the body and is located about two inches below the navel. It is also the symbolic centre of the top and bottom halves of the body, a point where the physical and mental spheres meet.

Aikido is usually taught in classes of about 20 people. Tuition is given in the 'dojo' or practice hall, a word which also means the hall where Zen monks practise meditation. Teachers have their own approach to discipline in the dojo; some are stricter than others and require a certain etiquette to be maintained inside. Keeping a formal etiquette is in itself a kind of discipline which is seen to reinforce the discipline involved in learning a martial art. A class usually lasts about an hour, and there is a uniform of jacket, belt and baggy trousers. As with most martial arts beginners move up through a series of 'gradings' or examinations to attain higher levels of proficiency. Because the emphasis is on developing inner strength, there is no need to be physically strong to practice Aikido.

READING

Aikido: The Way of Harmony *by John Stevens, Shambhala £12.95.* This definitive, profusely illustrated book covers the essential elements of the philosophy and practice of Aikido, the Japanese martial art that has been embraced by modern psychology and many western bodywork therapies. Useful to beginners and experienced practitioners, with descriptions and photographs of the main Aikido techniques and interesting insights into the history of Aikido and the life of its founder, Uyeshiba Morihei. Written by one of the main western Aikido teachers in Japan, under the direction of one of the founder's ealiest students.

CENTRES OFFERING AIKIDO

British Ki Aikido Association. Apply to Martial Arts Commission for list of approved local clubs.

Alexander Technique

Named after the creator, Australian F. Matthias Alexander, the Alexander technique is the application of a subtle guidance by a practitioner in the movement of the client. Alexander practitioners call themselves 'teachers' and their clients 'students'. They aim to re-educate the students by enabling them to 'unlearn' their habitual poor habits of movement.

Observing a teacher and student at work, it looks as if very little is happening. Imagine a typical scene: the teacher seems to spend much time holding the back of the student's head with one hand and jaw of the student with another, and guiding the student gently out of a chair, little by little, then sitting him or her down again. What is happening is that the student is learning by being taken slowly through a simple movement, in this case standing up. When the student is about to fall into a poor use of the body, the teacher will stop them and make them aware of what they are doing. The teacher will lead the student through these movements time and time again until the student learns a new way of moving and the misuse disappears.

The student may be asked to take up other positions such as as 'the monkey' (standing like a monkey), or asked to lie down on a table whereupon the teacher may lift and gently rotate the arms and move the legs.

At about the seventh session many people experience a feeling of walking on air. As the sessions continue they may report more energy and an ease in physical mobility.

Many of the students are actors or musicians. Musicians practise it because they are prone to bad posture huddled over their instruments and actors because they need to claim more versatility in their movements.

Some people notice alterations in the structure of their body, such as the disappearance of stoops and the hollow back. Some people claim to notice little difference.

The usual arrangement for lessons is three times a week for the first two weeks, twice a week for the next five weeks and once a week thereafter until about thirty visits have occurred. There are enormous variations upon the figures just quoted, mainly depending on the progress of the student. Students are asked to dress in loose clothing.

Each lesson lasts for half an hour. Many teachers practise outside of normal working hours. Alexander technique is also sometimes taught in week long intensives.

READING

Body Learning *by Michael Gelb Aurum Press £5.95.* The approach to learning and the techniques outlined herein can transform your life if you read and practise the methods outlined in this extremely well illustrated introduction to the Alexander Technique. **Art of Changing** *by Glen Park, Ashgrove Book £9.50 Cassette £6.95.* This book takes a deeper look at the Alexander technique introducing the basic exercises to aid personal growth and transformation, and to deal with physical and mental stress. Glen Park then develops this study to encompass the way in which the emotional and spiritual dimensions may be furthered with reference to Alexander's system of working. The cassette is a useful adjunct to the book, helping the student to work through the exercises and combine them with awareness of the chakra centres.

CENTRES OFFERING ALEXANDER TECHNIQUE

Acupuncture and Osteopathy Clinic SW1, Alexander Teaching Centre EC1, Augenblick Centre, Bloomsbury Alexander Centre, Bodywise E2, Brackenbury Natural Health Centre W6, Bumblebees Natural Remedies N7, CAER (Centre For Alternative Education And Research), City Health Centre EC1, Clapham Common Clinic SW4, Clissold Park Natural Health Centre N16, Constructive Teaching Centre, Edgware Centre for Natural Health, Hale Clinic W1, Highbury Centre N5, IBISS, Institute of Holistic Therapies SW6, Kingston Natural Healing Centre, Living Centre, Natural Healing Centre E7, Neal's Yard Therapy Rooms WC2, New Cross Natural Therapy Centre, Primrose Healing Centre NW1, South Camden Women's Centre, South London Natural Health Centre SW4, Westminster Natural Health Centre SW1, Wimbledon Clinic of Natural Medicine SW19, Women and Health NW1, Wood Street Clinic EN5.

TRAININGS IN ALEXANDER TECHNIQUE

Apply to the **Society of Teachers of the Alexander Technique**. They have a list of the training schools in London. The waiting list at all of these centres is typically longer than four years.

Allergy Therapy

It has been accepted for a long time now that pollen can cause an allergic reaction called hayfever which can spoil the sufferer's enjoyment of summer. It was not until recently however that research carried out by a London hospital convinced the medical profession that common foods could also cause a wide range of physical and mental symptoms in some people. Formerly such symptoms might have gone unrecognised and been treated by painkillers or tranquillisers.

An allergic reaction takes place when the body reacts to a substance which has been eaten, inhaled or in contact with the body in some other way, as if it were harmful, even though the substance is not in any way a threat to the organism. The immune system rejects the substance, and in its attempts to do so causes allergic symptoms. White flour, dairy products and food additives are often the culprits in food allergy.

Allergy can be involved in ill health in different ways. Sometimes the patient's symptoms, which can range from headaches, digestive problems, depression, palpitations and arthritic pains, are due to the allergy alone, and by not eating the food which causes the allergic reaction the symptoms are cured. Sometimes allergy is implicated in a particular illness, and helps to aggravate the symptoms. This is more controversial, and research has not been at all conclusive. An example of this was the claim that schizophrenia could be precipitated by food allergy. While this is debatable, it is certainly true that if the immune system is weakened by allergy, it may be less able to contend with any other disturbance which is present in the body.

The increase in environmental pollutants such a car fumes, industrial waste and pesticides has also had its part to play in causing ill health. These substances can be harmful, and the body's reaction may represent a response to a genuine threat, rather than being a strictly allergic reaction. Dr Peter Mansfield and Dr Jean Monro have investigated the effects of chemicals in the environment on chemically sensitive children. Although it is a moot point whether reactions to these substances are allergic or simply intolerant, allergy therapy can still be used here to identify the possible source of the patient's symptoms.

There are various methods used to diagnose an allergy. The patient may be put on a very restricted diet of foods which are usually non-allergenic. Then other foods will be reintroduced into the diet one by one, and the reactions of the patient to each food are charted. Another method is the 'scratch test' where the surface of the skin is lightly scratched and different substances are applied to it. Any irritation or inflammation may be an indication of an allergic reaction. A variant of this test is the introduction of the substances by injection into the skin and noting any skin reactions. The cytotoxic blood test uses a sample of blood to which the suspected allergens are introduced, and the effects monitored. Analysis of hair will show the long term effects of allergy, although it will not show recent developments. Applied kinesiology can be used to test muscle strength in the presence of a potential allergen.

Once the cause has been found, the foods or substances which cause the allergy can be eliminated from the diet or environment. One form of treatment offered by some therapists is the 'neutralising dose'. If the allergen is greatly diluted to the level of a homoeopathic potency and injected, the body will build up a resistance to the substance and be able to tolerate it again. However, to many people it may seem easier just to stop eating what the body rejects.

For information about allergy, contact Action Against Allergy.

READING

Food Allergy and Intolerance *by Jonathan Brostoff and Linda Gamlin, Bloomsbury Publishing £4.99.* This explains comprehensively and simply how certain foods can cause problems for some people and how by identifying and eliminating the culprits they can improve their health. Includes chapters on chemical sensitivity, the mind and body connection and problems in childhood. Also links common ailments with food allergies and details elimination diets to be followed. **Arthritis - The Allergy Connection** *by John Mansfield, Thorsons £4.99.* Dr. Mansfield explores a revolutionary new approach to alleviating one of the most crippling diseases known. He describes effective ways of dealing with the way in which food allergy may affect the development of arthritis including desensitisation and avoidance of stimulants. His ideas are reinforced by the results of clinical trials and scientific evidence.

CENTRES OFFERING ALLERGY THERAPY

Action Against Allergy, All Hallows House EC3, Alternative Medicine Clinic NW15, Association of Natural Medicines, Barbican Natural Health Centre EC1, Bayswater Clinic W2, Brackenbury Natural Health Centre W6, Breakspear Hospital, Clinics Health International SW6, Colon Health W9, Edgware Centre for Natural Health, Food and Chemical Allergy Clinic CR0, Holistic Health Consultancy SW1, Institute of Allergy Therapists, Living Centre, Natural Healing Centre E7, Natural Healing Centre, Natural Health Clinic, Natureworks, Wimbledon Clinic of Natural Medicine SW19.

Applied Kinesiology / Touch for Health

Applied Kinesiology is a manipulative therapy. It involves testing muscles with the hands for any signs of weakness, which if present may show a disturbance in the fuctioning of an organ. In this way, it is useful as a diagnostic technique. Kinesiologists are particularly interested in this weakness if it occurs in a set of muscles on only one side of the body, for this indicates an imbalance which, they believe, can be the first stage in the development of a particular health problem.

The technique was first developed by Dr George Goodheart, an American

BODY THERAPIES

chiropractor. He linked his discoveries about muscular weakness with oriental medical ideas of energy flow through the body in 'meridians' (see 'Acupuncture'). Through the meridians, the muscles are linked to particular organs. Whatever underlying problem is revealed by the muscle tests, it is usually treated by working on the reflexes to strengthen the muscles, massaging meridians and in some cases by diet.

Applied kinesiology is often used to diagnose food allergies. Muscles are tested before and after the ingestion of foods suspected of causing allergy. If the muscles are weaker a few seconds after the patient has chewed the suspected food, this indicates the presence of an allergy.

The difference between Applied Kinesiology and Touch for Health is that the former is used by professionals for diagnosis and treatment of patients, while Touch for Health is taught to the general public as a self-help technique for preventative health care.

TRAININGS IN APPLIED KINESIOLOGY

Academy of Systematic Kinesiology *Title of Training* Basic Kinesiology, certificate and diploma courses in Kinesiology. *Duration* From basic weekend classes to 1 or 2 years part-time, 8 weekends plus one eight day course. *Entry Requirements* Suitability assessed through screening for personality, ethical approach and integrity. *Fees* £80 per weekend, £500 advanced communications week long course, £1250 certificate course.

Aromatherapy

Aromatherapy is a treatment method which uses essential oils extracted from flowers, plants, trees or spices. These are massaged into the body, inhaled, sprinkled in baths or in some cases ingested.

Aromatic substances were used in healing throughout the ancient world, notably by the Egyptians who buried jars of frankinsense and myrrh alongside their pharohs in their tombs, and who used the same perfumes for both medical and cosmetic effect. Proponents of aromatherapy have to this day developed the art for purposes as diverse as the healing of wounds, treating skin cancer and banishing wrinkles.

The essential oils used in aromatherapy are highly concentrated and have to be extracted from large quantities of the mother plant. They are expensive to buy and need to be stored carefully in the right conditions and temperature, and these factors place some limitation on the popular use of aromatherapy. The oils are absorbed into the body through the skin. Although it is not known how aromatherapy works, since research has shown that if a drug is administered in this way its effects may be different from those it produces if it is taken orally, it may be that it is the method of application used in aromatherapy which enables the therapeutic effect of the oils.

The practitioner will decide on the essential oils which will be most efficacious for the client. Sometimes diagnosis is made using radiesthesia. This technique uses a pendulum - a small object such as a ring or a bead used as a weight and attached to a length of string or thread about a foot long. The therapist then asks questions, either about the health of the patient, or about what particular remedy is indicated and the pendulum responds with a 'yes' or 'no' answer.

Having selected the appropriate oil the aromatherapist will probably want to spend some time preparing the skin because diet, pollution and make-up have dulled the receptivity of the modern skin. Inhalation is used for the treatment of head and lung complaints. About six to ten treatments may be required, although beneficial effects may be felt earlier.

As might be expected, aromatherapy is most effective used in the treatment of the skin, in healing wounds and burns, and treating shingles, acne and stress related conditions. The massage with which the oils are applied adds to the therapeutic effect of the treatment.

BODY THERAPIES

READING

Practical Aromatherapy *by Shirley Price, Thorsons £3.50.* A simple explanation of all aspects of aromatherapy and how it can be used to good effect as a self-help therapy. Included is an illustrated section on aromatherapy massage techniques and also how to blend pure essential oils for different purposes. Suitable for the lay person and practitioner alike. **Aromatherapy, An A-Z** *by Patricia Davies, C.W. Daniel £9.95.* A book which provides the answers to such questions as: 'can I combine aromatherapy with other therapies or even conventional medicine? Which oil could help my skin? How are essential oils obtained from plants?' A popular and suitable reference work for students and practitioners of aromatherapy.

CENTRES OFFERING AROMATHERAPY

Acupuncture and Osteopathy Clinic SW1, All Hallows House EC3, Aromatherapy Associates SW6, Aromatherapy Training Centre SW16, Barbican Natural Health Centre EC1, Belgravia Beauty SW1, Bennet and Luck Natural Health Centre N1, Bexleyheath Natural Health Clinic, Bluestone Clinic, Body Clinic NW11, Body Harmony SW16, Bodyworks Natural Therapies, Brackenbury Natural Health Centre W6, Bretforton Hall, Bumblebees Natural Remedies N7, Centre for Health and Healing W1, Chessington Hypnotherapy Clinic, Clapham Common Clinic SW4, Clissold Park Natural Health Centre N16, College of Natural Therapies SE6, Falcons SW11, Green Wood college W6, Guild of Aromatherapy Practitioners, Healthy Living, IBISS, Institute of Clinical Aromatherapy SE6, Institute of Traditional Herbal Medicine and Aromatherapy NW1, International Federation of Aromatherapists SE21, Jeyrani Health Centre E18, Kingston Natural Healing Centre, Lavender Hill Homoeopathic Centre SW11, Lifeworks, Living Centre, London College of Massage W1, London Natural Health Clinic W8, Lotus Healing Centre, McCarthy Westwood Consultants SW11, Micheline Arcier Aromatherapy SW1, Muswell Healing Arts N10, Natural Healing Centre E7, Natural Medicine Centre, Naturecare, Natureworks, Neal's Yard Therapy Rooms WC2, Portobello Green Fitness Centre W10, Primrose Healing Centre NW1, Putney Natural Therapy Clinic, Raphael Clinic NW6, Register of Qualified Aromatherapists NW1, Resonance SW17, Shirley Goldstein, Silver Birch Centre NW10, South Camden Women's Centre, South London Natural Health Centre SW4, Sunnyholt Natural Health Centre W3, Sunra SW12, Therapy Made Unique E18, Tisserand Institute, Tyers St. Centre SE11, Wellspring Clinic SW6, West London School of Therapeutic Massage W11, Westminster Natural Health Centre SW1, Wholistic Health and Life Extension, Wholistic Health Centre, Wimbledon Clinic of Natural Medicine SW19, Women and Health NW1, Wood Street Clinic EN5, Yoga Dham, Ziva Belic Aromatherapy International School W5.

TRAININGS IN AROMATHERAPY

Aromatherapy Associates *Title of Training* (1) Foundation Course (2) Advanced Course *Duration* (1) Ten days full time. (2) Vary *Entry requirements* (1) Knowledge of massage and anatomy and physiology. (2) Must have done the

Foundation course. *Fees* (1) £610 incl VAT. (2) Varies. *Comments* Course is accredited by the International Federation of Aromatherapists and upon successful completion of the course, graduates are entitled to apply for membership of the IFA.

Institute of Clinical Aromatherapy *Title of Training* (1) Clinical Aromatherapy (2) Advanced Essential Oils Course. *Duration* (1) 6-8 days (2) 6 days. *Entry requirements* (1) Applicants must have qualified in either the course in anatomy and physiology given by the College of Natural Therapies or in a recognised course elsewhere. *Fees* (1) £379.50 (including VAT). (2) £97.75 (including VAT). *Comments* Also run Aromatherapy for the Qualified Beauty Therapist Certificate course.

Jeyrani Health Centre *Title of Training* Scientific Aromatherapy *Duration* Three part course of long weekends. *Entry requirements* Preferably for already qualified aromatherapists. *Fees* £675.

London School of Herbology and Aromatherapy *Title of Training* (1) Herbal Medicine/Medical Aromatherapy Diploma Course. (2) Aromatherapy Massage Course. *Duration* (1) 3 years part-time (500 hours). (2) 9 months part-time (100 hours). *Entry Requirements* None: students are trained in all aspects of required knowledge. *Fees* (1) £1,000 per annum. (2) £575 for whole training. *Comments* Training in both Chinese traditional approach, and western medical approach. Both courses include clinical practice.

Micheline Arcier Aromatherapy *Title of Training* Aromatherapy Diploma Course. *Duration* 8 days over two long weekends. *Entry requirements* Applicants should be qualified in anatomy, physiology, face and body massage with 2 years practical experience. *Fees* £510 including VAT.

Shirley Price Aromatherapy *Title of Training* Aromatherapy training courses including diploma standard with reflexology techniques. Basic massage course, anatomy and physiology correspondence course, diploma course, 4 post-diploma courses. *Duration* Diploma course in two parts, 3-9 months depending on qualifications already held in anatomy and physiology and basic massage. *Entry requirements* For diploma course, students must have a recognised qualification in basic massage and anatomy and physiology. *Fees* Basic course £165 + VAT, Diploma course parts 1 and 2 (5 days each) £250 + VAT each. Post diploma courses £100-£195 + VAT depending on subject. *Comments* Accredited school of the International Federation of Aromatherapists. Courses held at venues throughout the UK including London.

Tisserand Institute *Title of Training* Holistic Aromatherapy *Duration* Nine months full time. Part time is two years. *Entry requirements* GCSE biology or equivalent. *Fees* £2390 + VAT *Comments* Incorporates massage and reflexology, touch for health. Training courses are held in London at Royal Masonic Hospital, Hammersmith, London W6.

Ziva Belic Aromatherapy International School *Title of Training* Three part course (1) Basic Aromatherapy, (2) Aromatherapy and Illness, (3) Aromatherapy and Beauty. *Duration* Weekends. *Entry requirements* None. *Fees* 1 weekend: £80, 3 weekends: £225, 6 weekends £750.

Institute of Traditional Herbal Medicine and Aromatherapy *Title of Training* Aromatherapy Bodywork Diploma Course. *Duration* One year (16 weekends). *Entry requirements* None specified. *Fees* £1,000 + VAT *Comments* Graduates may join a leading professional association - The Register of Qualified Aromatherapists.

Ayurvedic Medicine

Ayurveda (which means 'science of life') is the traditional medicine of India which has been practised for over two and a half thousand years. It is based on texts which, among other things, describe operative techniques, how infection can be transmitted during surgery and even describes the body as being composed of cells long before Western medicine had made such important discoveries.

According to this system of medicine there are five elements (doshas) - earth, air, fire, water and ether. There are also three basic qualities of energy - rajas (active), ramas (passive) and sattva (unifying, wise). It is the correct balance of these, constantly changing with environmental conditions, which constitutes health.

Diagnosis involves observing the quality of 32 pulses, taking a personal history, considering astrological information and observing the condition of the body. Treatment can be with herbs, exercises, diet, breathing techniques, massage, urine treatment, yogic cleansing techniques or surgery.

Ayurvedic medicine is the main form of medicine available to people living in India. The training is long and thorough, and involves some knowledge of western medicine.

Unani medicine is an offshoot of Ayurveda, and includes ideas based on Greek and Arab sources. Siddha medicine is another form which has incorporated the use of minerals for treatment.

CENTRES OFFERING AYURVEDIC MEDICINE
Association of Ayurvedic Practitioners, Lotus Healing Centre, Private Polyclinic .

Bach Flower Remedies

These are herbal remedies derived from the flowers of plants. They are prescribed to treat the underlying negative emotional states which are seen as the cause of disease.

This system was devised by Dr Edward Bach, a doctor who practised at the beginning of this century. Working first as a pathologist and bacteriologist he found that different diseases seemed to be linked to the different temperaments of his patients, and classified these character types into seven categories which can be recognised by a predominant emotional state. These states are: fear, uncertainty or indecision, lack of interest in the present, despondency and despair, over concern for the welfare of others, loneliness and over-sensitivity. While he saw each type as possessing positive qualities which could be developed, it is the characteristic negative emotions of each which become apparent in illness.

Each category is further sub-divided for the prescription of the various flower remedies, so that for instance under the heading of 'over-sensitivity' there are four remedies: Agrimony for anxiety and mental torment hidden under a brave face; Centaury for weak will and a 'doormat tendency'; Walnut for major life changes and Holly for jealousy and suspicion.

There are no 'official' practitioners of Bach flower remedies. There are a few doctors who will prescribe them. Since they are completely safe most people who use them will select a remedy for themselves by self diagnosis, using the *Handbook of Bach Flower Remedies* which is available from the Edward Bach Healing Centre and some health food shops. The remedies themselves are available from these two sources. Bach himself discovered the remedies by intuition, often working himself into the same state of mind for which a remedy was required and, walking among the flowers and plants growing locally, he would feel drawn to the one which offered some relief. Prescribing the appropriate remedy for yourself can also be done in this intuitive way, especially since it can be difficult to decide among the long list of mental symptoms described in the handbook which ones are really at the root of your condition. To do this some people use radiesthesia - dowsing with a pendulum (q.v.).

An invaluable item for the first aid kit is 'Rescue Remedy' which is a mixture of five of the flower remedies and can be used after a shock, or in any emotional crisis. To take the remedies, put two or three drops in a glass of water or fruit juice.

More information about Bach Flower Remedies can be obtained from the **Dr Edward Bach Centre.**

READING

A Guide to the Bach Flower Remedies *by Julian Barnard, C.W. Daniel £1.50.* A thorough and straightforward guide to the remedies in pocket size for instant reference. **Bach Flower Therapy** *by Mechthild Scheffer, Thorsons £6.99.* This is the most popular of the Bach Flower books and has a chapter on each of the remedies and also describes how to choose the right remedy. It is suitable for practitioner's reference but clear and simple enough to be of benefit to the layman.

CENTRES OFFERING BACH FLOWER REMEDIES

Aetherius Society SW6, Augenblick Centre, Bennet and Luck Natural Health Centre N1, Brackenbury Natural Health Centre W6, Dr Edward Bach Centre, Foundation for Holistic Consciousness SE25, Hampstead Healing Centre NW3, Healing Fields Practice N7, Holistic Health Consultancy SW1, Homoeopathic Centre W13, Kingston Natural Healing Centre, Naturecare, Nutribiotics , Primrose Healing Centre NW1, Shirley Goldstein, Silver Birch Centre NW10, Therapy Made Unique E18, Wholistic Health Centre, Yoga Dham HA2.

Bates Eyesight Training

This is a natural method of eyesight improvement through eye exercises. It was devised by Dr William H Bates, an eye specialist who gave up orthodox methods in order to find a more satisfactory way of treating bad eyesight. He published his bestseller, *Better Eyesight Without Glasses*, detailing these exercises in 1919. Various exercises are recommended. 'Palming' involves covering the eyes with the palms of the hands for 10 minutes at a time, two or three times a day. This excludes all light and relaxes the eyes. 'Shifting and swinging' involve deliberatly imitating the natural minute and constant shifting movements of the eyes around an object, or objects. 'Splashing' involves splashing the eyes with hot and cold water repeatedly morning and night. Bates believed blinking reguarly - once or twice every ten seconds - was also of great importance. He also recommended remembering colours or beautiful scenes while 'palming', because he found this improved vision in actuality. A practitioner of the Bates eyesight training will give these and other exercises to be practised every day.

Aldous Huxley, who as a young man could hardly see to read, is perhaps the most famous of those who have been helped by this method, as he explains in his book, *The Art of Seeing*.

CENTRES OFFERING BATES EYESIGHT TRAINING

Bates Association of Great Britain.

Biodynamic Massage and Psychology

Biodynamic massage and biodynamic psychology were formulated by Gerda Boyesen, a Norweigan psychologist, physiotherapist and Reichian analyst. As in Reich's psychology, Biodynamics works on the premise that the mind and body function together in any emotional process, and that shocks, traumas and continually repressed feelings can build up chronic physical and psychological blocks. This is especially true if during childhood the growing child did not feel in a safe enough environment to be able to express its feelings. The modern world too tends to exacerbate these feelings of insecurity and stress, and the body may be holding itself in a permanent state of alert and tension.

Boyesen, through her work as a physiotherapist, found that blocked energy builds up in the form of fluids trapped between muscles and nerves. Her unique contribution to Reichian therapy was that she found that in massaging the patient to disperse this build up of fluids, the intestine was activated in a spontaneous peristaltic movement. This movement was not to eliminate foods, but rather a kind of psychic clearing process which occurs when emotion is allowed to follow its natural process of expression. This she likened to the concept in Chinese medicine that every organ has two functions. One function is physical, and one is esoteric or 'meaningful'. According to Boyesen, the meaningful function of the intestine is to digest stress.

The cornerstone of the theory and practice of biodynamic massage is that the healthy organism has the power to express and resolve, to digest all emotional traumas and shocks once the body has ceased to armour itself in patterns of chronic tension and blocks.

The therapist works using a stethoscope to listen to the noises inside the abdomen. There are many different sounds made by the intestines and the therapist is guided by these which are not just the sound of food being digested, but responses to the massage. The sounds mean that the therapist has been able to set free the emotional energy that has become trapped in a particular part of the body. The therapist may massage any part of the body. If enough energy is being released in a 'biodynamic updrift' the therapist may stop the massage, and instead encourage the client to tune in to his or her own 'stimuli from within'. These may take the form of memories, emotions, physical movements or expansive breathing.

Biodynamic massage is helpful in the treatment of migraines, high blood pressure, digestive problems and muscular pain as well as stress, anxiety and depression. It helps to maintain good health and brings about a greater sense of aliveness.

CENTRES OFFERING BIODYNAMIC MASSAGE
All Hallows House EC3, Association of Biodynamic Psychotherapists NW6, Biodynamic Clinic W5, Biodynamic Psychotherapy and Teaching W3, Brackenbury Natural Health Centre W6, Chiron W5, Gerda Boyesen Centre for Biodynamic Psychology and Psychotherapy W3, Healing Fields Practice N7, Hidden Strengths, Highbury Centre N5, Hillside Practice, Mental Development Ltd E5, Neal's Yard Therapy Rooms WC2, New Life Lodge N4, Psychotherapy Workshops for Women, Westminster Natural Health Centre SW1.

TRAININGS IN BIODYNAMIC MASSAGE AND PSYCHOLOGY
Gerda Boyesen Centre for Biodynamic Psychology and Psychotherapy *Title of Training* (1) Two Year Certificate Course in Biodynamic Psysiatry. (2) Two Year Advanced Training Course in Biodynamic Psychology and Psychotherapy. *Duration* (1) Two years (2) Two years. *Entry Requirements* None specified for (1). For (2) completion of (1). *Fees* £1410 per annum. Individual sessions at £15.

❝There are an amazing number of ways to get treatment. Should you go herbal? Or risk life, limb and sanity with conventional medicines? There will be small help from your orthodox doctor should you decide to go for 'fringe' medicine. He sees patients requiring other types of treatment in the same light that the commandant of Colditz saw escapees.

The Wise Woman will need to retain her wits if she is to tight rope walk between the vast gulf of conventional and alternative methods. If it's the body that needs a little help do try to resist the urge to make your own herbal concoctions unless you are very sussed about what you are doing. You run the risk of giving yourself a bad case of the wretched retching should you mistake the herb or spice. Never, never if you have to call the doctor tell him you were trying to cure yourself. Merely tell him you made a mistake putting the salad together. The penalty for admitting to your G.P. that you have been tampering with nature will be enemas and an edifying lecture on what a silly little girl you have been. If you live in the country it will be a lot easier to find yourself a herbalist or witch doctor. Country folk have less inhibitions about using old granny Moles' receipes that have cured everything from the plague to rabies since time began.

Even the fittest of us have our off days, so it's wise to know what kind of treatment we can expect when we lurch towards our nearest psychotherapist's surgery. Choosing is no light matter. Too handsome and you won't want to see him with a bad case of depression; too ugly he may make you fell worse. A woman doctor may or may not be the answer. Always interview your therapist's receptionist, just strike up a casual conversation and it won't take you long to discover if:

"Doctor is a very, very busy person and certainly hasn't time to waste on patients" or "Doctor is tied up a lot of the time". This means the consulting rooms are permanently closed as the doctor is using the couch for other types of practice. "Doctor is permanently attached to a maximum security unit for the hopelessly bewildered", means that Doctor is, in fact, an inmate.

Remember to take a good look at your surroundings, early giveaways of things amiss include stuffed birds, particularly if there's a raven on display. Any pieces of strange equipment, black boxes, couches with straps? Is there a family retainer crouched in the corner with a moving hump? Any or all of these things mean you should be prepared to decamp unless of course you are a Sun reporter, in which case pack a cross. Always be prepared to interview your doctor. Does he ever go out during the day? Does your perfume 'scent of wild garlic' make him feel faint? Does he salivate when he looks at your neck? All these things are little signs of future problems. ❞

Sue Anne Deakin

Institute of Biodynamic Psychology and Psychotherapy *Title of Training* (1) Certificate in Biodynamic Massage Methods and Biodynamic Physiatry (Basic Methods). (2) Certificate in Biodynamic Psychotherapy (Advanced Course). (3) Certificate in Biodynamic Psychology and Psychotherapy *Duration* (1) Two years part-time, one weekend per month, one full day per week, five day seminars in spring and summer holidays. One year post-graduate clinical practice and supervision leading to Practicing Certificate and Register of Practitioners. (2) Two years part-time. One weekend per month, one day per week during three ten week terms. Five day seminars in spring and summer holidays. (3) Four years part-time, one weekend a month, one full day per week. Five day seminars in spring and summer holidays each year. *Entry requirements* (1) All professional and academic qualifications acknowledged. Good general basic education and/or life experience essential. Experience of biodynamic therapy and/or other therapeutic approaches an advantage. All applicants interviewed and considered. (2) Certificate in Biodynamic Massage Methods and Biodynamic Physiatry. (3) All professional and academic qualifications acknowledged. Good general basic education and/or life experience essential. Experience of biodynamic therapy and/or other therapeutic approaches an advantage. All applicants interviewed and considered. *Fees* (1) £2100 per annum. If paid in advance £2000, or each term £700 or monthly standing orders of £210 x 10 months. (2) £2100 per annum. If paid in advance £2000, or each term £700, or monthly standing orders of £210 x 10 months. (3) £2100 per annum. If paid in advance £2000, or each term £700, or monthly standing orders of £210 x 10 months. *Comments* 1, 2 & (3) Regular Biodynamic Psychotherapy sessions during training compulsory (exclusive of *fees*).

Chiropractic

Chiropractic is a method which uses manipulation of the joints and especially the spine by the hands to restore and maintain health.

The system was devised by Dr Daniel David Palmer at the turn of the century when he cured his janitor of deafness by manipulating his spine. Although there are obvious similarities between chiropractic and osteopathy, the main differences lie in the slightly different styles of manipulation used, and that chiropractors are more likely to use X-rays and orthodox physiological tests such as blood samples and neurological examination for diagnosis. Like osteopathy it is based on the idea that displacement of the vertebrae causes disease, but while traditional chiropractic theory states that these impair the functioning of the nervous system, osteopaths maintain that the resultant disease is caused by impaired circulation.

The chiropractor will take a detailed medical history and make a physical examination, possibly using the tests outlined above. He or she will also feel the spine and joints with their hands to locate tissue changes and assess the range of mobility present. Then the appropriate manipulation is carried out. This takes the form of twists and pulls with the chiropractor and patient in a number of different positions.

A chiropractor should have undergone an intensive 4 year training at a recognised college. Conditions which respond well to chiropractic are not surprisingly low back pain, slipped discs, sciatica, headaches, migraines, digestive disorders and even asthma. Some cases of arthritis may be suitable and respond to treatment.

CENTRES OFFERING CHIROPRACTIC

British Chiropractic Association SW1, Bumblebees Natural Remedies N7, Chiropractic Advancement Association, Chiropractic Clinic W8, Hale Clinic W1, Hampton Healing Centre, Institute of Pure Chiropractic, Napier Chiropractic Clinic NW11, Neal's Yard Therapy Rooms WC2, Refuah Shelaymah Natural Health Centre N16, Sayer Clinic, South London Natural Health Centre SW4, Wellspring Clinic SW6, Westminster Natural Health Centre SW1, Wood Street Clinic EN5.

TRAINING IN CHIROPRACTIC

Anglo-European College of Chiropractic *Title of Training* Bsc. Chiropractic (CNAA). *Duration* Fours year full time *Entry requirements* 3 'A' levels or equivalent or over 23 years of age (consideration is given to each individual case). Must have some chemistry qualification/background. *Fees* £4,560 pa. *Comments* Qualifies you to practice as a chiropractor in most parts of the world.

Colonic Irrigation

Sometimes also called colonic hydrotherapy, colonic irrigation is the cleansing of the large intestine (or bowel) by passing water through and out of it via the rectum.

The function of the colon is to extract minerals, nutrients and excess water from food after is has passed, partly digested, out of the stomach and small intestine. Food is moved through the intestine by means of regular muscular contractions (called 'peristalsis') towards the rectum from which it is excreted. However, bad diet, stress, emotional trauma or the side-effects of medicines and drugs can interfere both with this movement, and with the colon's ability to absorb and it can become blocked with toxic waste matter. This not only further interferes with digestion, but is also believed to fester and release poisonous substances into the blood stream. These eventually reach and affect the vital organs, and this, according to the theory of colonics, is the cause of bad health. The aim of colonic irrigation is to unblock the colon and flush out the toxins so that it is restored to healthy functioning.

A series of four to eight colonic irrigations is usually suggested for new clients. A sterile speculum is placed in the rectum, and then a small tube through which water flows into the colon. The water is extracted through a separate tube, and the contents on the colon can be watched through a transparent window as they come out.

The process itself is not unpleasant. The recipient's lower half is kept covered throughout so that they do not feel undignified or embarrassed. The temperature and pressure of water is monitored by the practitioner, and hot and cold water may be alternated to stimulate the bowel. It should take about half and hour.

Immediately afterwards, recipients may need to open their bowels. Bacteria which normally lives in the gut and which is important to the digestion of food is replaced with an implant.

With the initial course of treatment, the practitioner may recommend a change of diet, or the taking of a particular dietary supplement to maintain the healthy functioning of the colon. Treatments are often taken two to four times a year.

While in trained hands, colonic irrigation is safe, in the hands of untrained people it can be dangerous and should *never* be attempted at home. The Colonic International Association has a list of trained practitioners.

READING

Tissue Cleansing through Bowel Management *by Bernard Jensen, Bernard Jensen £4.95*. Includes chapters on imbalances of the intestine and the benefits of colonic cleansing. Describes specific methods of cleansing and detoxification using supplements, colonic irrigation and diet. The book also offers insights into connection between mind and body and inner cleanliness. **The Colon Health Handbook** *by Robert Gray, Emerald Publishing £5.50*. This book is written by a nutrition counsellor and covers the use of supplements, bran and psyllium husks to strip the inside of the colon of waste materials. The methods are clearly explained and also included are notes on iris diagnosis to follow the progress of benefits gained from following the plan.

CENTRES OFFERING COLONIC IRRIGATION

Brackenbury Natural Health Centre W6, Colon Health W9, Colonic International Association, Hampton Healing Centre, Lifeworks, Raphael Clinic NW6, Refuah Shelaymah Natural Health Centre N16, South London Natural Health Centre SW4, Wellspring Clinic SW6, Wholeness E18, Wimbledon Clinic of Natural Medicine SW19.

TRAINING IN COLONIC IRRIGATION

Colonic International Association *Duration* 1 weekend and 3 day extended weekend.

Colour Therapy

Colour therapy is the use of colour or coloured light for therapeutic purposes.

On the most basic level most people are aware that if the rooms they live in are painted different colours they will have a different affect on their moods. Research has shown that blue light lowers blood pressure and has a calming effect while red light puts blood pressure up and excites the nervous system. It has also been shown that some forms of depression may be due to the light deprivation we suffer either during winter, or in offices where there are only fluorescent lights. Daylight bulbs have been invented to correct this deficiency.

The use of colour as an aid to healing is a very subtle art, and the whole spectrum of colours is used. Colour therapists may diagnose what colour someone needs by noting what colours they like and dislike, or by looking at them to see what colour their 'aura' is, or by taking a medical history. The diagnosis of exactly what colours someone lacks is a complex matter, and self-treatment is not as easy as one might think.

There a many ways in which the colour may be administered. The colour therapist may advise you to eat certain foods which have the desired colour, or ask you to drink water which has been placed in coloured containers and exposed to sunlight, or you may be bathed in coloured light. Some colour therapists concentrate on colour in clothes, and help you to discover which colours are best for you to wear because they suit your physique and temperament.

Colour therapy is perhaps best used as a supplement to other forms of treatment, and has been used for a variety of complaints, from physical disorders to depression and anxiety states. Colour visualisation can also be used as a method of self help.

The Luscher Colour Test, devised by Dr Max Luscher is a personality test which can be self administered. Here, colour preferences are used to uncover psychological make up, and this is an interesting way to find out how colour reflects one's personality.

READING

Healing Through Colour *by Theo Gimbel, C.W. Daniel £7.95*. A complete book on colour therapy. The author explains the historical background to the use of colour and the use of healing in the ancient temples. In addition the modern approach to colour is discussed in detail including uses in decoration, clothing, stage illumination and as a supplementary therapy in medical work. **The Healing Power of Colour** *by Magda Palmer, Thorsons/Aquarian £3.99*. This book examines what colour does to us, how it can be used in magic and dream interpretation and how we can use it to improve our behaviour and our health. It will help you to gain an expanded understanding of the nature of colour and how it can be used to enhance your life.

CENTRES OFFERING COLOUR THERAPY

Aetherius Society SW6, Association of Colour Therapists W1, Brackenbury Natural Health Centre W6, Bretforton Hall, Bumblebees Natural Remedies N7, Healing Fields Practice N7, Hygeia College of Colour Therapy, Image Impact W8, International Association of Colour Healers SW14, Kingston Natural Healing Centre, Living Colour NW3, Natureworks, Neal's Yard Therapy Rooms WC2, Pearl Healing Centre, South London Natural Health Centre SW4.

TRAININGS IN COLOUR THERAPY

Hygeia Studios *Apply to organisers for details*.
Living Colour *Title of Training* Colour Therapy Training Programme. *Duration*

Twenty weekends over two and half years. *Entry requirements* Completion of Foundation Colour Courses. *Fees* £2,750 incl. VAT for the whole course. Burseries available. *Comments* The course is stepped so that you can graduate from colour awareness to being a colour counsellor. Primarily for people interested in pursuing colour therapy as a career.

The course is stepped so that you can graduate from colour awareness to being a colour counsellor.

Crystal/Gem Therapy

This is the therapeutic use of semi-precious and precious stones in a number of different ways.

Gemstones have been used for healing, or revered as having special powers through the ages. The Chinese have used jade to treat kidney and bladder complaints for at least 5,000 years. The American Indians were given personal stones at birth which had special powers and significance. These would be carried around in pouches worn on the owners' body.

Each variety of stone is believed to have specific therapeutic properties, though the same stone can have different effects on different people. Quartz and amethyst crystals are both used for general healing and are believed to magnify healing energies so that they become more effective, whether transmitted by some mechanical means or by a human being. The crystals or gems can be worn, carried and used as an adjunct to massage, or sometimes to focus thoughts and wishes for healing.

They can also be used in conjunction with colour therapy, using a crystal light box. This is a box with a light inside it and a hole on the outside covered with different coloured filters or gels through which the light is projected. Crystals are placed on the filter to intensify the energy of the light emitted.

Electro-crystal therapy has also been developed. This involves the transmission of different pulses of high frequency electromagnetic energy through crystals and onto the part of the body which needs to be treated. Gem elixirs are another way in which the healing energy of crystals and gems are believed to be absorbed.

Many people like to have crystals in their homes, because they feel they have a positive effect on the atmosphere. Prices for these 'domestic' crystals can range from 50p for a very small one, to five thousand pounds for a very large cluster.

READING

The Healing Power of Crystals *by Magda Palmer, Arrow £3.99*. In this book the author reveals how we can forge a link through crystals and gems to the energies of the solar system and lists a number of stones appropriate to each birthsign. Also included are the particular healing properties of specific stones and the ailments most susceptible to crystal healing. **The Power of Gems and Crystals** *by Soozi Holbeche, Piatkus £7.95*. This charming book, now in paperback, is written by one of Britain's pioneers in crystal healing. The book is packed with the most interesting historical facts and illustrated exercises. It also offers information on dowsing and healing. Just about everything you would want to know about gems and crystals.

CENTRES OFFERING CRYSTAL/GEM HEALING
Care-Healing Centre W9, Crystal 2000, Crystal Connection NW1, Foundation for Holistic Consciousness SE25, London College of Crystal Healing, Nutribiotics, Pearl Healing Centre , School of Electro-Crystal Therapy, Wholistic Health and Life Extension.

Feldenkrais Method

In the Feldenkrais method gentle sequences of movement are taught so that students can learn how to reorganise patterns of action.

Moshe Feldenkrais was a Russian born Jew who escaped to England in 1940 from Nazi occupied France where he was working as an atomic physicist. When a knee injury prevented him from playing football he started to explore the dynamics of movement in the human body.

As with the Alexander technique much of the work involves letting go of ways of moving and holding the body which are habitual and restrictive. The process of re-learning freer movement is facilitated by slow exercises which should involve no strain or pain at all. They resemble the ways in which babies and young children learn to move. To release the 'pupil' from the pressure of gravity which puts added strain on the body, the lessons are at first carried out lying on the floor. By becoming more relaxed and more aware of how the individual body moves, the pupil has more freedom to choose a range of movements.

The Feldenkrais method is taught in two ways. 'awareness through movement' is taught in classes with a teacher verbally leading the class through a lesson. 'Functional integration' is a term used for an individual session where the teacher will guide the pupil's body through touch and gentle manipulation. These individual sessions are especially useful for those with disabilities or painful injuries.

The benefits of the method are not confined to the body. Feldenkrais felt that physical movement and posture can have a profound effect on the mind and emotions. The body not only reflects mental and emotional states but can also in turn affect them. Feldenkrais felt that by changing negative physical patterns the state of mind that produced them could be changed too.

Anyone can benefit from the Feldenkrais method. It has been used with those who have disabilities, including stroke patients and children with cerebral palsy and stiffness or injuries. The gentleness of the method makes it particularly suitable in such cases. People whose professions involve skilful, expressive movement such as dancers, singers, actors and athletes can also benefit.

CENTRES OFFERING THE FELDENKRAIS METHOD

Bodywise E2, Brackenbury Natural Health Centre W6, Feldenkrais Guild UK N10, Feldenkrais Method EC1, Feldenkrais Method NW3, Little Grove Education, Open Centre EC1, Playspace NW1, Silver Birch Centre NW10, South London Natural Health Centre SW4.

TRAININGS IN THE FELDENKRAIS METHOD

Feldenkrais Method *Title of Training* Professional Training Programme. *Duration* Four years part-time. *Entry requirements* None specified. *Fees* £2,000 per eight weeks full-time per year. *Comments* Training in segments of 3-5 weeks.
Feldenkrais Guild UK *Title of Training* Feldenkrais Professional Training Programme. *Duration* Four years part-time. *Entry requirements)* None *Fees* £2000 p.a.

Floatation Tank Therapy

A floatation tank is a bath or pool containing a concentrated saline solution of about a foot's depth, enclosed in a sound proof and light proof capsule or cubicle. The water is maintained at body temperature, and supports the body because the high concentration of Epsom salts makes the water extremly buoyant, and prevents the crinkling of the skin normally caused by prolonged immersion in water.

Floating in such an environment, where stimulation of the senses is reduced to a minimum, promotes relaxation. Some studies have shown that floating can lower blood pressure and reduce levels of stress-related biochemicals in the body. It can also help to alleviate pain, because it stimulates production by the body of endorphins - hormones which act to reduce pain.

Before floating it is necessary to wash or shower the whole body and shampoo the hair, so that body oils are not deposited in the pool. Vaseline should be applied to any wounds or scratches because the saline solution can sting on contact with breaks in the skin, although it is perfectly safe and can even promote healing. Floaters are also instructed not to touch their eyes during floating, because the water will sting these also, though once again it will not harm them. Once floating in the water on his or her back, the floater should be able to choose whether to be in total darkness, or whether to have a low level of light for reassurance. Those who suffer from claustraphobia are usually able to keep the door of the tank ajar, and the floater is able to leave the tank at any time, simply by opening the door. During the float, many floaters report feeling able to let go of tensions and anxiety, a sense of relaxation and peacefulness, and the sensation of being cosy. After the float it is common for this sense of relaxation to endure. Floats can last from fifty minutes to two hours.

One benefit of floating is that while other relaxation methods require effort to relax, floating is passive and may be an easier way to relax for those who find other methods such as meditation or biofeedback more difficult.

❝ I had my first float at a time when my work was very stressful an intensive. I really believed that nothing, but nothing could make me relax. But even before I got into the tank, the whole feeling of being in a cosy, warm environment and being really looked after by the people running the tank set me up with a sense of being nurtured and safe. When I first got into the tank I became aware of how tense I really was. I though 'It's no good, nothing's going to work, the only thing that's going to relax me is a month on a tropical beach'. But then - it must have been about half an hour into the float - I started to have this sensation of slipping, very gently and slowly, into what seemed like an ocean of calm.

When the music started to signal the end of the float, I didn't want to get out - it seemed like miles to the door of the floatroom, and like I was moving in slow motion. Apparently it took me half and hour to get ready and reappear - it seemed like five minutes to me! The effects lasted for several days afterwards. I felt really as if I'd been mentally 'cleaned out', much more awake and calm.❞

Anne Turner

❝ I found floating very disappointing. It's supposed to take you to a different mental plane, but I felt totally bound to the physical plane. When the music was switched off, I felt very lonely and isolated. Then I got bored so I splashed around from side to side of the tank. My neck got quite sore, but you're told beforehand that this may happen and told to cradle your neck with your joined hands. I think enjoyment of a float is very mood-dependent, and I was told it does get better on subsequent sessions. However, I did feel very relaxed and calm *afterwards.*❞

Karin Grey

Floating can also be used as an aid to learning. Audio or visual tapes can be played to the floater while in the tank, and this can accelerate learning. Some people choose to listen to subliminal tapes to bring about therapeutic change.

CENTRES OFFERING FLOATATION TANK THERAPY
Float Centre NW8, Float Experience, Float Space (The) NW3, Ki Kai Shiatsu Centre, Raphael Clinic NW6, Resonance SW17, South London Natural Health Centre SW4, Sunra SW4.

Healing

Though the technique of the 'laying on of hands' is in practice the same for many healers who see themselves as mediums for a healing force, there is often a great difference in the way they see their role in this process, and experience the force or energy itself.

This kind of healing has a long history in the Christian tradition and some spiritual healers believe that it is the power of God working through them which brings about a cure. Another kind of spiritual healer would best be described as a spiritualist healer, and believes that this power is mediated by a spirit guide or guides. Some healers are secular in their approach and do not regard their power as divine in origin, but more as a natural manifestation of their own, or universal psychic energies. However individual healers may see it, healing is usually seen as involving the transmission of energy in some form from the healer to his or her client.

A session with a healer may or may not involve them physically laying hands on you. Some work off the body, and all follow their intuition in treating each individual patient. Subjects report feeling heat or cold under the healer's hand, or pins and needles, or tingling sensations, but everyone's reactions will be different. Some people feel better immediately, others may need repeated treatments. Sessions will probably last about 30 minutes. Some spiritual healers offer 'absent healing' where healing thoughts are 'sent' to the person wishing to be healed, without any physical contact being made. Some healers have extended their work and use guided imagery and visualisation, counselling and a variety of other techniques.

Reputable healers stress that there are few 'miracle cures', and much depends for a permanent improvement of the condition on the patient's attitude and efforts to get well.

Although some healers are ambivalent about charging for their work, particularly if they feel that their ability to heal is a gift, and as such something which in turn needs to be given to others, they have to eat and pay overheads like anyone else. Some may ask for a donation rather than a fixed fee, which can be a little confusing to the client, but does offer him or her the opportunity to make their own evaluation of the treatment. Healers are now allowed to visit patients in some hospitals, at patients' request, especially those who are gravely ill.

READING

The Seven Levels of Healing *by Lilla Bek and Philippa Pullar, Rider £5.99.* The two authors describe how healing capacities can be trained and developed by applying an understanding of the seven levels of energy to the process of healing, by training and forms of self-discipline including meditation, visualisation an relaxation. **Peace, Love and Healing** *by Bernie Siegel, Rider £6.99.* This new book by the author of *Love, Medicine and Miracles* teaches how to be receptive to the messages the mind gives the body through dreams and symbols. Supported by inspiring stores of patients who have achieved remissions and miraculous cures, Dr. Siegel shows how love, hope, joy and peace of mind have strong physiological effects just as powerful as those of depression and despair.

CENTRES OFFERING HEALING

Aetherius Society SW6, Body Harmony SW16, Brackenbury Natural Health Centre W6, Care-Healing Centre W9, Chalice Foundation, College of Healing, College of Nutribiotics NW3, College of Psychic Studies SW7, Confederation of Healing Organisations, Dancing on the Path, Foundation for Holistic Consciousness SE25, Greater World Christian Spiritual Association W1, Hampstead Healing Centre NW3, Harry Edwards Spiritual Healing Sanctuary, Healing Centre NW6, Healing Workshops NW5, Isis Centre for Holistic Health N17, Kingston Natural Healing Centre, Lifeworks, National Federation of Spiritual Healers, Natureworks, Neal's Yard Therapy Rooms WC2, Primrose Healing Centre NW1, Raphael Clinic NW6, School of T'ai-chi Ch'uan - Centre for Healing WC1, School of the Dancing Dragon N16, Shirley Goldstein, Silver Birch Centre NW10, South Camden Women's Centre, Spiritualist Association of Great Britain SW1, St James Centre for Health and Healing W1, Universitas Associates, White Eagle Lodge W8, Women's Natural Health Centre NW5.

TRAININGS IN HEALING

Le Plan Seminars/International Healing School *Title of Training* Healing

Training. *Duration* Four two week residential courses in France *Entry requirements* Application plus personal interview. *Fees* £525 for each of the four parts of the course. *Comments* Course covers a wide variety of subjects, including chakras, auras, counselling, guided imagery, crystals, colour healing, use of ritual, meditation and professional and personal issues involved in healing.

National Federation of Spiritual Healers: *Details* Apply to organisers.

School of the Dancing Dragon *Title of Training* Healer Training Course *Duration* One weekend a month over a year. *Entry requirements* None. *Fees* £450 approximately.

Herbalism

The use of herbal remedies to cure disease must be one of the oldest and most widespread of medical arts, and formed the basis of much of modern pharmacology. But while modern drugs which derive from plants are made by separating out the 'active' ingredient and concentrating it, herbal remedies use the whole plant. Supporters of herbal medicine say that the natural chemical balance present in the entire plant means that its effects on the body are in turn more balanced, and so the side effects caused by many modern drugs are avoided.

A herbalist may follow the western tradition and use herbs from this country and Europe, or he or she may be a Chinese herbalist and use traditional Chinese herbs.

A herbalist is not usually medically trained, though they should have undergone a training course lasting a few years. As with homoeopathy, the herbalist will take a detailed medical history and perhaps focus particularly on your diet to see whether you may be suffering from any allergies. However, unlike homoeopathic treatment, the remedies are usually prescribed for a particular complaint, rather than through building up a picture of your personality and symptoms.

Herbs are prescribed in different forms. They can be taken as an infusion, and prepared in a similar way to tea. Sometimes they need to be boiled for quite a long time. Some herbs are prescribed in tinctures, where they are suspended in alcohol, and they can also be prepared as lotions, tablets, liquids, poultices and suppositories. Often a combination of different herbs is prescribed, so that if one herb does not effect a cure, another might.

Many people take herbal remedies as a method of self-help. If you do, you can go to a specialist herbal shop (see below in the 'Resources' section) to ask advice, though it is possible to find out which herbs work for you by trial and error. Treating yourself involves infusing the plants as tea, and of course pre-prepared herbal remedies for such things as insomnia, stress and menstrual pain are available at chemist shops. One word of warning - some herbs can be toxic, especially if taken in large quantities, so if experimenting with a new herb, it is best to take advice.

READING

The Holistic Herbal *by David Hoffmann, Element £8.95.*
Illustrated with original line drawings and photographs, this book places herbs in the context of Gaia, the living earth, and offers a practical, comprehensive look at the use of herbs. It includes a detailed look at the systems of the body; circulation, respiration, digestion and nervous systems. There are sections on herb gathering, preparation and herbal chemistry. As well as being a complete traditional herbal, this is a fascinating practical guide for maintaining a healthy body and soul.
Complete Herbal Handbook for the Dog and Cat *Juliette de Bairácli Levy, Faber & Faber £4.95.* One of a series of herbals by this author covering herbal treatment for different types of patient. Cats and dogs respond well to natural medicine and this book, divided into three parts, concentrates first on the care and rearing of young animals, secondly on the use of herbs to cure disease. The third part is a general section focusing on disease prevention.

CENTRES OFFERING HERBALISM

Acumedic Centre, African Herbs Ltd , All Hallows House EC3, Brackenbury Natural Health Centre W6, British School of Oriental Therapy and Movement, Bumblebees Natural Remedies N7, C.H.I Clinic SW6, Chinese Clinic W1, City Health Centre EC1, Clinic of Herbal Medicine, Clinics Health International SW6, Clissold Park Natural Health Centre N16, East-West Clinic of Natural Healing, Edgware Centre for Natural Health, European Shiatsu School, Fook Sang Acupuncture and Chinese Herbal Practitioners Training College UK NW11, General Council and Register of Consultant Herbalists , Haelen Centre, Hale Clinic W1, Healthy Living, Herb Society SW11, Holistic Health Consultancy SW1, Hong Tao Acupuncture and Natural Health Clinic, Kingston Natural Healing Centre, London College of Shiatsu W1, London School of Acupuncture and Traditional Chinese Medicine EC1, Lotus Healing Centre, Marigold Treatment Centre, National Institute of Medical Herbalists, Natural Healing Centre, Natural Medicine Centre, Natureworks, Neal's Yard Therapy Rooms WC2, New Cross Natural Therapy Centre, Nutribiotics, Primrose Healing Centre NW1, Private Polyclinic, Putney Natural Therapy Clinic, Refuah Shelaymah Natural Health Centre N16, School of Complementary Medicine NW1, Silver Birch Centre NW10, South Camden Women's Centre, South London Natural Health Centre SW4, St James Centre for Health and Healing W1, Thames & Ganges Trading Co, Traditional Chinese Medicine Clinic , Tyers St. Centre SE11, Westminster Natural Health Centre SW1, Women and Health NW1, Women's Natural Health Centre NW5, Wood Street Clinic EN5.

TRAININGS IN HERBALISM
Fook Sang Acupuncture and Chinese Herbal Practitioners Training College UK *Title of Training* Acupuncture and Chinese Herbal Practitioners Training (including training in traditional diagnosis). *Duration* Three years. Weekend attendance. October start. *Entry requirements* Preferably degree level or vocational training. Minimum A level standard. Mature students must show enthusiasm and desire to learn. *Fees* Year 1 £950, year 2 £800, year 3 £700, payable in instalments. *Comments* Successful graduates eligible for membership of Acupuncture Practitioners Association and Hong Kong Chinese Acupuncture Association.

Herbs Hands Healing *Title of Training* (1) Natural Health Course (2) Master Herbalist (3) Doctorate in Herbal Medicine. *Duration* Residential weekends and fortnights plus home study. *Entry requirements* for (2), completion of (1).

London School of Herbology and Aromatherapy *Title of Training* Herbal Medicine/Medical Aromatherapy Diploma Course. *Duration* 3 years part-time (500 hours). *Entry Requirements* None: students are trained in all aspects of required knowledge. *Fees* £1,000 per annum. *Comments* Training in both Chinese traditional approach, and western medical approach. Course includes clinical practice.

School of Herbal Medicine *Title of Training* (1) One year course in herbal medicine (2) Four year tutorial course in herbal medicine (3) Full time course in herbal medicine (4) Specially structured course. *Duration* (1) 1 year (correspondence) (2) 4 years part-time (3) 4 years, 3 days a week. (4) 1 year (correspondence) *Entry requirements* (1) None (2) Intending students should have good educational background, with qualifications in relevant subjects including English language, chemistry and biology 'O' levels. Preliminary courses available for those with insufficient qualifications. (3) 2 'O' levels, preferably 2 'A' levels, or equivalents, in biological sciences and chemistry. (4) Course for professionals such as GPs and Osteopaths. *Fees* Vary - apply to organisers.

Homoeopathy

Homoeopathy is a system of medicine which is based on the idea that an illness which produces certain symptoms can be cured by a substance or drug which produces the same symptoms.

Homoeopathic remedies are substances which have been diluted sometimes up to tens of thousands of times. In their undiluted form they would produce similar symptoms to those for which they are prescribed. While conventional medicine treats with drugs which produce contrary, suppressive effects (for instance aspirin to suppress a temperature), homoeopathy follows the treatment of like by like. A simple parallel can be drawn to illustrate this contrast: if one had cold feet, one could either plunge them into hot water which would alleviate the feeling of cold for a while, or put them in cold water which might make them feel colder at first, but

136

would then stimulate the circulation so that the body would be working to heat itself up. In the same way, the homoeopathic remedy, by aggravating the symptoms very minutely, stimulates the body's own defences or 'vital force'. The concept is also similar to that of innoculation.

Critics of homoeopathy claim that the substances are so highly diluted (sometimes as if one were putting one drop of a liquid into the Baltic sea) that the original cannot be found in the remedy. Supporters claim that even highly diluted remedies still contain the energy of the substance, though they cannot be detected by existing chemical methods.

The founder of this system was Samuel Hahnemann, a German doctor who practised in the early 19th century. He tested hundreds of drugs on healthy volunteers or 'provers' as he called them (some of whom must have been dedicated since many of the substances produced unpleasant symptoms) and catalogued the effects they had. Since many of the drugs were poisons, when Hahnemann prescribed them for his patients he tried diluting them as much as possible, and through this he discovered that in fact the more he diluted them, the stronger they became in their curative effects.

Diagnosis in homoeopathy has to be made very carefully and precisely to find the right remedy not only for the disease, but also for the individual patient. On visiting a homoeopathic doctor, he or she will take a detailed history, not just about your complaint, but also about the sort of person you are, your likes and dislikes and your physical and emotional temperament. He or she will take important events in your life into consideration and your family's medical history. For this reason the initial consultation is usually the longest.

When the remedy has been prescribed the homoeopath will tell you when and how to take it. The remedies have to be stored and taken carefully to preserve their properties. Since conventional drugs work in a way which is directly contrary to the way in which homoeopathic remedies take effect, you may decide to stop taking ordinary medicines, although it is worth discussing this with your homoeopath if this will be difficult. Some homoeopaths also recommend that you do not drink coffee, eat sweets or consume peppermint around the time you take the remedy, but this varies with the practitioner.

Homoeopathic remedies can be used to treat most reversible illnesses. On the whole they are not suitable for diseases requiring surgery, though dedicated homoeopaths would probably disagree. Useful to have around the house is the 'homoeopathic first aid kit' since all the remedies are safe enough to be self-administered. Homoeopathy has even be used with success on animals.

READING

Everybody's Guide to Homoeopathic Medicines *by Stephen Cummings and Dana Ullman Gollancz £4.95*. The authors explain in clear terms how to treat yourself and your family with safe and effective remedies. Learn about 'casetaking'

BODY THERAPIES

and how to prescribe for ailments such as colds, digestive problems, headaches and cystitis. Remedies for first aid use are also described as well as instructions for when it is necessary to seek outside help. The book begins with a brief outline of the fundamental ideas behind homoeopathy. **The Science of Homoeopathy** *by George Vithoulkas Thorsons £7.99.* Written by one of the world's leading homoeopaths, this work outlines both theory and practice of homoeopathy. The clear, concise language, inclusion of case histories, references and illustrations make it an excellent reference work for physicians and an informative introduction for the lay reader.

CENTRES OFFERING HOMOEOPATHY
Acupuncture and Osteopathy Clinic SW1, Aetherius Society SW6, Association of Natural Medicines, Barbican Natural Health Centre EC1, Bayswater Clinic W2, Bexleyheath Natural Health Clinic, Bodywise E2, Brackenbury Natural Health Centre W6, British Homoeopathic Association W1, Bumblebees Natural Remedies N7, Centre for Health and Healing W1, City Health Centre EC1, Clissold Park Natural Health Centre N16, College of Homoeopathy Clinic SE13, College of Homoeopathy NW1, College of Nutribiotics NW3, Drakefield Homoeopathic Centre SW17, Edgware Centre for Natural Health, Faculty of Homoeopathy WC1, Haelen Centre, Hahnemann College of Homoeopathy E13, Hahnemann College of Homoeopathy, Hampton Healing Centre, Hillside Practice, Holistic Health Consultancy SW1, Homoeopathic Centre W13, Homoeopathic Health Clinic, Insight Care N1, Kingston Natural Healing Centre, Lavender Hill Homoeopathic Centre SW11, Lifeworks, Living Centre, London College of Classical Homoeopathy SE1, London Lighthouse W11, London Natural Health Clinic W8, Marigold Trust WC1, Melissa Morant Centre NW3, Natural Healing Centre E7, Natural Healing Centre, Natural Health Clinic, Natural Medicine Centre, Natureworks, New Cross Natural Therapy Centre, Nutribiotics, Portobello Green Fitness Centre W10, Private Health Centre E7, Private Polyclinic, Putney Natural Therapy Clinic, Raphael Clinic NW6, Royal London Homoeopathic Hospital, Sayer Clinic, South Camden Women's Centre, South London Natural Health Centre SW4, Spectrum N4, Sunra SW12, Therapy Made Unique E18, Tyers St. Centre SE11, Women and Health NW1, Wood Street Clinic EN5.

TRAININGS IN HOMOEOPATHY
British Institute of Homoeopathy *Title of Training* Classical and Modern Homoeopathy. *Duration* Three years. *Entry requirements* Good general education plus some knowledge of anatomy and physiology. *Fees* £600 inclusive.
College of Homoeopathy *Title of Training* Professional Course in Homoeopathy. *Duration* Part-time course: one weekend per month over min 4 years. Full-time course: three days per week over min 3 years. *Entry requirements* Education to 'A' level standard and above. (Specific subjects not required). Students should usually be over 21 years. Mature students without 'A' levels but with relevant experience considered. *Fees* Part time: £940 + VAT p.a. Full-time: £2,820 + VAT p.a..

138

❝ I had developed a dry barking cough. The doctor gave me a ten day course of antibiotics, then, when that failed, he gave me a course of different treatment. There was no change so he sent me to the chest hospital where they examined my chest, said it was clear and sent me to a specialist. He X-rayed my head, noted my sinuses were blocked causing draining onto my throat, hence the cough. He suggested washing out my sinuses. No thanks! Well OK, 'we can dry them out' - by shining an infra-red beam into them four times a week. This was tedious and lengthy and gave some relief, but in the wet weather they filled up again. The doctor suggested a hot, dry climate. So I took a holiday in Greece and they healed completely.

When I got back to England they filled up even worse than before and the cough was unbearable. The doctor put me on a course of decongestants. This worked for a time, but as soon as the weather changed, the sinuses would fill up and the cough return. I suffered this for four years.

Eventually I went to a homoeopath, who gave me a single dose of pulsatilla. I developed a streaming cold which lasted eight days and several boxes of tissues. At the end my ears popped, my hearing improved and my cough vanished. **❞**

Gill Stow

Faculty of Homoeopathy *Title of Training* Postgraduate Training in Homoeopathy *Entry requirements* Applicants must be qualified MB or BS (Batchelor of Medicine or Surgery). *Comments* Refer to organisers for details.

Hahnemann College of Homoeopathy *Title of Training* (1) Beginners course (2) Paramedics course (3) Postgraduate *Duration* Generally courses are two weekends a month, but a combination of full time and part time study is possible. (1) 3 years, (2) 2 years, (3) 1 year. *Entry requirements* (1) Four GCE passes which must include one 'A' level in a science subject. (2) Must be qualified, registered paramedical practitioner with sufficient knowledge of anatomy, physiology and diagnosis. (3) Applicants myst be qualified homoeopathic pracititioners from abroad or from recognised institutes. *Fees* (1) £750 per year approx. (2) £1,500, for two years. (3) £750, including a non-refundable admission fee of £100. Examination £40. *Comments* Fees may be paid in instalments. Exceptional cases not meeting entry requirements may be admitted, subject to an interview by the education committee.

London College of Classical Homoeopathy *Title of Training* Four Year Full Time Professional Training Course *Duration* Three years full-time, four years part-time *Entry requirements* If under 21 then 5 'O' levels and 3 'A's. Otherwise 'O' level or equivalent in human biology. *Fees* £2090 excl VAT for full-time. £1050 excl VAT for part-time. *Comments* Discretionary grants are available from many boroughs.

London School of Homoeopathy *Title of Training* Homoeopathy Diploma *Duration* Four years part-time. *Entry requirements* 'A' level education or equivalent. *Fees* £1,000 p.a.

BODY THERAPIES

Iridology

Iridology is a method of diagnosis in which the eyes, especially the iris, indicate the physical and psychological condition of the patient. Iridologists claim that the whole body is reflected in the eye, because this is where the entire nervous system comes to the surface.

Dr Bernard Jensen, in developing this technique, has mapped the iris and correlated different segments with parts of the body. If a segment has an unusual colour or markings, or is flecked, this is an indication that the corresponding part is not functioning properly. As a diagnostic technique, Iridologists claim that not only past disorders can be recognised, but tendencies towards disease in the future can be spotted and remedied before developing. The eyes are also examined for their condition: bright or dull, coarse or fine.

Iridologists may employ a magnifying glass to examine the eyes, or take photographs and make slides from which a diagnosis can be made.

Iridology can be used as a diagnostic aid in conjunction with any other therapy.

READING
Iridology - Personality and Health Analysis through the Iris *by Dorothy Hall, Angus & Robertson £4.95.* Dorothy Hall, an experienced practitioner, introduces the way to use this diagnostic technique by detailing how to recognise the signs shown in the iris. Using this book you can attempt to find your own pattern of good health and well-being, a pattern as distinct as a fingerprint for each one of us. **The Science and Practice of Iridology** *by Bernard Jensen, Bernard Jensen £20.00.* The classic textbook for serious students of iridology. The colour photographs clearly illustrate the diagnostic techniques and the comprehensive text aids the development of skills in the student's powers of diagnosis. There is also a second volume of this work which is in even greater detail and costs approximately £80.

CENTRES OFFERING IRIDOLOGY
Alternative Medicine Clinic NW15, British School of Iridology, City Health Centre EC1, College of Opthalmic Somatology N1, Community Health Foundation EC1, European Shiatsu School SW5, Holistic Health Consultancy SW1, Insight Care N1, Institute of Holistic Therapies SW6, Kingston Natural Healing Centre, National Council and Register of Iridologists, Neal's Yard Therapy Rooms WC2, Wholistic Health Centre.

TRAININGS IN IRIDOLOGY
British School of Iridology Apply to organisers for details.
College of Opthalmic Somatology *Title of Training* Diploma Course and Advanced Course in Opthalmic Somatology. *Duration* (1) Diploma: 1 year part-time. One day per month plus 15 hours home study per week. (2) Advanced Course: part-time. One seminar per quarter (3 years) plus research, thesis and 15 hours home

140

study per week. *Entry requirements* Assessed on individual merit. *Fees* (1) Diploma: £1,200 payable in 3 instalments. (2) Advanced: £400 per year. *Comments* The course is aimed at homoeopaths and students of homoeopathy.

Kirlian Photography

This is high-frequency photography used to produce a photograph of the 'aura' of energy around the body, and from this some people believe that diagnosis of illness can be made, whether manifest or latent.

It was discovered by Semyon and Valentina Kirlian, from the Kuban in the Soviet Union. They found that photographs made using this technique would show differences in the energy field of healthy and diseased subjects.

A Kirlian photograph is usually taken using the two hands of the subject. A furry or hairy effect can be observed in the photographs, following the outline of the palm and fingers. This is believed to be the energy emitted from the hand. However, while in strictly controlled conditions Kirlian photography can be used to diagnose certain illnesses, in normal conditions the photograph can be affected by many extraneous factors such as the condition of the film, humidity of the air and so on. It is also not at all clear whether a Kirlian picture can accurately diagnose *potential* illness, as some enthusiasts claim.

CENTRES OFFERING KIRLIAN PHOTOGRAPHY
London Natural Health Clinic W8, Resonance SW17.

Massage

Massage is a way of working on the soft tissues, the muscles and skin, to relieve tension held in the body. There are many different massage techniques and individual practitioners may use or have been influenced by different body therapies like shiatsu, rolfing, physiotherapy or hand healing. Some masseurs (masculine) or masseuses (feminine) may rely very much on a technique, and others may use 'intuitive' massage. In 'intuitive' massage the practitioner is guided by the way the client's body feels to apply basic techniques where they are most needed - in areas where there is a build-up of tension.

A masseur/se might come to the home of the client if they are elderly or bedridden, but usually the client will visit them in their home or a health centre. Some work with the client lying on the floor but most will use a massage table. The room should be kept very warm or the cold will make the recipient of the massage tense up. The masseur/se will use oil to help their hands move smoothly over the skin and will use a variety of strokes, such as kneading, rubbing, pummelling, circling, or stroking using fingertips, thumbs or the whole hand. You may not realise how tense your muscles are until the masseur/se begins to touch them, because tension gives rise not only to feelings of pain or stiffness, but sometimes shows itself just in numbness.

Individual practitioners have different ideas on pain. A few feel that a certain amount of pain in necessary if the massage is to be effective in releasing tension. Most would feel that while working on areas which have become very tense can give rise to a feeling of discomfort, they would be careful to keep this to a minimum. While a muscle may be sore to the touch, there is also a feeling of relief which usually overrides any discomfort. Individual clients have different tastes too; some prefer a vigorous massage while others may want something more soothing. The most important thing as a client is to feel that you can discuss this with the masseur/se and they will be responsive to your needs.

Having a massage is a pleasant experience. It is a way of being nurtured, it is relaxing and, in releasing energy which has become stored up in tension, it can also be invigorating. Massage is useful as part of a programme for combating stress.

Self-massage is also possible, although it is not as effective as being massaged by someone else. Relieving a friend's stiff neck can be a very satisfying way of giving and receiving physical contact - something which can be neglected. Most people can learn how to do the basic strokes and there are many weekend courses for beginners who want to learn to use massage on family and friends. The centres listed below may offer individual massage, courses for those who want to learn to give massage or both.

READING

The Massage Book *by George Downing, Penguin £5.99.* This well known simple manual of massage has been recently republished, a testament to its popularity. Massage is an art of healing and a powerful means of communicating without words. In order to convey the full range and effect of the art, the author outlines its wider philosophy and its links with oriental cults. Included are chapters on meditation, zone therapy and massage for lovers. **The Book of Massage** *by*

Lucinda Lidell, Ebury Press £7.95. A classic guide to the relaxing and healing skills of the hands. It is beautifully illustrated with drawings and photographs and includes step-by-step instructions with authoritative advice on all aspects. This book teaches the effects of the power of human touch.

CENTRES OFFERING MASSAGE

Abshot Holistic Centre, Augenblick Centre, Carrie Bates N4, Belgravia Beauty SW1, Bennet and Luck Natural Health Centre N1, Bluestone Clinic, Body Clinic NW11, Bodywise E2, Bodyworks Natural Therapies, Brackenbury Natural Health Centre W6, Bretforton Hall, Bumblebees Natural Remedies N7, CAER (Centre For Alternative Education And Research), Centre for Health and Healing W1, Centre for Massage and Movement Studies SW2, Chalice Foundation, Chiron W5, Churchill Centre W1, City Health Centre EC1, Clapham Common Clinic SW4, Clare Maxwell Hudson NW2, Community Health Foundation EC1, Community Massage SW2, Cortijo Romero UK W3, Creative Journey, Edgware Centre for Natural Health, Food and Chemical Allergy Clinic, Gerda Boyesen Centre for Biodynamic Psychology and Psychotherapy W3, Green Wood college W6, Haelen Centre, Hale Clinic W1, Hampstead Healing Centre NW3, Healing Fields Practice N7, Health Management NW3, Highbury Centre N5, IBISS, Institute of Holistic Massage, Institute of Holistic Therapies SW6, Isis Centre for Holistic Health N17, Kingston Natural Healing Centre, Lifeworks, Living Centre, Living Centre, London College of Massage W1, London Lighthouse W11, London Natural Health Clinic W8, Mehta Method of Therapeutic Head Massage N1, Muswell Healing Arts N10, Napier Chiropractic Clinic NW11, Natural Healing Centre E7, Natural Health Clinic, Natural Medicine Centre, Nature Cure Clinic W1, Natureworks, Neal's Yard Therapy Rooms WC2, New Cross Natural Therapy Centre, New Life Lodge N4, Open Centre EC1, Portobello Green Fitness Centre W10, Primrose Healing Centre NW1, Private Health Centre E7, Private Polyclinic, Putney Natural Therapy Clinic, Raphael Clinic NW6, Resonance SW17, Sayer Clinic, School of the Dancing Dragon N16, Shirley Goldstein, Silver Birch Centre NW10, South London Natural Health Centre SW4, Sunra SW12,

Time to Unwind, Tyers St. Centre SE11, Wellspring Clinic SW6, West London Buddhist Centre W11, West London School of Therapeutic Massage W11, West London School of Therapeutic Massage W11, Westminster Natural Health Centre SW1, Wild Goose Company NW3, Wimbledon Clinic of Natural Medicine SW19, Women and Health NW1, Women's Natural Health Centre NW5, Women's Therapy Centre N7, Wood Street Clinic EN5.

TRAININGS IN MASSAGE

Bodywise *Title of Training* Bodywise Massage Diploma Course *Duration* Three terms of three weeks each. *Entry requirements* No experience necessary. *Fees* £150 per term, £450 in total. *Comments* To get diploma students complete a paper on anatomy and physiology and do 60-80 hours of massage in their own time.

Centre for Massage and Movement Studies *Title of Training* The Eyerman technique training in massage. *Duration* 3-year diploma course. 6 weekends a year plus 6 practical days per year. *Entry requirements* None for first year of diploma course, but for 2nd and 3rd years must have completed first year. *Fees* £475 per year. *Comments* Eyerman technique is a synthesis of massage and movement utilising techniques from eastern and western massage forms. Also weekend workshops.

Churchill Centre *Title of Training* Advanced massage course. Churchill Centre Certificate in Health Care and Relaxation with Massage. *Duration* Basic training three weekends for ITEC certificate. Advanced course two weekends *Entry requirements* None specified *Fees* approximately £50 to £60 per weekend.

Clare Maxwell Hudson *Title of Training* Introductory through to advanced techniques including basic massage, reflexology, shiatsu, sports massage, facials, etc. ITEC. *Duration* Vary. *Fees* Vary depending on length of course. Weekend £115 including VAT.

School of the Dancing Dragon *Title of Training* Basic Massage Course *Duration* Four weekends and four evenings. *Entry requirements* None. *Fees* £275

Comments Also introductory massage courses plus psychic development. Advanced massage training also.

Shirley Goldstein Holistic Therapies *Title of Training* Holistic Massage Diploma Course. *Duration* 3 weekends. *Fees* £195.

South London Natural Health Centre (Academy of Natural Health) *Title of Training* Holistic massage courses, from introductory to practitioner level, leading to ITEC and AMP qualifications. *Duration* For practitioner level, 5 weekends plus homework, case studies etc, or 12 evenings plus 2 weekends. *Entry requirements* Must do introductory weekend or evening. *Fees* £55-60 per weekend or £240 for 12 evenings.

Sunra *Duration* Five half days (20 hours). Refer to organisers for details.

West London School of Therapeutic Massage and Reflexology *Title of Training* Training in massage, anatomy and physiology, reflex zone therapy and sports therapy. ITEC. *Duration* Various. *Entry requirements* None specified *Fees* £75 to £1000 depending upon duration.

West London Buddhist Centre *Title of Training* Massage Training *Duration* One year. *Fees* By arrangement.

Metamorphic Technique

Metamorphic technique was originally developed from foot reflexology by Robert St John, but evolved into a completely different therapy. Rather than positing that each area of the foot corresponds to a part of the body, metamorphic techique is based on the idea that the foot from toe to heel corresponds to the pre-natal period from conception to birth. This is also seen to correspond to the spine from base to head. By massaging the foot it is believed that physical and psychological traumas incurred in the womb can be healed. For it is in the nine months of gestation, according to the theory of metamorphic technique, that all our mental, physical, emotional and spiritual patterns and responses are set.

Each foot is massaged for about half an hour, generally starting at the toe and working on the arch of the foot, down to the heel. The practitioner may also work on the hands and the back of the head.

Though it was originally devised to help handicapped children, it is a gentle technique which can be used by anyone.

CENTRES OFFERING METAMORPHIC TECHNIQUE
Jeyrani Health Centre E18, Metamorphic Association SW17, New Cross Natural Therapy Centre .

Natural Birth Control

There are various methods of natural birth control, but they all work on the theory that the fertile period in a woman's menstrual cycle can be worked out, either on certain principals, or by observing signs and changes in the body. During this time, the couple can either abstain from penetrative sex or use barrier methods of birth control (e.g. condom or diaphragm with spermicide). Couples wanting to conceive can also use them to indicate when it's likely, and, according to some theories (still unproven) can try to determine the sex of their child by making love just before ovulation (for a girl) or just after ovulation (for a boy).

Natural birth control doesn't involve taking substances or putting devices into the body, nor does it have the side effects sometimes associated with orthodox methods of birth control. However, they do require a degree of commitment by both the woman and her partner if they are to be effective. Though perhaps somewhat time consuming, natural birth control methods may provide a woman with the opportunity to get to know her own body and natural cycles more, to share responsibility for contraception and for both partners to communicate more with each other about sex. A combination of methods outlined below should be used, and *it is very important to get an expert in natural birth control to teach you.* Contacts for this are listed at the end of this section.

In general with all these methods you are more likely to avoid conceiving if you have unprotected intercourse only in the time after ovulation (a woman's fertile time) up to the next period, than if you have unprotected sex in the time after a period up to ovulation. They are only suitable for those in a long-term, monogamous relationship since they offer no protection against AIDS and sexually transmitted diseases.

Mucus Method

This involves observing the changes in quality and quantity of the mucus in the vagina throughout the menstrual cycle.

During menstruation this mucus (called 'cervical mucus') can't be observed easily, so these are not necessarily safe days. After menstruation, there may be a couple of days of no mucus, and a sensation of dryness in the vagina (however, if yours is a short cycle, you may have mucus straight away). Then the mucus will start to become more profuse, starting off whitish or yellowish, thick and tacky and becoming clearer, more slippery and stringy like raw egg white (you can stretch a strand of it between two fingers). These changes start about five days before ovulation and on the most fertile days you may have a sensation of slippery wetness and lubrication. Unprotected intercourse should be avoided from the first time you see or feel the mucus until four days after the slippery, wet sensation has gone. After this, the mucus will resume a whitish, yellowish, cloudy appearance and tacky consistency. A properly trained natural family planning teacher will enable you to learn the difference between these different kinds of mucus.

Basal Body Temperature

Just before ovulation, a woman's temperature drops slightly, and after ovulation it rises. By taking your temperature every day at the same time on waking with a basal fertility thermometer which can measure minute temperature changes, you can tell when you have ovulated. When you have recorded a temperature for three days in a row which is higher than all the previous six days the fertile time is over. Charts can be obtained from the Family Planning Association to note these temperature changes.

Because many things affect body temperature (even taking aspirin), expert help is needed to interpret the chart. This method by itself does not predict which are the infertile days before ovulation.

Calendar method

This should only be used as a cross-check with the above two methods. Before using this, you need to keep a chart of your periods for at least 6 consecutive cycles. Work out the number of days in the shortest cycle and subtract 19 - this gives you the probable first fertile and therefore unsafe day after the first day of your period. Then work out the number of days in the longest cycle and subtract 10 - this gives the probable last day of the fertile time after which it is safer to have sex again. If your cycle changes you will need to alter your calculations.

Astrological birth control

This method cannot be recommended unless you are happy to get pregnant, since there is no proof at all that it works! The fertile time, according to this method is when the sun and moon are the same distance apart in degrees as they were when the woman was born. This happens once every twenty nine and a half day lunar cycle. It is calculated with an ephemeris (an astrological table of the planets' positions).

Centres offering Natural Birth Control

Natural Family Planning Teachers (register).

Naturopathy

Fundamental to the practice of naturopathy is the idea that if provided with favourable conditions, nature itself can heal the body. Illness is a result of toxins accumulating in the system and symptoms of disease are the attempts of the body to throw off these harmful waste products. We need only co-operate with this process to establish and maintain good health because nature itself is always striving for the good of the organism. While animals are in tune with this and will instinctively fast or eat foods which contain medicinal substances when they are ill, human beings, according to Naturopathy, have lost contact with this instinct for health.

BODY THERAPIES

Naturopaths use different methods to restore the body to a natural state. Fasting is an important way of clearing out the substances which cause disease, and maintaining a healthy, natural diet afterwards consolidates the benefits gained from fasting. Naturopaths often use osteopathy (q.v.) as well, and hydrotherapy which is treatment with water such as the taking of hot and cold baths or showers, taking spa waters and so on.

Naturopathy is essentially a self-help therapy. Though the naturopath can prescribe a regime which will suit the individual, it requires work on the part of the patient to stick to it. While fasting can have unpleasant side-effects at first, naturopaths stress that these are the results of the body throwing off harmful waste and are part of the healing process. The fast may not be total, fruit juice or fruit may be recommended, and the naturopath will take into account your age and disposition when advising you of how to go about it. He or she may suggest ways to ease in and out of the fast so that the exercise is not too much of a shock to the system. Diets may be rigourous at first, but once the system becomes sensitive to what it really needs, healthy eating becomes more instinctive.

Naturopathy emphasises the importance of maintaining good health by eating well and exercising rather than taking action when symptoms develop and a cure is harder to achieve. Increasingly orthodox medicine is also now emphasising that prevention is better than cure.

READING
Natural Therapeutics *by Henry Lindlahr and Jocelyn Probyn* Volume 1 Philosophy of Natural Therapeutics £12.00 Volume 2 Practice of Natural Therapeutics £8.95. Volume 3 Dietetics £6.50 Volume 4 Iridiagnosis £8.75. These four volumes are concerned with laying down the general principles of natural therapeutics and go on to give guidance and directions on the application and combination of the methods which can be used to prevent disease, promote health and help to bring about cure.

CENTRES OFFERING NATUROPATHY
Barbican Natural Health Centre EC1, Bennet and Luck Natural Health Centre N1, Body Clinic NW11, Body-Mind Health Private Clinic, Bodywise E2, Brackenbury Natural Health Centre W6, British College of Naturopathy and Osteopathy NW3, Bumblebees Natural Remedies N7, Camden Osteopathic and Natural Health Practice NW5, Edgware Centre for Natural Health, Forty Hill Natural Therapy Centre, General Council and Register of Osteopaths, Hale Clinic W1, Hocroft Clinic NW2, Holistic Health Consultancy SW1, Institute of Botanic Medicine E17, Lifeworks, Nature Cure Clinic W1, Natureworks, Neal's Yard Therapy Rooms WC2, Primrose Healing Centre NW1, Putney Natural Therapy Clinic, Raphael Clinic NW6, South London Natural Health Centre SW4, Sunnyholt Natural Health Centre W3, Westminster Natural Health Centre SW1.

148

BODY THERAPIES

TRAININGS IN NATUROPATHY
British College of Naturopathy and Osteopathy *Title of Training* Diploma Course in Osteopathy and Naturopathy *Duration* 4 years full time. *Entry requirements* Two 'A' Levels (preferably including a biological science and chemistry) plus minimum 2 GCE/GCSE 'O' level passes (including at least 1 of English Language, Physics, Maths or Science or Biological Science BTech or equivalent). *Fees* Approximately £4,000 per annum.

Osteopathy

Osteopathy uses manipulation of the spine and joints to restore the bones, muscles, ligaments and nerves to their proper alignment and thus the patient to health.

The founder of osteopathy, Dr Andrew Taylor Still, had studied engineering as well as medicine. In developing osteopathic techniques, he approached the human body as if it fitted together like a machine, and found that disease was caused by the spinal vertebrae slipping out of position. When this happens 'lesions' appear where the muscles round the displaced vertebrae are so stressed that they pass on inaccurate information to the central nervous system, or the nerves around them become over sensitive and affect the surrounding tissue. This then affects the circulation of the blood. Since the blood was seen by Still as carrying the substances which protect us from disease, illness is then the result of blocked circulation.

On a visit to an osteopath, he or she will take your medical history, and will also be looking at the way you walk, sit and stand to see where the vertebrae may be out of alignment. Examination is also carried out with the hands, and the osteopath will feel the bones and joints. Some may also use X-rays. Treatment itself is very active and physical and may involve you in taking a variety of positions while the osteopath pulls, pushes or applies pressure to your head, arms, legs or back in a number of ways. While this may sound alarming, the treatment is usually painless. A session may last 20-30 minutes and how long you have to keep going back for depends on the severity of the problem. However, since most osteopaths are inundated with patients, they are unlikely to need to prolong your treatment unnecessarily for their own benefit! Sometimes the osteopath may give exercises to be done at home as a back up to the treatment sessions.

Osteopaths are rarely medically qualified, but should have undergone a thorough training of at least three years and be able to recognise medical conditions which lie outside their field of practice. Since osteopathy is one of the best organised therapies of the complementary medicines it is easy to get registers of qualified practitioners.

People usually go to osteopaths for 'bad backs'. and it is of course a good treatment for this ubiquitous complaint as well as for migraines and painful joints. The treatment was evolved to have a wide ranging application and can be helpful with other less obviously suitable complaints.

READING

Osteopathy - is it for you? *by Chris Belshaw, Element £5.95*. A simple worded guide to osteopathy for the patient which includes explanations of the technical terms. It explains how this manual therapy can influence the physiological mechanisms in the body that lead to healing and freedom from pain.

CENTRES OFFERING OSTEOPATHY

Acupuncture and Osteopathy Clinic SW1, Barbican Natural Health Centre EC1, Bennet and Luck Natural Health Centre N1, Bluestone Clinic, Body Clinic NW11, Bodywise E2, Bodyworks Natural Therapies , Brackenbury Natural Health Centre W6, British and European Osteopathic Association, British College of Naturopathy and Osteopathy NW3, British Osteopathic Association NW1, British School of Osteopathy SW1, Bumblebees Natural Remedies N7, Camden Osteopathic and Natural Health Practice NW5, Centre for Health and Healing W1, City Health Centre EC1, Clapham Common Clinic SW4, Clissold Park Natural Health Centre N16, College of Nutribiotics NW3, College of Osteopaths Education Trust, Cranial Osteopathy and Structural Therapy, Creative and Healing Arts W11, Edgware Centre for Natural Health, Equilibrium Therapy Centre SW18, European Shiatsu School, Fook Sang Acupuncture and Chinese Herbal Practitioners Training College UK NW11, General Council and Register of Osteopaths, Haelen Centre, Hale Clinic W1, Hocroft Clinic NW2, Independent Register of Manipulative Therapists N13, Institute of Botanic Medicine E17, Isis Centre for Holistic Health N17, Jeyrani Health Centre E18, Kingston Natural Healing Centre, Lavender Hill Homoeopathic Centre SW11, Lever Clinic, Lever Clinic EN1, Lifeworks, Living Centre, Living Centre, London College of Osteopathic Medicine NW1, London Natural Health Clinic W8, Lotus Healing Centre, Mehta Method of Therapeutic Head Massage N1, Natural Healing Centre E7, Nature Cure Clinic W1, Natureworks, Neal's Yard Therapy Rooms WC2, New Cross Natural Therapy Centre, Primrose Healing Centre NW1, Private Health Centre E7, Private Polyclinic, Putney Natural Therapy Clinic, Raphael Clinic NW6, Refuah Shelaymah Natural Health Centre N16, Sayer Clinic, South London Natural Health Centre SW4, St James Centre for Health and Healing W1, Sunnyholt Natural Health Centre W3, Sunra SW12, Wellspring Clinic SW6, Westminster Natural Health Centre SW1, Wholistic Health Centre, Wimbledon Clinic of Natural Medicine SW19, Women and Health NW1, Women's Natural Health Centre NW5, Wood Street Clinic EN5.

TRAININGS IN OSTEOPATHY

Andrew Still College of Osteopathy *Title of Training* Diploma in Osteopathy. *Duration* 5 years part time, weekends. *Entry requirements* Minimum of 5 GCEs, 2 of which should be 'A' levels, preferably one in a science subject. For mature students with sufficient experience these may be waived. *Fees* £750p.a..

British College of Naturopathy and Osteopathy *Title of Training* Diploma

Course in Osteopathy and Naturopathy *Duration* 4 years full time. *Entry requirements* Two 'A' Levels preferably (including a biological science and chemistry) plus minimum 2 GCE/GCSE 'O' level passes (including at least 1 of English Language, Physics, Maths or Science or Biological Science BTech or equivalent). *Fees* Approximately £3,400 per annum for 1990/91 entry.

British School of Osteopathy *Title of Training* BSc in Osteopathy *Duration* 4 years full-time. *Entry requirements* 2 science 'A' levels, preferably biology and chemistry. Will consider applicants without requirements, subject to interview. *Fees* For current academic year, first year fees £4,600. Since this is an academic course discretionary awards may be available from local authorities. *Comments* Write to the Registrar for further details.

College of Osteopaths Education Trust *Title of Training* Diploma in Osteopathy *Duration* 6 years part-time mostly weekends. *Entry requirements* 'A' Levels but for suitable applicants without these an Osteopathic Science Preparatory Course is available (six weekends). *Fees* Refer to organisers

London College of Osteopathic Medicine *Title of Training* Membership course MLCOM. *Duration* Thirteen months of 3 days per week. *Entry requirements* (1) Registered medical practitioner (2) 6 years at least post qualification (3) Must pass entry examination. *Fees* £2,000 for 13 months.

London School of Osteopathy *Title of Training* Diploma Course in Osteopathy *Duration* 5 years part-time (18 weekends per yr). *Entry requirements* 3 'A' levels in science subjects. *Fees* £1,750 payable by monthly bankers order. *Comments* Exceptions to the above entry requirements may be made in the case of mature students.

Polarity Therapy

In polarity therapy the body is seen as a made up of the universal energy which forms both the material and spiritual universe. It uses a variety of techniques including manipulation, stretching postures, and adjustment of diet to remove blocks in the flow of this energy through the body and to bring about the state of balance and health.

Randolph Stone, its originator, studied osteopathy, naturopathy and chiropractic and spent the last ten years of his life in India with his spiritual teacher.

He saw the body as having five energy centres which correspond to the elements of earth, water, fire, air and ether (ether is the fifth of five elements which according to Indian philosophical systems make up the universe). Specific exercises of 'polarity yoga' are prescribed to release and harmonise the energy of these centres, which may have become blocked through early emotional traumas, bad living habits or environmental influences. It is important that the energy is not only released, but also balanced between centres. The body's energies are seen as flowing in polarity between positive and negative poles. Good health is achieved when this flow reaches a point of equilibrium called 'neutral'.

Most of the work in polarity therapy is manipulation to balance the energies. This is sometimes done by the therapist by placing each hand on different parts of the body to facilitate the flow of energy between them. The body can be massaged in a clockwise or anti-clockwise direction or on the right or left side as is appropriate to the energy pattern of the recipient. Three types of pressure can be applied: positive, which makes the energy move, negative, which unblocks energy and can involve deep work on tissues, and neutral which is soothing. The therapist may also discuss the feelings which arise in the course of treatment, and any problems the client has.

The nutritional approach in polarity therapy usually begins with a cleansing programme. Natural, cleansing foods are eaten to purify and strengthen the body's own resources by expelling toxins from the system. Different foods are then reintroduced into the diet and monitored for the effects they have on the client's mental and physical well-being. Then a healthy eating programme is worked out for the individual client which will help to maintain this state of balance and health for life.

Polarity therapy requires some effort on the part of the client to change habits which are harmful, and for him or her to work on their own using the postures. Stone himself stressed that the achievement and maintenance of good health requires that we make this effort. It also asks for a positive attitude and willingness on the part of the client to change.

READING

The Polarity Process *by Franklyn Sills, Element £8.95.* This is a detailed explanation of how the theory of 'universal energy' can be understood and applied. Based on Dr. Randolph Stone's work in facilitating the free flow of life's finer energies. Franklyn Sills also provides a study guide to Dr. Stone's original writings, offering a new clarity to the subject. **Your Healing Hands** *by Richard Gordon, Wingbow £9.95.* This introduction to Polarity Therapy is well written and clearly illustrated and provides a practical hands-on approach to the therapeutic touch and natural healing. The book reinforces the feeling more than the intellect for those who want to practise polarity.

CENTRES OFFERING POLARITY THERAPY

Abshot Holistic Centre, All Hallows House EC3, Brackenbury Natural Health Centre W6, Foundation for Holistic Consciousness SE25, Highbury Centre N5, Jeyrani Health Centre E18, Natural Healing Centre E7, Neal's Yard Therapy Rooms WC2, New Cross Natural Therapy Centre, Polarity Therapy Association W1, Primrose Healing Centre NW1, Raphael Clinic NW6, Refuah Shelaymah Natural Health Centre N16, Shirley Goldstein .

TRAININGS IN POLARITY THERAPY
Polarity Therapy Education Trust: Apply to organisers for details.

Radionics

Radionics (in some cases known as radiesthesia or psionic medicine) is diagnosis and treatment which is carried out at a distance using particular instruments to aid the healer's own psychic faculties.

The principle involved is similar to dowsing, where a stick held by the dowser will twitch to show the hidden presence of water, oil or minerals underground, or can be used to find missing articles or persons. In radionics, a pendulum (a weight on the end of a lenght of thread) is often used. After getting the patient to fill in a detailed questionnaire, a 'witness' - a drop of blood on a piece of blotting paper or a lock of hair - is taken. This 'witness' is believed to act as a link between the practitioner and the patient. Diagnosis can then be carried out in a number of ways. The practitioner may ask questions about the patient's condition and the pendulum will indicate either a positive or negative answer depending on the way it swings. The pendulum may be used over diagrams of the body, to indicate which parts need treatment, and further questions will indicate how severely affected these parts are and what has caused them to malfunction. The pendulum may be used with special charts to show, on a scale of 0-100, how well or how feebly an organ is working. Practitioners vary in how much equipment they use; some prefer to use only a pendulum, while others may use boxes with dials, and an array of electronic equipment.

Once diagnosis has been made, a similar process is used to find the right treatment. Once again, different practitioners may use different methods, so that a wide range of treatments, and methods of 'transmitting' them to the patient may be used. Some will simply write and recommend that patients take a particular remedy or course of treament. Others may perform a kind of 'distant healing', by focussing on the patient and their particular complaint mentally.

Radiesthesia's beginnings were fraught with difficulty, largely because of the hostility of the medical establishment towards what they saw as 'quackery'. It was developed by a distinguished American neurologist, Dr Albert Abrahams. At the beginning of this century, Abrahams made a curious discovery while using the standard medical technique 'percussion' - tapping the body of a patient to determine the condition in the internal organs. He found that if the patient was facing west, the same sound would be given consistently by patients suffering the same disease, as long as they were tapped in the same area. Developing this, Abrahams then found that if a healthy person held a sample of blood from a diseased person, the sound given when he tapped them was characteristic of the disease suffered by the owner of the blood. Believing that the reaction was caused by electromagnetic force, he devised and marketed a box device to measure resistances from the patient's sample. However, results from 'the box' as it was called, were not always consistent, and it was even banned in some states in America. Ruth Drown, a Californian chiropractor in the 1930s developed her own kind of box and was prosecuted by the Food and Drug Adminstration. The pioneer of Radionics in the UK, George de la Warr narrowly escaped prosecution by someone who had bought his version of 'the box'.

The problem for exponents of radionics had been that they believed that the force involved was electromagnetic and could be measured under test conditions. In fact, results of such tests tended to be patchy except in one notable case. In 1924 a committee was set up to investigate a British version of the box, headed by Sir Thomas Horder. A Scottish homoeopath was asked to identify substances using the box, and to the surprise of the committee his results were almost completely correct.

Radionic theory is now less concerned with electromagnetic energy exclusively, but sees all life forms as part of and affected by a common field of energy which includes, in its grossest form, electromagnetic energy. It is by influencing this field that the healing is performed.

Radionics can be used for any condition, mainly because it does not interfere with any other form of treatment. It is best perhaps with chronic, mysterious complaints which conventional medicine has failed to diagnose. It is also frequently used by those with terminal illness to ease pain and provide psychic support. It is also used in agriculture to increase crop yields, and animals respond well to radionic treatment.

READING
Spiritual Dowsing *by Sig Lonegren, Gothic Image £4.95.* This is a book for all who approach dowsing in a spirit of openness and sincerity. A new and dynamic approach which makes explicit the link between this ancient art and inner growth. The approach is extremely practical, guiding the beginner into both usage and philosophy, empowering the reader to take personal responsibility in his or her action in dowsing either the earth's energies or for healing. **Radionics and the Subtle Anatomy of Man** *by David Tansley C.W. Daniel £2.95.* David Tansley believes that the time is ripe for radionics to bear witness to an energy field of a more subtle nature and to this end wrote an examination of the wider influences of radionic energy with regard to the probability of underlying force fields which may affect the health of the physical form.

CENTRES OFFERING RADIONICS OR RADIESTHESIA
International Federation for Radionics W1, Natural Healing Centre Wellspring Clinic SW6.

Reflexology

This is a technique in which particular areas on the soles and sides of the feet are seen to correspond to the organs of the body. These are massaged to promote the health of the organs. Reflexology can also be used as a diagnostic tool.

Reflexology is an art the origins of which stretch back to ancient China. It was Dr William Fitzgerald, an Ear, Nose and Throat specialist interested in acupuncture who started using it in the West. His ideas were developed and exported to the United States by Eunice D Ingham whose book, *Stories the Feet Can Tell*, was published in 1932.

Treatment is carried out with the patient lying bare footed on a couch. The reflexologist will feel for tiny lumps under the surface of the skin which are believed to be crystalline deposits. The place on the foot where these are found indicates which organ is not functioning properly. For instance, the big toe corresponds to the top of the head and brain, and various parts of the heel to the bladder, sciatic nerve and sexual organs. The reflexologist will massage these spots which can be surprisingly sensitive when touched, so it is not uncommon to feel some pain. Most people feel the discomfort is worth it to achieve the therapeutic results, and at least the very sensitivity of the spot convinces patients that the reflexologist is really 'onto' something. Treatments continue until the spot is no longer sensitive. A session may last from 15 to 45 minutes and a course of treatment a few weeks.

READING

Reflexology Today *by Doreen Bayly, Thorsons £3.99.* A well loved introduction to the practice of reflexology which is one of the most pleasant of all holistic therapies. This book is valuable for student and layman alike and includes charts of the feet and the body zones. **Better Health with Foot Reflexology** *by Dwight Byers, Ingham Publishing £10.95.* This book combines the use of both hand and foot reflexology and is the most accurate and complete guide to the subject. It has become the standard reference for the International Institute of Reflexology and is extensively illustrated with methods of treatment as well as the organs of the body and other functions. **Holistic Reflexology** *by Avi Grinberg Thorsons £20.00.* An authoritative and detailed fully illustrated guide designed to meet the need for in depth treatment. Mainly for therapists and their students, including case histories and the understanding of holistic treatment of patients. New and highly recommended.

CENTRES OFFERING REFLEXOLOGY

Acupuncture and Osteopathy Clinic SW1, All Hallows House EC3, Aromatherapy Training Centre SW16, Association of Natural Medicines, Association of Reflexologists WC1, Bennet and Luck Natural Health Centre N1, Bodywise E2, Bodyworks Natural Therapies, Brackenbury Natural Health Centre W6, British Reflexology Centre, British School - Reflex Zone Therapy of the Feet (Ann Lett Ltd), British School of

66 After the first reflexology session I ever had, I walked away feeling more 'grounded' than I have ever felt - as if I understood that word for the first time. It was a reflexologist who correctly pinpointed the cause of a long-standing back complaint I had. So impressed was I, I later became a reflexologist myself! **99**

Karin Grey

Reflexology, Bumblebees Natural Remedies N7, Churchill Centre W1, Clissold Park Natural Health Centre N16, College of Nutribiotics NW3, Edgware Centre for Natural Health, Equilibrium Therapy Centre SW18, Falcons SW11, Food and Chemical Allergy Clinic, Forty Hill Natural Therapy Centre, Green Wood college W6, Hampstead Healing Centre NW3, Institute of Clinical Aromatherapy SE6, Institute of Holistic Therapies SW6, Janice Ellicot School of Reflexology SW6, Jeyrani Health Centre E18, Kingston Natural Healing Centre, Lifeworks, Living Centre, Living Centre, London College of Massage W1, Mary Martin Shool of Reflexology, Mill Hill Health Care NW7, Natural Healing Centre E7, Natural Healing Centre, Natural Medicine Centre, Naturecare, Natureworks, Neal's Yard Therapy Rooms WC2, New Cross Natural Therapy Centre, Portobello Green Fitness Centre W10, Primrose Healing Centre NW1, Private Health Centre E7, Putney Natural Therapy Clinic, Raphael Clinic NW6, Resonance SW17, Sayer Clinic, School of Complementary Medicine NW1, Silver Birch Centre NW10, South London Natural Health Centre SW4, Sunnyholt Natural Health Centre W3, Sunra SW12, Therapy Made Unique E18, Wellspring Clinic SW6, West London School of Therapeutic Massage W11, Westminster Natural Health Centre SW1, Wimbledon Clinic of Natural Medicine SW19, Women and Health NW1, Women's Natural Health Centre NW5, Wood Street Clinic, Yoga Dham, Ziva Belic Aromatherapy International School W5.

TRAININGS IN REFLEXOLOGY
Bayly School of Reflexology *Title of Training* Introductory advanced courses in reflexology leading to certificate. *Duration* Minimum of 7-8 months, attendance at three weekends and home study. *Entry requirements* None. *Fees* £237 + VAT *Comments* Regular courses held in central London and regional venues. School is official teaching body the British School of Reflexology.
British School - Reflex Zone Therapy of the Feet (Ann Lett Ltd) *Title of Training* (1) Introductory and (2) Advanced Training in Reflex Zone Therapy of the Feet. (3) Midwives course (4) Reflex Zone Therapy of the Nervous System. *Duration* Courses are three days each. *Entry requirements* Applicants should have previous medical training, or training in nursing, physiotherapy, midwifery, acupuncture, osteopathy or naturopathy. *Fees* £125 per course.
British School of Reflexology *Title of Training* Reflexology training courses. *Duration* 8 months part-time. *Entry requirements* None at present, but shortly by questionnaire/interview. *Fees* £570 in three instalments of £190.

BODY THERAPIES

Churchill Centre *Title of Training* Basic and advanced trainings in Foot Reflexology. *Duration* Basic training two weekends or four days. Advanced training is two weekends. *Entry requirements* None specified. *Fees* approximately £50 to £60 per weekend.

Clare Maxwell Hudson *Title of Training* Introductory through to advanced techniques including basic massage, reflexology, shiatsu, sports massage, facials, etc. ITEC. *Duration* Vary. *Fees* Vary depending on length of course. Weekend £115 including VAT.

Crane School of Reflexology *Title of Training* Training in Reflexology. *Duration* Four weekends bi-monthly plus 100 hours home study. *Entry requirements* None. *Fees* £495 including VAT. *Comments* Venues around the country. Phone for details of London venue.

Reflexology Centre *Title of Training* Basic and advanced course in reflexology. *Duration* Weekend courses. Details on request.

Rolfing

Rolfing is a technique evolved by Ida Rolf, which is also sometimes called structural integration. It seeks to realign the body by manipulation of the connective tissue.

A useful rule of thumb in looking at body alignment is that the body should show a symmetry between the right side and the left, looking face on. Looking side on, one should be able to draw a straight line from the bottom of the ear to the ankles which should pass through the middle of the shoulders and middle of the hips. If the body is not in alignment extra energy is needed to maintain equilibrium. For instance if the head is protruding forward (sticking one's neck out) then the muscles in the back of the neck must work at holding the head in position. Whereas if the head is sitting centrally, balanced directly over the spine, little energy is needed to hold it in place. Thus if one's body is out of alignment, one is using more energy when simply standing than if the body were not out of alignment.

The experience of being rolfed is like having a very deep and sometimes painful massage. The rolfer uses not only his or her hands but elbows too.

There are a standard ten sessions of one hour duration. Each session builds on the last one and works on a different part of the body. Some rolfers take before and after photos to keep a record of the changes that happen and let you have duplicates.

Fritz Perls the founder of gestalt therapy swore it helped him reduce the pain of angina. However, like the Alexander technique, it is not a treatment for any particular disorder, but a system aimed at prevention.

In this country, rolfing usually comes under the umbrella of 'structural bodywork' which includes other techniques such as structural integration.

READING
The Power of Balance *by Brian Fahey, Metamorphous Press £13.95*. Dr. Fahey is a fine worker in the interdisciplinary effort to enhance mutual co-operation

❝ My sixth to tenth rolfing session took place in winter, (1972 I think), in Toronto, Canada. Snow had just begun to fall as I reached the Rolfer's consulting room.

I had previously had five Rolfing sessions at Esalen in California and knew full well how painful it was. I had heard rumours that there was a groundswell within the Rolfing Institute to make an anaesthetic available to clients as many of them had complained how painful the process was, but that Ida Rolf had crushed the idea. So it was with apprehension that I now embarked on my sixth session. I am not able to recall whether that particular session was more or less painful than any of the others.

What I do remember is the difficulty I had in walking at the end of the session. The Rolfer had spent an hour working mostly on my legs and it's difficult to describe the sensation of trying to walk after having my legs pummelled for an hour. It was as if my legs were not my own. That old familiar feeling of my legs being securely anchored to the rest of my body had gone. Instead I found that I could only take a step forward by throwing out a leg in front of me and waiting for it to land, being surprised when it did so. I am convinced that I looked like one of those puppets on a string which each part of the body moving separately from any other part, and look totally unco-ordinated. I 'walked' around the room exclaiming to him about the peculiar sensation and wondering whether it was an improvement over my old way of walking.

I left in a confused state of mind wondering about the confused state of my body. By then the snow had reached about three foot deep and the task of making it home with my 'funny' legs was like climbing Mount Everest. I must have cut a pretty sight that day. ❞

Mike Considine

between rolfing, medicine and chiropractic. This book reflects his comprehensive philosophy and provides dynamic information for all health professionals concerned with improving their patients' level of well-being. **Rolfing** *by Ida Rolf, Healing Arts Press £15.15.* This is the classic text on Ida Rolf's therapy which attempts to align and balance the physical body within its gravitational field. Rolfing is a system of massage of the connective tissue which releases physical and emotional stress and leaves the patient with both physical and emotional well-being. **Rolfing** is intended for the interested but untrained lay-person as well as the professional in need of specific technical information. Well illustrated with both photographs and line drawings.

CENTRES OFFERING ROLFING
Hakomi Institute W4, Institute of Structural Bodywork SW1, Rolfing Centre.

Shiatsu and Acupressure

Shiatsu is a massage technique which involves stimulating or relaxing the acupuncture points and meridians. The word shiatsu means 'finger pressure' in Japanese. It is like a form of acupuncture which does not use needles. The principle is the same: to release and balance the flow or ki (ch'i in Chinese) or life energy at points where it may have become blocked or over stimulated.

In Japan shiatsu is practised widely, often as a form of self help by one member of the family on another. The Chinese version is called acupressure, and in practice is virtually the same as shiatsu.

After the completion of the case history, diagnosis is usually carried out by palpation of the abdomen and observation of any abnormalities in the skin or muscles. Sometimes the practitioner may take the pulses, as in an acupuncture session (see section on acupuncture for an explanation of 'pulses'). In this way the practitioner decides which points and meridians need work to balance the energy flow. The massage itself is a mixture of general strokes over particular parts of the body to promote the harmonious flow of ki energy, and direct pressure on the acupuncture points with the fingertips or elbows. The intensity of the pressure also varies between gentle massage to a very strong pressure, but the recipient should not have to experience any more pain than is involved in the pleasurable release of tension. The practitioner may also use gentle manipulation to loosen joints and stretch the meridians, the energy pathways. A session may last from 45 minutes to an hour and a quarter.

Shiatsu helps to maintain health by toning up the body's energy, and can be used to treat a variety of complaints, such as tension, low vitality, pre-menstrual tension, lower back pains, stiffness in the neck and shoulders, digestion problems, asthma, headaches and insomnia. It can also help to promote greater emotional tranquillity. As will some other alternative therapies, there are contra-indications for some conditions.

If you know the right pressure points to use, you can practise shiatsu on yourself for first aid to relieve pain or cramps, and some people become so adept at this that they use it on trips to the dentist.

READING
Shiatzu *by Yukiko Irwin, Arkana/Penguin £7.99.* The line drawings and clear

❝ In the mid 1970s, I spent six months with a totally blocked nose. I had just become interested in things alternative, but at first I tried various doctors' prescriptions, but it soon became obvious that nothing I did was making the slightest difference to my condition.

I then beat a path to the door of every type of complementary practitioner - homoeopath, acupuncturist, naturopath, iridologist and psychotherapist - that I could think of. Nothing seemed to shift the condition and I resigned myself to the fact that breathing was going to continue to bother me for the forseeable future.

Some months later, I was visiting a friend in Devon, who remarked on my bunged up condition and suggested I went to see an elderly pendulum diagnostician who lived close by. With some scepticism, I went to see the lady who sat me down and asked me to point my finger down a page where many types of alternative treatments were listed. When my finger pointed at the word 'osteopathy' the pendulum she was holding began to circle dramatically. She then turned to another page where a picture of the spine was portrayed and the same process took place. At the first vertebrae (the axis) the pendulum again took off and I was told to go and see an osteopath she recommended.

When I went, the osteopath cradled my head in her hands and gave it a sharp jerk. At that second, my nose cleared and the problem never recurred. **❞**

Malcolm Stern

concise instructions in this book are intended to help anyone learn and use the shiatsu points to the best advantage. Aches and pains of everyday living can be relieved by this therapy at the hands of almost any sympathetic layman. **The Natural Healer's Acupressure Handbook** *by Michael Blate, Henry Holt £6.80.* This book illustrates how 'acupuncture without needles' can be used by the lay-practitioner as a alternative to aspirin and other commonly used drugs to alleviate pain and discomfort. Problems for which treatment is suggested include headaches, anxiety, nosebleeds, stagefright, cramps and exhaustion. Also included are first-aid treatments while awaiting medical attention. **Soft Tissue Manipulation** *by Leon Chaitow, Thorsons £19.95.* This is a practitioner's guide to the diagnosis and treatment of soft tissue dysfunction and reflex activity. The book provides students with a working knowledge of the diagnostic and therapeutic use of neuro-muscular, muscle energy and strain-counterstrain techniques. It also covers systems involving reflex points and trigger points.

CENTRES OFFERING SHIATSU

Abshot Holistic Centre, Acumedic Centre, Acupuncture and Osteopathy Clinic SW1, Bennet and Luck Natural Health Centre N1, Body Harmony SW16, Bodywise E2, Bodyworks Natural Therapies, Brackenbury Natural Health Centre W6, British School of Oriental Therapy and Movement, British School of Shiatsu-Do EC1, Bumblebees Natural Remedies N7, City Health Centre EC1, Clare Maxwell Hudson NW2, Clissold Park Natural Health Centre N16, Community Health Foundation EC1,

BODY THERAPIES

Creative and Healing Arts W11, East-West Clinic of Natural Healing, Equilibrium Therapy Centre SW18, European Shiatsu School, European Shiatsu School, European Shiatsu School, European Shiatsu School, European Shiatsu School SW5, Green Wood college W6, Haelen Centre, Hillside Practice, Institute of Holistic Therapies SW6, Ki Kai Shiatsu Centre, Kingston Natural Healing Centre, London Centre for Yoga and Shiatsu Studies N10, London College of Shiatsu W1, Melissa Morant Centre NW3, Natural Health Clinic, Natural Medicine Centre, Natureworks, Neal's Yard Therapy Rooms WC2, Nine Needles Health Care Centre, Portobello Green Fitness Centre W10, Primrose Healing Centre NW1, Putney Natural Therapy Clinic, Raphael Clinic NW6, Refuah Shelaymah Natural Health Centre N16, School of Complementary Medicine NW1, Shiatsu College NR2, Shiatsu Society, South Camden Women's Centre, South London Natural Health Centre SW4, Sunra SW12, West London School of Therapeutic Massage W11, Westminster Natural Health Centre SW1, Wholistic Health Centre, Women and Health NW1.

TRAININGS IN SHIATSU

British School of Oriental Therapy and Movement *Title of Training* (1) One Year Certificate Course in Shiatsu - Traditional Chinese Medicine and Ki-Development (Kitaiso). (2) Advanced Course in Shiatsu. *Duration* (1) One year consisting of 3 terms, 12 classes per term (Saturdays 2-6pm). *Entry requirements* None specified. *Fees* Approximately £200 per term. *Comments* Study background, philosophy and aetiology of traditional Chinese medicine. Students must complete a number of ongoing treaments for practical assessment, and taught Kitaiso (a 'movement system') to facilitate student's own healing powers. A self development ingredient is added to the course through the movement and Ki.

British School of Shiatsu-Do *Title of Training* (1) Beginners course in Shiatsu-Do. (2) Diploma Course in Shiatsu-Do. *Duration* (1) 99 Hours. Evening, weekend or daytime timetables. (2) Three years part-time. Evening, weekend or daytime timetables. *Entry requirements* Open to everyone. They have an equal opportunity policy covering gender, race, religion, sexual orientation. Limited access for disabled applicants. *Fees* (1) £348 + VAT (2) £2684.10. Instalments payable in advance. *Comments* Diploma course includes oriental diagnosis, philosophy, exercise, counselling, anatomy and physiology. Students may study a beginners course for self study/development or complete the course to practitioner level.

Clare Maxwell Hudson *Title of Training* Introductory through to advanced techniques including basic massage, reflexology, shiatsu, sports massage, facials, etc. ITEC. *Duration* Vary. *Entry requirements Fees* Vary depending on length of course. Weekend £115 including VAT. *Title of Training* Introductory through to advanced techniques including basic massage, reflexology, shiatsu, sports massage, facials, etc. ITEC. Duration Vary. *Entry requirements Fees* Vary depending on length of course. Weekend £115 including VAT.

European Shiatsu School *Title of Training* (1) Shiatsu Foundation Course (2)

Shiatsu Practitioner Diploma Course *Duration* (1) Four weekends, one weekend in every three. (2) Three years part time, average one weekend in every three. *Entry requirements* No entry requirements for the Foundation course. Practitioner Diploma courses requires completion of Foundation course. *Fees* (1) £222. (2) £777 per year. *Comments* Branches in London, Bath, Brighton, Bournemouth, Devon, Cantebury, Oxford, Marlborough, Reading, Wiltshire, Portugal and Spain. Most of the teaching staff have paramedical qualifications, mainly chartered physiotherapists. This address given above is the Wiltshire branch of the European Shiatsu School, plus the school's central administration.

Healing Shiatsu Education Centre *Title of Training* Professional training course in healing-shiatsu. *Duration* 3 years part-time. Choice of format: either weekends or series of 5-day residential workshops. *Entry requirements* None, but must have done one introductory weekend. *Fees* £165 plus VAT per term (3 terms per year) all inclusive of residential courses. *Comments* The training can also be undertaken purely as a form of personal development and self-healing.

Ki Kai Shiatsu Centre *Title of Training* 3 year Diploma Course in Shiatsu and Oriental Medicine. *Duration* 24 weekends spread over two and a half years. *Entry requirements* None *Fees* £666 per annum, payable by 3 post-dated cheques at commencement of course.

London College of Shiatsu *Title of Training* Shiatsu Practitioner Training *Duration* Two and half years, part time. Evenings and weekends. *Entry requirements* Must be over 18 years of age. *Fees* £300 per term approx.

London Centre for Yoga and Shiatsu Studies *Title of Training* Diploma in Yoga and Shiatsu Studies. *Duration* Three years. *Entry requirements* Ability and commitment are essential. *Fees* £1,500 per year, plus clinical practice fees £1,300.

Shiatsu College *Title of Training* Shiatsu training to professional standard, beginners classes and post graduate workshops. *Duration* 3 years, 12 weekends per year or 2 years, 2 days a week. *Entry requirements* Application forms considered individually. *Fees* 3 year course: £900 per annum in advance.

Tai Chi Chuan

Though tai chi is often bracketed with the martial arts, it is more akin to moving meditation. In tai chi slow, flowing movements which follow a set pattern enable practitioners to harmonise mind, body and spirit and become more deeply centred in themselves. Its applications can be as form of healing, for self-defence and as a spiritual discipline.

Legend has it that tai chi was originated by Chang Sanfeng, a thirteenth century Chinese Taoist monk, who adapted an earlier martial art form used by the monks for protection. The story goes that observing the movements animals make, Chang Sanfeng saw that they comprised of circular movements which he then formalised into a set of postures. These were then joined together and became the ritualised,

BODY THERAPIES

dance-like movements or 'forms' of tai chi. The practice of tai chi lies within a whole spiritual and philosophical tradition which is largely Taoist, but which also incorporates some aspects of Buddhism.

The emphasis in performing the movements is not on strength or exertion, but on relaxation, concentration and balance. The knees are kept bent and movement is achieved by shifting the greater part of the body's weight slowly from one foot to the other while the hands make careful and gentle pushing and circling gestures. Attention is also paid to correct breathing. Physically the aim is to develop muscle control, fluidity and grace. After mastering the techniques and much practice, the practitioner should become one with the movements to the extent that they are no longer exercising deliberate control, but letting the movements happen through them. This can occur if the practitioner has been able to open themselves up sufficiently to the chi energy, which in Chinese philosophy is the lifeforce present in everything.

As a form of self-defence the idea is that aggression can be neutralised through yielding. If one does not meet an attacker's force head on but instead gives way, the aggression will exhaust itself. Most people however do not take up tai chi primarily for self-defence, since one would probably have to be very experienced to use it successfully in this way.

Tai chi is often recommended therapeutically to those who suffer from tension and anxiety, high blood pressure and heart complaints because of its relaxing effect. It can promote and maintain good health both physically and mentally.

READING

Embrace Tiger, Return to Mountain *by Chungliang Al Huang, Celestial Arts, USA £9.95.* A popular classic first published in the USA, beautifully produced and illustrated with photographs and calligraphy. Not a martial arts manual, but a unique exploration of the basic principles. Al Huang writes: 'I remain interested less in the structure of exact positions, but more in the content and the spirit of dance in the form' and describes himself as a 'Tai Ji dancer'. **Way of Harmony: A Guide to the Soft Martial Arts** *by Howard Reid, Unwin Hyman £7.95.* Written by the producer of the 1983 BBC TV series *Way of the Warrior,* this book is a practical guide to Chi Kung, Tai Chi Chuan, Hsing I and Pa Kua systems of exercises which cultivate inner strength and vital energy and increase self-knowledge. It also includes a section on oriental paths to balance: diet, breathing exercises, meditation and therapeutic techniques. The book is aimed at those who want to combine the physical skills of the martial arts with a deeper mental approach. Profusely illustrated with colour photographs and drawings. **Tai Chi for Two: the Practice of Push Hands** *by Paul Crompton Shambala £11.95.* 'Push Hands' is a basic exercise for two partners practiced by Tai Chi students. This book presents it as a means of training oneself to relax under physical and mental pressure and to improve one's interactions with others in everyday life. Includes step-by-step instructions and photographs demonstrating the movements, plus chapters on Taoist philosophy and the concept of Tai Chi energy. Paul Crompton has been teaching Tai Chi in Britain since the early 1970s.

CENTRES OFFERING TAI CHI CHUAN
Bodywise E2, British T'ai Chi Association W1, Community Health Foundation EC1, Lifeworks NW5, London School of T'Ai Chi Chuan EC1, Martial Arts Commission SE8, Mushindokai N12, School of T'ai-chi Ch'uan - Centre for Healing WC1, Spira - Self Defence for Women W12, Studio E NW6, Sunra SW12.

Yoga
Yoga is a means of self help towards physical and mental health. It has been practised in India for over 3000 years, and can be used as a way of relaxing and keeping fit, as well as a kind of meditation technique.

Yoga comes from a Sanskrit word meaning 'union' which has the same root as the English word 'yolk'. The aim of yoga is union with the divine, with life. Though in the west we are most familiar with the form of yoga which involves physical postures ('hatha' yoga) the word yoga is used to describe many different disciplines which can be used to develop spiritual potential. For instance, there is karma yoga which is service to others through work and bhakti yoga which is union with the divine principle through religious devotion.

There are different systems of hatha yoga teaching too. However, all involve basic postures which have names like 'Cobra', 'Praying Mantis', 'Tree' and 'Corpse' pose. The poses are designed to stretch and strengthen muscles and ligaments, and to stimulate the internal organs and circulation. Though encountering the body's stiffness can be uncomfortable at times, yoga teachers stress that there should not be too much strain involved, and one should not try to push one's body beyond its limits. The temptation to push the body into the pose, rather than relaxing into it can be strong, and can even lead to injury. For this reason it is advisable to attend a yoga class, where the teacher will be able to show you the best way to do the pose.

Hatha yoga also involves attention to the breath. Proper breathing is seen as crucial to good health and to developing mental and emotional clarity. Breathing exercises are usually part of yoga practice, and the aim is to let go of the tension, particularly in the diaphragm, which leads to tense, shallow breathing and an overall sense of restriction. After a yoga session, the practitioner should relax fully. This may also involve some sort of meditation.

The benefits of yoga are increased relaxation, greater strength and suppleness, and better posture. Yoga has also had beneficial effects in the treatment of diseases, notably high blood pressure, multiple sclerosis, arthritis, asthma, backache (but care should be taken not to strain the back), painful periods, constipation and other chronic conditions. Some places hold classes specifically for handicapped people.

❝For me nothing has been more rewarding than the regular practice of yoga.

The form I practise is composed of a combination of postures *(assanas)*, breathing *(pranayama)*, meditation and a form of deep relaxation *(Yoga Nidra)*.

The postures reveal and work upon all the tensions in the body, in some positions parts of my body tremble and shake, presumably releasing energy in the same way as Reichian bodywork. Practiced with consciousness, I find them deeply centering, leaving me relaxed and in control of my body. The breathing vitalises and purifies the system - this can actually be felt, and with formal meditation takes me into an extremely calm and inward place (although sometimes I can overdo it and get a headache!). Afterwards, I feel joyful, view the world with equanimity, and everything in light - literally.

I practice Nidra usually before sleeping or on waking. Its beneficial results have been scientifically proven and is enough on its own to ward off minor illness, to guarantee a beautiful sleep and stress-less morning (I find that by lunch time a top-up is required). I know that only through regular practice can I be at my best. ❞

Andy Hilton

READING

Book of Yoga *by the Sivananda Yoga Centre, Ebury Press £7.95.* This classic guide to yoga is clear and comprehensive, superbly illustrated with full colour photographs. There are easy to follow instructions for working into the postures and authoritative teachings covering all aspects of this timeless discipline. The book is an inspiration for beginners and experts alike. **Yoga for A New Age** *by Bob Smith and Linda Boudreau Smith, Smith Productions £9.95.* Written by two yoga teachers this copiously illustrated book examines a modern approach to the discipline of yoga. The photographs include examples of bad posture and how to correct it. The yoga courses start at beginner's level and progress to an advanced standard. Included is a chapter on working in pairs and groups and some explanation of the way yoga practice helps the muscular system.

CENTRES OFFERING YOGA

3HO Kundalini Yoga Foundation NW4, All Hallows House EC3, Bhratiya Vidya Bhavan (Institute of Indian Culture) W14, Bodywise E2, CAER (Centre For Alternative Education And Research) TR19, Chinese Yoga Federation, Community Health Foundation EC1, Creative and Healing Arts W11, Croydon Buddhist Centre CR0, Health Management NW3, Hillside Practice, Holistic Yoga Centre MK19, IBISS TW7, Iyengar Yoga Institute W9, Jeyrani Health Centre E18, Khalsa Institute W1, Kingston Natural Healing Centre, London Centre for Yoga and Shiatsu Studies N10, New Cross Natural Therapy Centre, Private Polyclinic, Satyananda Yoga Centre, Shanti Sadan W11, South London Natural Health Centre SW4, Sri Aurobindo Circle (Ashram) SW16, Sunra SW12, Tyers St. Centre SE11, West London Buddhist Centre W11, Westminster Natural Health Centre SW1, White Eagle Lodge W8, Yoga Culture and Therapy Foundation WC1, Yoga Dham, Yoga for Health Foundation.

BODY THERAPIES

TRAININGS IN YOGA TEACHING

Iyengar Yoga Institute *Title of Training* Teacher Training Course in Yoga. *Duration* 2 years part-time, one class per week. *Entry requirements* Candidates must have studied with a qualified Iyengar teacher for 2 years previously, have a good grounding in the basic postures, and be able to maintain headbalance for 5 minutes. *Fees* £480 for 2 year course. *Comments* In addition to the basic Yoga teaching qualification, the Institute runs courses for teachers wishing to progress and gain higher certificates.

Synthesis of Light Holidays (SOL) *Title of Training* Yoga Teacher Training *Duration* One Month. *Fees* $1,500. *Comments* Held at the ashram of Swami Satchidananda, Virginia, USA. Food and accommodation included.

OTHER BODY APPROACHES

ACTIVE BIRTH

Active Birth Centre NW5, Dick Read School for Natural Birth, Highbury Centre N5, Splashdown Birth Pools.

ASTON PATTERNING

Institute of Structural Bodywork Various London locations, Reiki Centre NW3.

CRANIAL OSTEOPATHY

Bexleyheath Natural Health Clinic, Bumblebees Natural Remedies N7, Cranial Osteopathic Association, Forty Hill Natural Therapy Centre, Isis Centre for Holistic Health N17, Neal's Yard Therapy Rooms WC2, New Cross Natural Therapy Centre, Raphael Clinic NW6, South London Natural Health Centre SW4.

HELLERWORK

All Hallows House EC3, Institute of Structural Bodywork SW1.

LASER THERAPY

Body Clinic NW11, Insight Care N1, Natural Healing Centre E7, Wholistic Health Centre, Wimbledon Clinic of Natural Medicine SW19.

MAGNETIC THERAPY

Natural Healing Centre E7.

NUTRITIONAL COUNSELLING/DIET THERAPY

All Hallows House EC3, Bayswater Clinic W2, Bennet and Luck Natural Health Centre N1, Body-Mind Health Private Clinic, Brackenbury Natural Health Centre W6, Centre for Health and Healing W1, Chessington Hypnotherapy Clinic, Colon Health W9, Dietary Therapy Society N6, Edgware Centre for Natural Health, Equilibrium Therapy Centre SW18, Falcons SW11, Holistic Health Consultancy SW1, Homoeopathic Health Clinic, Institute for Optimum Nutrition SW6, Kingston

Natural Healing Centre, Living Centre, Lotus Healing Centre, Natural Health Clinic
HA3, Nature Cure Clinic W1, Neal's Yard Therapy Rooms WC2, New Cross Natural
Therapy Centre, Nutribiotics, Primrose Healing Centre NW1, Putney Natural Therapy
Clinic, Raphael Clinic NW6, Refuah Shelaymah Natural Health Centre N16, South
London Natural Health Centre SW4, Therapy Made Unique E18, Traditional Chinese
Medicine Clinic, Wholistic Health Centre.

POSTURAL INTEGRATION
Centre for Release and Integration , New Cross Natural Therapy Centre, Open
Centre EC1.

REBALANCING
Institute of Structural Bodywork (register).

REIKI
Kingston Natural Healing Centre, Lifeworks, New Cross Natural Therapy Centre,
Primrose Healing Centre NW1, Radiance Education Unlimited NW3, Reiki Centre
NW3.

TIBETAN MEDICINE
Tibet Foundation.

OTHER TRAININGS

ACTIVE BIRTH
Active Birth Centre *Title of Training* The Active Birth Teacher's Training Course.
Duration Two years part-time and can be done largely through correspondence if
you wish. Twelve study days per year. *Entry requirements.* Mostly for women. *Fees*
£500 p.a. all in. *Comments* Certificate given by the association. Intake in September
of each year. Would welcome Scottish applicants!
Jeyrani Health Centre *Title of Training* Midwifery Trends for the 1990s.
Duration Six days on day release. *Entry requirements* Must be professional
practising midwife with interest in natural childbirth and water births. Must produce
qualification certificate. *Fees* £125 *Comments* Run by a specialist in water births at
Whipps Cross hospital, and includes one day with Dr Michael Odent.

DIET THERAPY/NUTRITIONAL COUNSELLING
Centre for Nutritional Studies *Title of Training* Diploma course in nutritional
counselling. *Duration* 2 years part time, both home study and attendance. *Entry
requirements* Entry by interview. *Fees* Between £250-£750 per module. .
Institute for Optimum Nutrition *Title of Training* 2 year Course for
Nutritional Consultants. *Duration* 2 years,1 evening a week, plus 1 weekend a
month. (Satellite course also available for those who can't attend evenings). *Entry*

BODY THERAPIES

Requirements None specified. *Fees* £1,497 for the whole course, payable in instalments. *Comments* Students are expected to do 12 hours per week, have clinical experience and run a three-month research project.

MACROBIOTICS
Community Health Foundation *Title of Training* Kushi Institute Certificate Course *Duration* Level 1: 6 weekends and 6 day intensive or 4 weeks daytime. Level 2: 4 weekends and 9 day intensive or 6 weeks daytime. Level 3: 5 weeks daytime. *Entry requirements* Ideally completed an introductory Shiatsu or cooking course. *Fees* Level 1: £645 Level 2: £845 Level 3: £745 *Comments* Emphasis is on teaching students the deeper understanding behind macrobiotics and shiatsu, along with practical skills.

ECLECTIC/SPECIAL TRAININGS
Association of General Practitioners of Natural Medicine *Title of Training* (1) Foundation Course of Comprehensive Training in Natural Medicine. (2) Post graduate Diploma Specialist Courses *Duration* (1) One year foundation course 20 hours per week. (2) Three-four year Post Graduate Diploma specialist courses - 20 hours weekly of formal study. *Entry requirements* 1 and 2: A reasonable standard of English and an aptitude for learning. All applicants will be interviewed by the Principal of the College. (2) Must be a graduates of Foundation Course or have recognized training in natural medicine. *Fees* (1) £1500 plus registration fee £30. (2) £4000 approx. Scholarships and work awards are usually available on post graduate courses. *Comments* Prospectus £1 available from the Registrar.
Association of Natural Medicines *Title of Training* Training in Acupuncture, Homoeopathy, Naturopathy, Massage, Aromatherapy, Reflexology or Hypnotherapy. *Duration* Acupuncture, Homoeopathy, Naturopathy: 4 years, part-time, one weekend a month. Massage, Aromatherapy, Reflexology, Hypnotherapy: between 3 and 9 months part-time. *Entry requirements* Acceptance by interview. *Fees* 4 year courses: £640 p.a. Short courses prices vary, approx £200-£300. *Comments* For prospectus send £1 plus A5 size SAE to the Secretary.
Craniosacral Therapy Education Trust *Title of Training* Craniosacral Therapy. *Duration* One year. Course is held over nine 3-day seminars and one five day seminar. *Entry requirements* Post graduate course for example osteopaths, acupuncturists etc. *Fees* £1,250. *Comments* There is a London based and a Devon based training.
Creative Journey *Title of Training* Tama-Do (Sound, Colour, Movement). *Duration* One year part-time. *Fees* £850. *Comments* Students gain a thorough knowledge of the energy system of the human body and are expected to do their own research and practice during training. Suitable for therapists and all who seek for greater self awareness and improved health.
Institute of Emotio-Somatic Therapy *Title of Training* Emotio-Somatic Psychotherapy. *Duration* Two years. *Entry requirements* Previous qualification in

a helping profession. *Fees* £1090 per year.

Lotus Healing Centre *Title of Training* Chinese Medicine - Herbal and Acupuncture. *Duration* Four years. *Entry requirements* 5 'O' levels, 2 'A' levels and life experience. *Fees* £2,400 per year.

School of Complementary Medicine *Title of Training* Course in Complementary Medicine. *Duration* Three and half years, part-time starting in February of each year. A total of 60 weekends for the whole course. *Entry requirements* Love of life and people, reasonably good health, average academic ability, sensitivity and compassion, some intuition, inner sense of freedom, desire to heal, some time to study, ability to apply what you know. These qualities are more important than academic qualifications. *Fees* £140 per months for 44 months (no VAT). Cranial osteopathy. *Comments* It's a course to become a general practitioner in the field of Complementary Medicine. It takes a much more holistic approach than trainings which specialise in one subject only. Subjects covered are Chinese acupuncture, shiatsu , acupressure, massage, reflexology, touch for health, kinesiotherapy, cranial osteopathy, herbalism, Bach flower remedies, nutrition, psychosomatic medicine, counselling skills, transactional analysis techniques, NLP, chi kung exercises, anatomy and physiology.

INTRODUCTION TO SPIRIT

What Is Spiritual?
The word spiritual must be one of the most difficult to define in the English Language. The dictionary definition of 'spirit' alone ranges across the whole gamut of soul, ghost, animation, courage, breathing, mind and alcohol. The meaning it has for an individual tends to vary according to their particular values and beliefs. However, though the word may take different forms for different people, it is usually used to denote whatever is of greatest, highest or deepest value for that person, and how this is expressed in their lives.

The groups included here fall under the category of spiritual because their practices and beliefs all aim to take the practitioner beyond their normal, limited sense of themselves. Specifically they aim to take people beyond their sense of themselves as separate egos or selves, isolated from other people, from the world and the universe in which we live. In some way they aim directly to facilitate contact with the 'transpersonal'; that experience of the self as being part of a greater whole, and of partaking of what is spoken of in traditional religious systems as the divine, something which exists both within and beyond time and the particular. They may seek to do this in many different ways.

The Difference between Religion and Spirituality
Religions are one way in which spirituality can be expressed. They represent a system of beliefs and practices which have become recognisable as a particular tradition. Religion and the spiritual are *not* synonymous, and spirituality can be expressed and developed in many ways outside of religion.

The Search for a New Spirituality
In many people's minds the emergence of 'alternative' spiritual movements is associated with the sixties and the search of many people at that time for deeper, more lasting values than those offered by what seemed to them to be an over-materialistic society. Disaffected with a society which seemed to be obsessed with consumerism, achievement and conformity, and with orthodox religions which appeared irrelevant and stultified, some people turned to drugs, some to politics and others to religion, while some turned to all three.

The seeds of this collective change in consciousness were sown much earlier however. It was in 1893 that The League of Liberal Clergymen of Chicago, Illinois set up the World Parliament of Religions, a forum where followers of faiths from East and West could meet together and share perspectives. This assembly of Christians, Jews, Muslims, Buddhists, Hindus, Taoists, Confucians and Spiritualists led to the creation of the first centres of Hinduism, Buddhism and Islam in the U.S.

But it was not until 1965 when the U.S. government ended the restrictions on Asian immigration which had been in force for nearly fifty years that the dialogue between East and West was opened on a massive scale. Though this move was intended to allow refugees from Maoist China to take up residence in the U.S., many Asian teachers and holy men took the opportunity to make their voices heard in the heart of the West.

It was not only to the East that those in search of spiritual nourishment turned. At the same time Christianity experienced a revival in the form of 'born again' sects, who sought to rekindle enthusiasm for the religion that many Americans and Europeans had grown up with. There has also been a revival in interest in western occult traditions, and pre-christian or 'pagan' belief systems. At the turn of the century groups were formed which took some of their inspiration from the esoteric Judaic Kabbalah, and in some cases this was blended with the practice of ritual magic - notoriously in the case of Aleister Crowley. Today there are still practitioners of the 'old religion', witches and warlocks, who adhere to the folk religion of Europe which went underground with the advent of Christianity, but was never quite eradicated by it. Recently too there has been a growing interest in the religious beliefs and practices of the American Indians.

East meets West

Originally it was Europeans who went out to colonise what were then thought of as the less 'civilised' countries of the east, Africa and the 'New World 'of the Americas, or to convert their people to Christianity. Subsequently a strange reversal has taken place. Now the west is benefiting from a counter-colonisation and the ideas and philosophy of these countries seem to offer many people a different perspective. It seems as if many of the attitudes and beliefs which underpin the culture and religion of these countries are not only as valid as ours, but also offer an outlook which may complement the traditional emphasis of western culture. In the west a high value tends to be placed on individual achievement and activity, on science and the intellect, and on technical ability. Broadly speaking, the outlook of eastern religion speaks more of what is collective, and stresses the importance of looking inwards, of experience rather than mental knowledge. In addition to this, 'native' or pagan religions offer a profound sense of connection with the natural world of which we are a part - a sense which we urgently need to recapture if we are to avert ecological disaster. Broadly speaking, while the west strives, the 'new religions' accept and open to what is. The influx of these new ideas perhaps offers an opportunity for a balance between these two poles.

Some people in the West have been attracted to this complementary attitude and have found it an expansive, holistic way of being. However, perhaps there can be a danger here of rejecting western culture wholesale, which not only has a great deal of value within it, but also represents an integral part of a westerner's whole outlook and response to life.

Gurus and spiritual teachers

The guru-disciple or teacher/apprentice relationship has been important in many spiritual traditions. In the west however we tend to be sceptical about gurus and people who might be purporting to know more than we do. This scepticism may be by no means a bad thing sometimes as there are some teachers who have shown themselves to be simply more charismatic than wise. We are also very wary of leaders because while they can do great good they can also do great harm.

A common image of the guru is perhaps of an Indian swami, bearded and loinclothed who probably lives in a cave and holds forth to hundreds of faceless, adoring disciples. The whole idea seems very foreign. Most gurus are not in fact like this, and the mystique which surrounds them, not always of their own making, may obscure the wisdom they might have to offer. The only way to determine if a particular teacher has something for you is to follow your instinct about him or her.

Though the guru is in the main an eastern concept, there have been and still are western teachers in the same vein. Gurdjieff, the native Russian teacher who gathered a number of followers round him at the beginning of this century, and who is still influential, is an example.

There are also spiritual groups who do not emphasise the importance of a teacher or leader. Sometimes they take their inspiration from the writings of a teacher who is dead, or simply from a particular faith or set of beliefs.

Cults

One fear often expressed about spiritual groups is that they are cults designed to take away people's autonomy. Stories of dubious recruitment tactics and brainwashing techniques hit the headlines a few years ago. In some cases there have even been allegations of physical force being used on troublesome group members.

While some of these reports may be true, it is this kind of scandal which tends to get publicised. The groups which have operated in this kind of way represent a very small number indeed of the total. Perhas what has not been publicised as much is the very real benefits many people have derived, and satisfaction they have gained from their involvement with *bona fide* spiritual groups. If you come up against dogmatism, intolerance or authoritarianism it is to be hoped that you will recognise it, though of course this is sometimes easier with hindsight than when faced with a teacher, group or leader who seems to have it all worked out.

Different types of Groups

The groups included in this book have different beliefs and ways of organising themselves. They employ different practices and are organised differently, and some are large, some small. In some the emphasis is on community and there may even be residential communities associated with the group. In others importance may be placed on individual study and practice; in fact in some groups there are few or even no meetings at all. Some of the centres we have listed are less like groups but are individuals or organisations running courses and workshops with a strong spiritual dimension.

Another variable is the level of commitment seen as ideal by different groups. Some groups offer an alternative lifestyle to those deeply involved, and others are more informal. Some are much more closely knit as groups and others are much looser in structure. The centres range from those with residential communities, offices and commercial enterprises on the premises, to those which meet in members' own homes.

Some of these groups are religious in the traditional sense of the word. They follow a recognisable set of religious teachings such as Sufism, Buddhism, Hinduism or Christianity. Others may have a spiritual framework in the sense that they emphasise a universal perspective and the divinity present in humanity, perhaps using traditional religious terminology, but not subscribing to any one particular traditional religious philosophy. A group like the Theosophical Society is an example of this. Then there are others which are much more secular, and which do not have any religious context at all, but which see themselves as addressing the spiritual perspective. Enlightenment Intensives are an example of this approach.

What they do

Once again a very wide range of activities constitute the practices of spiritual groups in London.

Meditation: This came from the east and to a greater or lesser extent usually forms part of the practice of those groups which hail from the eastern tradition. However, meditation has also been practised in western traditions. In Christianity it usually takes the form of contemplation of a particular subject, though some people have also incorporated a less directed style into the traditional forms of Christian worship. Secular groups are also using meditation since it adapts itself well to a non-religious framework. More information about the different kinds of meditation is given in the section on the subject in this book.

Ritual and devotional practices: While meditation has gained a great deal of credibility with many people in the west and even some sections of the medical profession recognise its therapeutic value, ritual is often still regarded with a great deal of suspicion. Some people find such activities weird or esoteric, and others feel uncomfortably reminded of their own religious upbringing, especially if they have rejected it. Some people fear they will be taken over in some way if they let themselves get involved in rituals. Perhaps this is because we live in a society in which the rituals have to a certain extent lost the meaning they originally had. Weddings and funerals though they do in fact serve a useful purpose, socially, psychologically and spiritually, rarely act now as a way in which we can recognise and demonstrate the significance of important events in our lives. But ritual is an important way of focussing on feelings and values, and giving them a communal context.

Spiritually, ritual is used in this way. It serves to enable the participants to get in touch with their highest values and express these communally. It also places personal experience and emotion in the wider context of universal human experience. Many people enjoy ritual from the outset, finding that they recognise and respond to its use of the imaginative faculties. Others find they they prefer to know what is going on first before they engage.

Rituals are used by some Christian, Buddhist and Hindu groups, and in Paganism and Shamanism.

Chanting and prayer: Sound has been used in both east and west to express the spirit. The repetition of mantras (short phrases with spiritual significance or meaning) focuses the mind and also calls up deeper levels of energy. It can unite the physical (because singing, chanting or praying is a physical act), the emotional (because music evokes a strong emotional response) and the mental (especially if words are involved). Prayer is traditionally central in Christianity. Mantras are often used by Buddhist and Hindu groups. Music and chanting is important in the Sufi tradition.

Study: Some groups particularly emphasise study, talks and discussion. They may discuss the writings of a teacher or teachers and philosophers. They may have programmes of lectures by people on various topics. Taped lectures are becoming increasingly popular as a way in which people can make more contact with a teacher or lecturer, and absorb his or her teachings more fully by repeated listening. In some cases these methods are the only ones used by a particular group or association

Other methods: There are many other ways in which particular groups facilitate growth and communication. Some adapt therapeutic techniques, some meet together in different ways, some emphasise the importance of the arts and so on. This all points to the fact that the definition of what is spiritual is widening to include different aspects of culture.

Spiritual Groups in London

There are many spiritual groups in London practising in different ways. The decision to investigate the possibility of a spiritual path is very much a matter of instinct, of the heart. People usually become interested in a particular group because they have read something which seems to make sense to them, or because they have met someone involved in some sort of spiritual path, or because they feel attracted to a practice, like meditation or chanting. If you are drawn to this kind of search, don't be put off too soon by the vast array of groups which you may feel are not for you. As it says in the bible - 'seek, and ye shall find'!

Spirituality versus Psychology

Psychology has been called the modern religion. Freud's work exposed for the first time to much of the western world the depths of the human psyche, the inner world. What he saw there was the dark underside of experience, the unregenerated primitive instincts which had remained throughout the long process of civilisation seemingly untouched and merely pushed into unconsciousness. The resistance which Freud encountered in the course of publicising his work and ideas is a measure of how deeply his picture of human nature threatened the image of what it was to be human at the time. Yet paradoxically in many ways Freud's view echoed assumptions of the time - that man is essentially 'sinful', and his lower nature needs to be kept in check by society and religion. But while the orthodox solution was salvation by God and good works, Freud's was that knowledge of unconscious functioning through analysis would set the patient free of his or her own 'demons'.

With the development of Freud's original ideas, some psychologists and therapists have attempted to redress the balance, and in different ways have stressed that as well as hiding problems and complexes, the psyche also has hidden heights. While we may be largely unconscious of our instincts and repressed desires and hates, we are also unaware of our potential for joy and loving participation in the universe.

The question of when psychology and spirituality are similar, and when they are different is still being hotly debated as some psychologists turn to meditation and mysticism, and some gurus incorporate therapeutic techniques into their teachings. Both seek to offer practices and techniques which bring about individual growth, and both aim to free people from restrictive habitual ways of acting and being.

However, while it may often be difficult to distinguish the difference between spiritual and psychotherapeutic practice, it may be possible to distinguish different levels within both disciplines. Various theorists have suggested that it may be important to build a mature sense of one's individuality before going beyond the individual self. Some psychotherapies may concentrate more on developing a sense of 'who I am', and regard this as the limit of their work. Others have sought to include a more spiritual dimension into their work, or may have been founded on the premise that the spiritual quest is the most important one from a psychological point of view.

However, while there may be a great deal of overlap in practice, many psychologists and therapists are still quite wary of what they may see as an attempt to avoid painful feelings by going off into a cosmic 'bliss-out' in religion. Spiritual teachers too can be suspicious of therapy, feeling that it is simply equivalent to putting an elastoplast on the mortal wound of human suffering. It seems that the dialogue between psychology and spirituality has only just begun. It may take a long time for the two to settle their differences. However, in general more people are beginning to question what they see as an artificial division between what has in the past been called 'spiritual' and what has been called 'worldly'.

The 'New Age'

The last two decades has seen a growth in what has become known as 'New Age' activity and thinking. Even some sections of the media have hailed the 1990s as an era when society will turn away from the hard-edged, money-making 1980s and adopt caring, green, spiritual values.

The term 'New Age' can be used to cover a diverse number of attitudes, beliefs and activities, to the extent that it can be difficult to see what they have in common. As the name suggests, the central idea in New Age thinking is that humanity has reached a critical stage in its evolutionary development which will lead to a change in people's outlook and consciousness. New Age philosophy is characterised by various concerns:

1) The mystical nature of the universe: the fundamental reality of the universe is seen as love, and the universe is seen as ultimately benign and purposeful.

2) Global conciousness: belief in the oneness of humanity, and the importance of community and sharing.

3) Non sectarian spirituality: all religions are seen as expressions of the same vision, and great importance is placed on the individual's right to choose their own path, whether this takes a traditionally religious form or the form of secular spirituality.

4) Abundance rather than scarcity: the belief that that there are enough resources for everyone in the world both material and immaterial. 'Scarcity' mentality is seen as responsible for scarcity.

5) The importance of preserving natural environment, an ecologically sound lifestyle and a respect for nature.

6) Human potential and personal development: human beings have more potential than they realise, and are, in essence, divine. It is seen as our responsibility to develop this potential.

7) Human beings as creators of their own reality: the individual is seen as responsible for his or her own life, and as creating that reality through attitudes, thoughts, feelings etc.

8) Importance of the feminine: belief that it is necessary to redress the balance caused by over-valuing what is seen as the 'masculine' in our culture by reasserting the value of the 'feminine' and questioning the power of men.

9) 'Holistic' model in science, medicine etc: the belief that the universe is not a mechanism made up of randomly functioning parts but is a living organism which works as an indivisible whole.

In general, humanity is seen as progressing into a time of greater spirituality and world harmony.

There is much overlap between the New Age movement and the 'Human Potential' movement, which grew out of humanistic psychology in the 1960s. This is more psychotherapy and 'personal growth' oriented and less mystical in outlook, though in practice there are ideas, approaches and methodology common to both.

Critics of New Age philosophy have claimed that it concentrates too exclusively on the positive aspects of the universe, and therefore attempts to ignore, or at least deals inadequately with, the presence of suffering and evil in the world. New Agers have been criticised for being too credulous and subjective, and of attempting to dispense with reason and logic. Whatever the pros and cons of the movement, it is proving to have a steady following as evinced by the continuing popularity of New Age events.

Meditation

There are so many different kinds of meditation that it can seem hard sometimes to define what it is they all have in common. The benefits of meditation are being recognised in the west, though it is still sometimes seen as something strange or eccentric. However, it is more down to earth than going into some sort of psychedelic trance, or 'contemplating one's navel'.

Meditation is turning the attention inwards, away from all the external things which demand our attention. It involves focussing the mind, usually on one particular object or idea. In meditation the mind is cleared of all the extraneous thoughts which take up a lot of our energy, or for a little while at least our involvement with all those thoughts is suspended, so that a clearer, calmer experience of oneself is possible.

There are various ways of achieving this, depending on the particular meditation practice. Different kinds of meditation may be useful for different purposes, or temperaments. There are practices in which the meditator concentrates on the breath as it comes in and out of the body, without trying to change it in any way. This focuses the attention, and helps to bring together the awareness of mind and body. There are meditation techniques where a colour, shape or form is pictured and held in the attention. This 'visualisation' technique has been used in a very particular way to help in the treatment of illness, especially by cancer sufferers. Here the meditator will visualise his or her illness, and then see the body fighting that illness and suppressing it. Some yogic forms of meditation involve concentrating on an actual object such as a candle or a stone, and some use a 'mantra' or phrase repeated over and over again. There are meditation practices where there is no one object of concentration at all, and the meditator just tries to sit and be aware of all the changing thoughts and feelings passing through his or her mind. This is the Zen 'sitting' meditation.

Usually these kinds of meditation are done sitting down, often cross-legged or kneeling while sitting on cushions. However, this is by no means essential if it is difficult for you to do, and they can be done sitting in a chair. However, some practices involve movement. There are 'walking meditations' where concentration is on the body as you walk, and the processes involved in moving. The 'Dynamic Meditation' practised by followers of the Bhagwan Shree Rajneesh involves very vigorous whirling and dancing movement.

The benefits of meditation are just as diverse as the practices. One of the most immediate effects can be that the meditator feels more calm and relaxed. Many people take up meditation initially as a way of combating stress. It can also increase one's ability to concentrate, and helps the meditator develop a sense of a still, calm centre from which they feel more able to direct their lives creatively. It can also help to generate a greater sense of self-acceptance and warmth towards others. It can also be a way of achieving higher states of consciousness and heightened awareness.

Although there are quite a few books on the subject, as with learning any other skill, it is important to find a teacher who has experience themselves and can give you direct instruction and help. Centres which teach meditation are listed below, and will offer an explanation of their particular practices.

CENTRES OFFERING MEDITATION

Abshot Holistic Centre, Audio Limited, Barry Long Foundation, Bhratiya Vidya Bhavan (Institute of Indian Culture) W14, Brahma Kumaris World Spiritual University NW6, British Buddhist Association W9, British School of Oriental Therapy and Movement, Buddhapadipa Temple, Centre For Healing Through Forgiveness N15, Cortijo Romero UK W3, Croydon Buddhist Centre, Dharmadhatu (London), East-West Clinic of Natural Healing, Foundation for International Spiritual Unfoldment E7, Fountain London N14, Gaia House, Healing Workshops NW5, Health Management NW3, Heruka Buddhist Centre (central London), Jamyang Meditation Centre N4, Karma Kagyu Cho Khor Ling, Ki Kai Shiatsu Centre, Little Grove Education, Living Centre, London Buddhist Centre E2, London Kagyu Centre, London Serene Reflection Meditation Group, London Sufi Centre W11, London Zen Society NW1, Lotus Healing Centre, Raphael Clinic NW6, RIGPA Fellowship N1, Satyananda Yoga Centre, School of Meditation W11, School of T'ai-chi Ch'uan - Centre for Healing WC1, Shanti Sadan W11, Sri Aurobindo Circle (Ashram) SW16, St James Centre for Health and Healing W1, Studio E NW6, Sunra SW12, Teach Yourself Meditation WC1, Transcendental Meditation Baker Street Centre NW1, Transcendental Meditation National Office, Transcendental Meditation SW1, West London Buddhist Centre W11, White Eagle Lodge W8, Wild Goose Company NW3.

THE TRADITIONS

Buddhism

Buddhism has been dubbed 'Britain's fastest growing religion' by Arnold Toynbee. It has in fact been in existence for over 2,500 years. Its founder, the Buddha, saw suffering as central to the human condition, and his teaching concerned the ways in which people could transcend this suffering. These are the practice of an ethical lifestyle, and of meditation which then leads to insight into the nature of existence and the causes of human suffering.

Suffering is caused because according to Buddhism everything is impermanent. Human beings seek everlasting happiness by trying to hold onto what must fade or die. When this happens we experience pain, and try to avoid this pain by seeking another object of happiness in the world. Buddhist practices seek to take the practitioner beyond this cycle of holding on and running away, and to cultivate not a state of indifference, but one of joyful acceptance of the impermanent nature of existence. This understanding is not intellectual but a profound experience which leads to complete freedom. This state is called 'Nirvana'.

Buddhism emphasises the importance of the individual's own growth towards greater consciousness of him or herself. The development of 'mindfulness' is an important part of much of Buddhist meditation. Mindfulness starts with awareness of oneself - of one's body, one's feelings and emotions, and one's mind - and of other people and the world around one. It develops ultimately into awareness of absolute reality.

Alongside the emphasis on individual development, concern for other people and for life - the development of compassion - is also seen as crucial. In the later developments of Buddhism especially, Nirvana is not seen simply as a neutral state of being without passion or desires, but more positively as a dynamic state of joy, contentment and compassion.

As it spread to different countries from India where it started (and from where it has now virtually died out), Buddhism adapted itself to different cultures. This gave rise to very different approaches to the original teachings. The groups listed below reflect these approaches. The Theravada tradition emphasises morality, the monastic lifestyle and the original Pali scriptures. Tibetan Buddhism is part of the 'Vajrayana' or tantric tradition which is colourful, ritualistic and emphasises psychic energy and often visualisation meditations. Zen Buddhism is perhaps the form that most people in the West have heard of through pithy Zen stories or the cryptic sayings which abound in the tradition. Zen's approach is anti-rational with an emphasis on zazen (meditation) and direct experience.

READING

What the Buddha Taught *by Walpola Rahula, Evergreen/Grove Weidenfeld £7.15.* Addressed to the 'educated and intelligent reader' and written by Dr Rahula, himself a Buddhist monk and scholar, this is a lucid and comprehensive introduction to Buddhism. The new revised and expanded edition also contains selected texts from *sutras* and the *Dhammapada*. With sixteen black and white illustrations. **The Buddhist Handbook: a Complete Guide to Buddhist Teaching and Practice** *by John Snelling, Rider £6.95.* John Snelling is the editor of the Buddhist journal *The Middle Way* and uniquely placed to offer this overview of a vast subject. This is the first basic introduction to help the newcomer orientate him or herself to the many different schools, doctrines and organisations which comprise the world of Buddhism, as well as a useful addition to the library of the practising 'western' Buddhist. **A Buddhist Bible** *by Dwight Goddard, Beacon Press U.S.A. £11.95.* First published in 1932, this is one of the books which originally stimulated western interest in Buddhism. Goddard's preface states that his collection of major texts: 'is not intended to be a sourcebook for critical, literary and historical study; it is only intended to be a source of spiritual inspiration designed to awaken faith, and to develop faith into aspiration and full realisation'.

CENTRES OFFERING BUDDHISM

British Buddhist Association W9, British Shingon Buddhist Association N12, Buddhist Society SW1, Croydon Buddhist Centre, Dharmadhatu (London), Gaia House, Heruka Buddhist Centre (central London), Karma Kagyu Cho Khor Ling, London

SPIRIT

Buddhist Centre E2, London Kagyu Centre, London Serene Reflection Meditation Group, London Zen Society NW1, Mushindokai N12, Nichirin Shoshu of the United Kingdom, RIGPA Fellowship N1, Throssel Hole Priory, West London Buddhist Centre W11.

Christianity

Christianity is the majority and official religion of this country. Central to Christian belief is the importance of love (expressed in Christ's axiom 'love thy neighbour as thyself') which is seen as a divine attribute made manifest by god sending his son to earth to become man. This symbolises for Christians the possibility of humanity also expressing this love of god. The worship of the creator god in prayer and ritual is also central to Christian practice.

Acting in the world to help others is also stressed, and for this reason Christians have traditionally been involved in medical and charitable work, both in their native countries and abroad, often in Third World Countries.

As well as this emphasis on good works, there is also a strong mystical tradition within Christianity where solitary communion with, and personal experience of, god enables the believer to become receptive to the divinity, and thus enter a deeper union with him/her.

Some Christian groups today seek to re-interpret the original doctrines in a way which is relevant to modern life. One of these is Matthew Fox, proponent of 'creation spirituality' (see 'Reading' below). This is founded on the belief the human condition is not one of 'original sin' (implying that we are basically bad or separated from God), but one of 'original blessing' (implying that we are basically good and in harmony with God).

Christianity is rich in myth and symbol, and this has inspired many artists, writers and composers through the centuries.

READING

Meister Eckhart - The Man from whom God hid Nothing by Ursula Fleming, Fount £2.95. "God is a light shining in itself in silent stillness." These are words from the great German mystical theologian, Meister Eckhart (1260-1329). Ursula Fleming's incisive exploration into his teaching sheds light on this remarkable man who is one of the most controversial figures of Christian history. This is a selection from his writings which are as relevant today as they were six centuries ago. **A Lesson of Love: The Relevations of Julian of Norwich** Edited and translated by Fr. John-Julian OJN, Darton Longman and Todd £6.95. At the age of thirty, Dame Julian of Norwich (14th Century) was granted a series of sixteen mystical revelations of the

184

66 In 1966 when I was 22, I first meditated according to 'transcendental meditation'. The amazing effect was that I fell to the floor and was unconscious because 'my mind had touched the areas which had been polluted by medicine'. I still remember vividly the spiral that I followed downwards in my imagination, barely knowing that my body did the same by falling out of the chair.

When I was 29, I remember falling in a car thinking 'this must be the end, this must be the ocean'. I woke up with a dislocated hip which gave me permanent pain for some seven years and still occasionally now, 17 years later. Doctors said that my pain was 'psychological' and as I had considered my 4 year Jungian analysis finished, I decided to study humanistic and transpersonal psychology by attending all possible workshops and training groups. You name it, I did it and got so much out of it that I have been promoting the transformation of consciousness ever since 1976.

These two stepping stones come to mind as I remember what put me on the track of 'inner directedness'. As a teenager I began to ask questions about God, eternity and life after death. Now I may still not have answers, but at least I have an understanding that satisfies my curiosity.

I would not want to have lived without any of my workshop style experiences since I healed what doctors could not heal: myself. But I wonder how such ways of thinking and living can be made more commonplace. In particular, I wonder whether this is not the social responsibility of the Church which seems to experience a splendid isolation, while the non-organised mind-body-spirit movement surely by far exceeds in numbers what bishops would like to see in parishes . . . 99

Sabine Kurjo McNeill

66 I had been meditating regularly for about a year. Sometimes when I meditated I felt very good, calm, relaxed or contented. Other times I just felt bored, sleepy, tense or downright angry. One time I remember I settled myself down for a good meditation session, and as I sat there I just felt more and more filled with joy and contentment - I had never known anything like it. It was as if I was overflowing with this sense of happiness, and more kept flowing into me, like waves of light. I felt too that I was radiating love to everyone in the world, I didn't have to think about it or try, but it was just shining out of me. Then I had the sense of how powerful this light or love was. It seemed so powerful that suddenly I had the feeling that it didn't matter how much suffering there was in the world - and I knew there *was* a great deal of suffering - this love was somehow stronger than all that. It was as if the suffering was a flimsy veil over this powerful light and Julian of Norwich's words came into my mind: 'All shall be well, all shall be well, and all manner of thing shall be well'.

I felt the effects of this meditation very strongly for about three days afterwards. I felt uncharacteristically confident and able to perceive and relate to others. I never had another experience quite like it, inside or outside meditation, but it was a very important one and I felt it gave me a valuable perspective on life. 99

crucified Christ. She devoted the next twenty years to prayer and contemplation, and described her visions and her understanding of them in The Revelations of Divine Love, the first book written in the English language by a woman. **Original Blessing: A Primer of Creation Spirituality** by Matthew Fox, Bear & Co £8.50. Matthew Fox is a Dominican scholar and spiritual teacher, an eloquent advocate of Creation Spirituality. Original Blessing is an empowering and necessary book which leads us back to our own creativity and that deep ecstatic centre which resides beneath any fear of death.

Hinduism

Hinduism is not a homogenous religious system in itself. It is more a collection of different ideas, schools and cults. The word 'Hindu' is Persian for Indian, and was used by outsiders to lump together all the indigenous cults and religions of the Indian sub-continent.

It is difficult to isolate any one belief or practice which all Hindus have in common. For instance, though most Hindus believe in a creator god in some way, there are some who don't. Some are vegetarian, while others will eat meat. Most accept the authority of the Veda scriptures, which have been written over the 5,000 years of Hinduism's development.

However, the struggle for personal salvation is common to all Hinduism. The spirit or true self, Atman as it is called, is present in each individual. The Atman is the god within us, and is identified with Brahman, the Absolute, the origin and cause of all that exists. Maya, or human ignorance, keeps us from understanding our real nature, and realising our identity with this ultimate principle, and so we identify more with the phenomenal, ever changing world. The soul is seen as passing through countless births because it is attached to this world of appearances. Release from the cycle of incarnation is possible when the individual reaches a full

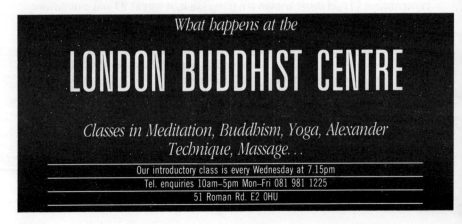

realisation that the real self is one with Brahman. This release is called moksha.

Because Brahman is seen as indefinable and unknowable, Hindus have traditionally worshipped the divine principle in more accessible forms. There are many more personal gods who are believed to be manifestations of Brahman, and who are worshipped because they are more human and act as a bridge between the relative world of human experience and the Absolute or god.

There are many different schools within Hinduism. Some have a very devotional approach, some see asceticism as a path to liberation, and others emphasise the importance of working in society for the collective good. Meditation, chanting and ritual are all practices employed by Hindu groups. The practice of Yoga is central in Hinduism. This is not just the Hatha Yoga we are familiar with in the West, which is the physical discipline of perfecting poses or Asanas (see 'Yoga' in Body section). Yoga means yoke or union, and it is a discipline which unites one with the universal or divine. Other forms of Yoga practised by the groups below include Bhakti Yoga, the discipline of devotion or love, Mantra Yoga, the chanting of Mantras, and Karma Yoga which is work as a spiritual practice.

In the personal struggle towards freedom, the teacher or guru is of great importance. Most modern Hindu groups centre around a teacher and their interpretation of the Hindu vision.

READING

Hinduism *by K M Sen, Penguin £4.50.* This book is an introduction to Hinduism and its sacred texts, the *Vedas*, the *Upanishads* and the *Bhagavad Gita*. Included is also a discussion of the three Hindu religious paths — the path of knowledge *(jnana)*, the path of work *(karma)* and the path of devotion *(bhakti)*. While giving insight into the caste system, the history of Hinduism and its nature and function, it also provides a look at current trends and customs and festivals. **Training the Mind through Yoga** *by M V Waterhouse, Shanti Sadan £3.00.* This collection of fourteen lectures introduces the general reader to the traditional methods of training the mind used in the spiritual science of *Adhyatma Yoga* and the 'yoga of self knowledge'. Beginning with an introduction to the *Bhagavad Gita* the lectures cover various aspects on refining the mind and emotions through discussing the stages in meditation the training of the yogi, awakening the higher consciousness and training and discipline. **Autobiography of A Yogi** *by Paramahansa Yogananda, Rider £5.95.* An authoritative introduction to the science of yoga, this book is a classic in its field, revealing the scientific foundation underlying the great religious paths of both east and west. It is an account of Yogananda's own search for truth which includes explanations of the laws governing miracles and recounts his meeting with many saints and sages throughout the world.

CENTRES OFFERING HINDUISM

Bhratiya Vidya Bhavan (Institute of Indian Culture) W14, International Society for

Krishna Consciousness (ISKON), Satyananda Yoga Centre, Shanti Sadan W11, Sri Aurobindo Circle (Ashram) SW16.

Paganism

The word 'pagan' derives from the Latin 'pagus' which simply means an inhabitant of the countryside. However, since the fourth century AD it has been used in a derogatory sense to denote those who subscribe to a creed other than the majority religion. In former times, the word inspired fear, hatred and the zeal to convert those who, in their primitive ignorance, did not know any better.

In reality Paganism is the natural religion, the native spirituality of the country, and it has been practised in Britain ever since the end of the last Ice Age 11,000 years ago. Any indigenous cult specific to a land and its culture may be called 'pagan'. British paganism was influenced by successive waves of pagan invaders over the centuries - Celtic, Scandinavian and Teutonic. Under its umbrella can be included the Celtic Druids, the Scandinavian godi, the medieval witchcult, Renaissance hermeticism and alchemy. Paganism still survives in the succession of 'New Age' cults and sects today.

The sense of continuity in Paganism derives from the magic of place, of myth and of music. It comes from the heart rather than the head, and a central feature of it is the celebration of Mother Earth and of nature. One expression of this is in the rituals which acknowledge the year's turning. These take place ideally at ancient sites such as Stonehenge and Glastonbury, which were specifically built to harness the stellar, lunar, solar and human energies in one harmony.

Modern British paganism is a revival of the old beliefs and practices, and today in many parts of the country there are cults of the Goddess, the Wicca, Odinism and Druidism. Imported varieties of paganism have also made their impact over the last decade (e.g.the shamanism of the North American Indians).

Common to all pagan cults are 'green' values - the promotion of an ecologically sound environment and the celebration of a transpersonal spirit through rite, dance, song and music. Paganism also explores the possibilities for empowering the individual through getting into a right relationship with the cosmos.

READING
Life and Times of a Modern Witch *by Janet and Stewart Farrar, Headline £2.95.* This book is written by two well known witches, as a result of a worldwide survey conducted to answer the many questions concerning their beliefs and rituals. Read this book to discover what kind of people become witches, what powers they possess, whether or not they worship Satan and a host of other things. **The Spiral Dance: A Rebirth of the Ancient Religion of the Great Goddess** *by Starhawk, Harper and Row £9.95.* A classic resource book for the women's spirituality movement, including rituals, invocations, exercises and magic. It is a brilliant

overview of the growth, suppression and modern day re-emergence of witchcraft as a Goddess worshipping religion. This is a book of tools, continually in the process of renewal in response to changing times. **Wicca: the Old Religion in the New Age** *by Vivianne Crowley, Aquarian/Thorsons.* Vivianne Crowley here explains the 'way of the witch', the quest for the self, showing how wicca — rapidly regaining its former popularity — has relevance in today's world. Included are the subjects of black and white magic, nudity, the God and Goddess within, the future of witchcraft and more. Additionally there is an explanation of the relationship between Witchcraft and Jungian psychology.

CENTRES OFFERING PAGANISM

Acca and Adda WC1, Asatru Folk Runic Workshop, Centre for Pagan Studies SW2, Eagle's Wing Centre for Contemporary Shamanism NW2, House of the Goddess SW12, London Group WC1, Pagan Link N16.

Qabalah

The Qabalah (alternatively spelt Kabbalah or Cabala) is primarily based on esoteric Jewish teachings and is at the heart of the western esoteric tradition. It is a philosophy and psychology of great theoretical and practical depth, its essential doctrine being that each individual person has the potential to realise their inner divinity and express this in all walks of life. There is evidence in the Old Testament of the existence of the Quabalah in pre-Christian times. It was not committed to writing until the Middle Ages, however, and most development has taken place in the nineteenth and twentieth centuries.

The Qabalah uses the 'Tree of Life' as a complete map of different levels of consciousness. There are may ways to use the Tree of Life. Being easy to both visualise and memorise, it can serve as a guide to personal development.

The Tree of Life is composed of eleven spheres, which represent everything from the body and the physical world through to the most central, or deepest aspect of our spiritual being, the place where individuality blurs into union with all other consciousness. In learning to have practical experience of these different spheres, so the individual can add to his/her knowledge of the different parts of him/herself.

In the Qabalah, each individual is believed to have their own Tree of Life inside them which has to be directly experienced rather than believed as a matter of dogma. Just as human beings have experiences common, so there are also group or collective Trees. It can thus be seen as relevant to both the evolution of the individual, and through the individual, the whole planet.

(Will Parfitt)

READING

Kabbalah and Psychology *by Z'ev ben Shimon Halevi, Gateway £6.95.* The author examines psychology as the study of the archetypal world which hovers between

Earth and Heaven. Psychology here is set against the scheme of Kabbalah which takes into account the divine origin of the human being, reincarnation, mystical experience as well as madness. The Tree of Life is studied in relation to both Freudian and Jungian psychology. **The Mystical Qabalah** *by Dion Fortune, Aquarian/Thorsons £7.95.* Of the books that Dion Fortune wrote, this one stands out as a seminal work in the development of the Qabalah and its incorporation into the Western Mystery Tradition. This is a useful reference book for those involved in the esoteric philosophy of the West and the study of the psychology of mystical experience. **The Living Qabalah: A Practical and Experiential Guide to Understanding the Tree of Life** *by Will Parfitt, Element £8.95.* Fully understood, the Qabalah offers a unique system of personal exploration and development, allowing us to examine all aspects of ourselves - our personality, soul and spirit. Using practical and experiential exercises designed for newcomer and expert alike, this illustrated manual provides a new way of using Qabalah in daily life.

CENTRES OFFERING QUABALAH
International Order of Kabbalists SW19, Living Qabalah SE22.

Shamanism

This is found as part of the native cultures of many different societies all over the world, for instance among the Aborigines of Australia, Lapplanders, American Indians and the Bon Po priests of Tibet. Traditionally the shaman uses rhythmic drumming and chanting, or more rarely, hallucinogenic drugs to alter consciousness and journey into 'non-ordinary reality' (as Carlos Castaneda called it in his popular Don Juan shamanic books) in order to gain insight, heal the sick or make contact with guides or teachers. Ritual and mask-making may also be used by modern shamans to facilitate this dialogue with what, in modern psychological terms, might be called the unconscious.

It is largely the shamanism of the North American Indians which has made the most impact here, with their *sweat lodge* tradition (a sort of do-it-yourself sauna in which participants chant for long periods) and the *medicine wheel* teachings. This tradition particularly stresses the importance of nature as teacher, healer and guide.

Shamanic ritual and journeying to 'non-ordinary reality' has also been taken up for psychotherapeutic purposes, notably by Stanislav Grof in his *holotropic therapy*. Grof uses various techniques to induce hallucinations in his clients, and has evolved a system of psychotherapy around their experiences.

READING
Way of the Shaman *by Michael Harner Bantam (U.S.A.)*

£3.60. Written by an experienced healer and widely travelled field worker, the Way of the Shaman is the most popular guide for the beginner on the shamanic path. Clearly explained practical techniques lead us up to the the understanding and practice of deep physical and spiritual healing, as practised by shamans everywhere. **Medicine Woman** *by Lynn Andrews, Penguin £5.99.* Neither Lynn Andrews nor Carlos Castaneda have escaped controversy in their books but the value of their accounts grows out of the potential for personal transformation they demonstrate which is available to us all. Andrews' first book describes her initiation by Agnes Whistling Elk. In later books she goes on to work with shamans and medicine people all over the world. **Shamanic Voices** *by Joan Halifax, Dutton U.S.A. £9.55.* This anthology allows shamans from as far afield as Australia, Africa and Alaska to speak for themselves about the rituals they guard and the experiences they have undergone. Their altered states of consciousness act as a bridge for those they serve between everyday life and the eternal. Dr, Halifax provides an excellent introductory essay and brief prefaces to every individual account.

CENTRES OFFERING SHAMANISM
CAER (Centre For Alternative Education And Research), Eagle's Wing Centre for Contemporary Shamanism NW2.

Spiritualism

Spiritualism is centred round the belief of the survival of the personality after death, and that there can be communication between the living and those 'on the other side'. This communication takes place through 'mediums', or 'sensitives' as they are sometimes known, who channel the messages of the dead. The messages may take the form of words of comfort or advice to friends or relatives, and spiritualists believe that this proves that they are still in existence, but in another 'plane' or world .

Many spiritualists are also involved in spiritual healing, which involves either the

---

THE CENTRE FOR PAGAN STUDIES

The Centre has been established for educational, therapeutic and spiritual purposes. It provides theoretical classes and experiential workshops in north European shamanism and ritual mythic drama. At a counselling level it aims to act as a guide to seekers through the occult labyrinth of competing wares in the esoteric marketplace. The research function of the Centre is well developed and provision can be made to people requiring a more one-to-one training after the manner of an apprentice.

Flat B, 5 Trinity Rise, London SW2. 081 671 6372

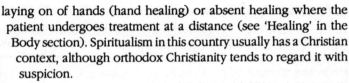

laying on of hands (hand healing) or absent healing where the patient undergoes treatment at a distance (see 'Healing' in the Body section). Spiritualism in this country usually has a Christian context, although orthodox Christianity tends to regard it with suspicion.

There are a number of spiritualist churches throughout London, where services are held. These involve a service similar to a church service, but at a paticular point a medium will give messages from the 'other side' to particular members of the congregation.

Spiritualism is an organised religion, and is therefore distinct from other forms of psychism, where mediums contact what they believe are spirits in order to make predictions and/or give advice. Another example of psychism is the 'channelling' of books or philosophical or religious teachings through someone who belives themselves to be in touch with a spirit guide.

READING

The Wanderings of a Spiritualist *by Sir Arthur Conan Doyle, Ronin £5.95.* This is a personal account of spiritualism or communication with the dead by the popular writer of the Sherlock Holmes stories. It includes meetings with remarkable people, geographical accounts and political musing from a spiritualist perspective. **The Book on Mediums** *by Allan Kardec, Weiser £9.95.* Although over a century has passed since its original publication, the Book on Mediums remains the most comprehensive and basic text on spiritualism, revealing the fundamental principles of communication with the spirit world. The book contains instruction on the theory of manifestations, the meaning of communicating with the invisible world, the development of mediumship, the difficulties and the dangers that are to be encountered in the practice of spiritism. **Testimony of Light** *by Helen Greaves, C.W. Daniel £4.95.* This book describes the after death experience through the communication given to Helen Greaves by her former friend and teacher, the late Frances Banks, through telepathy across the veil. The message given in the scripts is that the death of the body is but a gentle passing to a much freer and fuller life.

CENTRES OFFERING SPIRITUALISM
Spiritualist Association of Great Britain SW1.

Sufism

Sufism originated in Persia in the sixth century AD as a reaction against what the Sufis saw as the rigidity and worldliness of orthodox Islam. After the time of Mahommed the movement became unpopular with some Muslims, who thought it heretical, and many Sufis suffered condemnation and persecution. The word itself comes from 'suf' which is Persian for the white woollen cloaks the mystics wore. The term 'sufi' is actually correctly used to describe those who have attained knowledge of the divine. An individual who is still on the path is called 'faquir', which means poor, in the sense of spiritual poverty.

Like most mystical traditions the aim of Sufism is direct experience of, and ultimately union with, God, and this is achieved through love, both of other people and of God. Sufism has been called 'the religion of the heart'. There is no dogma, nor any highly structured philosophical system which defines the beliefs of Sufism. The approach is largely devotional, and the emphasis is on intuition and feeling. It stresses the idea of equilibrium and wholeness. The human being is potentially a microcosm of the balanced unity of the universe. The ideal is not to withdraw from the world, but to bring vision and insight into the world. Achieving knowledge of God, the practitioner becomes in turn a vessel for God's knowledge to act in the world.

It is a very fluid tradition and personal communication between teacher and pupil is of central importance. The Teacher initiates the pupil into a chain of Teacher-pupil relationships, the lineage of which stretches back to Mahommed.

The Sufis have always used many different methods to develop consciousness, as the groups which exist in the West today still do. Their practices include contemplative meditation, guided visualisation, breathing exercises, music and the 'whirling' which is associated with the dervishes.

Sufism has inspired much literature. Poetry and the use of symbolism figure largely in the tradition as a means of expressing the experience of the divine. *The Rubaiyat of Omar Khayyam* is perhaps the most famous Sufi inspired text in the West, though their influence is thought to be widespread in European culture. Some claim that Gurdjieff, the Russian mystic and philosopher, was taught by Sufis.

Today Sufi groups vary a great deal. Some are still very much rooted in Islam, and others are more eclectic in their approach. Some advertise their activities while others maintain the traditional secrecy about their activities, believing that those who are truly seeking will find them.

READING

What is Sufism? *by Martin Lings, Mandala/Unwin Hyman £4.95.* An eloquent and authoritative introduction to the mystical dimension of Islam. Martin Lings writes from his own personal experience and deep understanding of Arabic culture and religion: nine concise and powerful chapters convey the essence of Sufism. **Rumi and Sufism** *by Eva de Vitray-Meyerovitch, Post-Apollo Press, U.S.A. £9.95.* A beautifully illustrated book exploring the life thought and background of one of Islam's greatest mystics, written by a French scholar who became a believer in Islam through her works on Sufism. A clear and approachable introduction to the subject, with fascinating material on the *Mevlevi* brotherhood to which he belonged. **The World of Sufi** *by Idries Shah and others, Octagon £12.50.* An anthology of writings about Sufis and their work, with contributions from many authors, including Idries Shah, Doris Lessing and Peter Brent. Chapters on the classical tradition of the Sufis; Sufi humour; Sufi spiritual practices; modern psychology and Sufism; Sufi literature; and current study materials.

CENTRES OFFERING SUFISM

London Sufi Centre W11, Nimatullahi Sufi Order W2.

Modern Teachers

Anthroposophical Association   NW1

Rudolf Steiner, an Austrian living at the turn of the century, coined the term 'anthroposophy' (meaning awareness of one's humanity) to sum up his wide-ranging philosophy. Anthroposophy seeks to unite all of humanity's spiritual knowledge, covering the arts, science, philosophy and reilgion, and encompasses a whole social outlook emphasising the importance of human growth. Steiner applied his teaching to medicine, (see the Anthroposophical Medical Association), education (there are several Steiner Schools in the UK), science, and even agriculture where he devised a unique organic system of growing crops.

Barry Long Foundation

Barry Long is an Australian, born in 1926, who lived for 20 years in London and began teaching publicly in 1983. He now teaches in Australia, New Zealand, continental Europe and the UK through public meetings and seminars, and through books and tapes covering various aspects of 'life and living, death and dying, love and making love, meditation and the art of being'.

There is no formal practice, but Barry Long's teaching encourages the application of greater attention and stillness to all aspects of living to bring about greater self-knowledge and love. He stresses the importance of direct experience rather than religious forms or dogma, and of realising the truth for onself, rather than relying on a guru. No groups or gatherings as such except when Barry Long gives a seminar or talk. Books and tapes available mail order only.

Christian Community   W6

Set up by Rudolf Steiner in 1922 (see Anthroposophical Society, above), the Christian Community seeks to re-affirm the spirit of Christianity. Central ideas are the importance of the resurection as a symbol of individual growth; the inner meaning of the sacraments; reincarnation; freedom of thought. The arts and counselling are seen as an important part of spiritual practice.

Eckankar   W12

Eckankar takes its direction from Sri Harold Klemp, with the help of whom followers aim to make contact with the Light and Sound of God which is believed to purify the consciousness, and lift the individual into heavenly states. Three principles are important: firstly that the soul is eternal, secondly that travellers on the path of ECK dwell in the spiritual planes, and thirdly that the soul has no past or future, but lives in the present. ECK spiritual aides are provided to give spiritual assistance. Practice is through spiritual exercises (e.g. contemplation of the mantra 'HU', study of dreams and discourses, and service to life).

Foundation for International Spiritual Unfoldment E7

Non-denominational, non-sectarian organisation under the direction of Gururaj Ananda Yogi. Meditation is central, and spiritual practices are individually prescribed for each meditator. Spiritual unfoldment is seen as 'an unveiling of the patternings of the mind' and the dissolving away of unecessary conditionings and attachments which are believed to make us lose sight of our true divine nature or real self.

Free Daist Communion N10

Founded by Heart-Master Da Free John, a western born, living teacher. Disciples believe that he conducts the transforming power of the divine to those who relate to him in the traditional guru-devotee manner. Direct experience of the transcendental is made possible through contact with Heart-Master Da's spiritual company *(satsang yoga)* The teaching itself is about happiness - we are already happy but we don't know it because we are so involved in the self-absorbed quest for happiness. The teachings are studied and devotees then move onto awareness practice of how one separates oneself from happiness. Other practices include chanting, study, work and prayer.

Gurdjieff Ouspensky School

Now acknowledged as one of the spiritual masters of the twentieth century,

66 The American Indian who ran a native American shamanistic workshop I participated in looked well cast in the part of leader. When he donned his full headdress, painted his body and danced in a trance he looked as if he had been snatched straight from the Amazon and planted in our midst, which happened to be a country house in Devon. We were a newly formed tribe of twelve Westerners about to be initiated into the local religious practices of the Amazon jungle. I had not met any other members of the group before, other than one, who had been a friend for many years. I had booked that weekend to get out of London and into something different from the environment I was familiar with. I didn't realise just how different it would be.

Most of the Saturday was spent in a large room banging on a drum and chanting. I hated the chanting initially as it seemed monotonous and reminded me of singing chorus after chorus of hymns in church. Later I warmed to the chanting as I slowly got into the groove. I spent much of the day glancing at the beautiful women in the group, wondering when, if ever, I would get to talk to them. At the end of the day a 'sweat lodge' was planned and I was looking forward to this as an opportunity of talking to some of the other members of our group.

In preparation for the evening ritual we were instructed by our chief to build the sweat lodge next to a stream located on the grounds. We did this by foraging for branches which we used for the basic frame. We bent the long branches in the form of a semi-circle and put both ends into the ground. The branches were then tied together and blankets put over the frame so that it ended up igloo shaped. Inside, in the middle of the lodge, we dug a pit, to house the hot coals, which were to be used for the ritual. We then went back to the house to drink some tea (it's hard to drag the English away from their habits).

Most of our tribe had made their way down to the lodge while I lingered over a further cup of tea and made conversation with the few remaining dalliers. When I made my way down to the lodge it was turning dusk. At the bottom of the hill where the lodge lay, to my surprise, I could see the men standing naked in one group painting their bodies and the women standing fully clothed in another group. I wondered what was going on, as I had not been told that nakedness was on the agenda, nor could I fathom why the women were clothed and the men not.

I headed for the male camp and no sooner had I reached them than they started putting pressure on me to disrobe. I had nothing against going naked, but resented doing it on demand and without any mental preparation. It was my hesitancy (I think) that prompted the women to take off their clothes. At this point I took off my clothes too (how could I hold my head high as a red Indian warrior if I was afraid to do this?).

We were then instructed to dance round in a circle tapping a hand to the mouth making what seemed like common Red Indian warpath noises. As I looked around the group whilst we danced it was obvious how strange we must have appeared to any passers by (fortunately the grounds were private), and I thought 'if my mother could see me now, what would she say?'. I was very aware too, of how the extra flab round my waistline must be doing damage to my image as a virile warrior, as it wobbled when I danced, so I did my best to hold it in.

We then moved hot coals from a fire outside the lodge to the pit inside, then tumbled into the lodge. There were no lights and it was pitch black. Water was thrown on the coals and before long a strong heat developed, making me sweat profusely. We continued with the chants we had been rehearsing all day. The hot house became not only a hot house for my body, but my mind and soul also. The familiar gave way to an enveloping hypnotic overpowering rhythm. It was magical and I did not want it to end. The heat finally overcame me and I made my way to the door and was instructed to throw myself into the stream. It must have taken me five minutes in that freezing November water to cool down. I then had to go back into the lodge to heat up. We continued this chanting in the lodge for several hours and I made frequent visits to the natural splash pool. Near the end I was so exhausted that I was crawling out of the lodge on all fours to make my way to the pool. Here I was, naked, on all fours, covered in mud and paint, crawling out of a mud hut. I realised then that there was no way I could salvage my image. This in itself became a great freedom. **99**

Mike Considine

66My experiences in the framework of the Shamanistic/native American tradition have had a profound effect on my life. Through ritual, dance, teachings of the Medicine Wheels, sweatlodge and visionquest, the ancient wisdom came alive, and I contacted the 'Source' with a reality which was undeniably vivid and also unnerving. It was like the Real Thing! - a living 'therapy' rooted in nature, the earth and the body which made other therapies seem artificial, unnatural creations of our society. And it was fun!

My experiences included a mystical revelation of shamanistic flying (over South America!), visionary baptism and visions of archetypical symbols which I am still trying to understand. Three workshops over a span of nine months formed the basis of a journey of initiation and for me, it was the biggest trip of my life. It is only now, two years later that I have finally made the return to earth and mundane life, but with an inner richness which is constantly manifested by psychic and sychronistic events in the external world.

As city dwellers we struggle, sometimes desperately, to create a sense of community and connectedness. Shamanism is rooted, amongst other things, in a holistic experience of community. To reawaken this was both threatening to the alienated life I have led, and deep enough to make sense and give meaning to life, even in London. **99**

Andy Hilton

Gurdjieff brought a system of methods and ideas from the east to the west called The Fourth Way, or the Work. This ancient teaching is for ordinary, normal men and women who wish to work to achieve higher states of consciousness while staying in the circumstances of their everyday life. Ouspensky organised these ideas into a form which he thought would be especially suitable for the western intellect. The Fourth Way requires personal verification, understanding and efforts from everyone using it. Although very difficult, it aims to provide a short cut for modern men and women on the way of inner self development.

Lucis Trust SW1

Established by Alice A Bailey, an author and lecturer in the first half of this century who pioneered the idea of a New Age of global co-operation and wholeness. She wrote 24 books presenting an esoteric perspective on psychology, occult meditation and the evolution of humanity, which aim to help individuals be more effective in serving humanity and the Plan of Light and Love during what is seen as a time of transition into the Age of Aquarius. She founded the Lucis Trust as an international agency in the raising of human consciousness, and it now has consultative status with the United Nations. The Lucis trust administers a number of programmes: The Arcane School, a meditation school run by correspondence; Triangles, which is a global network of individuals from different spiritual paths who use prayer and meditation to spread goodwill in the world; World Goodwill, which publishes material presenting a global spiritual perspective on the issues facing humanity; and Lucis Press which publishes Alice Bailey's books.

Teilhard Centre W8

The Teilhard Centre works to extend understanding of the cosmic evolutionary thought of Pierre Teilhard de Chardin (1881-1955), a Jesuit priest and paleontologist. He believed that human evolution had not stopped but is continuing in the spiritual more than the physical aspect, effecting a gradual growth of the human community toward a highly differentiated, highly complex state of union.

The Teilhard Centre is a non-sectarian, educational charity with a diverse membership drawn together by interests in science, philosophy and religion, spirituality, personal growth and th desire to build a future where human beings love and respect not only one another but also their fellow creatures and their planetary, galactic and cosmic home.

Thomas Troward Society E11

A society based on the work of Thomas Troward, a man with a background in law who later became a judge. The society offers counselling and publications based on creative thought, spiritual psychology and 'Science of Mind'. They offer lessons in the 'Science of Mind', 'Mental Science' and spiritual counselling. Fees by donation according to arrangement. Their aim is to put people in touch with their inner creative source.

White Eagle Lodge W8
Founded in 1936 on the teachings of the spirit guide and teacher, White Eagle, who chanelled his message through Grace Cooke. The purpose of the teaching is to enable each individual to develop the light of Christ spirit which is believed to be in every human heart, so that it can radiate into the world. The teaching says that the basic law which controls life is love, expressed through love for God, humanity and nature, and this love is seen as leading people, through the experience of many lives, back to total awareness of the God within them.

OTHER GROUPS

3HO Kundalini Yoga Foundation   NW4
3HO stands for the healthy, happy, holy organisation. They practice Kundalini Yoga, the ancient, tantric technique which seeks to awaken the dormant cosmic energy in human beings and refine it by drawing it up through the seven chakras, or centres of consciousness and energy. The practices include adopting particular positions and movement, breathing techniques, meditation, chanting of mantras and use of mudras (symbolic gestures).

Aetherius Society SW6
Founded by Dr George King who was given the command: "Prepare yourself! You are to become the Voice of Interplanetary Parliament!" According to the Society, his previous practice of Yoga enabled him to go into a trance state and make contact with a being from the planet Venus, called Aetherius. The society aims to spread the teachings of this and other interplanetary guides, including Jesus and Buddha who they believe came from Venus. This solar system is believed to be ruled by an interplanetary parliament based on Saturn. Planets are seeen as classrooms where

---

RUDOLF STEINER HOUSE

Lectures, classes, performances

Bookshop & Library

Information about Steiner-based work in the U.K. and world-wide

35 Park Road, NW1 6XT
Tel: 071-723 4400/8219
Opening times: 10-1, 2-6 Mon-Fri.

LONDON SUFI CENTRE
Invites you:

Every Monday
7.30-9.30 pm	Sufi Teachings and Practices
6.30-7.30 pm	Sacred Dances
6.30-7.30 pm	Healing Course
6.00-6.30 pm	Healing Service

Every Thursday
7.00-8.30 pm   Meditation, Zikr & Sufi Practices

Every 1st Sunday of the month
5.00 pm   Universal Worship Service

All at 21 Lancaster Road, London W11 1QL
Tel: 071-229 1064 (071-221 3215 messages)

we learn various lessons through thousands of lives. A new master is to come shortly in a flying saucer to lead those who are ready into a New World. Various kinds of yoga, prayer, mantra yoga, pranayama, spiritual healing are practiced.

Baha'i Faith   SW7

According to the *Enclyclopaedia Britannica* this is the 'most widely spread independent religion in the world after Christianity'. Central to the Baha'i Faith is the belief in the oneness of mankind and of all religions. It originated in Persia through a succession of three teachers, a 'Forerunner' who prepared the way for the 'Founder', Baha'u'llah, who died in 1892. The 'Interpreter' then explained the teachings further. There are no priests or clergy, but there are local Baha'i communities practising together through prayer, meditation, service to humanity and worship through work. They have their own scriptures, holy places and parliament.

Beshara Trust   Oxon

The Beshara Trust was set up to provide an environment where any person who wishes to establish a spiritual dimension in their life can come together with others to study and work towards this. It seeks to do this without the restrictions of dogma or religion.

A Course in Miracles

'A Course in Miracles' is a 'self-study course in spiritual development'. The book was heard as a kind of 'inner dictation' over seven years by a professor of medical psychology at Columbia University, Dr Helen Schucman. The teachings posit that there are only two emotions: love and fear. Love is seen to unite us in our original unity with each other and God. Fear is seen as coming from the ego, and as separative. According to the Course, rather than holding onto emotions such as aggression, resentment and guilt, if perception is shifted towards forgiveness it is possible to recontact this love. It is structured as a text, a workbook of 365 lessons for students and a manual for teachers.

Centre For Healing Through Forgiveness   N15

College of Psychic Studies   SW7

The College of Psychic Studies runs courses, workshops and hosts lectures on a range of subjects which include healing, psychic phenomena, psychology of past lives, channelling etc. Training in healing and psychic unfoldment given. They believe that at the human level there is no single truth, but that truth can be found in all the great spiritual traditions, and also outside them.

Elizabeth Kubler Ross Foundation NW6

Founded by Elisabeth Kubler-Ross who has become renowed for her work with the dying. Holds workshops and seminars on aspects of death and dying. Non-sectarian.

Findhorn Foundation   SCOTLAND
Residential community founded in 1962 by Eileen and Peter Caddy and Dorothy Maclean on the principles that God, or the source of all life, is accessible to each of us at all times, and that nature, including the planet, has intelligence and is part of a much larger plan. Findhorn has no formal doctrine or creed, recognising that all major world religions share the same underlying principles. They subscribe to the 'New Age' belief that an evolutionary expansion of consciousness is taking place in the world, which will infuse humanity with spiritual values. Work, sacred dance and meditation are practised. However, it is daily life which is seen as the 'spiritual classroom' with an emphasis on living and working in community with others and developing a responsive relationship to the earth. A range of courses is run (see 'Residential Workshops').

Friends of Shanti Nilaya UK
Founded by Elisabeth Kubler-Ross who has become renowned for her work with the dying. Holds workshops and seminars on aspects of death and dying. Non-sectarian.

Graigian Society   NW5
The Graigian Society grew out of the first green party, and at its core is the 'first Green monstery', a spiritual community in a house full of the creative works of its occupants. They aim to 'bring about a caring and sensitive society'. Workshops and groups are held to facilitate self development through 'natural psychology' which stresses relating to others, creativity, the arts and has elements of the philosophy of Jung and Gurdjieff. They believe that human growth is as important as environmental measures to save the earth. Conduct local environmental campaigns and run groups on 'Being in a Group' and art therapy. Members of the community are easy to spot because of their green striped habits, friendliness and gentleness. They have a leaning towards the Celtic and medieval, and strong links with Wales. 'Graigian' comes from 'Y-Graig' which is Welsh for 'The Rock'.

International School of the Golden Rosycross Surrey
A group in the tradition of the Rosicrucians, who seek to work in the world to enable people to become receptive to Divine Truth, Wisdom and Love. They seek to penetrate ever more deeply into perfect knowledge, which they see as having been expressed by different seers at different times, and as part of an eternal process of universal development.

Open Gate   London
Open Gate are not a group, but run workshops on aspects of psychology, spirituality and the arts, and longer programmes in East/West studies, process-oriented psychology, Buddhist and Shamanic studies. They hold residentials and retreats, some with well-known spiritual teachers.

SPIRIT

66 The first retreat I went on was held in a boys' prep school in Sussex. I hadn't had any experience of anything like it before. We had to sleep in dormitories on lumpy mattresses on beds which were too short for anyone over 11. Then we had to get up at 6.30 am to meditate. I was thoroughly miserable the whole time because I was becoming more aware of how unhappy I was with the way I was living, and I spent a lot of the time wishing I could leave. However, when the 5 days I had booked for were up, to my own surprise I decided to stay on for another 5 days to the end of the retreat. Behind my decision to stay was the realisation that I was more in touch with what I really felt than I had probably ever been before, and this was in some way liberating. I also had a lot of support and a tremendous sense of community with the other people on the retreat. When I left and went back to my 'old life' I felt like a visitor from another planet - it was as if I was looking with new eyes. I felt much more centred in myself, my awareness of the environment and people seemed heightened, and some of the structures I had lived in seemed too small and badly fitting for me. It eventually led me to the decision to move and to change my job. 99

Imogen Fox

Order of Bards Ovates and Druids   Surrey
Druidism is one of the old traditions of British paganism (see above). Worship and working in harmony with nature expresses itself in ecological activity and veneration of natural elements: plants, stones, trees, sun, moon and stars. Druids celebrate eight festivals during the year which consist of the equinoxes and solstices, and the four 'fire' festivals. Traditional to druidry is the bardic tradition - story telling, poetry, music and song, which is seen as another form of worship and spiritual celebration.

Subud Central London   W9
Founded by Muhammad Subuh, (known to his followers as 'Bapak') an Indonesian who died in 1987. It is not a religion or teaching it itself - members are from all faiths - but aims to be a way of understanding and following the inner messages of religious teachings. This guidance is given through the 'latihan' or inner training, where an inner vibration is transmitted from person to person and causes illumination.

Theosophical Society   W1
This is one of the longest established of the non-denominational spiritual groups. Theosophical belief is that man is essentially a part of the all pervading spirit which energises all matter. It sees a common essence in all religion, and seeks to study the truth of these without dogma. The society encourages the study of comparative religion, philosophy and science and to promote the development of the latent powers in man.

Wrekin Trust (some events in London)
Educational charity concerned with the spiritual nature of humanity and the universe. It does not subscribe to any particular doctrine or dogma, but aims to help people find the paths most suited to them. Conferences with distinguished speakers from different traditions both spiritual and scientific, and workshops on a variety of themes.

COMMUNICATION

BOOKSHOPS

The bookshops below are specialists in some aspects of the areas covered by this book. Some may be general bookshops, but because they stock a largish supply of books in these fields we have included them.

A to Z Martial Arts Centre
Ground Floor
11 Kenway Rd
London SW5 0RP. (071) 370 0236.
Sell books and products on martial arts supplies.

Atlantis Bookshop
49A Museum Street
London WC1A 1LY. (071) 405 2120.
Mon, Tues, Wed, Fri 10-5.30, Thurs 10-8, Sat 11-5. Atlantis bookshop was closed for a while, but now back in business and expanded into the basement. It's the world's oldest occult bookshop, established in 1922. It covers all areas of occult, spiritualism, psychism, paganism and wicca, spirituality along with lighter subjects such as dowsing, ley lines and mythology.

Books Etc
120 Charing Cross Road
London WC2. (071) 379 6838.
General bookshop which has a good selection of books on Mind Body Spirit, psychology, psychotherapy, alternative medicine.

Books For A Change
52 Charing Cross Road
London WC2H 0BB. (071) 836 2315.
Jointly organised by CND, Friends of the Earth, the Unitied Nations Association and War on Want. A 'green' bookshop with books on practical and political aspects of ecology, plus recycled stationery, periodicals and some very nice postcards. Send SAE for comprehensive catalogue.

Books for Cooks
4 Blenheim Crescent
London W11 2EE. (071) 221 1992.
Comprehensive range of cookbooks. Vegetarian, vegan, macrobiotics, holistic. Secondhand section. 9.30-6 Mon-Sat.

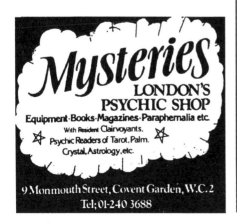

BOOKSHOPS

Changes Bookshop
242 Belsize Road
Kilburn
London NW6 4BT. (071) 328 5161.
Specialists in books on psychology, psychotherapy, counselling and personal growth. Very efficient mail order service. You can phone and pay by credit card. Mon-Fri 10-6, Sat 10-5. Friendly - may offer you a cup of tea while you browse. It's a small bookshop but they are big on enthusiasm and are knowledgeable about the subjects. They are eager to talk about psychological theories and the latest psychotherapies. Brian Wade at Changes did the book review for the 'Mind' section of this book. They provide useful lists of books on particular psychotherapies e.g. NLP, Jungian together with reviews of those books. Produce a newsheet four times a year of new titles. Shouldn't all bookshops be like this?

C O M P E N D I U M
L O N D O N S
L E A D I N G
C O N T E M P O R A R Y
B O O K S H O P
234 CAMDEN HIGH ST NW1
(071) 485 8944 / (071) 267 1525
(071) 267 0193 (FAX)

★★★★★★★★★★★★★★★★★★★★★★★★★★

try us for books on astrology, health &
healing, personal development, mysticism,
magic, mythology, humanistic & Jungian
psychology, women's studies, recovery &
co-dependence

U S I M P O R T S A R E O U R F O R T E

MAIL ORDER A SPECIALITY

Compendium Bookshop
234 Camden High St.
Camden
London NW1 8QS. (071) 267 1525 / 485 8944.
Mon-Sat 10-6, Sun 12-6. Has an extensive range of books on self help, psychology, astrology, new science, healing and related subjects. There is also a large range of books dealing with recovery, co-dependency and the subject of adult children of alcoholics. Large range of American imported material and a selection of self-help audio cassettes. Fast, efficient, mail order service. Credit card phone orders accepted. Special orders undertaken. Books supplied for conferences, groups etc.

Dillons Bookstore
82 Gower St
London WC1E 6EQ. (071) 636 1577.
Very large bookshop which is easy to browse round, the books being mostly in subject order. They have a comprehensive stock of alternative medicine, psychology, psychotherapy and spiritual books.

Family Planning Association
27-35 Mortimer Street
London W1N 7RJ. (071) 636 7866.
Mon-Thur 9-5, Fri 9-4.30. Books on birth control, conception, sexuality.

Friends Book Centre
Friends House
177 Euston Road
London NW1 2BJ. (071) 387 3601.
Mon-Fri 9.30-5.30, except Tues opens 10.30. Open occasionally on Sats. This is a bookshop run by the Quaker Society of Friends and covers religion, including comparative religion, peace studies, north-south issues, Quakerism, psychology, health, women, green issues and vegetarian cookery. Postcards. Also mail order.

Genesis Books
188 Old Street
London EC1V 9BP. (071) 250 1868.
Mon-Fri 11.30-7, Sat 11-3 (sometimes till 5pm if busy). Small bookshop situated in a therapy complex, with macrobiotic cafe located in building (the East West restaurant). They specialize in alternative medicine and macrobiotics books. Massage, psychology, herbalism, religion, Buddhism etc. Also sell crystals, new age cassettes and videos. Green issues.

BOOKSHOPS

Inspiration
28 Devonshire Road
Chiswick
London W4 2HD. (081) 994 0074.
Mon-Sat 10-6. New Age centre selling crystals, tarot cards and books, runes, relaxation, meditation and new age music tapes and jewellery. Astrological birth charts done.

Karnac (Books) Ltd.
118 Finchley Road
London
NW3. (071) 431 1075.
Mon-Sat 9-6. Stock a comprehensive range of books on psychoanalysis, psychotherapy, analytical psychology (Jung). Small section on women's studies and philosophy. Appropriately situated just round the corner from the Freud Museum (qv), and close to the Tavistock. They also publish books in the psychoanalytic and psychotherapy field. Mail order from the Gloucester Road Branch.

Karnac (Books) Ltd.
58 Gloucester Road
South Kensington
London SW7 4QY. (071) 584 3303.
Mon-Sat 9am-6pm. Specialise in books on psychoanalysis, analytical psychology and psychotherapy. Mail order available.

Mysteries
9 Monmouth Street
Covent Garden
London WC2H 9DA. (071) 240 3688.
Mainly a bookshop but they also sell pendulums, ritual magic candles, dakinis, pentagram rings, runes - you can make contact with the etheric just around the corner from John Le Carre's fictional home of MI5 at Cambridge Circus. It doesn't seem possible that anything else could be crammed into this lilac fronted shop - and indeed it's often so full of people it can be difficult to get inside. Though primarily a bookshop (esoteric, self help, spiritual, natural health etc.), there are also music and self help tapes and videos, jewellery, tarots and crystals. Tarot and palm readings are also carried out on the premises. Mail order.

Natural Medicine Centre
87 Beckenham Lane
Shortlands
Bromley BR2 0DN. (081) 460 1117.
This natural health centre has a bookshop on the premises covering wholistic health, self healing, complementary medicine, women's issues, personal development, family issues, ecology. They also sell herbs and herbal remedies and audio tapes.

Neal Street East
5 Neal Street
London WC2H 9UP. (071) 240 0135/6.
The bookshop on the first floor of this shop selling oriental arts and crafts specialises in books on all things oriental. This includes eastern religions, meditation and oriental mythology; oriental astrology and divination; health from chinese herbs, kiatsu to macrobiotics; martial arts and yoga; oriental customs, arts and culture. They also stock calligraphic inks and brushes and can show you how to use them in their Chinese brush painting workshops. Other events hosted by the bookshop are ikebana and cookery demonstrations, and Chinese New Year Celebrations.

BOOKSHOPS

Passage Bookshop

5 Canning Cross
Grove Lane
Camberwell
London SE5 8BH. (071) 274 7606.
General bookshop, but because it is next to the Maudsley Hospital carries titles chiefly on psychiatry, but also books on psychotherapy and psychology.

Silver Moon

68 Charing Cross Road
London WC2H OBB. (071) 836 7906.
Mon-Sat 10.30-6.30. Women's health, spirituality, religion, self help, healing. Tarot cards and jewellery in matriarchal symbols. Fiction is all women authors and there is a lesbian, black and political section.

Sister Write

190 Upper Street
Islington
London N1 1RQ. (071) 226 9782.
Mon-Sat 10-6, Thurs 10-7. Large section on women's spirituality and health, child care, also sections on black women, lesbians, fiction and a big children's section. Crafts made by women. Mail order.

Skoob

15 Sicilian Avenue
Southampton Row
Holborn
London WC1A 2QH. (071) 404 3063.
10.30-6.30 Mon. Second hand books on psychology.

Skoob 2

19 Bury Place
Bloomsbury
London WC1A 2JH. (071) 405 0030.
10.30 - 6.30 Mon to Sat. Secondhand bookshop covering magic, eastern philosophy, general religions, shamanism, alternative health, mysticism, mythology, astrology and tarot. Two floors.

Spiritualist Association of Great Britain

33 Belgrave Square
London SW1X 8QL. (071) 235 3351.

Sunpower Books

198 Blackstock Road
London N4. (071) 704 0247.
10-6 Mon to Sat. Small section on health and natural healing, spirituality, mysticism, wholefood, cookery and nutrition, women's health, pregnancy and childcare. Also sell aromatherapy oils, homoeopathic remedies and herbs.

Village Books

17 Shrubbery Road
Streatham
London SW16 2AS. (081) 677 2667.
General bookshop, but with an alternative slant. Psychology section.

W. & G. Foyle Ltd

113-119 Charing Cross Road
London WC2H OEB. (071) 437 5660.
Very large general bookshop. Covers the 'mind body spirit' field. Books are sorted by publisher so it's often difficult to browse.

Waterstone's Booksellers

193 Kensington High Street
Kensington
London W8 6SH. (071) 937 8432.
Largish bookshop with a large 'mind-body-spirit' section in the basement.

Waterstones (1)

99 Old Brompton Road
Kensington
London SW7 3LE. (071) 581 8522.
Mon-Sat 9.30-9, Sun 12-7. General bookshop with good sections on holistic health, psychology and self help, diet, religion, mysticism, psychism.

Waterstones (2)

121-125 Charing Cross Road
London WC2H OEA. (071) 434 4291.
Mon-Fri 9.30-7.30, Sat 10-7. Good general bookshop with sections on psychology and psychotherapy, self help, mystical, spirituality, divination.

Watkins Books Ltd

19-21 Cecil Court
Covent Garden
London WC2N 4HB. (071) 836 2182.
Mon-Sat 10-6 except Weds when they open at 10.30. Refurbished a year ago and expanded into the basement, Watkins is known for the breadth and depth of its selection of books on natural therapies, personal development, astrology, mysticism etc. One of the best sections in London on spirituality and religion including

eastern and western approaches, and the works of spiritual teachers. Bargains are to be had in the second hand section downstairs. If you need advice on which book to buy you'll be in good hands, because David Redstone and his staff at Watkins did the book reviews for the 'Body' and 'Spirit' section of this book.

Wholefood Books

24 Paddington Street
London W1M 4DR. (071) 935 3924.
Mon 8.30-6, Tues-Thurs 8.30-6.60, Sat 8.30-1.30. Specialises in nutrition and health, alternative therapies, natural childbirth and childrearing, organic gardening and farming, wholefood cookery. There also a wholefood shop.

Wisdom Publications

402 Hoe Street
London E17 9AA. (081) 520 5588.
Mon-Sat 10-6, shop located on first floor. Probably the largest selection of books on Buddhism and related art and culture in Europe. Also trade distribution. Publish the fabulous Tibetan art calendar, videos of Tibetan teachers, and audio cassettes on various subjects. Mail order, £2.50 for catalogue.

NEW AGE SHOPS

Abraxas

7 Shrubbery Road
Streatham
London SW16 2AS. (081) 769 4857.
They sell mostly arts and crafts and about 30% New Age products.

Inspiration

28 Devonshire Road
Chiswick
London W4 2HD. (081) 994 0074.
Mon-Sat 10-6. New Age centre selling crystals, tarot cards and books, runes, relaxation, meditation and new age music tapes and jewellery. Astrological birth charts done.

Mystic Trader

60 Chalk Farm Road
Camden Town
London NW1. (071) 284 0141.
Open every day 10.30-6.30. Sell books, audio tapes on personal empowerment and spiritual healing.

Mysteries

9 Monmouth St, Covent Garden WC2
(071) 240 3688

LIBRARIES

Church Street Library

Church Street
Kensington
London NW8. (071) 798 1480.
Section on religion.

Fulham Library

598 Fulham Road
London SW6 5NX. (081) 748 3020.
Christian religious collection.

Medical Library

Marylebone Library
Marylebone Road
London NW1 5PS. (071) 798 1039
Large collection of material on medicine, health and related topics. They are happy to answer telephone, written or personal enquiries.

Newham Bibliographical Services Department

62A Pond Road
Stratford
London E15. (071) 511 1332.
Section on Eastern Religion.

PUBLISHERS AND DISTRIBUTORS

The publishers listed below have recently published books in the holistic field. Some are large, general publishers who may have a small number of titles on health, self improvement or related subjects.

Arkana

27 Wrights Lane
London W8 5TZ. (071) 938 2200
Publish New Age books for Mind, Body and Spirit. Psychology, transformation, health, science and mysticism, women's spirituality and astrology.

Arrow Books

Random Century House
20 Vauxhall Bridge Rd
London SW1V 2SA. (071) 973 9700 ex 217.
A publisher of general titles, with some New Age, health and self help books.

Bantam Books

Transworld Publishers
61-63 Uxbridge Rd W5 5SA. (081) 579 2652/3
x442
General publishers with small range of self-help, popular psychology titles.

C W Daniel Comp Ltd

1 Church Path
Saffron Walden
Essex CB10 1JP. (0799) 21909
Publishers of books on natural healing, and the metaphysical and spiritual.

Dorling Kindersley

9 Henrietta Street
Covent Garden
London WC2E 8PS. (071) 836 5411.
Range of books strong on visuals covering health (including a series from the British Holistic Medical Association on common problems), yoga and massage, childcare, vegetarian cooking.

Element Books

The Old School House
The Courtyard, Bell St
Shaftesbury
Dorset SP7 8PL. (0747) 51448.
One of the largest publishers and distributers of books on eastern and western religious traditions, spiritual teachers, psychology, modern spirituality, healing etc.

Want to get your manuscript published?

We can supply you with our *Submissions Package* which gives full info of over 250 New Age/holistic health publishers complete with labels. Simply decide which publishers you want to approach, peel off the labels and attach to the envelopes containing copies of your sample chapter/synopsis and then post.

(071) 733 7883 or (071) 978 9062
BCM Raft, London WC1N 3XX
serving holistic business

Do you want your book or product reviewed?

We supply a *Reviewers Package* giving details of the types of reviews that New Age/holistic health publications do, complete with a set of mailing labels. You simply read the details about the reviewer, decide whether they are best suited to review your product or book and post off to them using the mailing labels provided.

(071) 733 7883 or (071) 978 9062
BCM Raft, London WC1N 3XX
serving holistic business

PUBLISHERS

Faber & Faber
3 Queens Square
London WC1N 3AU. (071) 465 0045.
Titles on religion, philosophy, health, medicine, nursing, midwifery and psychology.

Fontana Paperbacks
8 Grafton Street
London W1X 3LA. (071) 493 7070.
Some publications on health and green issues.

Foulsham
Yeovil Road
Slough
Berks SL1 4JH. (0753) 26769.
Publish various self help and health titles, and have just started a new imprint, Quantum, for 'the exploration of inner space and its practical application'.

Fowler & Co Ltd
1201 High Road
Chadwell Heath
Romford
Essex RM6 4DH. (081) 597 2491.
Shop open Mon-Fri 9-5. Astrology specialists and mind, body, spirit titles. Also carry cassette tapes. Small shop and mail order.

Free Association Books
26 Freegrove Road
London
N7 9RQ. 609 5646/0507.
Interesting range of books on psychoanalysis. There are titles exploring work of individuals, as well some attempting the worthy task of bringing psychology and politics closer together by exploring social issues and culture from a psychoanalytical viewpoint. Their journal, Free Associations, attempts to take this further by making psychoanalysis more relevant to urgent social issues and to contribute to a more socially conscious profession. Includes scholarly articles on women, race, power, group dynamics in institutions etc. £20 for 4 issues.

GAIA Books Ltd
20 High St
Stroud
Gloucestershire GL5 1AS. (0453) 752985
Titles on natural health and living, self development and ecology, including The Gaia Atlas of Planet Management. Independently owned company.

Grafton Books
8 Grafton Street
London W1. (071) 493 7070.
Some publications on green issues.

Macdonalds
3rd Floor
Greater London House
Hampstead Road
London NW1. (071) 377 4600.
Natural medicine, self help and green guides (including John Button's *Green Pages*).

Rider & Co
Random Century Group
20 Vauxhall Bridge Road
London SW1V 2SA. (071) 973 9000.
Publish books on ancient mysteries, divination, health and healing, martial arts, mysticism and religion, occult and personal growth.

Shanti Sadan
29 Chepstow Villas
Notting Hill Gate
London W11 3DR. (071) 727 7846.
Publications, books on yoga, Vedanta, poetry and the mysticism of the far east. Translations of Sanscrit classics. Publish 'Self Knowledge', a yoga quarterly journal devoted to spiritual thought and practice. Single copy including postage £1.50

Thorsons Publishing Group
77-85 Fulham Palace Road
Hammersmith
London W6 8JB. (081) 741 7070 x4735.
Large selection of titles in the Thorsons, Aquarian and Crucible range; health, self-help, spirituality, psychology, healing, psychism. Thorsons have cornered the health food shop market, where their bookstands are often to be seen on display.

University Associates International
45-47 Victoria Street
Mansfield
Notts NG18 5SU. 0623 640203.
Distribution centre of books on management training, organisation development, effective leadership etc.

Unwin & Hyman (Mandala)
15-17 Broadwick Street
London W1V 1FP. (071) 439 3126.
Publish the Mandala series, a large range of titles on personal growth, spirituality, healing etc.

Wellspring Publications Ltd
46 Cyril Mansions
Prince of Wales Drive
London SW11 4HW. (071) 720 3541.
Books and tapes on self discovery and the psychology of vision.

White Eagle Publishing Trust
9 St. Mary Abbots Place
Kensington
London W8 6LS. (0730) 893300.
Publishing wing of White Eagle Lodge (qv). Publish the work of White Eagle, a spirit guide, and others. Audio cassettes.

Wisebuy Publications
25 Rest Cottages
London NW6 1RJ. (071) 433 1121.
Publish three titles on food allergy, healthy eating and massage and relaxation.

FILMS

British Association for Counselling
37a Sheep Street
Rugby
Warwickshire CV21 3BX. (0788) 578328/9.
Catalogue can be purchased for £1 (including p&p) describing videos and films for hire.

Concord Video and Film Council
201 Felixstowe Road
Ipswich
Suffolk IP3 9BJ. (0473) 726012/715754.
Wide range of videos and films available for hire or purchase covering psychotherapy and counselling, alternative medicine, relationships, peace, social/global issues, the arts etc. Psychotherapy videos include famous therapists in action, coverage of issues such as death and bereavement, child abuse, eating disorders, drug addiction, group psychotherapy, counselling techniques etc. A real treat is the fly-on-the-wall's view of a Californian encounter group - get all the action without taking any of the risks! Hire charges range from £1 to £20, and sale from £20 to £200. Send £1 for video catalogue (includes updates).

MAGAZINES & PUBLICATIONS

Caduceus
38 Russell Terrace
Royal Leamington Spa
Warks
CV31 1HE. (0926) 451897.
Articles on holistic healing, natural health, spirituality and the connection between body, mind and spirit aimed at healers, health care professionals and members of the general public with an interest in exploring holistic health. Quarterly, £2.50 per issue, 38pp.

Directory of Occult Resources (DOOR)
Spiral Publications
8 King Street
Glastonbury
Somerset BA6 9JY.
Everything for the would-be Wiccan in here: groups, contacts and an impressive number of occult/pagan magazines and publications. £2.95 (UK) per year. Spiral also publish a journal, Starcraft, for £2 per issue.

Electromagnetics News
PO Box 25
Liphook
Hants GU30 7SE. (042) 877430.
Charts electromagnetic fields research, the effects of powerlines, VDUs and microwaves, and looks at safety guidelines and medical uses. Bi-monthly, subs £15 per annum.

Group Relations
152 Park St Lane
Park St
St Albans AL2 2AU. (0727) 872010.
A journal for people working in groups and teams. Published three times a year. £1.85 per issue. Sub £6.

Health Today
Queensway House
2 Queensway
Redhill, Surrey RH1 1QS. (0737) 768611.
Free magazine for shoppers in health food shops. Reports on health and green issues. Their special feature is 'The Green Hand Gang Pages' for kids.

Here's Health
Victory House
14 Leicester Place
London WC2H 7NB. (071) 437 9011.
Glossy monthly magazine available in newsagents with articles on natural medicine, nutrition, vegetarian cookery, holistic health, news, interviews and reviews.

Homoeopathy Today
Humane Education Centre
Avenue Lodge
Bounds Green Road
London N22 4EU. (081) 889 1595.
Articles about homoeopathy, research, history, institutions and uses and treatment of particular conditions. Published by the Hahnemann Society. Quarterly, subscription £8 per annum. Apply for specimen copy.

Human Potential
5 Layton Road
Islington
London N1. (071) 354 5792.
The who, what, where, when and why not of the 'growth' movement. Articles cover humanistic psychology, Jungian psychotherapy, sexuality, spirituality, controversy etc. with interviews and news, book reviews, and an extensive calendar of events with all the workshops and groups you could ever want to go to in the following three months. For subscription phone (081) 291 6254 . Quarterly, £5 per year.

Journal of Alternative and Complementary Medicine
Mariner House
53a High St
Bagshot
Surrey GU19 5AH. (0276) 51522.
Independent magazine devoted to alternative and complementary medicine. Published monthly by Green Library - £1.95. each issue. £25 sub.

Journal of Complementary Medicine
21 Portland Place
London W1N 3AF. (071) 636 9543.
An academic publication which focuses on research and hopes to promote complementary medicine to other fields of science. £3.95 per issue. Twice a year.

Kindred Spirit
Foxhole
Dartington
Totnes
Devon TQ9 6ED. (0803) 866686.
A 'New Age' magazine covering earth energies, meditation, healing, death, spiritual experiences, crystals, scientific breakthroughs, psychology, esoterica, complementary medicine, alternative therapies, environmental issues. Interviews with innovative thinkers, environmentalists, spiritual teachers and therapists, plus news, book reviews, a resource directory and mail order catalogue. Quarterly £2.40 per issue, or subscriptions £9.50 per annum. Full colour throughout.

Link Up

51 Northwick Business Centre
Blockley
Glos GL56 9RF. (0386) 701091.
Magazine with global perspective with articles on personal growth, spirituality etc. Qtly £1.85.

New Humanity

51A York Mansions
Prince of Wales Drive
London SW11 4BP. (071) 622 4013.
Envisages integrating the disciplines of science, philosophy, politics, the arts, religion and the humanities to promote closer co-operation and understanding among them. 'Endeavours to 'clarify a direction in which humanity might evolve towards harmony and integration through diversity of knowledge.' Bi-monthly, £1.50 per issue.

Open Mind

22 Harley St
London W1N 2ED. (071) 637 0741.
Published bi-monthly by MIND, the National Association for Mental Health. Now in it's eighth year of publication, the magazine has covered topics such as psychotherapy for troubled young people, complementary medicine, the politics of poverty, who should pick up the therapy bill... It has encouraged debate among health care professionals, patients and their relatives. OPEN MIND provides a regular 'benefits' column, an update on research in mental health publications, international developments and full listings of coming events. Yearly rates for six issues: £8 individuals, £10 organisations and institutions.

Psychic News

2 Tavistock Chambers
Bloomsbury Way
London WC1A 2SE. (071) 405 3340.
Established 1932. The world's only independent weekly Spiritualist paper containing news, reviews, events and comment. Price 24p. Obtainable from newsagents or direct subscription.

Rainbow Ark

PO Box 486
London SW1P 1AZ. (071) 828 2782.
Non profit making magazine with articles covering interesting and controversial ideas and possibilities: spiritual, ecological and humanitarian, green issues, health, new age, philosophy, esoterics, news, current affairs, reviews,

'odd thoughts spot'. Extensive diary listing holistic and green events. For free trial copy send 27p stamp to address above. Published quarterly. 50p per issue, £3 annual subs (incl p/p.).

Resurgence

Ford House
Bideford
Devon EX39 6EE. (0237) 441293.
Perhaps the most 'literary' of the magazines devoted to holistic topics, Resurgence can boast of contributors such as Kathleen Raine and James Hillman. A high standard of photography has recently been featured even more by the addition of colour pages. Subjects covered are ecology and its spiritual roots, cultural values, holistic education, world issues, religion, the countryside etc. Substantial book reviews section and a poetry section. Bi-monthly.

Skeptical Enquirer

10 Crescent View
Loughton
Essex IG10 4PZ.
Examines the claims of the paranormal world to expose frauds and charlatans. Subs £14 p.a. Four issues/yr.

Thomas Troward Society

20 Grove Park
London E11 2DL.
Publish 'New Light', the in-house journal of the Thomas Troward Society. £6/issue.

Transformer

New Life Designs Ltd
170 Campden Hill Road
London W8 7AS. (071) 938 3788.
Free resource guide of events, practitioners, products and services. Quarterly. Spring issue is also programme for Festival of Mind, Body, Spirit.

Vegan Society

7 Battle Road
St Leonards on Sea
East Sussex TN37 7AA. (0424) 427393.
The Vegan magazine is the Journal of the Vegan Society. 36 pages, quarterly. Single issue £1, subs £5 pa. News, articles, health and nutrition, recipes, young vegans pages, book and product reviews. Also publish books on aspects of veganism, including The Cruelty Free Shoppper (£3.99 from them) which contains comprehensive listings of products made and tested without cruelty to animals.

Vegetarian Magazine
ESG Publishing
3rd Floor
58 High Street
Sutton, Surrey. (081)770 7337.
Magazine of the Vegetarian Society, attractive format and articles on nutrition, environmental issues, news and as you might expect, lots of vegetarian recipes and mouth-watering pictures. Bi-monthly, £1.

Yoga and Health
21 Cadburn Crescent
Lewes
East Sussex BN7 1NR. (0273) 473495 / (0425)
616483.
Monthly magazine covering all aspects of yoga and its health aspects, alternative therapies, book reviews, reviews of new products. £1.50.

NETWORKS

Networks can range from highly structured organisations with strict membership criteria, to loose, informal contact groups. Some are simply information services, while others aim to help members exchange skills and resources.

Ace of Rods
Acca and Adda
BCM Akademia
London WC1N 3XX.
Contacts magazine for Wiccans/Pagans and for those who seek their vision. Contacts ads free to subscribers. 8 issues £7.50 pa.

Acorn Centre
Spindlewood
Watery Lane
Lower Westholme
Shepton Mallet, Somerset. (074 989) 338.
Events and conferences, meditation adventures around the British Isles. Also books mail order.

Association for Therapeutic Healers
Flat 5
54-56 Neal St
London WC2 9PH. (071) 240 0176.
A meeting point for the 'new' healers - support groups, courses, seminars, workshops, open days, talks and a regular newsletter. Register of practitioners. Membership £15 per year for newsletter, reduced fees for seminars, inclusion on register etc. Must be proposed and seconded by existing members.

Breakthrough Centre
7 Poplar Mews
Uxbridge Road
Shepherds Bush
London W12 7JS. (081) 749 8525.
Centre and network serving those who wish to combine personal growth, the sane, humane, ecological (SHE) enonomy and practical commercial approaches. Support for owner-managed small businesses, transforming large organisations, and career development courses and advice. Workshops on personal development in a commercial context. Open house time Tuesday to Saturday 5-7pm for contacts. Sunday evening meditation and sharing (second Sunday of the month, except August). Breakthrough club for owner managers. Noticeboards.

Business Network
18 Well Walk
Hampstead
London NW3 1LD. (071) 435 5000.
For the subscription of £35 per year, you get a register of members with whom to network, a monthly meeting with guest speakers and time for discussion and socialising, members' announcements or for browsing the networking tables, as well as a newsletter (bi- or tri-annually). Entry to meetings is £5 to members, £8 to non-members.

Centres Network
10-14 Macklin Street
London WC2B 5NG.

First Editions
PO Box 2578
Sedona AZ 86336
United States . (0101) 602/282 9574.
New marketing opportunities -international directory of 9,000 listings and newsletter. Cooperative mailings to the USA, metaphysical retailers. Mailing lists and workshops.

GAIA
2-4 High Street
Glastonbury
Somerset BA6 9DU. (0458) 34131.
They provide 'alternative information' on vegetarian Bed and Breakfasts, guides and tours, rooms for hire, festivals in the Glastonbury

area. They have 30 healers and therapists registered with them.

Gender Network
BM Network
London WC1N 3XX. (071) 923 1534 or (071) 372 5917.
A self-help group for people with gender dysphoria (transsexuals).

Holistic Health Contact Group
(071) 351 2726.

Ixia Ltd
PO Box 1255
London W4 3PX. 994 3010.
Ixia produce a monthly diary of events in the areas of personal growth, ecology, complementary medicine, earth mysteries, higher awareness and other related subjects, in date order. Events include lectures, seminars, weekends, workshops etc. Inclusion is free, and it costs £12 for you to subscribe to a year's posted bulletins, which come in booklet form with descriptions of each event. Also keep database of organisations dedicated to providing information or education on a sustainable basis (though counselling and treatments on their own are not included at present).

Neal's Yard Agency (for personal development)
14 Neal's Yard
Covent Garden
London WC2 9DP. (071) 379 0141.
An agency which can book you in to any workshop, training or personal development course and holidays on its books. There is no fee to the public. Drop in and browse through the brochures on display. You can also book over the phone, credit cards accepted. The staff can give informed and impartial advice. The agency also offers one-off consultancy sessions (£25) to individuals who are considering having counselling to help them decide which approach might be best. They also offer a 'personal audit' session (£30) to help clarify your personal assets, liabilities, aspirations and future directions.

Scientific and Medical Network
The Old School House
Hampnett
Northleach
Glos GL54 3NN. (0451) 60869.
Informal international group whose 600 strong membership consists mainly of qualified scientists and doctors, with some psychologists, engineers and philosophers. It aims to extend contemporary scientific and medical thinking beyond its current materialistic way of looking at the world, and include non-physical possibilities. Its main concerns include the Nature of consciousness; brain/mind interface, parapsychology, causality; healing, psychoneuro-immunology; science, ecology and spirituality; values in education and training. Publishes newsletter 3 times yearly. Associate membership open to those sympathetic with aims (£7.50 pa). Full membership by invitation only to scientists. Members receive members lists, and can participate in local groups, working groups and special seminars and lectures. Mail order tapes of lectures.

Whole Health Institute
Mickleton House
Mickleton
Chipping Campden
Glos GL55 6RY. (0386) 438727.
Aims to provide a focus and meeting ground for professionals and lay people interested in the cause of health, and promote a new spirit in the healing arts, from both a traditional and non-traditional standpoint. Headquarters are in the USA.

PRODUCTS

AIR PURIFIERS

Amcor Appliances Ltd
19 Woodfield Road
Paddington
London W9 2BA. (071) 289 4433.

Air Improvement Centre
23 Denbigh Street
London SW1V 2HF. (071) 834 2834.
Mon-Fri 9.30-5.30. Sat 10-1. Showroom stocking and supplying a wide range of air improvement products by different manufacturers. As well as air purifiers and ionisers, also stock humidifiers, de-humidifiers and mobile air conditioners. Also have stands in the electrical departments of Harrods and Selfridges.

AROMATHERAPY OILS

Aromatherapy oils or 'essential' oils are extracted from plants, flowers or trees and used in aromatherapy (see relevant entry in 'Body' section). Aromatherapy has recently become extremely popular and essential oils have even started appearing in some high street chain stores, often accompanied by leaflets on self-help use. However, while food and herbal medicine are regulated to a certain extent in terms of contents, standards and quality, at present there is no official standard by which the purity of essential oils can be measured, though some reputable essential oils manufacturers are now looking at this problem. The quality of the plants used and the conditions they have been grown in also affect the therapeutic potency of the oils. For instance, if artificial fertilizers or pesticides have been used, the oils could be adulterated with toxins. The best means of extracting the oils is through distillation, but adulteration can also take place in this process of extraction. Furthermore, the oils are suspended in vegetable oils and some manufacturers may dilute their oils much more than others, so it is difficult to tell which oils are good value for money. Some products called aromatherapy oils may not even contain the plant essence they are named after, because synthetic oils can be produced which contain the same active substances and smell the same as the original oil.

Perhaps the best way to ensure the

quality of oils is to buy from a supplier with a background in aromatherapy, or those who work closely with consultant trained aromatherapists. Get information from them about their oils, how they ensure quality and ask about dilution ratios.

Acumedic Centre
101-103 Camden High Street
Camden
London NW1. (071) 388 5783.
Shop on the main Camden High St. They sell books on acupuncture and Chinese medicine, with an assortment of alternative medicine aids such as ionisers, mas-

sage equipment, tapes and biofeedback machines.

Aromatique
Sarnett House
Repton Drive
Gidea Park
Essex RM2 5LP. (0708) 720289.
Mail order. Cosmetics and toiletries containing essential oils for different skin and hair conditions.

Cosmos Herbs
329 Chiswick High Road
London W4 4HS. (081) 995 7239.
11am-6pm Mon-Sat. Medicinal herbs and remedies sold, as well as occult ritual supplies and an intriguing range of incense and oils (from Luv Luv Luv oil to Graveyard dust). Member of British Herbal Medicine Association. Mail order available.

Baldwin and Co
173 Walworth Road
Camberwell
London SE17 1RW. (071) 703 5550.

Institute of Clinical Aromatherapy
22 Bromley Road
Catford
London SE6 2TP. (081) 690 2149.
Mail order essential oils and vegetable oils.

217

PRODUCTS

Hermitage Oils
East Morton
Keighley BD20 5UQ. (0274) 565957.
Retail and wholesale. Extensive range of oils of different qualities. Rapid turn round on orders. Telephone above number or send SAE for list and order form.

Fleur
8 Baden Rd
London N8. (081) 340 4097.
Can visit by appointment. They supply new age shops, health food shops and they do mail order.

Jolanta Health Products
78 Meadow Street
Preston PR1 1TS. (0722) 325177.
Vegetable oils, toiletries etc.

Ionisers (UK)
3 Gordon Cresent
Broad Meddows
South Normanton DE55 3AJ. (0773) 863034.
Ionisers range between £39-£495. They also sell a range of about 20 different Aromatherapy oils which are infused with Homoeopathic remedies.

Quinessence
3a Birch Avenue
Whitwick
Leicestershire LE6 3GB. (0530) 38358/180779.
Affiliated to the International Federation of Aromatherapists, mail order essential oils and essential oil remedies, ready mixed lotions and massage oils, vaporisers and mood enhancers - from 'wild passion' to 'celestial dream'! Free advice service from qualified aromatherapist.

Neal's Yard Apothecary
2 Neal's Yard
off Shorts Gardens
London WC2H 9DP. (071) 379 7222.
Mon, Tues, Thurs 10-6, Wed, Sat 10-5.30. Also at Chelsea Farmers Market, Sydney Street, London SW3 (which is also open Sun 11-4) and 68 Chalk Farm Road, London NW1. (071) 284 2039. Cosmetics and toiletries, nutritional supplements, essential oils, herbal tinctures (including Chinese), medicinal herbs and powders, gifts. Nice line in naturally scented vegetable oil soaps, and toiletries and preprations packed in cute blue bottles.

Micheline Arcier Aromatherapy
7 William Street
Knightsbridge
London SW1X 9HL. (071) 235 3545 .
The shop sells face oils, body oils and bath oils made from essential oils.

Shirley Price Aromatherapy
Wesley House
Stockwell Head
Hinckley LE10 1RD. (0455) 615466.
Comprehensive range of essential oils and aromatherapy skin care. Mail order.

BACK PRODUCTS

Alternative Sitting
PO Box 19
Chipping Norton
Oxford OX7 6NY. (0608) 658875.
Specialists in work and domestic ergonomic problems. Sell ergonomic furniture.

Back Store Ltd
330 King Street
Hammersmith
London W6. (081) 741 5022.
Mon-Fri 10-6, Sats 10-4. Everything for the back is here. Allow yourself some time to choose.

Back Shop
24 New Cavendish Street
London W1M 7LH. (071) 935 9120.
10am-6pm Mon-Sat. All manner of things for the back are here including chairs, pillows, beds, shoes, exercise equipment and meditation stools which give correct support to the back, and even a 'massage

pillow' — a cushion which vibrates to give you your own portable massage. Also books, videos, mail order

Pelvic Support Chairs
New Mill Lane
Eversley
Hants RG27 0RA. (0734) 732365.
Pelvic support chairs, car accessories and the Nada chair - not really a chair but a portable back support sling.

Banana Chair Company
Barton Road
Long Eaton
Nottingham NG10 2FN. (0602) 463616.
Sell the 'banana chair'. A revolutionary version of a rocking chair, but designed to be easy on the back.

Wholistic Research Company
Bright Haven
Robin's Lane
Lolworth
Cambridge CB3 8HH. (0954) 781074.
Enormous range of mail order holistic health equipment also includes grain mills, pulsors, biomagnetic therapy equipment, herbal tablet makers, reflex foot rollers, humane mouse traps, enema/douche kits, iridology equipment, and mail order books. They also publish a handy booklet which explains the use of each product, and gives instructions on benefits, and how to use them.

BIOFEEDBACK MACHINES
Biofeedback machines are electrical equipment which give information about mood and state of mind through either measuring brain wave patterns or muscle tension. The machine has to be in contact in some way with the body and measures physical changes which reflect emotional or mental changes. The so-called lie detector is an example of the biofeedback machine, as is equipment

used to measure the brain wave frequency of, for instance, people meditating.

Audio Limited
26-28 Wendell Road
London W12. (081) 743 1518 or 743 4352.
Sell several machines designed to measure brainwave frequencies and monitor states of mind. Also manufacture the therapeutic strobe to alter mood.

Healthwatch UK
4 Valley Road
Weaverham
Cheshire CW8 3PP. (0606) 853554.
Make a watch which monitors stress using biofeedback - it displays a number between 0 and 99 to let you know how stressed you are. Comes with book and costs £59.95 plus £1.25 p&p.

John Bell and Croyden
Medical Dept.
54 Wigmore Street
London W1. (071) 935 5555.
Sell Biofeedback machines that also have instruction tapes attached to them. They also have a wide range of aids for disabled people.

Euroneuro
Acorn Bookshop
17 Chatham Street
Reading RG1 7JF. (0734) 664914.
Sell their 'Light and Sound Machine' (mind machine) for inducing relaxation and creativity, and for increased learning ability. You wear thick sunglasses which emit light into the wearers eyes in rythym to the music played through earphones. Mail order. Will provide brochure.

BIORYTHM CHARTS

K Marks
170 Buckingham Road
Hampton
Middlesex .

London Biorhythm Co Ltd
Wickham House
10 Cleveland Way
London E1. (071) 790 2424.
Biorythm charts and the 'bio display unit', a do-it-yourself biorhythm kit. Also do research into biorhythms and their effects and publish newsletter (£9 per year for 6 issues).

BIRTHING POOLS

These are (usually circular or oval) pools filled with water in which women can give birth. Giving birth in water is said to ease the pain of contractions and provide an enviroment in which women can relax in the favoured position for active birth, crouching or kneeling. The agencies listed below provide pools for hire or sale.

Active Birth Centre
55 Dartmouth Park Road
Kentish Town
London NW5 1SL. (071) 267 5368.
Hire out portable water birth pools. Ring for catalogue.

Birthworks
4e Brent Mill Trading Estate
South Brent
Devon TQ10 9YT. (0364) 72802
Available for sale or hire at £35 per week. Two types available: circular one which can be dismantled, and fixed rectangular one for hospitals.

Splashdown Birth Pools
17 Wellington Terrace
Harrow-on-the-Hill
Middlesex HA1 3EP. (081) 422 9308.
Water birth pools for hire or sale, with a choice of round and oval. Pools measure 5ft in diameter by 26 ins deep. £125 plus £20 for sterilised liner for four weeks standby hire. Door-to-door delivery anywhere in the UK. Free advice and information packs on water birth to enquirers, free water birth workshops. Sell and loan books and cassettes.

Birthing Tub Company
Pakyns Lodge
Albourne Road
Hurstpierpoint
W Sussex BN6 9ET. (0273) 835245.
Manufacturers and suppliers of portable, collapsible, wooden water pools for use in labour and childbirth. The cost including delivery and return to anywhere in the U.K. is £150 for a period of two weeks before the birth until a suitable time afterwards.

BOOKS

Acumedic Centre
101-103 Camden High Street
Camden
London NW1. (071) 388 5783.
Shop on the main Camden High St. They sell books on acupuncture and Chinese medicine, with an assortment of alternative medicine aids such as ionisers, massage equipment, tapes and biofeedback machines.

Gale Centre for Creative Therapy
Stable Cottage
Whitakers Way
Loughton
Essex IG10 1SJ. (081) 508 9344.

Middle Earth
Unit 3 Trading World
131 Broadway
Bexley Heath
Kent
(081) 298 0246.

Lifeskills
3 Brighton Road
Finchley
London N2 8JU. (081) 346 9646 or 580 4972.
Mail order and telephone order only. Established 12 years. Typical prices £8 per tape (incl VAT).

Understanding
28 Hollyfield Avenue
London N11 3BY. (081) 368 0865.
A mail order business selling books and charts on reflexology. Send SAE for brochure.

Gale Centre
Whitakers Way
Loughton
Essex IG10 1BR. (081) 508 9344.
Sell by mail order a range of books and tapes on counselling and therapy. Slanted towards those in the caring professions, especially social workers.

CLOTHES AND SHOES

Back Shop
24 New Cavendish Street
London W1M 7LH. (071) 935 9120.
10am-6pm Mon-Sat. All manner of things for the back are here including chairs, pillows, beds, shoes, exercise equipment and meditation stools which give correct support to the back, and even a 'massage pillow' — a cushion which vibrates to give you your own portable massage. Also books, videos, mail order.

Green Farm Nutrition Centre
Burwash Common
East Sussex TN19 7LX. (0435) 882482/883457.
Large mail order catalogue with lambswool bedding, VDU screens also available. Large range of dietary supplements, and skin and hair care products.

Natural Shoe Store (2)
21 Neal Street
London WC2. (071) 836 5254.

Natural Shoe Store (1)
325 King's Road
London SW3. (071) 351 3721.
Range of shoes both British and American designed to be kind and easy on the feet. Branch at Neal Street.

CRUELTY FREE PRODUCTS

Sesonol Organic Hair Products
P O Box 14
Worthing
West Sussex BN11 1BR.
Organic hair preparations available mail order.

CRYSTALS

Delta Minerals
PO Box 1761
London W9 3BY. (081) 968 8496.
Crystals, minerals and gems; pyramids and other geometic dynamics, magical and healing wands. Mail order or phone for appointment.

Crystal 2000
37 Bromley Road
St Annes-on-Sea
Lancs FY8 1PQ. (0253) 723735.
Also crystal light torches for colour crystal healing and crystal light boxes.

PRODUCTS

British Lapidary and Mineral Dealers Association
Glenjoy
19/21 Sun Lane
Wakefield WR1 1JD. (0924) 373786.
One of the oldest established importers of crystals in the UK for wholesale and retail. As well as all the usual crystals and gems, supply aqua aura crystals which are coated with a transparent layer of gold, giving them a blue aura and appearance similar to aquamarine. Also arrange gem and mineral fairs.

Crystal Connection
23 Camden Lock
London NW1 8AF. (071) 267 4325.
Open seven days a week. 11.30-7.30. Crystals, balls, pyramids, gems, books, pictures, jewellery.

Kernowcraft
Bolingey
Perranporth
Cornwall TR6 0DH. (0872) 573888.
Mail order supplier, retail and wholesale. Precious and semi-precious stones, crystals, available also in bead form. Mounts, chains and fastenings for jewellery making, as well as silversmithing equipment. Pyramids, spheres, obelisks, wands, standing points etc. - ask for the crystal list when applying for information.

Everlasting Gems
Unit Q14/15, Antiquarius Antique Centre, 131/141 Kings Road
Chelsea
London SW3. (071) 351 6548.
Mon-Sat 10-6. Retail shop which specialises in selling spectacular crystals and mineral specimens. Also importers and wholesalers of minerals and crystals, specialising in unusual and spectacular pieces.

Middle Earth
Unit 3 Trading World
131 Broadway
Bexley Heath
Kent
(081) 298 0246.

Natural Art Gallery
Unit Q14-15, 131/141 King's Road
Chelsea
London SW3. (081) 949 8126.

Rainbow Gems
The Railway Arches
1st Rainbow Arch, Camden Lock Market
(off Chalk Farm Road) NW1. (081) 802 9196.
Rainbow Gems trades on Saturday and Sunday from 9.30-6 at Camden Lock market, and, as well as a selection of crystals and minerals, both polished and natural, sells pyramids, spheres, eggs and wands. Also do gem elixirs.

New World Aurora
16A Neal's Yard
Covent Garden
London WC2. (071) 379 0818.
Open Mon-Sat 10-6. This shop is open to the public and stocks a wide range of natural quartz crystals, dowsing pendulums, rainbow crystal jewellery and balls, cards and posters and 'New Age' music and videos. Also mail order.

Snapdragon
12 South Park
Sevenoaks
Kent TN13 1AN. (0732) 740252.
Mystical cards, tarot cards, crystal balls, special incense, healing pendants, pendulums. Keep a list of alternative medicine practitioners in the area. Tapes for healing.

Wessex Impex Ltd
Stonebridge Farmhouse
Breadsell Lane
St Leonards on Sea
East Sussex TN38 8EB. (042) 483 659.
Visitors by appointment only please. Importers of rough crystals. Manufac-

turers of crystal jewellery, gemmologists, lapidaries, wholesale and retail.

DAYLIGHT BULBS

Otherwise known as full spectrum lighting, this is used to treat seasonal affective disorder (shortened to 'SAD') which is a form of depression caused by lack of sunlight, and which some people get in the winter. The lack of sunlight affects the pineal gland, which starts to secrete too much of a hormone called melatonin, which causes depression.

Full Spectrum Lighting
Unit 5 Wye Industrial Estate
London Road
High Wycombe
Bucks HP11 1LH. (0494) 26051
Bulbs fitted with full spectrum light, particularly for the alleviation of Seasonal Affective Disorder (SAD) or 'Winter Depression', now a recognised medical condition that can be helped by exposure to a light level of 2500 lux which accurately simulates the spectrum of natural day light.

Hygeia College of Colour Therapy
Brook House
Tetbury
Glos GL8 8NS. (045383) 2150.
Health-oriented illumination: lamps, true-lite tubes. Also colour therapy instruments.

Wholistic Research Company
Bright Haven
Robin's Lane
Lolworth
Cambridge CB3 8HH. (0954) 781074.
Enormous range of mail order holistic health equipment also includes grain mills, pulsors, biomagnetic therapy equipment, herbal tablet makers, reflex foot rollers, humane mouse traps, enema/douche kits, iridology equipment, and

mail order books. They also publish a handy booklet which explains the use of each product, and gives instructions on benefits, and how to use them.

DIY ACUPUNCTURE

Acumedic Centre
101-103 Camden High Street
Camden
London NW1. (071) 388 5783.
Shop on the main Camden High St. They sell books on acupuncture and Chinese medicine, with an assortment of alternative medicine aids such as ionisers, massage equipment, tapes and biofeedback machines.

ETHICALLY SOUND INVESTMENTS

Acorn Ethical Unit Trusts
1 White Hart Yard
London
SE1 1NX. (071) 407 5966.

FLOAT TANKS

Floatarium Ltd
21 Bond Street
Brighton BN1 1RD. (0273) 679555.
Established 1988. Sphinx flotation tank sold, a deluxe size in which two people can float at the same time! Back-up information service for purchasers. Also available is the 'Dream Machine', which provides programmes of light and sound to promote different moods and mental states.

South London Natural Health Centre
7A Clapham Common South Side
Clapham Common
London SW4 7AA. (071) 720 8817.
Phone 720 9506 for Gracemill Ltd who are manufacturers and installers of the 'ocean float room'.

PRODUCTS

Float Centre
20 Blenheim Terrace
St Johns Wood
London NW8 OEB. (071) 328 7276.
Sell the 'Open Float Room' ™, which is 8ft high x 8ft long x 4ft wide. Can be custom built to suit your premises. Provide staff training and back up consultancy to those interested in starting up their own commercial centre. Staff training on how to run a float centre - £225 per day incl VAT. Contact Samantha O'Connor.

FOOD PRODUCTS

3HO Kundalini Yoga Foundation
55 Sunny Gardens Road
London NW4 1SJ. (081) 203 7302.
Sell their famous 'Yogi Tea'.

FUTONS

Futon Express
23-27 Pancras Road
London NW1 2QB. (071) 833 3945.
10-6pm Mon-Sat. Hand made, 100% cotton filled futons and futon sofa beds as well as the 'Party Paker' portable futon for those who don't want to risk a night on their host's camp bed. Branches at 56 Chalk Farm Road, NW1 (485 1000) and 149 St Johns Hill, SW11 (924 2517).

Futon Factory
192 Balls Pond Road
London N1 4AA. (071) 226 4477.
Pure cotton futons with stylish patterned covers, and the 'Floaton' - a futon on a special waterbed which distributes pressure evenly.

Futon Company
654A Fulham Road
London SW6 5RU. (071) 736 9190.

GAMES

Trading Centre
Findhorn Foundation
The Park
Forres
Scotland IV36 0TZ. (0309) 691074.
Produce the Transformation Game: "a playful yet substantial way of understanding and transforming the way you play your life. Just as life is filled with insights, setbacks, pain and miracles, so is the Transformation Game. It mirrors players' lives, highlighting strengths, identifying blind spots and bringing fresh perspectives to current challenges". Also sell Angel cards, nature and tree calendar, tree diary.

HERBS AND HERBAL REMEDIES

Culpeper Herbalists
8 The Market
Covent Garden
Piazza WC2. (071) 379 6698.
Mon-Sat 10-8, Sun 11.30-7. Range of herbs, also cruelty free toiletries.

Cosmos Herbs
329 Chiswick High Road
London W4 4HS. (081) 995 7239.
11am-6pm Mon-Sat. Medicinal herbs and remedies sold, as well as occult ritual supplies and an intriguing range of incense and oils (from Luv Luv Luv oil to Graveyard dust). Member of British Herbal Medicine Association. Mail order available.

Bioforce UK Ltd
Unit 8, Dukes Road
Branchline Industrial Estate
Troon, Ayshire
Scotland KA10 6QR. (0292) 316664.
Large manufacturer of natural health products such as foods and food supplements, tonics, herbal preparations etc.

Herbalists
74 Lee High Road
London SE13. (081) 852 9792.
They have been established since 1926 and offer herbal consultations. Open between 8.30am and 5.15pm.

East Asia Company
101 - 103 Camden High Street
Camden
London
(071) 388 5783 or 388 6704.
Wide range of books on Alternative Medicine as well as books on general health, symptom alleviation, natural living, oriental philosophy and lifestyle. They do charts (such as reflexology charts) on health for practitioners as well as for the public. Sell herbal and homoeopathic remedies.

Nutribiotics
35 Highview Avenue
Edgware
Middlesex HA8 9TX. (081) 958 7553.
Supply specially potentised homoeopathic and herbal remedies, and also stock aloe vera gel products. Sell a first aid homoeopathic kit.

Neal's Yard Apothecary
2 Neal's Yard
off Shorts Gardens
London WC2H 9DP. (071) 379 7222.
Mon, Tues, Thurs 10-6, Wed, Sat 10-5.30. Also at Chelsea Farmers Market, Sydney Street, London SW3 (which is also open Sun 11-4) and 68 Chalk Farm Road, London NW1. (071) 284 2039. Cosmetics and toiletries, nutritional supplements, essential oils, herbal tinctures (including Chinese), medicinal herbs and powders, gifts. Nice line in naturally scented vegetable oil soaps, and toiletries and preprations packed in cute blue bottles.

Bach Flower Remedies Ltd
Dr Bach Centre
Mount Vernon
Sotwell, Wallingford,
Oxon OX10 0PZ. (0491) 33712.
Sell a range of Bach flower remedies. If you wish to place an order then send to Bach Flower Remedies, Unit 6, Suffolk Way, Drayton Road, Abingdon, Oxon OX14 5JX.

HOMOEOPATHIC PHARMACIES

Ainsworths Homoeopathic Pharmacy
38 New Cavendish Street
London W1M 7LH. (071) 935 5330/(08833) 40332.
Same day postal supply of all traditional homoeopathic medicines including many novel remedies. Veterinary remedies as well.

E Gould and Son
14 Crowndale Road
London NW1 1TT. (071) 388 4752.
Mon-Fri 9-5.45. Closed Sats. Open Sun am.

East Asia Company
101 - 103 Camden High Street
Camden
London
(071) 388 5783 or 388 6704.
Wide range of books on Alternative Medicine as well as books on general health, symptom alleviation, natural living, oriental philosophy and lifestyle. They do charts (such as reflexology charts) on health for practitioners as well

as for the public. Sell herbal and homoeopathic remedies.

Nelson & Co
73 Duke Street
London W1. (071) 629 3118.

IONISERS

Ions are gas molecules present in the air which carry a positive or negative charge. Research has shown that positive ions have the effect of making people more irritable, tired and perform less well, and that negative ions in the air tend to make people more alert and perform better. Negative ions are produced by such things as plants, the breaking of water into droplets and by ultra-violet light from the sun. Positive ions are produced, among other things, by fluorescent lighting, electronic equipment, air conditioning and man-made fabrics - though humankind isn't to blame for all positive ions, because there are certain winds which blow in certain parts of the world, and are known to contain a high proportion of positive ions. When such winds blow, legend and experience show that crime and traffic accidents increase.

Ionisers increase the amount of negative ions in the air. They are usually small and fairly inexpensive, and are often used by people who work in office conditions to counteract the effect of the synthetic environment.

ClearAir
PO Box 83
Covent Garden
London WC2H 9AJ.

Air Improvement Centre
23 Denbigh Street
London SW1V 2HF. (071) 834 2834.
Mon-Fri 9.30-5.30. Sat 10-1. Showroom stocking and supplying a wide range of air improvement products by different manufacturers. As well as air purifiers and ionisers, also stock humidifiers, dehumidifiers and mobile air conditioners. Also have stands in the electrical departments of Harrods and Selfridges.

Ionisers (UK)
3 Gordon Crescent
Broad Meddows
South Normanton DE55 3AJ. (0773) 863034.
Ionisers range between £39-£495. They also sell a range of about 20 different Aromatherapy oils which are infused with Homoeopathic remedies.

Green Farm Nutrition Centre
Burwash Common
East Sussex TN19 7LX. (0435) 882482/883457.
Large mail order catalogue with lambswool bedding, VDU screens also available. Large range of dietary supplements, and skin and hair care products.

Mountain Breeze Air Ionizers
6 Priorswood Place
Skelmersdale
Lancashire WN8 9QB. (0695) 21155.
Room and car ionisers, air filters and an aromatherapy oil diffuser.

London Ioniser Centre
65 Endell Street
Covent Garden
London WC2H 9AJ. (071) 379 7323.
You can go and inspect and buy ionisers which can serve areas from 25 foot square to 50 foot square here. This shop is independent of manufucturers, and is involved in interesting research into the benefits of ionisers.

PRODUCTS

Surplus Value
Freepost
Stockport
Cheshire SK2 6YB. (061 483) 9436.

Wholistic Research Company
Bright Haven
Robin's Lane
Lolworth
Cambridge CB3 8HH. (0954) 781074.
Enormous range of mail order holistic
health equipment also includes grain
mills, pulsors, biomagnetic therapy
equipment, herbal tablet makers, reflex
foot rollers, humane mouse traps, en-
ema/douche kits, iridology equipment,
and mail order books. They also publish
a handy booklet which explains the use
of each product, and gives instructions
on benefits, and how to use them.

JEWELLERY

Crystal Connection
23 Camden Lock
London NW1 8AF. (071) 267 4325.
Open seven days a week. 11.30-7.30pm.
Crystals, balls, pyramids, gems, books,
pictures, jewellery.

Celtia Ltd
Celtia House
Longrock
Penzance
Cornwall TR20 8HX. (0736) 51680.
Celtic design jewellery, belts, purses,
bags, ornaments, cards and celtic inspired
compositions on tape.

Kernowcraft
Bolingey
Perranporth
Cornwall TR6 0DH. (0872) 573888.
Mail order supplier, retail and wholesale.
Precious and semi-precious stones,
crystals, available also in bead form.
Mounts, chains and fastenings for jew-
ellery making, as well as silversmithing

equipment. Pyramids, spheres, obelisks,
wands, standing points etc. - ask for the
crystal list when applying for information.

Rainbow Gems
The Railway Arches
1st Rainbow Arch, Camden Lock Market
(off Chalk Farm Road) NW1. (081) 802 9196.
Rainbow gems trades on Saturday and
Sunday from 9.30-6 at Camden Lock
market and, as well as a selection of
crystals and minerals, both polished and
natural, sells pyramids, spheres, eggs
and wands. Also do gem elixirs.

New World Aurora
16A Neal's Yard
Covent Garden
London WC2. (071) 379 0818.
Open Mon-Sat 10-6. This shop is open to
the public and stocks a wide range of
natural quartz crystals, dowsing pendulums, rainbow crystal jewellery and balls,
cards and posters and 'New Age' music
and videos. Also mail order.

Wessex Impex Ltd
Stonebridge Farmhouse
Breadsell Lane
St Leonards on Sea
East Sussex TN38 8EB. (042) 483 659 .
Visitors by appointment only please.
Importers of rough crystals. Manufac-
turers of crystal jewellery, gemmologists,
lapidaries, wholesale and retail.

JUICERS

Juicers extract the juices of fruit, vegetables and sometimes of herbs and plants.
Consuming fresh juice is a way of in-
gesting high doses of nutrients for
therapeutic purposes - for instance in the
Gerson cancer therapy diet which features fresh juice as part of the detoxification process. Many healthy people also
like to drink juice, because they feel it

helps to maintain good health.

There are different types of juicer. Centrifugal juicers grate the fruit or vegetable and then spin the pulp, forcing the juice out by centrifugal force. These are the cheapest juicers, but they tend not to extract such a high level of nutrients as other models. Nose cone pressure juicers break down the material with a cutter or masticator. This is then forced into a cone under high pressure, and the juice is forced out. This method produces juice which is rich in nutrients, but it is more expensive than the centrifugal juicer. With juice presses the material is first pulped, then put into a strong nylon cloth which retains the pulp when the juice is squeezed out by a press.

Green Farm Nutrition Centre
Burwash Common
East Sussex TN19 7LX. (0435) 882482/883457.
Large mail order catalogue with lambswool bedding, VDU screens also available. Large range of dietary supplements, and skin and hair care products.

Wholistic Research Company
Bright Haven
Robin's Lane
Lolworth
Cambridge CB3 8HH. (0954) 781074.
Enormous range of mail order holistic health equipment also includes grain mills, pulsors, biomagnetic therapy equipment, herbal tablet makers, reflex foot rollers, humane mouse traps, enema/douche kits, iridology equipment, and mail order books. They also publish a handy booklet which explains the use of each product, and gives instructions on benefits, and how to use them.

Dragon Martial Arts
128 Myddleton Road
London N22 4NQ. (081) 889 0965.
Weds, Thurs, Sats 9.30-5.30. Books, equipment, suits and martial arts weaponry.

Shaolin Way
10 Little Newport Street
London WC2. (071) 734 6391.
A shop which sells martial arts supplies of different designs. 11-7pm seven days a week.

Biocomfort Ltd
VC House
London Road
Sevenoaks
Kent TN13 2TE. (0732) 462816.

Back Shop
24 New Cavendish Street
London W1M 7LH. (071) 935 9120.
10am-6pm Mon-Sat. All manner of things for the back are here including chairs, pillows, beds, shoes, exercise equipment and meditation stools which give correct support to the back, and even a 'massage pillow' — a cushion which vibrates to give you your own portable massage. Also books, videos, mail order.

Green Farm Nutrition Centre
Burwash Common
East Sussex TN19 7LX. (0435) 882482/883457.
Large mail order catalogue with lambswool bedding, VDU screens also available. Large range of dietary supplements, and skin and hair care products.

PRODUCTS

Porta-Ped Mini Couch
28 Hollyfield Avenue
London N11 3BY. (081) 368 0865.

MISCELLANEOUS

Applied Technology Alternative Medicine Ltd
42 Ospringe Road
Faversham
Kent ME13 7IJ. (0795) 535143.
ATAM supply computer systems for homoeopathic prescribing for practitioners, but are now bringing out a system for self-diagnosis which can be used by non-professionals.

Lois Mary Blackburn
53 St John's Priory Park
Farringdon Road
Lechlade
Gloucestershire GL7 3EZ.
Stained glass artist with interest in the healing aspects of colour and symbolic images. Small or large pieces to commission.

Trading Centre
Findhorn Foundation
The Park
Forres
Scotland IV36 0TZ. (0309) 691074.
Produce the Transformation Game: "a playful yet substantial way of understanding and transforming the way you play your life. Just as life is filled with insights, setbacks, pain and miracles, so is the Transformation Game. It mirrors players lives, highlighting strenghts, identifying blind spots and bringing fresh perspectives to current challenges". Also sell Angel cards, nature and tree calendar, tree diary.

NATURAL BIRTH CONTROL EQUIPMENT

Wholistic Research Company
Bright Haven
Robin's Lane
Lolworth
Cambridge CB3 8HH. (0954) 781074.
Enormous range of mail order holistic health equipment also includes grain mills, pulsors, biomagnetic therapy equipment, herbal tablet makers, reflex foot rollers, humane mouse traps, enema/douche kits, iridology equipment, and mail order books. They also publish a handy booklet which explains the use of each product, and gives instructions on benefits, and how to use them.

NUTRITIONAL SUPPLEMENTS

Green Farm Nutrition Centre
Burwash Common
East Sussex TN19 7LX. (0435) 882482/883457.
Large mail order catalogue with lambswool bedding, VDU screens also available. Large range of dietary supplements, and skin and hair care products.

Emerald Life
5 Cheyne Place
Suite 4
London SW3 4HH. (071) 352 5665.
Sell 'Chlorella' which is a natural medicinal algae. It is a rich source of protein, chlorophyll, vitamins, minerals and is claimed to stregthen the immune system and aid in detoxification. Mail order only.

ORGANIC WINE

Organic wine is made from grapes grown without chemical fertilisers or weedkillers, and which have not been sprayed with insecticide. To earn the name of organic, no synthetic additives should be used to preserve or flavour the wine.

229

PRODUCTS

Farmers and producers of organic wine should use only ecologically sound techniques. Wine-producing countries have their own bodies which lay down guidelines for organic wine and monitor its production. Bottles of organic wine will display the symbol of approval by such a body as proof of their integrity.

Available now in addition to wine, are organic beers and spirits. Enthusiasts claim that drinks grown organically are less likely to cause hangovers because they don't contain harmful additives. However, this is a claim which hasn't as yet been put to clinical trials!

Organics
290 Fulham Palace Road
London SW6 6HP. (071) 381 9924.

Vinceremos Wines
Unit 10, Ashley Industrial Estate
Wakefield Road
Ossett
West Yorkshire WF5 9JD. (0924) 276393.
Range of organic wines, beers and spirits from around the world including rum from Cuba, Armenian brandy and sparkling white wine from India. Prices start from £2.85 per bottle.

Vintage Roots
25 Manchester Road
Reading
Berks RG1 3QE. (0734) 401222.
Range of organic wines mostly from France including the French 'classics'. They are planning to stock organic beer and vinegar in the near future. Also able to provide wines that are suitable for vegetarians, and some wines that are also bio-dynamic.

POLLUTION CONTROL

Future Concepts
198 High Road
London N22 4HH. (081) 883 0767.
Various subtle energy devices.

Green Farm Nutrition Centre
Burwash Common
East Sussex TN19 7LX. (0435) 882482/883457.
Large mail order catalogue with lambswool bedding, VDU screens also available. Large range of dietary supplements, and skin and hair care products.

Mountain Breeze Air Ionizers
6 Priorswood Place
Skelmersdale
Lancashire WN8 9QB. (0695) 21155.
Room and car ionisers, air filters and an aromatherapy oil diffuser.

Life Reharmonics
24 Chapel Market
Islington
London N1. (071) 278 4610.
Makers of 'Reharmoniser', which they claim helps to neutralise 'negative energy' (electromagnetic fields, geomagnetic energy, radiation etc).

POSTERS AND PRINTS

Middle Earth
Unit 3 Trading World
131 Broadway
Bexley Heath
Kent
(081) 298 0246.

TAPES - PERSONAL DEVELOPMENT

The tapes listed below are very different in their approach to personal development, and techniques range from subliminal messages to lectures and talks by renowned healers or teachers.

British Centre for Self-Hypnosis
59 Ashford Crescent
Ashford
Middlesex TW15 3EG.

Dharmachakra Tapes
PO Box 50
Cambridge
CB1 3BG.
Taped lectures by Ven. Sangharakshita, founder of Friends of the Western Buddhist Order, on many aspects of Buddhism.

New World Cassettes
Paradise Farm
Westhall
Halesworth
Suffolk IP19 8RH. (050) 279 279.

New World Aurora
16A Neal's Yard
Covent Garden
London WC2. (071) 379 0818.
Open Mon-Sat 10-6. This shop is open to the public and stocks a wide range of natural quartz crystals, dowsing pendulums, rainbow crystal jewellery and balls, cards and posters and 'New Age' music and videos. Also mail order.

Matthew Manning Centre
Buryfields
Cage End
Hatfield Broad Oak
Bishops Stortford, Herts CM22 7HT. (0279) 718330.
Personal development and relaxation tapes to promote healing by perhaps the most famous healer in Britain today.

Lifeskills
3 Brighton Road
Finchley
London N2 8JU. (081) 346 9646 or 580 4972.
Mail order and telephone order only. Established 12 years. Typical prices £8 per tape (incl VAT).

SCWL
55 Kellner Road
London SE28 OAX. (071) 630 7732 or (081) 855 8575.

Triangle Truth Ltd
PO Box 89
London SE3 7JN. (081) 305 2317.
Series of tapes on on subjects such as forgiveness, weight loss, confidence, prosperity, relationships etc. £8.95 per tape.

Tapewise
23 New Road
Brighton BN1 1WZ. (0273) 680281.
Tapes on the problems of teenage life for worried parents, produced by the Trust for the Study of Adolescence.

Gale Centre
Whitakers Way
Loughton
Essex IG10 1BR. (081) 508 9344.
Sell by mail order a range of books and tapes on counselling and therapy. Slanted towards those in the caring professions, especially social workers.

Stream
86 Wavertree Road
London SW2 3ST. (081) 674 4264.
Sell a range of cassettes produced by the Monroe Institute on personal development.

TAPES (MUSIC)

Dawn Awakening Music
PO Box 15
Totnes
Devon TQ9 6UD. (0804) 26336.
Distributors of New Age and relaxing music, and some relaxation tapes. Mail order catalogue available.

PRODUCTS

Cloud Nine Music
39 Abbeygate Street
Bury St Edmunds
Suffolk IP33 1BR.

Celtia Ltd
Celtia House
Longrock
Penzance
Cornwall TR20 8HX. (0736) 51680.
Celtic design jewellery, belts, purses, bags, ornaments, cards and celtic inspired compositions on tape.

Free Flow Music
The Cabin
Dorstone
Hereford HR3 6BL. (0981) 550786.
Distribute tapes from Voices of Silence group.

Earthsounds Music
Old Mill
Skeeby
Richmond
North Yorks DL10 5EB. (0748) 825959.
Series include 'Fire of Ritual', 'Seed Thoughts' and 'World Musics'.

Earthly Delights
Manor Farmhouse
Blackwell
Nr Buxton
Derbyshire SK17 9QT.
'Sounds' by Earthly Delights and Nocturnal Emissions. Truly alternative, not to say arcane, and even 'X' rated stuff.

Inner Harmonies
The Coach House
Park Hall
Salford Priors
Worcestershire
Northbleach
Glos WR11 5SG. (0789) 772255.
Relaxing music from four composers, including *Living Earth* by Annie Locke, copies of which have been presented by a US peace delegation to the Soviet Union.

Elfington Cassettes
The Old Forge Studio
Back Road
Wenhaston, Halesworth
Suffolk IP19 9EP. (050) 270 678
The music of Mike Rowland, composer of *The Fairy Ring*. Gentle music for relaxation and meditation.

Gale Centre for Creative Therapy
Stable Cottage
Whitakers Way
Loughton
Essex IG10 1SJ. (081) 508 9344.

Private Music
1 Bedford Avenue
London WC1B 3DT.
Independent label formed by Peter Baumann, founding member of the electronic music group, Tangerine Dream. Artists include Ravi Shankar, Jerry Goodman, Nona Hendryx, Yanni, and Tangerine Dream.

New World Aurora
16A Neal's Yard
Covent Garden
London WC2. (071) 379 0818.
Open Mon-Sat 10-6. This shop is open to the public and stocks a wide range of natural quartz crystals, dowsing pendulums, rainbow crystal jewellery and balls, cards and posters and 'New Age' music and videos. Also mail order.

New Era Music
10 Amhurst Terrace
London E8 2BT. (071) 278 0499.

Music Suite Ltd
Cenarth
Newcastle
Emlyn
Dyfed SA38 9JN. (0239) 710594 .
Original compositions by Adrian Wagner, Francis Monkman (ex of 'Curved Air' - remember them?), Prana, and various story tapes. Also offer bulk cassette and video duplicating service, CD and record

manufacturing and electronic music studio.

Snapdragon
12 South Park
Sevenoaks
Kent TN13 1AN. (0732) 740252.
Mystical cards, tarot cards, crystal balls, special incense, healing pendants, pendulums. Keep a list of alternative medicine practitioners in the area. Tapes for healing.

Seventh Wave Music
15 Broughton Rd
Thornton Heath
Croydon CR4 6AG. (081) 689 8721.
Uplifting atmospheric music, creating landscapes using sound and rhythm composed by Nigel Shaw. Four albums available.

TAPES (RELAXATION)

Dawn Awakening Music
PO Box 15
Totnes
Devon TQ9 6UD. (0804) 26336.
Distributors of New Age and relaxing music, and some relaxation tapes. Mail order catalogue available.

Matthew Manning Centre
Buryfields
Cage End
Hatfield Broad Oak
Bishops Stortford, Herts CM22 7HT. (0279) 718330.
Personal development and relaxation tapes to promote healing by perhaps the most famous healer in Britain today.

Shapetapes & Planet Tree Music
31 Redington Road
Hampstead
London NW3 7QY. (071) 435 9847.
Series of tapes which correlate to particular shapes (square, triangle etc) which aim to have a particular 'toning' effect on the body.

TREATMENT COUCHES

Marshcouch
36 Glebe Close
Hemel Hempstead
Herts HP3 9PA. (0442) 63199.
5 different models of treatment couch, can be custom built for individual's height with choice of fabric or vinyl covering at no extra charge. From £34 - £260 excluding VAT and small delivery charge.

VIDEOS

New World Aurora
16A Neal's Yard
Covent Garden
London WC2. (071) 379 0818.
Open Mon-Sat 10-6. This shop is open to the public and stocks a wide range of natural quartz crystals, dowsing pendulums, rainbow crystal jewellery and balls, cards and posters and 'New Age' music and videos. Also mail order.

Namaste Films
PO Box 351
Swindon
Wilts
(0793) 763666.
42 minute relaxation video of the ocean and coast of Australia.

Yoga Dham
67 Pinner Park Ave
North Harrow
Middlesex HA2 6JY. (081) 428 6691/9402.
Yoga video.

WATER PURIFIERS

If you want to find out what your water contains, apply to your local water authority for a report on its chemical and bacterial composition and compare these levels of metals and chemicals with permitted EC levels. Information on these levels can be obtained from your local water authority or by sending an SAE to

PRODUCTS

Friends of the Earth, 26-28 Underwood Street, London N1 7JQ (071 490 1555). If there are greater levels of impurity than the EC recommendations, then complain to the EC.

Water filters come in jug form, or can be fitted to the tap, or can be plumbed into the water supply pipe. They vary enormously in cost and effectiveness. The cheapest are jug filters which use charcoal to remove unpleasant tastes and smells, especially cholorine. The charcoal must be replaced regularly - usually at least once a month. Tests show that they are not as effective in removing a whole range of toxic pollutants as plumbed-in filters.

Plumbed-in filters can use a variety of methods to extract pollutants and bacteria from the water. Granular silver activated carbon filters remove some chemicals, including chlorine. The silver in this type of filter helps to remove bacteria, though only after the water has been left from 2 to 24 hours. Ultraviolet radiation is used in some filters to kill bacteria, though this is less effective if there is a lot of iron in the water. Microstraining purifiers are the most effective in cleaning water, and only they can really be called 'purifiers' rather than just 'filters'. They work using highly refined filtration and absorption to remove bacteria and chemicals. These systems also use electrokinetic attraction which draws the dissolved impurities to it. Since this then becomes clogged, the filtration unit must be replaced every 1 to 2 years with cartridges available from the supplier.

Appenstar Ltd
P O Box 679
Virginia Water
Surrey GU25 4AB. (0344) 842168.

General Ecology (UK) Ltd
Homelands
Unit 10
Leatherhead
Surrey KT22 8SU. (0372) 363555.
Market the Seagull range of non-chemical water purifiers, as used by many airline companies. Portable device also available.

Imperial Health Technologies
Courtview House
Hampton Court
Surrey KT8 9BY. (081) 977 5577.

EDUCATION

Centre for Continuing Education

City University
Northampton Square
London EC1. (071) 253 4399.
They run evening classes in psychology, psychotherapy and counselling.

Chequer Centre
Chequer Street
London EC1.
Adult education courses covering such subjects as Alexander technique, aromatherapy, compulsive eating support group, healing, herbal medicine, homoeopathy, massage, reflexology, shiatsu, tai chi, subtle energy
healing, confidence building for women and counselling. Open to all.

Holistic Early Learning School
2 Amgerst Road
Ealing
London W 13 8ND. (081) 998 2732.
A school for three month to five year olds. Part-time and full-time. With health food diet, homoeopathic first-aid facility for minor ailments. A wide range of educational activities. Offers an individual approach to the care and education of young children.

ADULT EDUCATION

London has a wealth of further education classes. These classes are still relatively cheap and cover subjects such as psychotherapy, counselling, health, alternative therapies, religion or philosophy. The departments listed below offer a good selection of courses in this field.

Birkbeck College - Centre for Extra-Mural Studies
26 Russell Square
London WC1B 5DQ. (071) 631 6669.
Day and evening adult education classes on psychology, psychotherapy, religion, myth etc. Typically courses on Counselling, Transactional Analysis, Gestalt, Family Therapy, Co-Counselling, Psychosynthesis and Personal Construct Therapy. Ring or write for prospectus which is published yearly in June. For a ten week course

of 20 hours the cost is £25. One third of the fee for OAPs and unemployed.

City University
Northampton Square, London EC1 (071) 253 4399.
They run evening classes in psychology, psychotherapy and counselling.

RECOGNISED ACADEMIC COURSES

British School of Osteopathy
1-4 Suffolk Street
London SW1Y 4HG. (071) 930 9254.
BSc in Osteopathy, 4 years full time. See 'Osteopathy' section for further details.

Centre for Complementary Health Studies
University of Exeter
Streatham Court
Rennes Drive
Exeter EX4 4PU. (0392) 433828.
(1) BPhil and (2) MPhil in Complementary Health Studies. (1) 2 years part-time. (2) 1 year full-time or two years part-time, although applicants are advised to allow at least 50% longer than these minimum requirements. (1) Applicants should be those working in complementary and orthodox medicine or other caring professions with day-to-day responsibility for patients. (2) Substantial academic study in the arts, sciences or social sciences. (1) £1,500 per annum, (2) £1,900, overseas students £5,000. The centre also runs a research programme, and offers certain information services.

Polytechnic of East London
School for Independent Study, Polytechnic of East London, Holbrook Centre
London E15 3EA. (081) 590 7722.
Title: (1) BA/BSc by Independent Study, (2) MA/MSc by Independent Study. (1) 3 years full-time, 5 years part-time. (2) Minimum: full-time 1 year, part-time 2 years. (1) 2 A levels required, or comparable qualifications. (2) Honours degree, or equivalent. Apply to course adminstrator for details of fees.

Roehampton Institute of Higher Education
Senate House
Roehampton Lane
London SW15 5PS. (081) 878 8117.
(1) Diploma in Psychological Counselling (2) MSc in Psychological Counselling. Duration:

ETHICALLY SOUND INVESTMENTS

(1) 1 year part-time (2) 2 year part-time. Entry: (1) Appropriate academic qualifications or experience in helping professions and counselling. (2) Candidates must be 25 years old and have a degree with a pass at 2.2 level or above. Special entry may be given to those with appropriate professional qualifications. Fees: Refer to organisers. Comments: also run Diploma in Counselling and Supervision Course and Certificate in Counselling in Formal and Informal Settings (mainly for those in youth or social work). Also offer Certificate in Counselling in Formal and Informal Settings (one year part-time), open to youth and community workers; Introduction to Music Therapy (ten week part-time); Diploma in Dance Movement Therapy (two years part-time).

School of Psychotherapy and Counselling

Regents College
Inner Circle
Regents Park
London NW1 4NS. (071) 487 7406.
MA in the Psychology of Therapy and Counselling Duration: 27 months with the possibility of 12 months extension in special cases. Entry Requirements: Combination of a Bachelor's degree or appropriate equivalent, some professional experience and experience of groups, self-exploration, own therapy or counselling. Candidates will be considered individually in terms of experience and may be accepted without all the formal entry requirements. Fees: £200 deposit plus six payments of £850 for the whole course. Comments: Course consists of academic seminars on Humanistic and Integrative Psychotherapy and Existential, Psychoanalytic and Transpersonal approaches plus a range of second year options. Training seminars. Supervised six month part-time placement and writing a thesis. Degree awarded by Antioch University and additional British validation sought.
Post Qualifying Diploma in Existential Psychotherapy once the Masters Degree (above) is obtained. Two years duration.

SERVICES

ETHICALLY SOUND INVESTMENTS

A number of ethical investment funds have sprung up over the last few years, just as 'green' products have become much more common. However, what is becoming evident is that one person's 'green' is another person's 'grey' area.

Different ethical investment funds have different criteria - some for instance are very clear on not investing in the tobacco industry, others have no investment at all in nuclear weapons or energy. It's best to check out what criteria are used, and make sure they are in agreement with your own. In unit trusts your money is spread across a number of companies to minimise risk. Because it is the nature of modern business to be mostly about large multi-nationals which have many subsidiary companies doing different things, it's very difficult to invest in the mainstream without including some investment in questionable areas, especially if your criteria are very tight. It can also be difficult to find out all the interests of a large company with many subsidiary companies.

If you decide to invest with a unit trust scheme, in addition to the sensible financial questions such as what degree of risk is involved, what charges are made and what the premium is, you can ask about what ethical criteria are used, how rigorously they are applied and whether the fund has an independent vetting committee and if so how it works. If the fund claims to be 'green', do they look only at the finished product, or do they take into account the processes of production, and even the company's general record on the environment?

Another way of researching your ethical investment is to apply to **EIRIS**, the Ethical Investment Research Service. They research companies' interests in several areas of concern, and cover all companies in the Financial Times All-Share index. Their address is *EIRIS, 401 Bondway Business Centre, 71 Bondway, London SW8 1SQ. (071) 735 1351.* Send SAE with enquiries.

If you don't want to take your chances with the multi-nationals, then you can invest in small schemes which loan money for small projects. This has the advantage of being very ethical, though the premium may not be as good.

Among the unit trust schemes they offer is the TSB Environmental Investor Fund. The investments are vetted by an independent committee set up under the auspices of the Conservation Foundation.

Allchurch's Investment Management Service

19-21 Billiter Street
London EC3N 2RY. (071) 528 7364.
Set up originally as the Ecclesiastical Insurance group to serve the church and clergy. Now run Amity fund for ethical investment.

Ecology Building Society

18 Station Road
Cross Hills
Keighley
West Yorkshire
BD20 8TB. (0535) 35933.
Lends money for property or projects which are likely 'to lead to the saving of non-renewable resources, the promotion of self-sufficiency in individuals or communities, or the most ecologically efficient use of land'. Examples are: small-scale workshops, back-to-back houses, homes for people running ecological busi-

nesses, organic farms, houses with special energy saving or energy efficient features, properties which will help to promote the life of small communities etc.

Ethical Investment Fund

10 Queen Street
Mayfair
London W1X 7PF. (071) 491 0558.
Unit Investment underwritten by Royal Heritage Life Assurance.

Ethical Investment Research Service

401 Bond Business Centre
71 Bondway
London
SW8 1SQ. (071) 735 1351

Friends Provident Unit Trust

Pixham End
Dorking
Surrey RH4 1QA. (0306) 740123.
Run the stewardship trust: includes unit trust, income trust, the north american stewardship trust, personal equity plan.

ICOF (Industrial Common Ownership Finance)

12-14 Gold Street
Northampton NN1 1RS. 0604 37563.
Lend money to co-operatives.

Mercury Provident

3 Orlingbury House
Lewes Road
Forest Row
Sussex RH18 5AA. (034282) 3739.
Founded on the principles of Rudolf Steiner (see Anthroposophical Society), supports projects which are of benefit to the community, have community support and are in some form of social ownership.

Merlin Jupiter Ecology Fund

Knightsbridge House 197 Knightsbridge SW7 1RB. (071) 581 8015.
Investment in companies which are environmentally concerned, have 'social commitment'. Avoids those with direct links with South Africa, armaments, nuclear power or tobacco.

Tilt Ltd
Birdwood House
44 High St
Totnes, Devon . 0803 867099.
A community company using local money to invest in local projects. Money is used to create ecologically and socially sustainable projects.

DATING AGENCIES

Consciousness Connection
PO Box 16539
Santa Fe
NM
USA. 87506-6539.

Contact Centre
BCM Cuddle
London WC1V 6XX.

British and international contact service for vegans/vegetarians, and international contact service open to non vegetarian/ vegans. £12.75 for life membership, plus small fee if you wish to advertise in broadsheets.

Frendz
PO Box 834
Sherborne
Dorset DT9 4YB.

Friendship Register
29 Goldstone Way
Hove
Sussex BN3 7PA.

Friendships
Apperley Court
Apperley
Gloucestershire GL19 4QD.
Is a nationwide friendship agency. For those people interested in meeting people involved in holistic medicine, new age, meditation, 'green issues', yoga, astrology, psychology etc.

Vegetarian Matchmakers
Johnson House
Coronation Road
London NW10 7QE. (081) 348 5229.
Provides a comprehensive service for unattached vegetarians, vegans, macro-

biotics and those of similar mind, nationwide. Introductions, friendship, gettogethers, weekend breaks/holidays etc. Hundreds of participating members, from teenage to sunset years. Has been bringing veggies happily together since 1980, and is a member of the Association of British Introduction Agencies.

ROOMS FOR HIRE

Association for Analytic and Bodymind Therapy and Training
8 Princes Avenue
Muswell Hill
London N10 3LR. (081) 883 5418.
Sound-proofed, pleasant therapy rooms with garden.

Bodywise
119 Roman Road
Bethnal Green
London E2 0QN. (081) 981 6938.
Small and large room for hire by groups or individuals. Large room £15/hr, £80/day, £140/ weekend. Small group room £7.50/hr, £45/day, £80/weekend.

Community Health Foundation
188-194 Old Street
London EC1V 9BP. (071) 251 4076.
Wide range of rooms to rent for workshops, courses and meetings. £25 for 18ft x 18ft room and £50 for 44ft x 30ft half day or evening. Good central location with restaurant downstairs and close to Old St tube station.

Gaunts House
Wimborne
Dorset
BH21 4JQ. (0202) 841522.
Large conference, seminar and retreat centre available for hire (can accommodate up to 200 people) by community wishing to promote 'individual growth and fulfilment from a nonsectarian basis'. Facilities include gym and heated pool.

Holnest House
Holnest
Sherbourne
Dorset DT9 6HA. (096) 321340.
Rooms and accomodation for workshops in Dorset. Set in the country: rolling hills, half an hour from the sea. £Neg. Large rooms and garden if workshop needed to be outside.

Lower Shaw Farm
Old Shaw Lane
Shaw
Nr Swindon
Wilts SN5. (0793) 771080.

Neal's Yard Agency (for personal development)
14 Neal's Yard
Covent Garden
London WC2 9DP. (071) 379 0141.
Two large rooms for hire at a central location. The rooms measure 22 x 27 feet and 14 square feet.

Penthouse 62
The Anchor Brew House
50 Shad Thames SE1 2AY. (071) 403 8991.
Large loft for hire. Suit group that needs lots of space. 4100 sq ft. £Neg. Set in Wapping.

Portobello Green Fitness Centre
3-5 Thorpe Close
North Kensington
London W10 5XL. (081) 960 2221.

RIGPA Fellowship
330 Caledonian Road
London N1 1BB. (071) 700 0185.
Centre available for occasional hire.

Sound Health
261 Grove Street
Deptford
London SE8 3PZ. (081) 691 7519.
Consulting rooms and space for workshops. Victorian house with garden in Wandsworth.

Sunnyholt Natural Health Centre
120 The Vale
London W3 7RQ. (081) 746 0499.
Rooms for practitioners and space for workshops.

Tyers St. Centre
121 Tyers St
London SE11 5HS. (071) 820 0580.
Workshop space available evenings and weekends.

PRACTITIONERS SERVICES

Bates, Carrie
c/o Spectrum
7 Endymion Road
London N4 1EE. (071) 263 5545.
Established 1991. 100% MBS/New Age. Aims to help holistic practitioners, small businesses and the self employed empower themselves and use radio to promote the benefits of their work. Runs workshops and one-to-one consultancy on helping prepare for, and make the most of, radio interviews. Also offers individual advice

RAINBOW EXPRESS

DO YOU NEED SUPPORT IN PROMOTING YOURSELF?

I offer Intuitive, Marketing Consultations based on my wide experience of 11 years self-employment.

Also available – inspired holistic products through mail order.

Contact Susan Lever on 081–992 5987 for further details.

on how to get on the radio. One day workshop costs £50, and one-to-one consultancy (which lasts one and quarter hours) is £40. Carrie is also an holistic massage practitioner.

HSC UK & Ireland Ltd
Silver Birches
Private Road, Rodborough Common
Stroud
Glos GL5 5BT. (045387) 3446, 3668, 2618.
Blood/urine analysis and remedies, service for medical doctors and natural medicine practitioners. £50, £99 and £185 depending on type of analysis. Remedies last for about 3 months.

Neal's Yard Agency (for personal development)
14 Neal's Yard
Covent Garden
London WC2 9DP. (071) 379 0141.
Are an agency which matches up the public with holistic businesses running courses, events, dance, art, psychotherapy, counselling, trainings, martial arts, men's and women's groups etc. If you have a course, training, event, holiday etc you wish to find clients for, Neal's Yard Agency will do their best to find them for you. The public come into the shop and browse around and talk to somebody about further advice. There is no fee to participants, businesses pay a 10% booking fee (min £10). Also large and small meeting rooms for hire (14 ft square and 22 ft x 27 ft).

PATHWAYS
Publicity and Information Service
for practitioners and organisations involved in therapy, growth and healing

The Network that works for you!

• Practitioner briefing • Events and resources bulletin • Exhibition representation • Leaflet distribution

For your information pack write or phone Mary Fee Pathways (MOD), 12 Southcote Road, London N19 5BJ Tel: (071) 607 7852

FOOD

MACROBIOTICS

Macrobiotics is familiar to most people as a kind of diet. But it is also a whole theory of health and well-being based on the balancing of the opposite and complementary energies of Yin and Yang. Literally the word Macrobiotics means 'large life'.

Macrobiotic theory is based in the Oriental belief that good health is based on the balance of life energy. Yin energy is feminine, receptive, damp, cold and is symbolised by the moon. Yang energy is masculine, active, dry, hot and symbolised by the sun. Everything that exists partakes more or less of the qualities of these elemental energies. As in acupuncture, illness is seen as an imbalance of these forces in the body. Since food can be classified as Yin or Yang, a Macrobiotic diet is a way or restoring this balance through eating the right foods.

Cereals and brown rice form the basis of the Macrobiotic diet because they contain the best balance of Yin and Yang. Yin foods are those which contain a lot of water, grow above the ground and tend to be hot, sour or sweet in taste. They tend to be blue, green or purple. Yang foods tend to be hard, dense, dry, grow below ground and are often red or yellow in colour. Different methods of cooking can also increase the tendency towards Yin or Yang: quick cooking increases Yin, and slow cooking, Yang. Foods that will promote this balance depend on the temperament of the eater and his or her environment. It is better to eat local foods too, because there is a natural affinity between the food of a region and its people. But it is important to stress that each individual is unique and has his or her own requirements for healthy eating.

Although Macrobiotics is a good way of healing oneself, at first it is important to consult a trained macrobiotic dietitian, especially if you have a particular complaint. Diagnosis is carried out by observation of the colour and shape of the

patient's body, an assessment of their temperament, and by taking the 'pulses' (see Acupuncture section for an explanation of the pulses). Emphasis is not only placed on eating healthily, but also on lifestyle. Disease can also be a result of not looking after the body properly, of having a negative attitude to life or of being in the wrong environment.

Though it can be hard to keep to a macrobiotic diet - if you like eating out then you may find it harder - many people have found it can help in treatment of very stubborn conditions, as well as promoting increased vitality and better digestion.

MACROBIOTICS/VEGETARIANISM

Bumblebee Natural Foods
30,32,33 Brecknock Road
London N7. (071) 607 1936.

Bumblebees Natural Remedies
35 Brecknock Road
London N7 0AD. (071) 267 3884.
Three neighbouring shops, each shop specialising in different produce.
No. 30 sell a wide range of macrobiotic food, fruit and nuts, beans, jams, honeys, spreads, pastas, oils, teas, and soya milk.
No. 32 is the takeaway section with hot dishes prepared in their kitchen. Also breads, grains, juices, cereals and a large selection of O.G. wines.
No. 33 is the O.G. fruit and vegetable shop. It also stocks herbs and spice and herb teas. The dairy is sited towards the back of the shop.
No. 10 Caledonian Road (previously Peacemeal) does take-aways and a large selection of wholefoods.

Bushwacker
59 Goldhawk Road
London W12. (081) 743 2359.
Wholefood shop sells range of wholefood, organic fruit and vegetables, medicines, books and also macrobiotic specialities.

VEGETARIANISM AND VEGANISM

A vegetarian diet is one which excludes all meat. A vegan diet excludes not only meat but also all animal products, such as milk, eggs and sometimes honey. Most vegans also prefer not to use or wear leather.

The past few years have seen an increasing number of people becoming vegetarian or vegan. A number of different factors have contributed to this change in eating habits. Recent publicity about the possible harmful effects of meat and dairy products has added to the argument that a vegetarian diet is healthier and has offset the popular and unfounded fear that unless your diet includes a lot of meat you will become undernourished in some way. The satu-

rated fats present in animal products have been found to be contributory to the development of heart disease, and links appparently exist between high meat consumption and low fibre intake and breast and bowel cancer. Research shows that a high fibre, vegetable and fruit based diet is also less fattening and promotes healthy functioning of the digestive system.

However, most people who adopt a vegan or vegetarian diet do so for ethical reasons. Since the consumption of meat and dairy products is no longer necessary for our survival, it is argued that the suffering inflicted upon animals in the food creating process is also unnecessary. Factory farming and mass production of meat means that in the modern world animals are subjected to greater suffering that in the days of the smallholding. The publicity which has been given to the way in which meat is produced has left many people feeling that since they cannot condone the process, they cannot eat the product either.

Ecological awareness too has played its part in the change in eating habits. Animal farming tends to use up more resources than plant farming and requires more acres of land for less food production. Forests throughout the world have been cleared for animal grazing and this has led to further ecological problems.

In the 1990s it is far easier to be a vegan or vegetarian than it was 20 years ago. Health food shops have sprung up all over the country, and vegetarian restaurants have become commonplace, at least in the big cities. Many restaurants offer special vegetarian dishes or a vegetarian menu. The growth of high quality vegetarian cuisine means that fewer people are cracking the old nut rissole and lentil jokes, and vegetarians are not seen as 'cranks' any more. Life can still be difficult for the vegan who wants to eat out though milk substitute products such as soya milk are available even in some local supermarkets in London.

Some people who would like to exclude meat from their diet still feel unsure about what they would eat instead, or still feel anxious about the prospect of a vegetarian coming for dinner. For further information on this and on other aspects of vegetarianism and veganism, contact the centres below.

Vegetarian Society
Parkdale
Dunham Road
Altrincham
Cheshire WA14 4QG. (061) 928 0793.
Campaigns to promote vegetarianism, gives information and advice, publishes books, leaflets and Vegetarian magazine, produces range of merchandise, supports non-animal research into the benefits of vegetarianism. Also runs cookery courses (see Vegetarian Society Cookery School in Residential Workshops section).

VEGETARIAN RESTAURANTS

Angel Gate
51 Queen Caroline Street
Hammersmith
London W6. (081) 748 8388.
Vegan, wholefood and vegetarian.

Baba Bhelpoori House
118 Westbourne Grove
Bayswater
London W2. (071) 221 7502.
Closed Mon. Open 12-3, 6-10.45.

Bunjie's Coffee House
27 Litchfield Street
London WC2. (071) 240 1796.
12-11 every day. Sunday 5-11. Wholefood. Cheap, folk music some nights.

Cherry Orchard
241 Globe Road
Bethnal Green
London E2 0JD. (081) 980 6678.
Tues-Fri 12-3 and 6.30-10.30, Sat 12-10.30, Sun & Mon closed. Vegan and vegetarian dishes at reasonable prices, canteen service at lunchtime changes to waitress service at night. Very pleasant garden in the Summer. Run by women members of the Buddhist centre next door.

Country Life
1 Heddon Street
London W1. (071) 434 2922.
11.30-3.00, Fri 11.30-2.00. Closed Sat and Sun. Vegan/wholefood. Buffet. Cheap.

Cranks Health Foods (1)

1 Central Avenue
Covent Garden Plaza
London WC2. (071) 379 6508.
9.30-8.00, Sun 9.30-7. Covent Garden tube.

Cranks Health Foods (2)

17-18 Great Newport Street
London W1.
Leicester Square, wholefood, vegan 8am - 10.30pm Mon to Fri.

Cranks Health Foods (3)

8 Marshal Street
London W1. (071) 437 9431.
Mon to Fri. 8-10.30pm Vegan/wholefood.

Cranks Health Foods (4)

9-11 Tottenham Street
London W1. (071) 631 3912.
8-8pm Mon-Fri, 9-8pm Sat, closed Sun. Vegan/wholefood.

De Las Casas

153 Clapham High Street
London SW4.
Vegetarian and vegan dishes. 48 seats and small health food shop at the front. Open evenings except Sundays. All food is cooked with filtered water, and is made with organically grown ingredients wherever possible. Licence applied for, so bring your own bottle.

Dining Room

Winchester Walk
London Bridge
London SE1. (071) 407 0337.
Tues-Fri 7-10. Vegan/wholefood.

Diwana Bhelpoori House (1)

121 Drummond Street
Euston
London NW1. (071) 387 5556.
12-11.45 daily. Indian. Cheap.

Diwana Bhelpoori House (2)

50 Westbourne Grove
Bayswater
London W2. (071) 221 0721.
12-3 and 6-10.30 daily. Indian. Cheap.

East West Restaurant

188 Old Street
London EC1. (071) 608 0300.
Mon-Fri 11am-9.30pm. The only macrobiotic restaurant in town.

Fallen Angel

65 Graham Street
Islington
London N1. (071) 253 3996.
Mon-Sat 12-12, Sun 12-11.30. Wine bar/Cafe.

Food for Thought

31 Neal Street
Covent Garden
London WC2. (071) 836 0239.
Covent Garden. Wholefood/vegan , 12-8, Sat 12-8 closed Sun.

Full of Beans

127 Rushey Green
Catford
London SE6. (081) 698 3283.
9.30-5.30 Mon-Sat. Wholefood, hot meals, snacks, cakes. Vegan dishes sometimes available.

Gate Vegetarian Restaurant

51 Queen Caroline Street
Hammersmith
London W6. (081) 748 6932.
12 noon-11.30pm Mon-Fri, 12 noon-12 midnight Sats. Licensed (organic and non-organic wines). Private parties catered for. Linked to the Rudolf Steiner inspired Christian Community.

Govinda's

9 Soho Street
Soho
London W1. (071) 437 3662.
Purely vegetarian restaurant

Greenhouse

16 Chenies Street
London WC1. (071) 637 8038.
Goodge Street tube. Mon 10-6pm, Tues-Fri 10-10pm, Sat 1-8.30pm. Reasonable prices, vegan dishes available.

Hare Krishna Curry House

1 Hanway Street
London W1. (071) 636 5262.
10.30-11pm all week. Has just re-opened and seats 50. Gujarati vegetarian dishes and wholefood. Licensed.

Health Place Cafe

17 Strutton Ground
London SW1. (071) 222 4588.
Mon-Fri 9-9pm. Home made vegetarian food
and organic wines and beers. Healthfood shop
two doors up.

Hearth Cafe At Earthworks

132 Kings Street
Hammersmith
London W6 OQU. (081) 846 9357.
Wholefood, Mon-Wed 11am-6pm. Fri & Sat
11am-10.30 pm.,

Hockney's

98 High Street
Croydon, Surrey. (081) 688 2899.
Purely vegetarian. Vega meals also available.
Tue - Sat 12 noon-5.30pm counter lunch.   5.30
- 9.00pm supper served by a waiter.

London Ecology Centre

45 Shelton Street
Covent Garden
London WC2. (071) 379 4324.
10.30am-10.30pm. Covent Garden. Wholefood
and vegan. Licensed.

Mandeer

21 Hanway Place
London W1. (071) 323 0660.
10.30 Mon-Sat, closed Sun. Indian. Excellent
food and cheap too. Well worth a visit.

Manna

4 Erskine Road
Chalk Farm
London NW3. (071) 722 8028.
6.30pm-12am daily. Wholefood, sometimes
vegan.

Millwall

30 Stoke Newington Church St.
Stoke Newington
London N16. (071) 254 1025.
12-3pm and 6-12am Mon-Thur, 12-3pm and 6-
1am Fri, 12-1am Sat, 12-12 Sun. Vegan/
wholefood.

Milward's

97 Stoke Newington Church St.
Stoke Newington
London N16. (071) 254 1025.
Mon-Fri 6-12, Sat and Sun 12-12. Vegan/
wholefood.

Neal's Yard Bakery and Tea Room

6 Neal's Yard
Covent Garden
London WC2. (071) 836 5199.
10.30-8 Mon Tue Thur Fri. Covent Garden.
Wholefood, vegan dishes available and as many
different types of tea as you could wish.

Nuthouse

26 Kingley Street
London W1. (071) 437 9471.
10.30-7.00 Mon-Fri, 10.30-6 Sat, closed Sun.
Vegan/wholefood. Cheap.

Ravi Shankar

133 Drummond Street
Euston
London NW1. (071) 388 6458.
12-11 daily. Indian food.

Raw Deal

65 York Street
London W1. (071) 262 4841.
Baker Street. 10-10 Mon-Fri. Wholefood.

Shan

200 Shaftesbury Avenue
Soho
London WC2. (071) 240 3348.
12-10 Mon-Sat, closed Sun.

Something Else

49 Cross Street
Islington
London N1. (071) 226 6579.
6.30-11 Mon to Thur, 6.30-11.30 Fri and Sat, Sun
7-10.30. Vegan.

Well Bean

10 Old Dover Road
Blackheath
London SE3. (081) 858 1319.
Mon-Fri 9-6, Sat 9-5.30. Wholefood: main dish
and soup every day, pies, pizzas, salads. Bring
your own bottle.

Wholemeal Cafe

1 Shrubbery Road
Streatham
London SW16. (081) 769 2423.
Midday to 10pm, 7 days a week. Open Sat and
Sun 9-11.30am for breakfast. Wholemeal. Fully
licensed. No smoking.

Wilkins Natural Foods
61 Marsham Street
Victoria
London SW1. (071) 222 4038.
Mon-Fri 8-6. Wholefood cafe, mainly lunctime trade. Some vegan dishes.

Woodlands Restaurant
37 Panton Street Off
Haymarket
London W1. (071) 839 7258.
12-2.45 and 6-10.30 daily, Indian food.

Woodlands Restaurant
77 Marylebone Lane
London W1. (071) 486 3862.
12-2.45 and 6 - 10.30 daily, Indian food.

Woodlands Restaurant
402 High Road
Wembley
Middlesex . (071) 930 8200.
12-2.45 and 6-10.30 daily, Indian food.

LONDON GETAWAY

RESIDENTIAL COMMUNITIES

Lauriston Hall
Castle Douglas
South West Scotland
Though no longer a 'commune', the 20 adults and 11 children at Lauriston Hall live together as individual members of a housing co-op, some in families, some by themselves, and others in small, non-family 'living groups' and share some aspects of their work. Hold visitors weeks when people can come and experience first hand what goes on. Run a number of residential workshops as well such as gay men's weeks, Reichian weeks, tai chi, music, alchemy and taoist weeks, and 'maximising our immunity' workshop. Sliding scale from £8.50 per day up to £15, depending on income. Workshops may cost more.

Lower Shaw Farm
Old Shaw Lane
Shaw
Nr Swindon
Wilts SN5. (0793) 771080.
Community with no collectively stated religious or party political base. Workshops and holidays, as well as working weekends etc. Prices are cheap - £55 per weekend workshop which includes food and accommodation. Some of the weekend workshops they do are Shiatsu, fools weekend, yoga, massage, death exploration, pottery, women and crafts (such as photography), rug making etc. Offer concessions up to one third full price.

Monkton Wyld Court
Nr. Charmouth
Bridport
Dorset DT6 6DQ. (0297) 60342.
Holistic education centre and the home of 10 adults, 2 teenagers, 5 young children plus 2 or 3 short term volunteers. They work co-operatively, taking care of a wide range of groups involved in therapy, healing, yoga, tai-chi, dance, theatre and the arts as well as children's groups, youth groups, mentally handicapped and other community groups. They maintain their own land and grow their own food. Weekend workshops range from Drums, Rhythm and Voices to Dreamwork and Psychosynthesis. Appetising vegetarian dishes

cooked in a big communal pot. The all-in prices make it good value.

Seekers Trust

The Close
Addington
West Malling
Kent ME19 5BL. (0732) 843589.
Prayer (Christian) and spiritual healing is offered at this residential community. Self catering flats available for long or short stay. Centre situated at Addington Park in Kent within 37 acres of gardens and woodlands. The work entails constant prayer and very considerable clerical routine, most of which is carried out by voluntary helpers within the community. In some hundred half hour sessions each week, groups of dedicated reident members of the Trust meet in small chapels linking by concentrated prayer with the people who have asked for help and healing, who say the identical prayers at precisely the same times. No fees but donations accepted. Also conference hall.

RESIDENTIAL HEALTH CENTRES

Bethany Vegetarian and Vegan Nursing Homes

7/9 Oak Park Villas
Dawlish
Devon EX7 0DE. (0626) 862794.
Run on Christian principles, it offers care to all vegetarians and vegans, and is registered with the local health authority as a Nursing home and rest home with 23 beds. Special diets such as diabetes, wholefood, Gerson type cancer therapy and gluten free are catered for. Visiting chiropodist, hairdresser, masseuse, occupational therapist, homoeopath and acupuncturist. Aim to give residents holistic health care with a choice of naturopathic or allopathic therapy. Non smoking environment. Nursing bed £250 per week, rest home bed £175 per week. Also accept DSS patients.

Breakspear Hospital

1 High Street
Abbots Langley
Herts WD5 0PU. (0923) 261333.
Private hospital opened March 1988 with in-patient, day-patient and out-patient facilities. Environmental control, filtered water and organic food. Patients seen by appointment only. Monthly seminars, lectures. Sale of books and vitamins. Prices £85 for initial consultation with

doctor, thereafter prices individually ascertained. No concessions. Register of practitioners. Wheelchair access. Allergy desensitisation, sleep monitoring. Sauna and excercise programmes. Will perform home surveys for environmental contaminants.

Park Attwood Therapeutic Centre

Trimpley
Bewdley
Worcs DY12 1RE. (02997) 444.
Nursing home run by qualified doctors using Anthroposophical Medicine - 'a therapeutic community in a clinical setting'. Have treated people for conditions both physical and mental. Also run in-service training for nurses, and are open to visits from interested health professionals.

Raphael Medical Centre

Coldharbour Lane
Hildenborough
Tonbridge
Kent TN11 9LE. (0732) 833924.
In- and out-patient facilities for Anthroposophical therapies.

Tyringham Naturopathic Clinic

Newport Pagnell
Milton Keynes
Bucks MK16 9ER. (0908) 610450x204.
Osteopathy, acupuncture, massage, naturopathy, indoor pool with sauna and jacuzzi, gymnasium, hydrotherapy. Outdoor sports facilities. £228 -£465 per week. Are a charity.

RESIDENTIAL WORKSHOPS

A residential is a workshop which takes place over a weekend or longer, and in which the participants stay together in accommodation provided, usually because the venue is in the country. This builds up a more intensive atmosphere, and can enable people to enter more fully into the workshop. See also 'Residential Communities' in this section.

Abshot Holistic Centre
Little Abshott Road
Titchfield Common
Fareham
Hants PO14 4LN. (0489) 572451.
'Maitri' means 'friend to oneself' and here they run self development courses including stress management, regression therapy, polarity therapy, synergetics, meditation and channelling. Centre used to be the stables of the old Abshott Manor, which were converted 6 years ago. Swimming pool, vegetarian food, special diets catered for with prior notice. Training centre for the International School of Polarity Therapy. £65 per weekend, £90 for a four day course.

Ashtanga Centre
9 Vallis Way
Frome
Somerset
BA11 3BD. (0373) 72205.
Residential centre running residential weekend courses on yoga, massage (ITEC), meditation, shiatsu, touch for health. £80 for weekend inclusive of food. accommodation and tuition.

Aura Soma
Dev Aura
Little London Tetford
Nr Horncastle
Lincs LN9 6QL. (0507) 533781.
Colour therapy and its healing adjuncts. 6-day residential courses cost £370.

Bartragh
Bartragh Island
Lillala Bay
County
MAYO EIRE. 010 353 9632285/32514.

Beacon Centre
Cutteridge Farm
Whitestone
Exeter
Devon EX4 2HE. (039281) 203.
The centre is committed to personal, interpersonal and planetary healing and transformation. Courses on self enlightenment and transformation, yoga, meditation, tai chi, circle dancing, crystal healing and psychotherapy. Fully centrally heated with sauna and olympic size trampoline for those who are feeling 'bouncy'. Situated within 20 mins drive of Dartmoor, the sea and Exeter city centre. Working organic farm. Long weekend is approx £75, plus £4 (+ VAT) per night for shared accommodation - includes hire of self catering kitchen. Bed and breakfast also available. Write for programme. Available for hire for groups.

CAER (Centre For Alternative Education And Research)
Rosemerryn
Lamorna
Penzance
Cornwall TR19 6BN. (0736) 810530.
Wide range of workshops including Alexander Technique, gestalt, massage, rebirthing, resonance therapy, stress management, yoga, Shamanism, women's and men's groups and body-oriented approaches, groupwork, RSA certified courses in groupwork and counselling etc. One

of the longest established centres for residential workshops in personal and professional development in Europe. It is situated in seven acres of woods and gardens, near the sea in an area of outstanding natural beauty. The house itself is an old Cornish manor house. When there are no groups there, you can stay on a nightly basis. Wheelchair access. £35 per person daily including residential costs and VAT. Average price of a 5 day group £250 (includes residential costs), 3 day group £90. Concessions for low waged and unwaged.

Centre of Light
Tighnabruaich
Stuy, by Beauly
Inverness-shire IV4 7JU. (046) 376 254.
Residential healing and therapy centre in the peace and beauty of the Scottish highlands. Practise healing, channelling, kinesiology, massage, healing with colour and light. Week long courses and individual sessions. £425 per week. £130 per weekend. Healing sessions with three healers £45. Individual sessions £20 per hour.

Eden Centre
Eden House
38 Lee Road, Lyton
Devon EX35 6BS. (0598) 53440.
A centre for holistic approach to health and creative development. Holiday retreats £56 per week, accommodation only. £112 including food. Week workshops all-in £170. Weekend workshops £75. Minimum booking is for one week. Offer a wide range of therapies - massage, aromatherapy, relaxation, meditation, colour therapy, writing/poetry, Alexander technique and stress management. The house is available for small groups in August.

Findhorn Foundation
The Park
Forres
Scotland IV36 OTZ . (0309) 73655.
Courses include Learning to Love, Letting Go - Unfolding Your Inner Self, Massage, Deep Ecology, Primal Painting, Towards Sexual Wholeness, Myths we Live By, Gestalt to name but a few. Participants live and work in the Findhorn Community in the 'Experience Week', completion of which is a requirement for participation in most courses longer than a weekend. For prices see under List of Centres sec-

tion. For details of the philosophy of Findhorn see Other Groups in Spirit section.

Gablecroft College of Natural Therapy
Church Street
Whittington
Shropshire SY11 4DT. (0691) 659631.
Residential training in massage, reflexology, aromatherapy, sports injury treatment, healing and dowsing. ITEC recognised. Finnish sauna and organic, vegetarian meals.

Grimstone Manor
Yelverton
Devon PL20 7QY. (0822) 854358.
Residential group training centre run by Grimstone Community. The Community runs several workshops each year and hosts many more. Courses on rebirthing, yoga, reflexology, massage, shiatsu, gestalt, psychodrama, tai chi. Also retreats, holiday breaks and season celebrations. The manor is situated in 27 acres on the edge of Dartmoor and has an indoor swimming pool, jacuzzi and sauna. Prices vary according to nature of the workshop. Short stays, bed and breakfast sometimes possible.

Hazelwood
Loddiswell
Nr Kingsbridge
S Devon TQ7 4EB. (0548) 82232 / (081) 883 2124.
Workshops on voice work, and music weekends with classical performers in concert (£175 per weeknd for the latter).

Holwell Centre for Psychodrama and Sociodrama
East Down
Barnstaple
Devon EX31 3NZ. 0271 850 267/597.
Weekend and week long courses covering Living Without the Hurt Child, Learn to Love the Devil in You, Couples, Dreams, Journal Process, Cancer/AIDS and Psychodrama, How do Psychotherapists Handle Their Own Anxiety? and more. £120 per residential weekend, £315 per week. Centre also available for hire. No wheelchair access at present, but changes are being made. Creche facilities by arrangement.

RESIDENTIAL WORKSHOPS

Hourne Farm
Steel Cross
Crowborough
Sussex
(0892) 661093.
Set in the Sussex countryside, they offer a programme of weekend workshops, courses, open weekends and summer schools. Study of leylines, divination, yoga, holistic therapies, crystals. Approx £55 per weekend workshop.

Laughing Otter Retreat
95 Devon Port Road
Shepherds Bush
London W12 8PB. (081) 740 4991.
Workshops on native American Indian practices. They are held in Suffolk and Dorset. Weekend retreats in different locations. £120 per weekend. Concs. Offer massage, medicine wheel therapy, past life healing, sweat lodge ceremonies, vision questing, shamanic drumming, crystal and colour therapy. Men and women only groups available.

Le Plan Seminars
10 Irene Road
London SW6 4AL. (071) 736 2460.
Weekend courses in Provence, France, on aspects of healing and spirituality both individual and global. Teach people to be healers. Large enough for 24 students. Also run 4-part diploma course in healing (cost £2,100). Partial bursaries available.

Musicosophia
25 Hatch End
Forest Row
E. Sussex RH18 5DT. (0342) 822511.
Located near East Grinstead. An international group of music lovers exploring an innovative approach to conscious and creative music listening which helps to increase powers of concentration and sensitivity to classical music. No technical knowledge of music required. £50 - £60 per weekend workshop, non residential. Residential costs more.

Okido Natural Health Education Trust
Basement Flat
45 Elgin Crescent
London W11. (071) 727 1575.
Yoga holidays in Holland.

Pegasus Foundation
Runnings Park
Croft Bank
West Malvern
Worcs WR14 8BR. (06845) 65253.
Weekends about aspects of healing such as counselling skills, developing healing potential, healing relationships. Residential fees £95-£110.

Pellin Training Courses
15 Killyon Road
London SW8 2XS. (071) 720 4499.
Intestive residential personal and professional growth programme in southern Italy. Described by the organisers as 'arduous and challenging' in a safe and nourishing environment. Morning and evening group for individual Gestalt work. £275 per programme week, including full board, excluding air fares.

Studio 8
10 Wycliffe Row
Totterdown
Bristol BS3 4RU. (0272) 713488.
Open arts workshops, tutorial groups, Art Synthesis course exploring creativity, imagination and adventure through drawing, painting and other visual arts - 'awareness through art'. Venues are London, Wales, Kent and Italy. £43.50 for non-residential London weekends, £190 for a week in Wales or Kent inclusive.

Taraloka
Cornhill Farm
Bettisfield
Nr Whitchurch
N. Shropshire SY13 2LV. (094875) 646.
Buddhist retreat centre for women. Part of 'Friends of the Western Buddhist Order'. A year round programme of events. Meditation and an introduction to Buddhism. £60 per weekend. Concs.

Tighnabruaich
Tigh na bruaich
Struy
by Beauly, Inverness-shire
Scotland IV4 7JU. (0463) 76254.
Healing centre in Scotland. Run 'The Watershed', a course exploring the self through nature. Can take up to 4 people to stay combining holiday with daily two-three hour therapy session. Vegetarian organic food. Watershed £350, stay £305 per week.

Vegetarian Society Cookery School
Co-ordinator Parkdale
Dunham Road
Altrincham
Cheshire WA14 4QG. (061 928) 0793.
Courses at various levels on how to cook vegetarian food for vegetarians and non-vegetarian participants. Weekends, weeks and the 'Cordon Vert' Diploma course.

Yoga for Health Foundation
Ickwell Bury
Ickwell Green
Nr Biggleswade
Bedfordshire SG18 9EF. (0767) 27271.
Residential, generally short stay (one/two weeks) yoga centre. Day and overnight guests also welcome. Please notify in advance of day visits.
Also run special courses for the disabled. £33 per day, £60 per weekend.

RETREATS

A retreat is an intensive period of meditation, study or other religious practices which is residential. They almost always take place in the country. All retreats have a programme of activities. There are usually set times for meditation or prayer, and this structure provides a framework within which the retreatant can let go of having to organise his or her life and concentrate on inner spiritual experience.

Retreats can vary enormously in terms of what the programme is and whether the organisers expect you to participate fully in all activities, or whether you can just be there and join in as you wish. It is as well to decide beforehand what you do want and to check with the organisers about the programme.

Some retreats have an intensive programme with a great deal of meditation or prayer, and others may be silent some, or all, of the time. Others have a looser programme. There may be an early start,

as early as 4am on certain retreats, and accommodation may be in dormitories or occasionally in smaller rooms. You may be asked to bring a sleeping bag. Sometimes participants are expected to work on the retreat, sometimes all the work is done for them. Food is usually vegetarian.

A good publication for finding a place for a retreat, even in central London, is **The Vision**, the Journal of the National Retreat Association *(24 South Audley Street, London W1 (071) 493 3534)*, which costs £1 plus post and packing. This lists all the Christian retreat houses in Britain and group and individual retreat facilities.

Creative and Healing Arts
222 Westbourne Park Road
London W11 1EP. (071) 229 9400.
Mainly weekend retreats in the country with yoga, shiatsu, dance and music.

Four Winds Centre
High Thicket Rd
Temple Hill
Dockenfield
Farnham, Surrey GU10 4HB. (025125) 3990.
Directed by Frank Kevlin, a Sufi leader, Four Winds runs a 'Summer Experience', a series of workshops on spiritual and psychotherapeutic themes. It's a transpersonal and humanistic growth centre. Programmes include Nirtan: Music, Meditation and Dance, Communicating Using NLP, Spiritual Retreat, Love, Anger and Confict etc. The centre is also available for hire, and for individual retreats.

Gaia House
Woodland Road
Denbury
Nr. Newton Abbot
Devon TQ12 6DY. (0803) 813188.
Buddhist vipassana (insight) meditation retreats, as well as working retreats, yoga, reiki, zen etc. Facilities for solitary retreats also available. Voluntary donations for teachings. Cost is for board and lodging £13 per day (cheaper for

HOLIDAYS

longer stays or for those who can provide needed skills).

Insight
Lighthouse Road
St. Brides, Wentlooge
Nr. Newport
Gwent NP1 9SF. (0633) 815582 (0633) 810126.
New Age centre retreat in a lighthouse. Situated on ley lines, near the sea. Wedge shaped bedrooms and a meditation pyramid room. Individual or group visits.

Patanjali Yoga Centre
The Cott
Marley Lane
Battle
East Sussex (0424) 870538. (0424) 870538.
The centre was started in North West London in 1972 to encourage people to cure themselves through yoga exercises and breathing etc. It changed its name and moved to Battle, East Sussex in 1989 where an Ashram was established.

HOLIDAYS

The centres listed below provide the opportunity for residential workshops or healthy activities coupled with a holiday location. For more information about wholesome breaks, try **The Complete Healthy Holiday Guide** *by Catherine Mooney, Headway Books £6.95* which lists over 300 places to stay where healthy food is served and healthy activities are on offer.

Churchill Centre
22 Montagu Street
Marble Arch
London W1H 1TB. (071) 402 9475.
Massage learning holidays in Lanzarote.

Cortijo Romero UK
4 Maldon Road
London W3 6SU. (081) 993 4898.
Holistic holiday courses in the foothills of the Sierra Nevada. From £260 per week. Courses include massage, dance, yoga, meditation. Set in the mountains. Swimming pool. Vegetarian food. A holiday in the sun.

Dove Centre
Henton Wells
Somerset BA5 1PD. (0749) 74604
Offer advice, information and support to those wishing to visit sacred sites (such as Glastonbury) in the South West of Britain. Can suggest itineraries or escort you to the site, and even lead you through a guided meditation when you get there if you want. Can give telephone advice, or you can visit and stay taking advantage of their bed and breakfast facilities and meditation room. If you want they can give you meditation/yoga instruction or book you up with a local alternative medical practitioner. Stone cottage, 200 years old; a quiet haven for personal retreats, healing and Kripalu Yoga.

HOLIDAYS

Fasting Walks
41b Haringey Park
Crouch End
London N8 9JD. (081) 341 7696.
Arrange walks and holidays throughout Europe where participants fast while enjoying the scenery and each other's company. Participants usually cover 25 kilometres a day after a 7am start, and find accommodation in the evening for the whole group. They are based in Germany and mainly German-speaker oriented, but are keen to have British people on the walks and are looking for a person in Britain who could act as a contact.

Gateway
c/o 76 Nelson Road Central
Great Yarmouth . (0493) 844458.
Centre in South West France offering limited accommodation in tranquil setting. There's a swimming pool, and a resident psychic adviser and dream counsellor are always on hand.

Hatha
33 Percy Road
Pocklington
York YO4 2LZ. (0759) 304140.
Arrange yoga holidays in different venues.

Health Holidays
31 Rosslyn Hill
London NW3 5UJ. (071) 431 0760.
Mediterranean holidays and country weekend breaks include yoga, meditation, massage etc. Vegetarian cuisine.

Le Val Dieu
11 Meadow Green
Welwyn Garden City
Herts. (0707) 324631.
Workshop holidays in southern France. Typically: yoga, meditation, art, medicine wheel, circle dancing. Workshops are held on a farm. Vegetable garden, horse riding, cows, good food. The address is 11190 Rennes-le-Chateau, (from UK phone 010-33-6874-2321).

Living Planet Travel Ltd
PO Box 922
London N10 3UZ. (0582) 429365.
Adventure holidays to Peru, India, Mexico and Nepal. Will arrange individual itineraries - for instance will introduce you to the Buddhist kingdom of Zanskar and Ladakh and their tradition Tibeten culture (£1600 for a 34 day holiday).

Millennium Institute
PO Box 935
Palo Alto
CA 94301 USA. (415) 321 2169.
Residential courses on personal growth and spirituality in Bali in a purpose built local-style complex. Two weeks in this idyllic setting will set you back £2974 including flight. Also run journeys and expeditions to the ancient power places of Peru, the Inca trail, Egypt and Greece, India and Nepal etc.

Oak Dragon Camps
PO Box 5
Castle Cary
Somerset BA7 7YQ. (0269) 870959.
Run a yearly series of outdoor, educational camps centred around various subjects such as spirituality, myth, creative arts, healing and green issues for both adults and children. Camp facilities include vegetarian food, children's funspace, hot showers, etc. Each day there is a camp pow-wow, workshops in marquees, ongoing practical projects, celebrations and spontaneously arising events. Numbers limited to 70-100 people. £70 - £95 for 8 days adults, small charge for children. Half price for low incomes.

Skyros Centre
92 Prince of Wales Road
London NW5 2NE. (071) 267 4424.
There are three centres on the island of Skyros in Greece - Atsitsa, Skyros Centre and the Skyros Institute. Atsitsa offers holistic health holidays where participants can join in a programme of yoga, massage, meditation etc. £395-£495 (depending on season), includes courses, accommodation and full board, flight not included. Skyros Centre offers personal development courses such as psychodrama, gestalt, bioenergetics etc. £385-£450 includes courses accommodation and half board, flight not included. Skyros Institute offers training courses in personal development and holistic health. £415-£515 includes courses, accommodation and half board, flight not included. Prices given are for two weeks.

Sunra
26 Balham Hill
Clapham South
London SW12 9EB. (081) 675 9224.
Health holidays in the sun. £520 including flight for two week holiday. Yoga and meditation and massage. Also yoga holidays in the UK.

LECTURES

Synthesis of Light Holidays (SOL)
112 Wood Vue
Spennymoor
Co Durham DL16 6RZ. (0388) 818151.
Yoga holidays in India and USA. Spiritual tours of India. Also Greek and South American holistic holidays. £125-£290 per week. Bursaries available at short notice.

Vegi Ventures
17 Lilian Road
Burnham-on-Crouch
Essex CM0 8DS. (0621) 784285.
Activity and sightseeing holidays in Britain and abroad for people who prefer a vegetarian diet. Samples of what is on offer are a Scottish Highland adventure on the Isle of Rasaay (£198 inclusive of board and lodging and tuition), canal cruising in France and Austrian ski parties. Small friendly groups. Holidays range from £94 for a weekend houseparty to £599 for a fortnight on an Adriatic Island. Also macrobiotic cooking.

Vinyasa Yoga
17 De Montfort
Merley
Wimborne
Dorset BH21 1TG. (0202) 842853.
Two week yoga vacations in Southern Greece. £395-£450.

EVENTS

LECTURES

Alternatives
St James's Church
197 Piccadilly
London W1V 9LF. (071) 287 6711.
This is a project dedicated to providing a platform for New Age ideas - creative and spiritual alternatives to currently accepted Western thought. It does this through a regular lecture series, workshops, meditations and sacred dance. It also provides a counselling service for other New Age groups, advising them how to start their own projects or helping them with any group dynamics problems.

Centre for Creation Spirituality
St James's Church
197 Piccadilly
London W1V 9LF. (071) 734 4511 (2-5pm).
The centre has a programme of workshops, talks and courses on green issues, sexuality, spirituality, creativity etc. £4, concs £2. Workshops £20 per day.

Hahnemann College of Homoeopathy
243 The Broadway
Southhall
Middlesex
UB1 1NF. (081) 574 4281.
Lectures on homoeopathy are held at the Polytechnic of Central London, 35 Marylebone Road, London, on alternative Sundays.

London Earth Mysteries Circle
18 Christchurch Avenue
London NW6 7QN. (081) 459 0652.
Talks by speakers on a wide range of earth mystery subjects. Held 2nd and 4th Tuesdays of each month (except August). £2 per lecture (unwaged, £1.50, members £1). They arrange mini-bus trips to ancient sites and related conferences around the country.

Rainbow Ark
PO Box 486
London SW1P 1AZ. (071) 828 2782.
For details of venue phone the above number. Free lectures every Thursday at 6.30pm at a central London venue. All welcome. Speakers on a wide range of new age and holistic subjects from tarot and prophecy to healing, UFO's,

Zen, green economics and the millennium. There is time for questions, discussion and socialising. Also run 'Wholology' courses and workshops.

Turning Points
Office: 21a Goldhurst Terrace
London NW6 3HB. (071) 625 8804.
Tuesdays 7-10pm. Established in 1982, originally at St James's, Piccadilly, then branching out to include other venues in central London, Wales and Greece. Topics include personal and planetary change, healing, creativity, men and women, etc. Light refreshments are served and there is time for socialising. Workshops and conferences. Sell tapes and books. Wheelchair access sometimes. £3 per evening, £25-£30 per day. Concessions.

FESTIVALS

New Life Designs
170 Campden Hill Road
London W8 7AS. (071) 938 3788.
Organise 1) Festival for Mind, Body, Spirit (May bank holiday weekend) - the original 'New Age' festival which has been going for 13 years. Covers natural health, personal growth, spiritual/philosophical organisations, psychic arts, ecology, crafts and products. As well as the stalls, there's an ongoing programme of lectures, demonstrations and workshops. 2) The Healing Arts Exhibition (usually held in the autumn). Alternative medicine and complementary therapies exhibition - therapies, products, training bodies etc. Lectures and workshops, and a physical therapy room where a team of bodyworkers will give you a taste of the technique of your choice.

Swan House Special Events
Holly Road
Hampton Hill
Middlesex TW12 1PZ. (081) 783 0055.
Organise *The Health Show* (formerly *Here's Health Exhibition*). Now covers green living (who doesn't these days?), fitness, beauty and healthy eating as well as natural remedies and therapies.

GALLERIES AND MUSEUMS

Freud Museum
20 Maresfield Gardens
Hampstead
London NW3. (071) 435 2002.
Weds-Sun 12-5. Admission £2 adults, £1 concessions (children under 12 free). Freud lived here for the last year of his life after fleeing Nazi-occupied Vienna with his family in 1938. His library and study house his collection of Greek, Egyptian, Oriental and Roman antiquities and here you can also see the famous analytic couch. The museum also runs exhibitions, lectures and seminars and shows videos based on Freud's own home movies.

EVENTS

OTHER EVENTS

Barefoot Boogie

Jacksons Lane Community Centre
Archway Rd and Jacksons Lane
London N6. (081) 883 2966.
No smoking, barefoot boogie perrier drinking
folks only. Great place to let your hair hang
down on a Friday night. Large hall, world music
and rock. Bring an instrument if you wish. 7.30
-11pm. £4.

Circle Dance

Old Hall Community
East Bergholt
Colchester
Essex CO7 6TG. (0206) 298294.
Celebrate the seasons with dances and songs of
unity from many lands. Stefan Freedman cho-
reographs dances and accompanies on the
accordion, flute and guitar. Holidays, weekends
and day workshops. Write for details.

Gaia Limited

2-4 High Street
Glastonbury
Somerset BA6 9DU. (0458) 34131.
Week of events, lectures, discussions, stalls,
exhibitions and celebrations to explore the
topic of how personal and community responsibility can further the evolutions of strategies supporting planetary recovery.

Hold Back The Night

The Feathers Club
Dalgarno Way
London W10. (081) 208 1983.
New venue, last Saturday of every month 9pm-
2am. Multi-event club: dance floor with 'world
grooves' (Latin, African, jazz and soul music),
acoustic live sound room, cabaret (featuring
the like of John Hegley and Josie Lawrence),
chill-out room, trampolines and inflatables, juice
bar (for those wanting something a bit stronger,
bring your own), vegetarian and vegan cuisine.
For those who can't stand the strain, masseur
and reflexologist will be in attendance for foot
first aid. Creche from 9-12. £4.50 entrance,
£3.50 concessions.

Tibet Foundation

43 New Oxford Street
London WC1A 1BH. (071) 379 0634.
Organise Tibetan cultural events, such as the
World Tour of Sacred Music and Sacred Dance
by the Tibetan monks of Gaden Shartse Monas-

tery. Send SAE for details of other cultural
events.

Urasenke Foundation

4 Langton Way
London SE3. (081) 853 2595.
Traditional Japanese tea ceremony - sessions
are £10 and you have to be a member of the
society. Membership £23 p.a. Established 1976.

Whirl-Y-Gig

75 Herga Court
Sudbury Hill
Harrow
Middx HA1 3RT. (081) 864 6760.
Wednesday nights and alternate Saturdays. The
alternative disco. A place to dance to World
Music and refresh yourself at the cafe selling
Norfolk Punch and a range of health drinks.
While Whirl-y-Gig used to take place in Notre

EVERY SATURDAY NIGHT

**except Aug - Sept & Xmas break; please
phone 081 864 6760 for more details**

Dame Hall in Leicester Square, this venue has been temporarily closed, so ring for details of venue - Old Hampstead Town Hall is usually used.

Woodie's
32 Hillmarton Road
London N7 9JS. (071) 609 1586.
Phone before you boogie on down to check Woodie's is happening.

HELP

ORGANISATIONS FOR

SPECIFIC PROBLEMS

Alternative Centre
The White House
Roxby Place
Fulham
London SW6 1RS. (071) 381 2298.
Specialise in the treatment of psoriasis and eczema.

Cancer Help Centre
Grove House
Cornwallis Grove
Clifton
Bristol BS8 4PG. (0272) 743216.
Provides a complementary/holistic approach to cancer, which can be used alongside orthodox medical treatment. Programme includes counselling, dietary advice, relaxation and meditation, healing by touch. Patients can make day visits or stay over a longer period and participate in both one-to-one and group sessions, and are put in touch with local support group. Fees are £100 for patient plus one relative for initial day, £25 for subsequent days. £605 for one week patient, £165 for one week relative. Two bursaries available, one for day and one for residential patients.

Clinics Health International
Riverbank House
Putney Bridge Approach
London SW6 3JD. (071) 371 9717/371 9590.
Clinic specialising in the treatment of eczema, acne, psoriasis, dermatitis and other skin conditions through Chinese herbal medicine. Consultants are two professors from China.

Fellowship of Sports Masseurs and Therapists
B M Soigneur
London WC1N 3XX. 886 3120.
Run training courses for those wishing to become masseurs for sportspeople.

London Headache and Migraine Clinic

7 Park Crescent
London W1N 3HE. (071) 637 1491.
Offers a range of safe and natural therapies for the treatment and relief of headaches, migraines and related conditions. Uses acupuncture, herbal medicine, osteopathy and counselling as well as stress management, exercise and dietary advice if appropriate.

New Approaches To Cancer

5, Larksfield, Egham
Surrey TW20 ORB. (0784) 433610.
National and international charity which promotes the positive benefits of holistic and self-help methods of healing to cancer patients, which they see as complementing hospital treatment. Has national referral network linking support groups and individuals. They can refer those with cancer to their nearest local support group or clinic. The service is free, but the clinics they refer you to may not be. They provide advice over the whole spectrum of holistic healing therapies, yoga etc. and where it is available.

St James's Centre for Health and Healing

197 Piccadilly
London W1V 9LF. (071) 287 6711.
As well as offering a range of therapies and counselling, St James's Centre also runs free cancer support groups.

Traditional Chinese Medicine Clinic

10 Sandown Way
Northolt
Middx UB5 4HY. (081) 743 0706.
Specialise in treating gynaecological problems and cancer patients that cannot be treated by orthodox medicine. Appointment only. Patients are seen by Dr Hsu who also tries to prevent the side effects of western drugs on cancer patients. Children's problems also treated. First visit £55, subsequent visits £35. Unemployed and low waged get up to 25% discount.

Wandsworth Cancer Support Centre

PO Box 17
14/28 York Rd
London SW11 3QE. (071) 924 3924.
A cancer support centre offering one-to-one counselling and massage courses. Newsletter and resource library. Offer a holistic approach to those with cancer, their relatives, friends and health professionals. Run courses in relaxation and visualisation, workshops, on-going groups, counselling service. Offer healing and massage, also workshops for health professionals. There are books, tapes, periodicals and videos about cancer available on loan to members. Membership £5 per annum for individuals (£2 concessions). Established 1983. Run educational workshops and courses for health care professionals as well.

USEFUL ORGANISATIONS

Action Against Allergy

24-26 High St
Hampton Hill
Middx TW12.
Information centre (by mail only) and also charity headquarters for AAA membership and fundraising for research. Receive approximately 100 letters a week from allergic people needing advice of various kinds. They are not a medical body but they try to indicate where and how people might get medical help. Annual meeting with prominent speaker. Mail order sales of books. Membership £10 per year, members get magazine 3 times per year and access to postal lending library.

Appropriate Health Resources and Technologies Action Group

1 London Bridge Street
London SE1 9SG. (071) 378 1403.
AHRTAG supports and provides information on the primary health care approach (PHC) around the world. The aim of PHC is to provide comprehensive health care for everyone with an emphasis on preventive care, co-operation between different sectors of society, community participation and a fair distribution of resources.

Association for Humanistic Psychology

c/o 26 Huddlestone Road
London E7 OAN. (081) 555 3077.
AHP is an organisation for people from all walks of life interested in the values of Humanistic Psychology. There are workshops, lectures and social events regularly. Has its own journal 'Self and Society' and a separate section for practitioners e.g. therapists, counsellors etc.

USEFUL ORGANISATIONS

Association for Improvements in the Maternity Service (AIMS)
40 Kingswood Avenue
London NW6 6LS. 960 5585.
Advise and support for all parents on maternity rights and home birth. Pressure group. The volunteers work from home. Produce a quality pamphlet. Have a feminist, empowering holistic approach to birth.

Association of General Practitioners of Natural Medicine
The Hon Secretary
38 Nigel House
Portpool Lane
London EC1N 7UR. (071) 405 2781.
The association controls the standard of teaching and practice of a GP of Natural Medicine. Membership £20pa. Conferences and training sessions. Fund raising activities: sponsored walks, annual gatherings etc. Concs.

Association of Humanistic Psychology Practitioners (AHPP)
14 Mornington Grove
London E3 4NS. (081) 983 1492.
A professional organisation existing to promote the highest standards of excellence among humanistic psychology practitioners. Practitioners have to satisfy strict criteria of training and professional competence and are required to adhere to high standards of practice and ethics. They produce a membership directory (free) listing practitioners who are members as well as a list of training organisations of humanistic psychotherapy.

Balint Society
Tollgate Health Centre
Tollgate Rd
Beckton. (071) 474 5656.
The Society promotes learning about, and research into the understanding of, the Doctor-patient relationship. Meetings and lectures. Trainees and young practitioners welcome. Journal to members free. £20 membership.

British Association for the Person-Centred Approach
BAPCA
London WC1N 3XX.
A newly formed organisation whose aims include bringing together all people, groups and organisations who work in the tradition of the person-centred approach based on the work of Carl Rogers. It is part of a European wide organisation - there are similar associations in France, Germany, Italy and Hungary. Details of events can be obtained from the above address.

British Association of Art Therapists Ltd
11a Richmond Road
Brighton BN2 3RL.
Supply information about courses and training available in art therapy. Publish journal £7 subs (individual), £14 subs (organisation). Provide a folder of information on Art Therapy as a profession in Great Britain £5.

British Herbal Medicine Association
Field House
Lye Hole Lane
Redhill
Avon BS18 7TB. (0934) 862994.
Association for herbal practitioners, manufacturers and retailers of herbal medicines set up to promote and monitor herbal remedies and their sale. Publish British Herbal Pharmacopoeia (2 volumes at £35 each, less for members).

British Natural Health Directory
49 Ossington Street
Bayswater
London W1 4LY.

British Nutrition Foundation
15 Belgrave Square
London SW1X 8PS. (071) 235 4904.
Leaflets and briefing papers on various aspects of nutrition, send SAE for list. Seminars on nutrition.

British Register of Naturopaths
1 Albermarle Road
York YO2 1EN.

British Society of Dowsers
Sycamore Cottage
Hastingleigh
Ashford
Kent TN25 5HW. (0233) 75253.
Seminars and residentials on dowsing for beginners and old hands. Also lectures in London. Disseminates information on dowsing, network of local groups, lending library, journal to members, books and dowsing equipment for sale. Membership £16.50 per annum (UK).

College of Health
18 Victoria Park Square
London E2 9PF. (081) 980 6263.
Was set up in 1983 to represent the interests of users of the health service. The college keeps a register of over 1200 self help groups and voluntary organisations for people who suffer from particular diseases, disabilities and handicaps. Campaign. Publish 'Guide to Hospital Waiting Lists', 'Guide to Homes for the Elderly', 'Guide to Going into Hospital'.

Council for Complementary and Alternative Medicine
Suite 1
19A Cavendish Square
London W1M 9AD. (071) 409 1440.
Set up to provide a forum for communication and co-operation between professional associations of complementary practitioners.

Cranial Osteopathic Association
478 Baker Street
Enfield
Middlesex EN1 3QS. (081) 367 5561.
Professional body for cranial osteopathy. Register of members and training.

Doctor-Healer Network
27 Priory Terrace
London NW6 4DG. (071) 624 3874.
Membership/networking organisation for those interested in promoting holistic approaches to healthcare. Produce quarterly newsletter and professional journal, organise conferences and workshops. Produce self-help books and tapes and general information about holistic medicine, available mail order. Send SAE for full details. Members receive the quarterly 36-page newsletter Holistic Health, get discounts on self-help tapes, books and events and details of regional group activities. Membership for different categories: healthcare professional, healthcare student, and open membership for the public. Sliding scale from £15-£45 depending on income.

Dulwich Health Society
130 Gypsy Hill
London SE19 1PL. (081) 670 5883.
Promotes information and action on geopathic stress and magnetic therapy. According to the theory of geopathic stress, illness is caused by sleeping long term in an area of harmful 'earth radiation'.

Emerson College
Forest Row
Sussex RH18 5JX. (0342) 822238.
Training in Waldorf education, educational eurythmy, biodynamic agriculture, rural development, social development, sculpture, voice development, speech and drama - all are applications of Rudolf Steiner's anthroposophy (qv). Also run some residential workshops.

FACT - Food Additives Information
Room W
25 Horsell Road
London N5 1XL.

Floatation Tank Association (UK)
3A Elms Crescent
London SW4 8QE. (071) 350 1001.
Is a professional body for people offering float tank facilities for public use. It sets professional standards and disseminates information. Membership subscription: £75 professional membership, £30 individual membership. Information and literature about floating. Workshops.

Green Paths Centre
13 Croftdown Road
London
NW5 1EL. (071) 485 9981/4870.
Programme of workshops, discussions, lectures, meetings for people 'greening' their lives, lifestyles and businesses. Aims to facilitate personal growth and social renewal from a green perspective.

Hahnemann Society
Humane Education Centre
Avenue Lodge
Bounds Green Road
London N22 4EU. (081) 889 1595.
Publish Homeopathy Today / see Homeopathy Today

Health Practitioners' Association
181 Erith Road
Bexley Health
Kent DA7 6HS.
Advice on training in Complementary therapies. Register of practitioners. Post-graduate training seminars in London.

Holistic Health Association
42 Mansfield Road
Worthing
West Sussex BN11 2QN.

Holistic Health Concessions Register
36 Broadway Market
Hackney
London E8 4QJ. (071) 254 1158.
List of 250 qualified practitioners offering complementary therapies and psychotherapy at reduced fees for the low waged. Ring for details or write enclosing SAE because they are completely unfunded and can't afford to pay for stamps. Have worked with Angel Drug Project to make complementary therapies available to drug users. Lowest £5, and some practitioners will work free with people who are HIV positive or have AIDS.

Homoeopathic Trust
Hahneman House
Great Ormond Street
Bloomsbury
London WC1N 2HR. (071) 837 2495.
Located next to the Great Ormond St Hospital, the Trust will supply you with a list of GP's who practice homoeopathy. This list is contained within an info pack which costs £1.50.

Identity Counselling Service
2 Warwick Crescent
London W2 6NE. (071) 289 6175.
Specialise in counselling for personal and relationship issues, and those confused about their sexual identity and orientation.

INFORM
London School of Economics and Political Science
Houghton St, Aldwych
London WC2A 2AE. (071) 955 7654.

International Psychoanalytic Association
Broomhills
Woodside Lane
London N12. (081) 446 8324.
Keep a register of trained psychoanalysts throughout the world.

London Convivium for Archetypal Studies
PO Box 417
London NW3 6YE. (071) 431 1515.
Registered charity. Disseminate new ideas on archetypal psychology (Jung) and the arts. Yearly conference, usually in June. Produce an annual book called 'Sphinx' £10. Concs.

London Food Commission
88 Old Street
London EC1V 9AR. (071) 253 9513.
Researches the state of food in the capital, information on what goes in and out of food. Campaigns against harmful practices in production. Publications, available mail order, cover fast food, food adulteration, additives, food irradiation etc. Also publishes quarterly 'Food Magazine'.

Marylebone Centre
17 Marylebone Road
London NW1 5LT. (071) 935 6328.
This is an ordinary GP practice which employs an acupuncturist, osteopath, homoeopath and masseur to treat patients when appropriate. While they usually only treat patients registered with them from their catchment areas, they will take referals from other GPs for those who need an assessment of which complementary therapy could help them. Would that all GP surgeries were like this!

Medical Information Service
Boston Spa
Wetherby
W Yorks LS23 7BQ. (0937) 843434/210926.
Research articles from specialist journals in their Complementary Medicine Index - part of their Current Awareness Topics Services. £29 per year membership plus fee for search.

Pagan Funeral Trust
BM Box 3337
Lonon WC1N 3XX.
Information and advice about arranging a pagan funeral. Newsletter.

Pathways Publicity and Information Service
12 Southcote Road
London N19 5BJ. (071) 607 7852.
Regular bulletin of events and resources for growth and healing. £3 pa. members. Information on individual therapy, group work,

USEFUL ORGANISATIONS

training courses, organisations and journals. Introductory booklets and videos. Brochure design and distribution service offered to practitioners. Send SAE to above address.

Refuah Shelaymah Natural Health Centre
42c Braydon Road
London
N16 6QB. (081) 800 2200
Provides word processing facilities for therapists and is also a networking point for exchange sessions of any therapy.

Society for Existential Analysis
Regents College
Inner Circle, Regents Park
London NW1 4NS. (071) 487 7556.
Provides a forum for the expression of views and the exchange of ideas amongst those interested in the analysis of existence from philosophical and psychological perspectives. Its aim is to be a professional association which will seek to develop and expand existential-phenomenological approaches to psychotherapy and counselling. Membership is open to anyone interested in this field and includes psychotherapists, psychiatrists, psychoanalysts, counsellors and students.

Society of Teachers of The Alexander Technique
10 London House
266 Fulham Road
London SW10 9EL. (071) 351 0828.
This is a governing body for Alexander Technique which does not refer people to practitioners.

Topaz Line
BM Topaz
London WC1N 3XX.
Free, friendly and confidential postal counselling and support, for those who prefer this method of 'talking through' their problems, or who perhaps cannot reach or afford other facilities. They take into account the belief system of the individual, and offer help with practical strategies for coping. A postal service only which is entirely free of charge, though people may make a donation if they wish, which goes towards costs. They are looking for volunteers, so if you wish to help, contact them.

UK Homoeopathic Medical Association
243 The Broadway
Southall
Middlesex UB1 3AN. (081) 574 4281.
Mainly for practitioners who have qualified in homoeopathy, who go on to a register of practitioners, which is made available to the public. £40 pa. members. You can ring up to find a local practitioner. They will send free a directory of members. Quicker response if you send SAE. Publish journal.

United Kingdom Standing Conference for Psychotherapy
167 Sumartra Road
London NW6 1PN. (071) 431 4379.
A federation of psychotherapy organisations representing the profession of psychotherapy in the UK. The aims of the Conference are to protect the public by the promotion of high standards of training, research and education; to foster the dissemination of knowledge about psychotherapy; and to increase its availability. The Conference is in the process of setting up a Register of Psychotherapists. (They regret they can only deal with enquiries from organisations, not from individuals.)

Alphabetical List of Centres

We have included when possible, information on what each organisation offers and a breakdown of costs, including concessionary rates

3HO Kundalini Yoga Foundation
55 Sunny Gardens Road
London NW4 1SJ. (081) 203
7302.
Spiritual teacher is Yogi Bhajan who is resident in USA and teaches around the world. Many members of 3HO are practising Sikhs. Run evening, weekend courses, seminar, residentials and retreats in France and the USA. Have residential communities and some people involved are natural healing practitioners. They also run a health food business and sell 'Yogi Tea' a healthy tea drink. They offer Yoga.

5 to Midnight
Nappers Crossing
Staverton
South Devon
TQ9 6PD. (080426) 655.
Ritual theatre, photo therapy. Residential workshops at various locations, some in London. Weekend workshops £40-50. They offer Dance therapy.

Abraxas
27 Bathhurst Mews
London W2 2SB. (071) 402
0290.
Run seminars and workshops on dreams. Ongoing evening and weekend workshops. Broadly Jungian but gestalt, art therapy and music is embraced. £100 for 10 evenings or £100 for two weekends. They offer Dream Therapy and Jungian Psychotherapy.

Abshot Holistic Centre
Little Abshott Road
Titchfield Common
Fareham
Hants PO14 4LN. (0489)
572451.
Run a variety of residential growth workshops in Hants. They offer Bioenergetics, Massage, Polarity Therapy, Resonance Therapy, Shiatsu, Meditation.

Academy of Systematic Kinesiology
39 Browns Rd
Surbiton
Surrey KT5 8ST. (081) 399
3215.
A natural health centre. Run workshop on balanced health. They offer Touch For Health therapy and training plus Acupuncture.

Acca and Adda
BCM Akademia
London WC1N 3XX. (081) 677
5837.
Workshops, tuition in esoteric subjects, magic and Wicca. Consultations in tarot, runes, palmistry, geomancy, I-Ching etc. Also publish *O Fortuna*, journal of spiritual, magickal and ecological progress. Esoteric subjects, beliefs and philosophies (of all kinds). Challenging (and impossible) big prize crossword every time. Quarterly. Sample issue £1.50 plus stamp, or £6 subscription . Day workshop £20 includes full vegetarian lunch and refreshments. No concessions, but may accept work (e.g. gardening, filing etc) in lieu. They offer Paganism.

Action Against Allergy
24-26 High St
Hampton Hill
Middx TW12.
A self help group for people with allergic illness. Newsletter. £5 subs. SAE to above address. Provide information only; leaflets, booklets, advice etc. £10 subs. They offer Allergy Therapy.

Active Birth Centre
55 Dartmouth Park Road
Kentish Town
London NW5 1SL. (071) 267
5368.
Provides an educational service for expectant parents which centres around yoga in pregnancy and preparation for an active birth. Full programme of workshops and seminars. Programme for mums and babies such as baby gymnastics and baby massage. Free national information and networking service by post or telephone. Sell books, pregnancy clothes, natural pregnancy and babycare products. Catalogues on request. They offer Active Birth therapy and training.

Acumedic Centre
101-103 Camden High Street
Camden
London NW1. (071) 388 5783.
Specialist supplies and health products sold in shop on the premises. Bookshop.
Chinese acupuncture and Chinese herbs. Professional supply showroom for equipment and products. See East Asia Company in this book. £20 per session typical. They offer Biofeedback, Stress Management, Acupuncture, Herbalism, Shiatsu.

Acupuncture and Osteopathy Clinic
34 Alderney Street
Pimlico
London SW1V 4EU. (071) 834
6229/1012.
£35 for acupuncture and osteopathy, initial consultation, £25 thereafter, £25 subsequent. They offer Hypnotherapy, Acupuncture, Osteopathy, Shiatsu, Aromatherapy, Reflexology, Homoeopathy, Alexander Technique.

Acupuncture Clinic
Number 7
31 Craven Park
London NW10 8SU. (081) 961
4736.

No consultation fee. £20 per session, £10-£15 concs. They offer Acupuncture.

Acupuncture Clinic of North London
Winchester Court
237 Green Lanes
London N13. (081) 886 9494.
They offer Acupuncture.

Adlerian Society for Individual Psychology
55 Mayhill Road
London SE7 7JG. (081) 858 7299.
Counselling and psychotherapy based on principles of individual psychology. They are a UK association of practitioners and associate members interested in Alfred Adler and the movement based upon his work called 'individual psychology'. Aim to advance public knowledge of the work of Alfred Adler and train counsellors and psychotherapists to practise in this tradition. They hold a programme of public lectures, a conference in Oxford and one day sessions in various parts of the country. The counselling centre, based in Swiss Cottage, London, is open Monday evenings 7-9. Typically £18 per one day workshop, £10 individuals sessions. Concs. Wheelchair access to public meetings and counselling centre in Swiss Cottage. They offer Adlerian Therapy and training.

Aetherius Society
757 Fulham Road
London SW6 5UU. (071) 736 4187.
Open to public Mon-Sat 9am-10pm. Centre where lectures/healing services and personal instructional courses are held with a health food shop nearby. Also have a northern headquarters and groups throughout the country. Sell books and have a mail order service. Manufacture and sell radionic pendulums and holy stone shapes. Give spiritual counselling. Run a 'UFO hotline' on (071) 731 1094. Hold conferences and seminars. Wheelchair access. Services/healing free, donations welcome. Lectures £2.50. Senior Citizens £1.50. Courses £20-50 (one-two day). They offer Colour Therapy, Hand Healing,

Homoeopathy, Bach Flower Remedies.

African Herbs Ltd
104 Kingsley Road
Hounslow East
Middlesex TW3 4AH. (081) 570 5795.
Astrology, spiritualism. They offer Herbalism.

Alexander Teaching Centre
188 Old Street
London EC1V 9BP. (071) 250 3038.
Established since 1983. Register of practitioners. Concs. Bookshop in the main building. £15-£16 an individual lesson. Workshops from £45. Introductory evening classes £45. They offer Alexander Technique.

All Hallows House
St Dunstan-in-the-East
Idol Lane
London EC3R 5DD. (071) 283 8908.
Holistic health centre in the Wren Tower in the City of London. Open Mon-Fri 9-7pm. Concessions for long term treatment. They offer Allergy Therapy, Stress Management, Acupuncture, Biodynamic Massage, Autogenic Training, Hellerwork, Counselling, Aromatherapy, Herbalism, Reflexology, Polarity Therapy, Yoga, Diet Therapy.

Alternative Medical Trust
Tintagel
Camblesforth
Selby YO8 8HW.

Alternative Medicine Clinic
56 Harley House
Marylebone Road
London NW15 HW. (071) 486 7490.
Complementary health centre. One level apartment with lift facility. the client is seen at consultation as a whole person and the problem is assessed. £25 per session. They offer Allergy Therapy, Iridology, Kinesiotherapy, Hypnotherapy, Stress Management.

Andrew Still College of Osteopathy
30 Rosebank Road
London W7 2EN.

They offer a training in Osteopathy.

Anglo-European College of Chiropractic
13-15 Parkwood Road
Boscombe
Bournemouth
Dorset BH5 2DF. (0202) 431021.
They offer a training in Chiropractic.

Anna Freud Centre
21 Maresfield Gdns
Hampstead
London NW3 5SH. 794 2313.
They offer Child psychotherapy plus the relevant training.

Anthroposophical Association
Rudolf Steiner House
35 Park Road
Regents Park
London NW1. (071) 723 4400.
Office open 10-1, 2-6. Lectures, performances, classes in eurythmy, painting, drawing, creative speech, groups, workshops and courses exploring Rudolf Steiner's anthroposophy and its implications. Opened in 1926, bookshop, library open to public. Information about Steiner schools, homes and other activities. Weekend seminars for Teachers in Steiner schools. Wheelchair access. Lectures and evening workshops £3.00 (£1.50 concs). Day workshops.

Arbours Association
6 Church Lane
London N8. (081) 340 7646.
They offer a training in Psychoanalytic Therapy.

Arbours Consultation Service
6 Church Lane
London N8. (081) 340 8125.
£Neg with individual therapist. Concs. They offer Psychoanalytic Therapy.

Arcadia SE6 Creative Therapy Centre
130 Wellmeadow Road
London SE6 1HP. (081) 698 6312.
Radical psychoanalysis and advocacy. £23/session. They offer Psychoanalysis, Gestalt Therapy.

Aromatherapy Associates
68 Maltings Place

Bagleys Lane
Fulham
London SW6 2BY. (071) 371
9878/(071) 731 8129.
Nine practitioners and three treatment rooms. All associates are fully qualified, insured members of the International Federation of Aromatherapists. Mail order - body and bath and face oils. £37 initial consultation, £32 subsequent treatment. They offer Aromatherapy treatments and training.

Aromatherapy Training Centre

56a Riggindale Road
Streatham
London SW16 1QJ. (081) 677
1293.
Wheelchair access. £15-£30 per session. They offer Aromatherapy, Reflexology.

Art from Within

119 Grosvenor Avenue
Highbury
London N5 2NL. (071) 354
1603.
Groups held at the Highbury Centre at above address. Booking necessary. Groups are a maximum of 10 people and are not drop-in. Individual sessions are usually six initial sessions after which it is open ended. Short term and long term in-depth work. £20-£30 for individual sessions. £80 per weekend. £100 for 8 three hour sessions (evenings) They offer Art Therapy, Psychosynthesis.

Art of Dream Fulfilment

28 Woodlea Road
London N16 0TH. (071) 241
6415.
Creative visualisation and life improvement. Workshops and courses and metaphysical counselling and healing. Counselling with the Tarot. £10 for healing to £80 for longer courses. Counselling £18. They offer Dream Therapy.

Art of Movement

9 Aynhoe Mansions
Aynhoe Road
London W14. (071) 603 5122.
Creative dance workshops. Gabriel Roth's system of dance - 5 rhythms to release. £25 per day. £18-£25 per hour individual work. Astrological counselling £50 chart reading of one and half hour's duration. They offer Dance therapy, Astrological Psychotherapy.

Arts Psychology Consultants

29 Argyll Mansions
London W14 . (071) 602 2707.
An eclectic, humanistic, arts based psychology and counselling service to anyone working in the performing or creative arts. Established in 1988. Staff are psychologists and counsellors with background in the arts. Also offer training, career guidance, creativity and personality testing. Database service available for specialist referrals. Concessions for the low income. All appointments by telephone. Phone for prices. They offer a psychotherapy training.

Asatru Folk Runic Workshop

43 St Georges Avenue
London N7. (071) 607 9695.
Northern mysteries study group. Courses in runecraft, lectures, consultations. They offer Paganism.

Association for Analytic and Bodymind Therapy and Training

8 Princes Avenue
Muswell Hill
London N10 3LR. (081) 883
5418.
The centre is small, personal, friendly and supportive. An association of caring men and women, each with a distinctive style and expertise. It has been established for 20 years. There are also talks on the principles and methods therapists use. £25 - £38 for individual sessions. Approx £8-£10 per session for group therapy. Concs.They run a training in psychotherapy. They offer Couple Therapy, Hypnotherapy, Primal Therapy, Gestalt Therapy, Group Oriented Therapy.

Association for Group and Individual Psychotherapy

1 Fairbridge Road
Upper Holloway
London N19 3EW. (071) 272
7013.
They run a training in Psychoanalytic Therapy and Group Oriented Therapy. They offer Group Oriented Therapy, Psychoanalytic Therapy.

Association for Marriage Enrichment

c/o Westminster Pastoral Foundation
23 Kensington Square
London W8 5HN. (071) 937
6956.
Hold residentials through the UK for couples in 'marriage enrichment'. Non-residential activities can be arranged for suitable groups. Small selection of books from USA available. Offer a three weekend training course in marriage enrichment. £100 per couple per weekend. Concs. They offer Couple Therapy.

Association for Neuro-Linguistic Programming

100b Carysfort Road
London N16 9AP. (071) 241
3664.
Umbrella organisation. Register of practitioners of NLP. Contact and information point for general public and practitioners. Introductory and applications seminars on NLP. Two conferences a year. £ vary.
They offer Neuro-linguistic Programming.

Association of Ayurvedic Practitioners

7 Ravenscroft Avenue
Golders Green
London
NW110SA. (081) 455 3909.
They offer Ayurvedic Medicine.

Association of Biodynamic Psychotherapists

153 Goldhurst Terrace
London NW6 3EU. (071) 328
3868.
Referral list only for biodynamic psychotherapy. Professional newsletter, discussion with other psychotherapists. £15-20 per session. They offer Biodynamic Massage.

Association of Colour Therapists

c/o ICM
21 Portland Place
London W1 3AS. 636 9543.

LIST OF CENTRES

They offer Colour Therapy.

Association of General Practitioners of Natural Medicine
The Hon Secretary
38 Nigel House
Portpool Lane
London EC1N 7UR. (071) 405 2781.
They offer a training in Miscellaneous Body.

Association of Independent Psychotherapists
PO Box 1194
London N6 5PW. (081) 340 5441.
Aim to support people in coming to terms with early life difficulties and discovering their own sense of identity and purpose. A group of psychotherapists whose work draws on psychoanalytic, Jungian and transpersonal perspectives. £20-£30 per session for individual, £10-£16 for group work. Each therapist has a sliding scale of fees.They run a training in Psychotherapy. They offer Jungian Psychotherapy, Psychoanalytic Therapy, Transpersonal therapy.

Association of Jungian Analysts
3-7 Eton Avenue
South Hampstead
London NW3. (071) 794 8711.
They offer Jungian Psychotherapy and the associated training.

Association of Natural Medicines
27 Braintree Road
Witham
Essex CM8 2DD. (0376) 511069 / (0621) 892650.
Natural healing centre. £15-£25. Concessions to unemployed and OAPs. They run a training in Complementary medicine. They offer Acupuncture, Allergy Therapy, Hypnotherapy, Homoeopathy, Reflexology.

Association of Reflexologists
27 Old Gloucester Street
London WC1N 3XX. (081) 445 0154.
Professional association for reflexologists. Gives information to general public, and on schools for those wishing to train. Instructional meetings on other therapies and quarterly newsletter to members. Meetings arranged at various venues. Register. Workshops £20. They offer Reflexology.

Astro-Psychotherapeutic Practice
23 Whitehall Gardens
London W3. (081) 992 9514.
Established 1986. Ring for appointment. They also do mail order tape horoscope readings. Psychotherapy session from £25 . Horoscope readings from £45 . Workshops from £65. They offer Astrological Psychotherapy, Jungian Psychotherapy, Men's Therapy.

Audio Limited
26-28 Wendell Road
London W12. (081) 743 1518 or 743 4352.
Day and evening courses. Also individual biofeedback training, massage. £25 for a day workshop. They offer Biofeedback, Relaxation Training, Meditation.

Augenblick Centre
39b Bonnington Square
London SW8. (071) 735 4513.
Friendly centre run in a communal setting. Individual and group work. £20 for individual sessions, but depends on income and social situation. Run workshops such as 'Free Your Voice', 'The Healing Voice' and 'An Introduction for Bach Flower Remedies'. They offer Massage, Voice Therapy, Biodynamic Psychotherapy, Alexander Technique, Bach Flower Remedies.

B

Baha'i Faith
27 Rutland Gate
Knightsbridge
London SW7 1PD. (071) 584 2566.
Contact for details of local meetings.

Barbican Natural Health Centre
105 Whitecross Street
Barbican
London EC1Y 8JD. (071) 628 6139.
Established 1983. Six rooms on 2nd and 3rd floors. From £30 per hour. They offer Hypnotherapy, Acupuncture, Allergy Therapy, Aromatherapy, Homoeopathy, Naturopathy, Osteopathy.

Barnes Physiotherapy Clinic
2a Elm Bank Gardens
Barnes
London SW13 ONT. (081) 876 5690.
Established 1983. Physiotherapy, psychotherapy. £20. They offer Counselling.

Barry Long Foundation
Whistlands
Langley Marsh
Wiveliscombe
Taunton TA4 2UJ. (0984) 23426.
Mail order books and tapes of Barry Long. No callers or activities on site. They offer Meditation.

Bates Association of Great Britain
11 Tarmount Lane
Shoreham-by-Sea
West Sussex
BN43 6RQ. (0273) 452623.
Professional body for teachers of the Bates method. Can put you in touch with practitioners (send SAE). Can give general information on the method and supply booklist. Visiting lectures and workshops can be arranged. £15-25 per session. Workshops vary. Most teachers work with children at reduced fees. Low cost training clinics. They offer Bates Eyesight Training.

Bates Eyesight Training
128 Merton Road
London
SW18 5SP. (081) 874 7337.

Bates, Carrie
c/o Spectrum
7 Endymion Road
London N4 1EE. (071) 263 5545.
Offers holistic massage - helping people re-connect and get back in touch with their bodies. Carrie is a qualified massage practitioner, who aims to create a sense of well-being that can have far reaching physical,

LIST OF CENTRES

mental and emotional benefits. She believes in the importance of ongoing personal growth and professional development. £30 per hour and quarter for an individual session. Concessions on a negotiable basis. She offers Massage.

Bayly School of Reflexology
Monks Orchard
Whitbourne
Worcs WR6 5RB. (0886) 21207.
They offer a training in Reflexology.

Bayswater Clinic
25B Clanricarde Gardens
Bayswater
London W2 4JL. (071) 229 9078.
Natural holistic treatment for environmentally induced illnesses, such as food and chemical allergy. Biochemical testing for food and chemical allergies, nutrition and treatment of candidosis. Correction of diet and dietary counselling. £75 per hour consultation fee.
They offer Allergy Therapy, Diet Therapy, Homoeopathy.

Belgravia Beauty
11 West Halkin St
London SW1X 8JL. (071) 259 6033.
Beauty salon specialising in holistic therapy. £15-£45. They offer Aromatherapy, Massage, Relaxation Training, Biofeedback.

Bennet and Luck Natural Health Centre
54 Islington Park Street
Islington
London N1 1PX. (071) 226 3422.
Established for 3 years, this centre is also a health food shop selling books and a range of organic produce. Can refer if necessary. Wheelchair access to building but not to toilets. Range between £16- 25 per session. They offer Counselling, Acupuncture, Aromatherapy, Bach Flower Remedies, Diet Therapy, Massage, Naturopathy, Osteopathy, Reflexology, Shiatsu.

Bereavement and Loss Workshops
107 Antill Road
London N15 4AR. (081) 801 2296.

They offer Bereavement Counselling.

Beshara Trust
Frilford Grange
Frilford
Near Abingdon
Oxon OX13 5NX. (0865) 391344.
Runs seminars with visiting leaders.

Better Health Centre
129 Kentish Town Road
London NW1. (071) 485 7493.

Bexleyheath Natural Health Clinic
6 Sandford Road
Bexleyheath
Kent DA7 4AX. (081) 303 9571.
Established for 4 years, there are four practice rooms and waiting area. Consultations are by appointment only, but they are open to visitors. Sell books, tapes, cosmetics, dietary supplements and a selection of health foods.
Homoeopathy £20/£30 for initial consultation, subsequently £11/£15. Osteopathy £20.50 initially, then £17.50, Hypnotherapy £25, Acupuncture £18 initial consultation, then £14.50, Regression £50, Massage £20-£18. They offer Hypnotherapy, Regression, Acupuncture, Aromatherapy, Cranial Osteopathy, Homoeopathy.

Bhratiya Vidya Bhavan (Institute of Indian Culture)
4a Castletown Road
West Kensington
London W14 9HQ. (071) 381 3086/4608.
The philosophy of the Bharatiya Vidya Bhavan is summed up in their mottos: "Let noble thoughts come to us from all sides', and "The world is one family'. Spiritual director is Mathoor Krishnamurti. Celebrate with music, prayer and sacred dance. Every weekend, hold gatherings of people to sing bhajans (religious songs). Also discourses and seminars by well-known scholars and swamis. Hindu religious festivals are observed with prayers and offerings. Meditation hall for those of all religions, bookshop with sections on various religions and philosophy. Sell tapes, records and CDs of religious songs. Concs to students and the elderly. Bookshop on

premises. £2.50-£3.00. They offer Yoga, Hinduism, Meditation.

Biodynamic Clinic
23 High St
The Green
Ealing
London W5 5DF. (081) 579 1904.
Mon-Sat 9-9. Pleasant reception and large treatment area. Drop-in or by appointment. Established December 1989. Mother and baby clinic and childrens clinic. Monthly talks given at local town hall. Wheelchair access. £20 per hour pro rata. £12 per hour apprentice clinic. £30 per hour with senior practitioners. Weekend workshops £60. They offer Biodynamic Massage.

Biodynamic Psychotherapy and Teaching
13 Mansell Road
London W3 7QH. (081) 749 4388.
Two psychotherapists with 10 and 15 years of clinical experience offering Jungian psychotherapy which includes the body-dimension. Work with individuals, couples and groups; supervision available, especially for body therapists who want more analytical input: hypnotic trance work (past-life regression) available. Foreign languages available: German, some French and Spanish spoken. Sale of publications/ video by A B and G Heuer. £23 per session; group prices depending on size of group, average £10 per 3 hour session. They offer Jungian Psychotherapy, Biodynamic Massage.

Bioenergetic Partnership
22 Fitzjohn's Avenue
Swiss Cottage
London NW3. (071) 435 1079.
Bioenergetic Analysis as developed by Dr Alexander Lowen and his trainers with an analytic orientation. They offer an on-going evening group, weekly, subject to initial interview. Open to all. Individual ongoing bioenergetic therapy offered. Advanced monthly group to therapists and trainees. Workshops £15 evening, £30 day. Individual therapy £25 - £35 by negotiation. They offer Bioenergetics.

Bloomsbury Alexander Centre
Bristol House

LIST OF CENTRES

80a Southampton Row
Bloomsbury
London WC1. (071) 404 5348.
Lessons are on a one to one basis, so appointments have to be made. A course of lessons can be from 10 to infinity! People are welcome to drop in for information or to book appointments, and teachers are at the centre from 8am-8pm. There are five rooms, with about fifteen teachers using the centre, which has been established since 1987. The longest qualified teacher has been teaching for 13 years, and the centre provides a home for two senior teachers who have been teaching since the 1930s. Occasional introductory courses, courses for those with some experience, and for qualified teachers. Speakers on request. Books. Training starting in 1993 approximately. Access: ground floor, 2 steps to manage, slightly awkward door. Also run workshops and evening classes. £15-£20 per session (half hour), ranging down to £12 according to experience of teacher. Concessions arranged by discussion in the first session.
They offer Alexander Technique.

Bluestone Clinic
16 Harley House
Marylebone Road
Marylebone
London NW1. (071) 935 7933
or 935 8958.
Pulsed electromagnetic energy (PEME) which it is claimed speeds up healing in the body by 50%. Cold beam laser treatment and remedial beauty treatments. Visiting spiritual healers. 2 hour treatment £52 (includes remedial massage £20, plus osteopathy £20, and treatment on PEME which is charged at £20 per hour). Subsequently, if you don't require osteopathy, treatment is £40. Aromatherapy massage is £42 per hour. They offer Aromatherapy, Massage, Complementary medicine, Osteopathy.

Body Balance
14 Golders Rise
London NW4 2HR.

Body Clinic
32 The Market Place
Falloden Way
Hampstead Garden Suburbs
London NW11 6JJ. (081) 458 9412.

Electrolysis, neuro-muscular massage, Faradic therapy, G5 massage, facials, leg waxing, paraffin wax therapy, manicures, steam cabinet, sunbed, specialists in sports injuries and back problems. Has been established since January 1987. It is open 7 days a week and has late evenings Tues, Weds and Thurs till 9pm. There are 5 therapy rooms and 8 practitioners. Clients can usually pop in without an appointment, but this is not so on the late evenings or Sunday as these tend to get booked up in advance. Sell range of vitamins, essential oils, sports aids, therapeutic bath salts and books. Wheelchair access. One hour full body massage would cost £19.50. If you book a course of 5 therapies you get one free. Special rates for students. Concessions. They offer Hypnotherapy, Acupuncture, Aromatherapy, Chiropody, Laser Therapy, Massage, Naturopathy, Osteopathy.

Body Harmony
124 Streatham High Road
London SW16 1BW. (081) 769 9917.
Healing room at the back of their new age/body shop. £20-£25. They offer Aromatherapy, Touch for Health (Kinesiology), Hand Healing, Shiatsu.

Body Power
11 Merton Road
London SW2 1DP.

Body-Mind Centering
Flat 5
64 Sinclair Road
London
W14. (071) 602 8637/(0223) 894041.
Body-mind centering uses the movements of infancy, individual rhythms and expressive qualities of the body to release patterns and correct imbalances in the body. Methods used include touch, anatomical imagery and guided and improvised movements to bring about a more harmonious, responsive and expressive ways of moving and being. It can help with conditions such as low back pain due to chronic misuse, and can promote grace and co-ordination. Individual session and group workshops in London and Cambridge. Workshops can be arranged for special interest groups. Individual

sessions £18. They offer Complementary medicine.

Body-Mind Health Private Clinic
631 Green Lanes
Hornsey
London N8. (081) 340 0509.
The centre was established 11 years ago. They also treat people with spiritual difficulties.
Between £22-£30 for consultation and treatment. They offer Hypnotherapy, Acupuncture, Diet Therapy, Naturopathy.

Bodyspace
Guy Gladstone
The Open Centre
188 Old St. London EC1. (071) 254 8047.
£25/one hour session. One day workshop £25. Drop-in evening talks on bioenergetics. They offer Bioenergetics, Psychodrama and Pulsing.

Bodywise
119 Roman Road
Bethnal Green
London E2 0QN. (081) 981 6938.
Tai chi, aikido, yoga, Alexander and massage courses. Established 1983. Alternative health centre with five practice rooms, two group rooms. Reception cover from 9am-7pm and Sat mornings. Quiet friendly atmosphere. Yoga class £2.50 (1 hour). Average costs of therapies on offer is £18-£23 per hour. Concessions available. They run a training in Massage. They offer Counselling, Acupuncture, Alexander Technique, Feldenkrais, Homoeopathy, Martial Arts, Massage, Naturopathy, Osteopathy, Reflexology, Shiatsu, Yoga.

Bodyworks Natural Therapies
Greyhound House
23-24 George Street
Richmond
Surrey TW9 1JY. (081) 332 1751.
Acupuncture, kinesiology, diet therapy and shen tao can be arranged with advanced notice. Launched March '89, Bodyworks provides a home visiting complementary practitioner service covering central and greater London. Treatments are given

268

LIST OF CENTRES

either in clients homes, or their places of work.
1 hour £28, one and a half hour £35. A small fee may be added for visits outside London. They offer Aromatherapy, Massage, Osteopathy, Reflexology, Shiatsu.

Brackenbury Natural Health Centre
30 Brackenbury Road
Hammersmith
London W6 OBA. (081) 741 9264.
9am-9pm Mon-Fri, 9am-1pm Sat. Established in 1983, this is a large centre with over 25 qualified therapists and seven treatment rooms with cane furniture and indoor plants. Offer free advice to anyone unsure about treatment. Friendly, welcoming atmosphere. Some natural products sold, give talks and Qi Gong sessions in local church hall, hold workshops and occasional open days. Baby massage taught to two mums at a time. Register. Creche. No access. £20-£40. Concs available for students, OAPs, UB40s, low income.
They offer Counselling, Acupuncture, Alexander Technique, Allergy Therapy, Aromatherapy, Bach Flower Remedies, Biodynamic Massage, Colonic Irrigation, Colour Therapy, Diet Therapy, Herbalism, Homoeopathy, Massage, Naturopathy, Osteopathy, Polarity Therapy, Reflexology, Shiatsu, Couple Therapy, Feldenkrais, Hypnotherapy, Stress Management, Hand Healing.

Brahma Kumaris World Spiritual University
98 Tennyson Road
London NW6 7SB. (081) 459 1400.
Courses in positive thinking, meditation and interpersonal skills. Non-governmental organisation affiliated to the U.N. Centres in sixty countries. Working for peace based on change in human values. Free of charge. They offer Meditation.

Breakspear Hospital
1 High Street
Abbots Langley
Herts WD5 0PU. (0923) 261333.
They offer Allergy Therapy.

Bretforton Hall
Bretforton
Vale of Evesham

Worcs WR11 5JH. 0386 830537. Cymatics (acoustic treatment), (treatment by sound). £16 per session. They offer Aromatherapy, Colour Therapy, Massage.

British Acupuncture Association and Register
34 Alderney Street
London SW1V 4EU. (071) 834 1012.
Controlling body for acupuncture. They have a handbook with the list of the practitioners in London, £1.50. They offer Acupuncture.

British and European Osteopathic Association
6 Adele Road
Teddington
Middlesex
(081) 977 8532.
They keep a register of members. They offer Osteopathy.

British Association for Counselling
37a Sheep Street
Rugby
Warwickshire CV21 3BX.
(0788) 578328/9.
They keep a nationwide register of counsellors. Send £12 plus £2 postage for book listing counsellors throughout the UK. Produce journal 'Counselling' (£15 subs, £4 individual copies), and publications on counselling such as 'Careers in Counselling' and 'Guide to Training Courses in Counselling'. They sell cassettes and videos (also for hire) on counselling. They do a useful resource pack for those involved in AIDS counselling (£100). In London there is the North London Branch and the South London branch (listed in this book). You can become a member, phone or write for details. Prices are determined by the counsellor who is recommended to you, but the fees are usually very reasonable. They offer Counselling.

British Association for Counselling (North London Branch)
72 Great North Road
London N2 ONL. (081) 340 3924.
They have a local resource list of personal counsellors in private practice in North London, available at no charge by post. The branch has been established 5 years. They have an

ethical code of practice. They also publish information about counselling for the general public. This branch of the BAC offers a support network for counsellors: monthly meetings with speakers on counselling topics and access to the decision making of the BAC. £5-£30 per session, often negotiable according to the individual practitioner. They offer Counselling.

British Association for Counselling (South London Branch)
33 Crantock Rd
London SE6 2QS. (081) 698 3205.
Hold a monthly support group for counsellors. They offer Counselling.

British Association for Social Psychiatry
112A Harley Street
London W1. (081) 555 2603.
They offer Art Therapy, Bereavement Counselling, Family Therapy.

British Association of Analytical Body Psychotherapists
22 Fitzjohn's Avenue
Swiss Cottage
London NW3. (071) 435 1079.
Bioenergetic Analysis as developed by Dr Alexander Lowen and his trainers. They offer an on-going evening group, weekly, subject to initial interview. Open to all. Individual on-going bioenergetic therapy offered. Workshops £15 evening, £30 day. Individual therapy £25 - £35 by negotiation. They offer Bioenergetics therapy and training.

British Association of Psychotherapists
37 Mapesbury Road
London NW2. (081) 346 1747.
Individual psycho-analytic psychotherapy for adults and children. The BAP was founded in 1951 and in 1981 became a charity. The secretary will answer enquiries about the clinical service. The Clinical Service offers advice and information through consultation to adults and adolescents and children suffering from emotional and psychological problems. Those seeking help can discuss with an experienced psychotherapist, whether psychotherapy would be an appropriate form of help and treatment. There are some external

courses for people wanting to understand more about working in a psycho-dynamically orientated way. Consultation fee £30. On-going therapy between £18-£22. A few places are available in the Reduced Fee Scheme with trainee psychotherapists. They run a training in Psychoanalytic Therapy and Jungian Psychotherapy. They offer Child psychotherapy, Psychoanalytic Therapy.

British Buddhist Association
11 Biddulph Road
Maida Vale
London W9 1JA. (071) 286 5575.
Non-sectarian Buddhist group under direction of A Haviland-Nye Dhammacariya. Teach meditation and run part-time study courses for various levels of experience and knowledge. Shrine room for meditation, bookshop. Open by appointment. They offer Buddhism, Meditation.

British Chiropractic Association
Premier House
10 Greycoat Place
London SW1P 1SB. (071) 222 8866.
Will provide a range of leaflets on the treatments of different symptoms. Comprehensive list of practitioners. They offer Chiropractic.

British College of Acupuncture
8 Hunter Street
London WC1N 1BN. (071) 833 8164.
Have clinic where students work. Register of practitioners. They offer Acupuncture treatments and training.

British College of Naturopathy and Osteopathy
Frazer House
6 Netherhall Gardens
Hampstead
London NW3 5RR. (071) 435 7830 (clinic), 435 6464 (college).
Founded in 1935, this is a private training college with clinic open to general public. Register. Wheelchair access. They have available a register of practitioner members: send large

SAE for 28p and £1.50 for list plus leaflets. £12 initial consultation, £6 each subsequent consultation. They offer Naturopathy and Osteopathy treatments and training.

British Foundation for Past Life Therapy and Research
95 Prospect Road
Woodford Green
Essex IG8 7MD. (081) 505 8720.
Relaxation, pastoral counselling, stress control, past life regression therapy, divine/metaphysical healing, reincarnation. By appointment only. Quiet residence in East London. Clients can be visited. Initial consultation of one hour £15. Two hour therapy session £35. They offer Hypnotherapy.

British Homoeopathic Association
27A Devonshire Street
London W1N 1RJ. (071) 935 2163.
Register of qualified medical doctors trained in homoeopathy, and homoeopathic vets and chemists. Send SAE for list. They offer Homoeopathy.

British Hypnosis Research
8 Paston Place
Brighton BN2 1HA. (0273) 693622.
Centre at St Ann's Hospital, London (appointments through Brighton centre). Training videos and books available. Training in Eriksonian hypnosis, psychotherapy and NLP. Register. No wheelchair access. Therapy with director £50; with trainees free of charge. They run a training in Neuro-linguistic Programming. They offer Hypnotherapy, Neuro-linguistic Programming.

British Hypnotherapy Association
1 Wythburn Place
London W1H 5WL. (071) 723 4443.
Emotional and psychosexual difficulties, migraine and anxieties. Write giving a brief indication of your problem, stating area in London where you work or study and enclose £2. You will receive a list of practitioners and a pamphlet. Produce publications and give talks. £variable

per 50 minute hour. They offer Hypnotherapy.

British Institute of Homoeopathy
427 Great West Road
Hounslow
Middx TW5 0BY. (081) 577 7781.
They offer a training in Homoeopathy.

British Institute of Practical Psychology
67 Highbury New Park
London N5 2EZ.

British Ki Aikido Association
c/o The Secretary
48 Oakshott Court
Polygon Road
London NW1 1ST. (071) 281 0877.
Classes mainly in north London. They offer Aikido.

British Osteopathic Association
8-10 Boston Place
Marylebone
London NW1 6QH. (071) 262 5250.
Run clinic (see London College of Osteopathic Medicine) which specialises in offering low-cost treatment to those with low income. Register. They offer Osteopathy.

British Psycho-Analytical Society and The Institute of Psycho-analysis
63 New Cavendish Street
London W1. (071) 580 4952 or (071) 636 2322.
This establishment was founded by Ernest Jones, the biographer of Freud. They offer Psychoanalysis (and associated training) and Psychoanalytic Therapy.

British Reflexology Centre
Monks Orchard
Whitbourne
Worcs WR6 5RB. (0886) 21207.
Will provide a register of members for £1.50. Newsletter, books and charts. Details of Reflexology trainings and courses on related subjects. £10-

£25 per session. They offer Reflexology.

British School - Reflex Zone Therapy of the Feet (Ann Lett Ltd)
87 Oakington Avenue
Wembley Park
London HA9 8HY. (081) 908 2201.
Established in 1980 to train nurses, physiotherapists, midwives and doctors in reflex zone therapy. Affiliated to European schools in Holland, Scandinavia, Belgium, Spain, France, Italy, Israel, Switzerland and Germany with the same training programme. 20,000 practising therapists most of whom use their training in hospitals, clinics, and some in private practice. Register. Wheelchair access. They offer Reflexology treatments and training.

British School of Iridology
Dolfin House
6 Gold Street
Saffron Walden
Essex CB10 1EJ. (0799) 26138.
Register. They offer Iridology consultations and training.

British School of Oriental Therapy and Movement
46 Whitton Rd
Twickenham
Middx TW1 1BS. (081) 744 1974.
Drop in classes in Kitaiso, Tues (advanced) and Thurs (beginners). Training in Shiatsu. They use a large hall five minutes from Richmond tube station. Register of practitioners. No wheelchair access. The cost per term is £200. Concs. They run a training in Shiatsu. They offer Complementary medicine, Shiatsu, Acupuncture, Meditation, Herbalism.

British School of Osteopathy
1-4 Suffolk Street
London SW1Y 4HG. (071) 930 9254.
The British School of Osteopathy is a registered charity. Open Mon-Fri 9-6pm, and Sat 10-1. £8-£15, concs £4-£8. Sports clinic £18. They offer Osteopathy treatment and training.

British School of Reflexology
92 Sheering Road

Old Harlow
Essex CM17 0JW. (0279) 429060.
Register. Clinic and training school for 18 students, established 15 years. Wheelchair access. £13 for 45 minutes. They offer Reflexology treatments and training.

British School of Shiatsu-Do
188 Old Street
London EC1V 9BP. (071) 251 0831.
Treatments by appointment. Send SAE to their office for full details of courses. Established 1983. Hold open evenings for lectures. Sell books, videos, special clothes, futons and neck rolls. Talks and demonstrations by arrangement. Treatments: £18 for students of BSS. £25 for prospective students. Concs. They offer Shiatsu treatment and training.

British Shingon Buddhist Association
'Kongosatta'
12 Finchley Park
London N12 9JN.
Linked with the British Cheirological Society (qv). They offer Buddhism.

British Society of Hypnotherapists (1950)
37 Orbane Road
Fulham
London
SW6 7JZ. (071) 385 1166.
Established 1950. Register of practitioners. Training for treatment of neurotic behavioural problems, traumas and psychosomatic illness. They offer Hypnotherapy.

British T'ai Chi Association
7 Upper Wimpole Street
Marylebone
London W1M 7TD. (071) 935 8444.
Tai Chi. Original Yang and Cheng forms. For health, meditation and self defence. £80 for a course of ten two hour classes. They offer Martial Arts.

Brothers
207 Waller Road
London SE14 5LX. (071) 639 9732.
Growth programme for men using psychosynthesis, education and analytic techniques. Established for 5 years, Brothers runs introductory and

on-going workshops. Admission is based on written application. Also offer individual sessions for men. Annual conference 'Embodying the Masculine'. £60 per weekend. They offer Men's Therapy, Psychosynthesis.

Brunel Management Programme
Brunel University
Uxbridge
Middlesex UB8 3PH. (0895) 812058 or 256461.
Courses on self knowledge and self development for managers. Stress at work. Courses on interpersonal effectiveness in management and on organisational design and development. Plus other short courses. £150 - £200 per day for the management courses. They offer Management and Stress Management Courses.

Buddhapadipa Temple
14 Calonne Road
Wimbledon
London SW19. (081) 946 1357.
This is a Tai Buddhist Temple where they offer free Vipassana Meditation. It is also a retreat where people can stay.
Meditation free. Minimal cost for the retreat. They offer Meditation, Retreats.

Buddhist Society
58 Eccleston Square
Victoria
London SW1V 1PH. (071) 834 5858.
Introducing Buddhism course open to public - a series of 8 lectures running continuously throughout the year. Library open to public to browse, but not to borrow. Members may attend courses on Zen, Theravadin and Tibetan Buddhism. Residential summer school. Correspondence course in basic Buddhism, cassettes and bookstall. Seminars, lectures. Quarterly journal, 'The Middle Way', free to members . Basic Buddhism course free. Membership £16 per annum in London, £11.50 for those outside a 50 mile radius. Summer school £175 per week. They offer Buddhism, Retreats.

Bumblebees Natural Remedies
35 Brecknock Road

London N7 0AD. (071) 267 3884.
Chinese herbalism. Offer a wide range of treatments and have a shop on the premises. The shop sells natural medicines including: herbal, homoeopathic medicine, nutritional items, cruelty free products and aromatherapy oils. Near Kentish Town tube station. They offer Acupuncture, Alexander Technique, Aromatherapy, Colour Therapy, Cranial Osteopathy, Herbalism, Chiropractic, Homoeopathy, Massage, Naturopathy, Osteopathy, Reflexology, Regression, Shiatsu.

C

C.H.I Clinic
River Bank House
Putney Bridge Approach
London SW6 3JD. (071) 371 9590.
They are dealing with skin complaints like Psoriasis and Eczema. The treatment includes consultation and herbs. The clinic has 3 practitioners from China. Psychotherapy is also available alongside the herbs treatment. First consultation including first week herbs is £50 and after that it is £35 per week just for the herbs and the treatment; the consultation is free. They offer Stress Management, Herbalism.

CAER (Centre For Alternative Education And Research)
Rosemerryn
Lamorna
Penzance
Cornwall TR19 6BN. (0736) 810530.
One of the longest established centres for residential workshops in personal and professional development in Europe. They run a training in Counselling and Psychotherapy. They offer Feminist Therapy, Gestalt Therapy, Men's Therapy, Psychotherapy, Rebirthing, Stress Management, Alexander Technique, Mas-

sage, Resonance Therapy, Yoga, Shamanism.

Camden Osteopathic and Natural Health Practice
96 Malden Rd.
Camden Town
London NW5 4DA. (071) 482 1248.
They offer Acupuncture, Naturopathy, Osteopathy.

Camden Psychotherapy Unit
25/31 Tavistock Place
London WC1H 9SE. (071) 837 5628.
Offers therapy to Camden residents experiencing psychological and emotional difficulties. Free. They offer Family Therapy, Psychoanalytic Therapy.

Capital Hypnotherapy Centre
Temple Lodge
51 Queen Caroline Street
Hammersmith
London W6 9QL. (071) 737 1929.
Counselling, hypnotherapy, primary cause analysis.
Approximately £35. They offer Anti-smoking Therapy, Hypnotherapy.

Care-Healing Centre
3 Bristol Gardens
Little Venice
London W9 2JG. (071) 286 2003.
Run a training in hands-on spiritual healing which can be adjusted to a persons requirements. £45 per one and half hour session. Healing free or donation for charities. They offer Hand Healing, Hypnotherapy, Neuro-linguistic Programming, Crystal Therapy.

Central School of Counselling and Therapy
56b Hale Lane
London NW7 3PR. (081) 906 4833.
They offer Counselling.

Centre for 'A Course In Miracles'
56b Sotheby Road
London
N5 2UR. (071) 704 6197.

Study, prayer, meditation and group sharing around 'A Course In Miracles'. Evening courses and seminars.

Centre for Autogenic Training
Positive Health Centre
101 Harley Street
London W1. (071) 935 1811.
Individual or group session, also in-house programmes for groups from one company or area can be arranged. £40 for pre-course assessment, £140 for the course. They offer Autogenic Training.

Centre for Biosynthesis
BCM CHESIL
London WC1.

Centre for Counselling and Psychotherapy Education
21 Lancaster Road
Notting Hill
London W11 1QL. (071) 221 3215.
Professional training. Individual, couple and group therapy. Centre established 1983; comprising two houses (130 students). Holistic approach which includes the spiritual dimension.
Weekend workshops (£50 and short-term groups). £6-£30 per session (average £15; sliding scale). Concessions.
They run a training in Counselling. They offer Counselling, Couple Therapy, Transpersonal therapy.

Centre For Healing Through Forgiveness
22 Conway Road
Harringay
London N15 3BD. (081) 542 5567.
Centre for study, prayer, meditation, interactive group exercises, song and sacred dance based around 'A Course in Miracles'. Director is Simon Christopher who runs some events. Evening, weekend groups, courses and seminars. Run regular retreats in South Devon. Counselling also available. Aims to teach the meaning of true forgiveness and its value in the healing process. £25 per hour for individual sessions. Concessions on

LIST OF CENTRES

application. They offer Rebirthing, Meditation.

Centre for Health and Healing
St James's Church
197 Piccadilly
W1V 9LF. (071) 437 7118.
This centre is attached to St James's Church, Piccadilly and offers holistic therapies. Includes cancer care and women's group. Drop-in in the caravan. £25 per hour. Concs. They offer Counselling, Music therapy, Diet Therapy, Massage, Homoeopathy, Osteopathy, Aromatherapy.

Centre for Massage and Movement Studies
17 Beechdale Road
London SW2 2BN. (0903) 204893.
Weekend workshops as well as training in the Eyerman technique. They offer Massage treatments and training.

Centre for Nutritional Studies
The Garden House
Rufford Abbey
Newark
Notts NG22 9DE. (0623) 822004.
They offer a training in Diet Therapy.

Centre for Pagan Studies
Flat b
5 Trinity Rise
Tulse Hill
London SW2 2QP. (081) 671 6372.
Healing, pathworking and meditation. Established for educational, therapeutic and spiritual purposes to provide academic classes and experiential workshops in north European shamanism, wicca and ritual mythic drama. Also aims to act as a guide to seekers through the labyrinth of competing wares in the esoteric marketplace. Classes, workshops, apprenticeship training. Practice through ritual drama, mythic re-enactment, ecstatic dance, pathworking, chanting, making music etc. Consultation and advice available for seekers trying to find their way through the confused labyrinth of the New Age marketplace. Offers free information on different current strands in the esoteric field, particularly in London. Fees are standard Adult

Education Institute fees plus concessionary rates. They offer Paganism.

Centre for Personal Construct Psychology
132 Warwick Way
Pimlico
London SW1V 4JD. (071) 834 8875.
Approximately £92 per weekend workshop. They offer Personal Construct Therapy and a training in the subject.

Centre for Psychoanalytical Psychotherapy
20 Renters Avenue
London NW4 3RB. (081) 202 8351.
Individual work at £35 per session. Fees negotiable. They offer Psychoanalytic Therapy and training.

Centre for Psychological Astrology
PO Box 890
London NW3 2JZ. (071) 223 2478.
They offer Astrological Psychotherapy.

Centre for Release and Integration
62 Twickenham Road
Teddington TW11 8AW. (081) 892 1121.
The office is in Teddington but they can refer you to practitioners in London and through the UK. £40-£50 per one and half to two hour session. They offer Postural Integration therapy and training.

Centre for Stress Management
156 Westcombe Hill
Blackheath
London SE3 7DH. (081) 293 4114.
Cognitive/behavioural therapy, anxiety management, psychodynamic counselling. Established 1987, includes training room and two counselling rooms. Training in cognitive/behavioural approaches to psychotherapy, and counselling and stress management. Mail order, books, relaxation tapes, hypnosis tapes, videos on health, daily logs, biofeedback machines, biodots. In house workshops for organisations. Free leaflets on health (send SAE).

Lectures, workshops. Management consultancy for industrial stress. No wheelchair access. Sliding scale £10-£50 per session. Various prices for workshops. They offer Assertion Therapy, Biofeedback, Counselling, Hypnotherapy, Stress Management.

Centre for Therapeutic Communication
46 Antrim Mansions
Antrim Road
London NW3.

Centre for Transpersonal Psychology
7 Pembridge Place
Bayswater
London W2 4XB.
The centre is a co-operative of like-minded psychologists, counsellors, psychotherapists and members of related professions that have a commitment to the path of self realisation. They offer Transpersonal therapy and training.

Centre of Integral Psychoanalysis
6 Colville Road
London W11 2BP. (071) 727 4404.
Health and personal growth. Psychoanalytic treatment for adults, children and adolescents; individual analysis and group therapy. Founded in San Paulo, Brazil, branches throughout the world. Lectures every Monday 7.30pm, admission free - please drop-in. A scientific cultural organisation aimed at improving the quality of life for both the individual and society at large, by promoting the application of trilogical concepts in all spheres of human endeavour. The first interview is free. £15 per half hour individual therapy. £10 group therapy per session. Sliding scale of fees. They run a training in Psychotherapy. They offer Psychoanalytic Therapy.

Chalice Foundation
P.O. Box 3
Dartmouth
Devon
TQ6 9TY. (0803) 834406
Runs courses to develop practical skills in the healing arts. Courses on healing development and self healing. Massage (ITEC). Small friendly informal groups. Appointment needed. Courses are held at Regent's College in NW1. Two weekend healing de-

273

velopment course cost £115. Holistic massage weekend £55. Five day massage £165. They offer Hand Healing, Massage.

Chantraine School of Dance
47 Compayne Gardens
West Hampstead
London NW6 3DB. (071) 624 5881.
They teach the dance of contemporary expression, an approach to dance and movement created by Francoise and Alain Chantraine. Established in France in 1958 and in England in 1977. Emphasis is on the development of the person as the dancer and towards a unity of mind, body and spirit. There is no one building; classes are held at Adult Education institutes mostly in North London, but also in South Kensington. Not so much dance therapy, more dance as a way of expression. Currently set at ILEA Adult Education rates (i.e. very reasonable). £1-£2 per hour. Concs. They offer Dance therapy.

Cheirological Society
16 Bridge St
Osney
Oxford OX2 0BA. (0865) 241086.
Teaches cheirology (hand analysis) in the fields of psychological diagnosis, emotional integration, vocational and medical analysis and spiritual evolution. Founded in 1889 and incorporated Chinese Buddhist methods of analysis in its training programme within a western tradition and holistic perspective. Runs regular courses at introductory, intermediate and advanced levels. Publishes newsletter, journal, research papers and text books. Register of practitioners and consultants. Also centres in east London (Dagenham), Ealing, Finchley, Surbiton and Hammersmith. They offer Astrological Psychotherapy.

Chequer Centre
Chequer Street
London EC1.
They offer a training in Massage.

Chelsea Pastoral Foundation
155A Kings Road
Chelsea
London SW3 5TX. (071) 351 0839.
Young persons' counselling service, for those aged between 17 to 24. They offer Counselling.

Chessington Hypnotherapy Clinic
130 Guilders Road
Chessington
Surrey
(081) 397 3146.
Psychologist. Wheelchair access, one step on entry.
£35 per session (1 hour). Free consultation. They offer Hypnotherapy, Aromatherapy, Diet Therapy.

Children's Hours Trust
28 Wallace House
410 Caledonian Road
London N7 8TL. (071) 609 5568.
They listen to children and their play. Client-centred approach based on Rachel Pinney's theories of 'creative listening'. Full attention and no interpretation. Small centre. Registered charity formed in 1983. You can visit by appointment. Workshops twice a month in London and by arrangement elsewhere, children welcome. Creche. Wheelchair access. Register of practitioners. Mail order. Library. Volunteers welcomed. £15 per session (negotiable). £25 for day long workshop. Concessions. They offer Child psychotherapy.

Chinese Clinic
12 Bateman Street
London W1V 5TD. (071) 494 3593.
Chinese herbalism and western orthodox medicine practised by two doctors. £20-£25 for one session. Concessions. They offer Acupuncture, Herbalism.

Chinese Yoga Federation
44 Albany Mansions
Albert Bridge Road
London SW11.
They offer Yoga.

Chiron
26 Eaton Rise
Ealing
London W5 2ER. (081) 997 5219.
Offers body psychotherapy drawing on the work of Lowen (bioenergetics), biodynamic psychology (Boyesen), gestalt body therapy (Rosenberg) and core energetics (Pierrakas). On going evening psychotherapy groups. Weekend workshops. Member of UK standing conference for psychotherapy. £45 approx.They run a training in Psychotherapy. They offer Bioenergetics, Couple Therapy, Gestalt Therapy, Biodynamic Massage, Massage.

Chiropractic Advancement Association
56 Barnes Crescent
Wimborne
Dorset BH21 2AZ.
Register of members of the British Chiropractic Association. Publish newsletter for members 'Back Chat'. They offer Chiropractic.

Chiropractic Clinic
8 Sunningdale Gardens
Stratford Road
Kensington W8 6PX. (071) 937 4836.
Has X-Ray facilities. £25 per session. They offer Chiropractic.

Christian Community
Temple Lodge
51 Queen Caroline Street
London W6 9QL. (081) 748 8388.
Set up by Rudolf Steiner in 1922 to practise the spirit of Christianity rather than merely to uphold the traditional forms. Celebrate the sacraments, Christian festivals, hold study groups, services, workshops. Counselling is available, and a homoeopathic doctor visits on Thursday (phone 458 4304 for appointment). Bookshop and vegetarian restaurant. Donations for services, talks. They offer Christianity.

Chung San Acupuncture School
15 Porchester Gardens
Maida Vale
London W2 4DB. 727 6778/229 0136.
Clinic on Sunday with students of school. Treatment also available from qualified practitioners. Treatment by student £10, by qualified practitioner £20. They offer Acupuncture treatments and training.

Churchill Centre
22 Montagu Street
Marble Arch

London W1H 1TB. (071) 402 9475.
Mainly part-time courses in health care and relaxation with massage for Churchill and ITEC certificate. Individual treatments by appointment. The centre was founded in 1973 by Ken Holme. Design and make treatment couches to order, including backrests, cover and cushions. Sell books, tapes and oils. £15-£25 individual sessions (one to one and half hours). Concs. They offer Massage and Reflexology treatments and training.

Circle of Creative Arts Therapy
1 Ravenstone Road
London N8 0JT. (081) 888 4259.
Workshop on various themes to do with self-development and spirituality, inspiring new ideas from creative art images. Group and individual work. By negotiation, £10-£18. They offer Art Therapy, Creativity Courses.

City Health Centre
36-37 Featherstone Street
London EC1Y 8QX. (071) 251 4429.
Western and Chinese herbal pharmacy, iris photography and consultation service, vega diagnosis. Established 1982, 6 treatment rooms, consultations by appointment. Practitioners available for short free consultations to help people decide the best form of treatment or therapy. Mail order herbal pharmacy. Treatment fees £18-25 (half to one hour), consultation fee (one to one-and-a-half hours) £30-£35. They offer Counselling, Neuro-linguistic Programming, Acupuncture, Alexander Technique, Herbalism, Homoeopathy, Iridology, Massage, Osteopathy, Shiatsu.

Clapham Common Clinic
1st Floor
151/153 Clapham High Street
Clapham Common
London SW4 7SS. (071) 627 8890 or 622 4382.
Also offers psychotherapy. Established for 3 years. Open Mon-Fri 9-9pm. Sat 10-6. £18-£28 per session. They offer Counselling, Acupuncture,

Alexander Technique, Aromatherapy, Massage, Osteopathy.

Clare Maxwell Hudson
NW2 .(081) 450 6494.
All forms of massage. Clinic for members of the public. Home visiting service for those living in London. Sessions from £25. They run a training in Massage and Reflexology and Shiatsu. They offer Massage, Shiatsu.

Clinic of Alternative Therapies
18 The Drive
South Woodford
London E18 2BL. (081) 989 2216.
Treatment for arthritis, rheumatism, migraine. £15 initial consultation. They offer Acupuncture and also do Vegatesting

Clinic of Herbal Medicine
8 Whitgift Street
Croydon
Surrey CR0 1DH. (081) 681 0924.
Herbal medicine. Member of National Institute of Medical Herbalists. £20 first visit, £12 subsequent visits. Concessions.

Clinic of Herbal Medicine
61 Fernside Road
Balham
London SW12. (081) 675 6405.
Open Tue-Sat inclusive with one practitioner and a variable number of students in attendance. The clinic is a training centre manned by senior students under the supervision of a qualified medical herbalist. Appointment only for sessions but you are welcome to drop-in to get the feel of the place.
First consultation waged £10, unwaged £6. Subsequent consultations waged £6. Plus the cost of medicines. Creche. Wheelchair access. They offer Herbalism.

Clinics Health International
Riverbank House
Putney Bridge Approach
London SW6 3JD. (071) 371 9717/371 9590.
They offer traditional Chinese medicine and will treat all skin conditions including eczema and psoriasis. Two

resident dermatologists. They offer Allergy Therapy, Herbalism.

Clissold Park Natural Health Centre
154 Stoke Newington Church Street
Stoke Newington
London N16 0JU. (071) 249 2990.
Have been established since 1984 and have 5 treatment rooms where patients may be seen by appointment. Offer an acute 'homoeopathic drop-in' 3 evenings a week on Monday, Wednesday and Friday at 5pm where patients can be seen without an appointment. Also offer various evening and weekend courses on different aspects of health. Sell homoeopathic first aid kits and books. £20-£30. They offer Counselling, Acupuncture, Aromatherapy, Herbalism, Osteopathy, Alexander Technique, Homoeopathy, Reflexology, Shiatsu.

Co-Counselling
17 Lisburne Road
London NW3 2NS. (071) 485 0005.
Part of a network, Co-counselling Community International. The therapy is self help, so it's free. They offer Co-counselling sessions and training.

College of Healing
Runnings Park
Croft Bank
West Malvern
Worcs WR14 4DU. (0684) 565253.
Offer a three year part-time diploma course in the art of healing. They offer Hand Healing.

College of Homoeopathy
Regents College
Inner Circle
Regents Park
London NW1 4NS. (071) 487 7416.
College and clinic of homoeopathy. £20 initial appointment, £10 thereafter. They offer Homoeopathy consultations and training.

College of Homoeopathy Clinic
26 Clarendon Rise
London SE13 5EY. (081) 852 0573.

Teaching clinic for students. Four practice rooms. Open six days a week. Initial appointment £30, thereafter £18. Concessions to children and others by negotiation. They offer Homoeopathy.

College of Natural Therapies

22 Bromley Road
Catford
London SE6 2TP. (081) 690
2149.
They offer Aromatherapy.

College of Nutribiotics

15-17 South End Road
Hampstead Heath
London NW3 2PY. (071) 794
0848.
Aloe Vera, potentised homoeopathy, Spagyrik therapy, Homoeopathic chiropody. Run courses in homoeopathy and chiropody, and homoeopathy and nutrition. Run research institute into homoeopathic medicine. See also other centre at 129 Kentish Town Road, NW1. Practitioners have many years experience and some are qualified doctors as well as complementary practitioners. Also sell health foods, vitamins and minerals. £25-£35. Discounts for children, the elderly and the unemployed. Up to 50% discount. They offer Acupuncture, Hand Healing, Homoeopathy, Osteopathy, Reflexology.

College of Ophthalmic Somatology

24 Chapel Market
Islington
London N1 9E2. (071) 278
1212/4610.
A lecture takes place in central London at Regent's College, one Sunday per month. They offer Iridology treatments and training.

College of Osteopaths Education Trust

Administrative Services
110 Thorkill Road
Thames Ditton
Surrey KT7 0UW. (081) 398
3308.
NB Teaching Clinic is at Neals Yard Therapy Rooms. The above address

is the admin office only. They offer Osteopathy treatment and training.

College of Psychic Studies

16 Queensberry Place
London SW7 2EB. (071) 589
3292/3.
Training for mediumship, healing; consultations with sensitives. Send A5 SAE for complete programme. Publish Light three times yearly, £1.50 each. Membership £7.50, £12 or £18 per year depending on level. They offer Hand Healing.

College of Traditional Chinese Acupuncture

Tao House
Queensway
Leamington Spa
Warks CV31 3LZ. (0926)
422121.
They offer a training in Acupuncture.

Colon Health

27 Warwick Avenue
London W9 2PS. (071) 289
7000.
Uses colonic irrigation to help with many disorders such as skin and heavy toxic conditions. Free implants and free charts. £40 per session. They offer Allergy Therapy, Colonic Irrigation, Diet Therapy.

Colonic International Association

26 Sea Road
Boscombe
Bournemouth
Dorset BH5 1DF. (0202) 36354.
They offer Colonic Irrigation treatments and training.

Communication and Counselling Foundation

Haflodas
Tregoran
Dyfed
Wales SY25 6UG. (0974)
298998/(0570) 470831
Programme of workshops, some residential: The Psychology of Transition and Envisioning the Future Retreat. Also run the Women, Earth and Spirit programme, a series of workshops and retreats for women. Wheelchair access. Apply to organisers. They run a training in

Psychosynthesis. They offer Feminist Therapy, Psychosynthesis.

Community Health Foundation

188-194 Old Street
London EC1V 9BP. (071) 251
4076.
Established in 1976 this is one of the largest natural health centres. They aim to provide health education by concentrating on cooking, exercise and massage. They run a wide range of courses dedicated to natural health care. There is a popular clinic for individual advice on macrobiotics, shiatsu and massage. Also have rooms to rent for workshops/courses. There is a macrobiotic/vegan restaurant on the premises as well as a book and food shop. They hold open days and free introductory evenings. £60 for a weekend course. £20 per shiatsu massage. £25 for a macrobiotic consultation. Concs 10% reduction. Course fees: Shiatsu, 12 Monday evenings or three weekends or a six day intensive costs £135; Macrobiotic cooking, six Tuesday evenings or one weekend £60; Yoga and Meditation, six evenings or one weekend, £40; Tai Chi, evening classes, £4 per class; Swedish Massage, twelve Monday evenings, £220, successful graduates receive an ITEC certificate. They run a training in Macrobiotics. They offer Macrobiotics, Martial Arts, Massage, Shiatsu, Yoga, Iridology, Hypnotherapy, Neuro-linguistic Programming.

Community Massage

27 Helix Gdns
Brixton
SW2 2JL. (081) 674 7933
They offer Massage.

Confederation of Healing Organisations

The Red and White House
113 High St
Berkhamstead
Herts
HP4 2DJ. (0442) 870667.
Head office of a confederation of 16 associations deploying about 8,500 healers in the UK and others abroad. Their aim is to make healing available

on the NHS and in private medicine. They offer Hand Healing.

Constructive Teaching Centre
18 Landsdowne Road
Holland Park
London W11. (071) 727 7222.
They offer Alexander Technique.

Core Trust (The)
1-12 Lisson Cottages
Lisson Grove
London NW1 6UD. (071) 258 3031.
An holistic treatment centre for people with problems with addiction.

Cortijo Romero UK
4 Maldon Road
London W3 6SU. (081) 993 4898.
One to two week residential courses in the foothills of the Sierra Nevada, Spain. £260-£300 per week depending on the time of year. Occasional bursary. They offer Creativity courses, Psychosynthesis, Meditation, Dance therapy, Massage.

Counselling in North London
c/o 2 Hemington Ave
Friern Barnet
London N11 3LR. (081) 368 2144.
Psychodynamic, humanistic and existential therapy. Appointments available day and evening, weekdays and weekends. £12-25 negotiable. They offer Counselling.

Crane School of Reflexology
135 Collins Meadow
Harlow
Essex CM19 4EJ. (0279) 21682.
They offer a training in Reflexology.

Cranial Osteopathic Association
478 Baker Street
Enfield
Middlesex EN1 3QS. (081) 367 5561.
Aim to undo cranial lesions i.e. damage to the head. Register of members. £20-£25. They offer Cranial Osteopathy treatments and training.

Cranial Osteopathy and Structural Therapy
Primrose Hill

28 Oppidans Road
Chalk Farm
London NW3. (071) 379 7662.
They offer Osteopathy.

Craniosacral Therapy Education Trust
29 Dollis Park
Finchley
London N3 1HJ. (081) 349 0297.
They offer Complementary medicine treatments and training.

Creation-Centred Spirituality
St. James's Church
197 Piccadilly
London W1V. (071) 734 4511.
Experiential workshops on Creation Centred Spirituality, including women's spirituality, creativity, dreams etc., using various media to explore Christian themes. Talks, ongoing courses, celebrations. £14-20 for a day workshop (Concessions £14, £7). £3 talks (concessions £1.50). They offer Christianity.

Creative and Healing Arts
222 Westbourne Park Road
London W11 1EP. (071) 229 9400.
Individual sessions, classes and workshops. Weekend retreats doing shiatsu, yoga, dance, music. Treatments £20 for an hour. Classes vary from £2 for group class and £20 for one to one tuition. Workshops vary, £45 average per weekend. Concessions. They offer Osteopathy, Shiatsu, Yoga.

Creative Arts and Therapy Consultants
Terpsichore
70 Cranwich Road
London N16 5JD. (081) 809 5866.
They run a training in Psychotherapy. They offer Dance therapy.

Creative Journey
55 Washington Road
Worcester Park
Surrey KT4 8JG. (081) 330 7217.
Group and individual work focussing on the body, through sound, colour and movement. Researches into effects of sound-colour-movement on energy fields and physical body. Teaches systematic methods for

clearing and maintaining energy fields in full health. £20-£35 per session. Groups £3-£25 per person depending on the length of the session. They run a training in Complementary medicine. They offer Voice Therapy, Massage.

Croydon Buddhist Centre
98 High St
Croydon CR0 1ND. (081) 688 8624
A centre of the Friends of the Western Buddhist Order (see London Buddhist centre for details), with an emphasis on meditation, study, devotional ceremonies. Evenings, weekends, retreats at their centre in Sussex. Run Hockney's, a vegetarian restaurant, a wholefood shop and a bookshop. £3 per meditation class. £45 per weekend retreat. Concs. They offer Yoga, Buddhism, Meditation.

Crystal 2000
37 Bromley Road
St Annes-on-Sea
Lancs FY8 1PQ. (0253) 723735.
Run crystal healing training, also correspondence courses. Publish Crystal News (£1.25). They offer Crystal Therapy.

Crystal Connection
23 Camden Lock
London NW1 8AF. (071) 267 4325.
Electro-crystal healing and light touch healing. Wheelchair access. Workshops. Monday to Friday. £15 upwards.
They offer Crystal Therapy.

Dancing on the Path
Flat 1
39A Glengarry Road
London SE22. (081) 693 6953.
Individual sessions and shamanic dance workshops by psychotherapist trained in the Dancing Path by Gabrielle Roth. £30 day workshop. £25 per hour individual work. They offer Counselling, Dance therapy,

LIST OF CENTRES

Transpersonal therapy, Hand Healing.

Demigod
2 Berenger Towers
off Kings Road
Chelsea
London SW10 0EF. (071) 351 2220.
£108 for two day workshops. £50 for individual sessions. They offer Counselling, Dream analysis and therapy. Also Clairvoyance, Crystal ball readings and Psychometry.

Dharmadhatu (London)
27 Belmont Close
Clapham
London SW4. (071) 720 3207.
Part of Vajradhatu, an international Buddhist organisation founded by the Tibetan teacher the Ven Chogyam Trungpa Rinpoche of the Kagyu School. His books such as *Cutting Through Spiritual Materialism,* and *Shambhala* are an excellent guide to the spirit of Buddhism framed in western terms. Provide Shambhala Training, a secular meditation programme of ten weekends. Retreats in Ireland. Study and meditation practice. Meditation practice free. Meditation instruction free. Study courses £2 per week. Concs, students and unwaged half price. They offer Buddhism, Meditation, Retreats.

Dick Read School for Natural Birth
14 Pitt Street
London W8. (071) 937 4140.
Established 1976. Natural childbirth procedures according to the Dick Read approach. Individual tuition given. Visiting speakers to groups. Book and teaching cassette also available. Sliding scale, average £10 per 2 hour session. Concs. They offer Active Birth.

Dietary Therapy Society
33 Priory Gardens
London N6 5QU. (081) 341 7260.
Organisation of professional dietary therapists. Register. £15-25. They offer Diet Therapy.

DMA UK Technologies for Creating
1/12 Belgravia Workshops
157-161 Marlborough Rd

London N19 4NF. (071) 281 7496.
They do not offer a therapy. Affiliated with the arts rather than the human potential movement. They offer a variety of courses for learning the skill of creating. The organisation was formed in 1985. Hold regular introductory evenings. Varies from course to course. 'Path of Least Resistance' available for £7.50 + £1.50 p&p. They offer Creativity courses.

Dr Edward Bach Centre
Mount Vernon
Sotwell
Wallingford
Oxon OX10 0PZ. (0491) 34678.
Bach Flower Remedies available by post, books, free advice service, consultations by appointment. They offer Bach Flower Remedies.

Drakefield Homoeopathic Centre
122a Drakefield Road
London SW17 8RR. (081) 672 5253.
They offer Homoeopathy.

Druid Order
161 Auckland Road
London SE19 2RH.
Public meetings at London Ecology centre fortnightly on Fridays at 7.15 .Public ceremonies on Tower Hill at Spring equinox (12 noon GMT), at Stonehenge at Summer solstice, on Primrose Hill at Autumn equinox (12 noon GMT). Teaching and training given to companions in Groves and classes, available to those who wish to be initiated into the Druid order. Collection at evening meeting.

E

Eagle's Wing Centre for Contemporary Shamanism
58 Westbere Road
West Hampstead
London
NW2 3RU. (071) 435 8174.
Courses in Shamanism and teachings of American Indians run in London and Devon. Also run 'Playworld'. One year course in elements of Shamanism. Based on the medicine wheel

teachings of the American Indian. Courses run from a weekend to a year in duration. Typical weekend £45/50, residential £65. One year course (7 weekends and one week residential) £750 (concessions available). They offer Paganism, Shamanism.

Ealing Psychotherapy Centre
St Martin's Rooms
Hale Gardens
Acton
London W3 9SQ. (081) 993 5185.
Individual and group analytic psychotherapy. Established for ten years with around twenty psychotherapists. Appointments need to be made in advance by letter or telephone to the general administrator. Therapists at the centre are available for teaching, lecturing, staff group consultancy etc. Wheelchair access. £18 - £25 per session. Group psychotherapy around £10 per session. Limited concs (they try to be earnings related) They offer Psychoanalytic Therapy, Couple Therapy.

East-West Clinic of Natural Healing
46 Whitton Rd
Twickenham
Middlesex TW1 1BS. (081) 744 1974.
Small clinic established one and a half years. Movement classes and meditation classes. £20 first consultation, £18 subsequent consultations. Herbs individually priced. Concessions.They run a training in Shiatsu. They offer Acupuncture, Herbalism, Chinese Herbalism, Shiatsu, Meditation.

Eckankar
8 Godolphin Road
Shepherds Bush
London W12 8JE. (081) 746 0131.
Contact only for local group. Classes and courses by donation.

Edgware Centre for Natural Health
128 High Street
Edgware
Middx
HA6 1HP. (081) 952 9566.
Dispensary and reception with clinics at rear of building. Average £15

278

per half hour session, £20 per one hour session. They offer Acupuncture, Alexander Technique, Herbalism, Massage, Naturopathy, Osteopathy, Allergy Therapy, Counselling, Diet Therapy, Homoeopathy, Hypnotherapy, Reflexology.

Edmonton Acupuncture Clinic
322 Fore Street
Edmonton
London N9 OPN. (081) 803 8102.
Established 8 years. £20 per session. £16 OAP. £15 students. Home visits £25 (within 20 min drive). They offer Acupuncture.

Elgenwelt London
12 Howitt Rd
London NW3 3LL. (071) 586 3254.
Weekend courses in London run by nationwide organisation based in Newcastle. Run courses in Edinburgh, Cumbria, Ilkeston, Worcester etc. Also offer in-service training. £45 per weekend for self funding; £52 if sponsored. They offer Client-centered Therapy, Counselling, Existential Psychotherapy, Psychodrama.

Elizabeth Kubler Ross Foundation
PO Box 212
London NW6 7NW.
Founded by Elisabeth Kubler-Ross. Established in 1984. Run workshops to promote relief of suffering from terminal illness and bereavement. £350 per five day residential. Concessions according to need. They offer Bereavement Counselling.

Equillbrium Therapy Centre
117 Granville Road
Southfields
London SW18 5SF. (081) 870 8761.
Dietry advice. Hypnotherapy workshops. Team of practitioners. £12-£26. Concessions. They offer Counselling, Couple Therapy, Eating Problem Support, Relaxation Training, Acupuncture, Osteopathy, Hypnotherapy, Reflexology, Shiatsu, Diet Therapy.

European Shiatsu School
222 Westbourne Park Road
London W11. (071) 229 9400.

£15 - £25 approx per treatment They offer Osteopathy, Shiatsu.

European Shiatsu School
13 North Common Road
Ealing
London W5. (067) 286 459.
Deep tissue bodywork, physiotherapy. Wheelchair access. £25 approx per treatment. They offer Herbalism, Shiatsu.

European Shiatsu School
163 Cromwell Road
London SW5 0SQ. (071) 370 6772.
£25 per treatment approx. They offer Iridology, Shiatsu.

European Shiatsu School
Neal's Yard
Covent Garden
London WC2. (0672) 86 362.
They offer Shiatsu.

European Shiatsu School
10 Rideley Road
London NW10. (081) 969 8283.
They offer Shiatsu.

European Shiatsu School
High Banks
Lockeridge
Nr Marlborough
Wilts SN8 4EQ. (0672) 86362.
They offer a training in Shiatsu.

Faculty of Homoeopathy
2 Powis Place
Great Ormond Street
Bloomsbury
London WC1N 2HR. (071) 837 2495.
Must be referred by your GP because it is a national health hospital. Treatment is free. They offer Homoeopathy treatments and training.

Faculty of Traditional Chinese Medicine of the UK
13 Gunnersbury Avenue
London W5. (081) 993 2549.

They offer Acupuncture treatments and training.

Falcons
25 Kite House
Grant Road
London SW11 2NJ. (071) 585 3445.
Consultation and facilities for small groups. Use of leisure complex: swimming, jacuzzi, sauna by arrangement. Initial session £30, subsequent £25. They offer Stress Management, Aromatherapy, Diet Therapy, Reflexology.

Family Planning Association
27-35 Mortimer Street
London W1N 7RJ. (071) 636 7866.
They can put you in touch with your local family planning clinic. Will answer all queries about contraception, sexuality and health over the phone. Leaflets. They offer Natural Birth Control.

Feldenkrais Guild UK
PO Box 370
London N10 3XA.
No centre at the above address. Members scattered throughout the country, so they can put you in touch with a teacher. Awareness through movement classes and workshops given by members throughout the UK, as well as individual functional integration lessons. £5-£8 per group lesson. £20-£35 per day workshop. They offer Feldenkrais treatments and training.

Feldenkrais Method
188 Old Street
London EC1V 9BP. (081) 549 9583.
Can refer you to a practitioner. They offer Feldenkrais treatments and training.

Feldenkrais Method
28a Hampstead High St
London NW3 1QA. (071) 794 4066.
£30 per session. Weekend course £50. They offer Feldenkrais.

Finchley Alternative Medicine Centre
253 Ballards Lane
Finchley

LIST OF CENTRES

London N3 1NG. (081) 445 2631.
Practise Bioresonance which is a combination of homoeopathy and acupuncture. £40 per session.

Findhorn Foundation
The Park
Forres
Scotland IV36 0TZ . (0309) 73655.
Very large community in northeast Scotland, situated in and around the seaside village of Findhorn. Courses attract up to 4,000 visitors per year. Residents of the 200 strong 'open' community run various businesses, including solar panel making, a computer consultancy, a Steiner school and Meadowlark nursing home. Experience week £180-240, weekend workshop £50-£110, week course £200-290, retreat weeks from £80-210.

Float Centre
20 Blenheim Terrace
St Johns Wood
London NW8 0EB. (071) 328 7276.
Float tanks (8ft x 7 ft x 4ft wide) in secluded rooms. There are four private rooms with showers, towels, shampoos, aromatherapy oils etc. Hair drying rooms with cosmetics (all inclusive). Library with refreshments. Open 10-7, seven days a week. Sessions must be booked at least two days in advance. Subliminal audio tapes while you float. One week introductory course (3 x 1 hour sessions) £48.
Each one hour session costs £22, but discounts apply if you book more than one. Half price for students, nurses/doctors, police and fire service men/women. They offer Flotation Tank Therapy.

Float Experience
Battersea SW. (071) 350 1001.
One tank, an 'ocean floatroom'. Small private centre established five years ago. Information about floating available. By appointment only. £15-£25 per session. Concessions for students and non-waged. They offer Flotation Tank Therapy, Jungian Psychotherapy.

Float Space (The)
22 Shirlock Road
London NW3 2HS. (071) 485 7420.

Natural therapy centre. Bed and breakfast also available. They offer Flotation Tank Therapy.

Food and Chemical Allergy Clinic
149 Primrose Lane
Shirley Oaks
Croydon
Surrey CR0 8YP. 081 654 1700.
Established 8 years. Testing for allergies, desensitisation. Also treat asthma, eczema, ME, candida, multiple sclerosis, hayfever. Ring for appointment. Wheelchair access. £15 per 45 minute session. They offer Allergy Therapy, Massage, Reflexology.

Fook Sang Acupuncture and Chinese Herbal Practitioners Training College UK
1037B Finchley Road
Golders Green
London NW11 7ES. (081) 455 5508.
Chinese osteopathy. Traditional Chinese diagnosis. Acupuncture treatments last from 1-3 hours, depending on the severity of the condition. Associated clinic in Reading, and affiliated training college. Initial consultation £15, subsequent acupuncture treatments £20, herbal medicine £25, combined treatments £30. These prices are per session (1-3 hours)They run a training in Acupuncture and Herbalism. They offer Acupuncture, Herbalism, Osteopathy.

Forty Hill Natural Therapy Centre
478 Baker Street
Enfield
Middlesex . (081) 367 5561.
Relaxation and bee venom therapy (in which the patient is stung by a bee - used to relieve arthritis). Also supervised fasts. Wheelchair access. £20-£25. Concessions. They offer Acupuncture, Cranial Osteopathy, Naturopathy, Reflexology.

Foundation for Holistic Consciousness
25b South Norwood Hill
London SE25 6BS. (081) 653 8453.
Workshops on healing with flower essences. £15-£25 per session. £150 per 48 hour workshop. They offer

Bach Flower Remedies, Polarity Therapy, Crystal Therapy, Hand Healing.

Foundation for International Spiritual Unfoldment
71 Trumpington Road
Forest Gate
London E7 9EH. (081) 555 4643.
Courses by appointment. Residential courses bi-annually. Open evening Wednesdays 8pm, except first week of month when held on Friday at 8pm. No wheelchair access. Twelve week meditation and spiritual unfoldment course; payment by donation, £100. They offer Meditation.

Fountain London
PO 1383
London N14 6LF.
They offer Meditation.

Free Daist Communion
32 Church Crescent
London N10 3NE. (081) 444 5292.
Teacher is Heart-Master Da Love-Ananda who sometimes visits the UK. Evenings, weekends, courses and regular retreats at home (London, Kent, Hampshire) and abroad (USA, Canada, New Zealand, Australia, Holland, Fiji, Hawaii). Many co-operatively run businesses worldwide. Centre has meeting rooms, video rooms, meditation halls, bookshop, retreat rooms. Bimonthly newsletter on request (free).

G

Gaia House
Woodland Road
Denbury
Nr. Newton Abbot
Devon TQ12 6DY. (0803) 813188.
Founded by Christopher Titmuss and Christina Feldman, Buddhist Vipassana (insight) meditation is taught here on retreat. Zen and Reiki energy balancing. There is a residential community here too, and facilities for solitary retreats. Working retreats at a reduced rate. Some

concessions. They offer Buddhism, Meditation, Retreats.

Gale Centre for Creative Therapy
Stable Cottage
Whitakers Way
Loughton
Essex IG10 1SJ. (081) 508 9344.
Voice therapy, individual therapy, short courses for members of the helping professions. Mail order books and tapes. Low cost concessions available. They offer Family Therapy, Group Oriented Therapy, Psychodrama.

General Council and Register of Consultant Herbalists
Marlborough House
Swanpool
Falmouth
Cornwall TR11 4HW. (0326) 317321.
Register of practitioners. They offer Herbalism.

General Council and Register of Osteopaths
56 London Street
Reading
(0734) 576585.
Professional association linked with British College of Naturopathy and Osteopathy. Register. They offer Naturopathy, Osteopathy.

Gerda Boyesen Centre for Biodynamic Psychology and Psychotherapy
Acacia House
Centre Avenue, Acton Park
London W3 7JX. (081) 743 2437.
Evening, weekends and long courses. ITEC Diploma courses. Psychoperistaltic massage. £variable. Low cost massage given by trainees. Concessions. They run a training in Biodynamic Massage. They offer Biodynamic Massage, Massage.

Gestalt Centre London
64 Warwick Road
St Albans
Herts AL1 4DL. (0727) 864806.
Established in 1983 the centre's initial focus was on gestalt therapy and training. With a growing number of graduates the associate programme now offers a wide range of workshops from peace building to encounter

marathons within a variety of formats i.e. one day events to week long residentials. The centre is an association of accredited therapists working throughout London and the home counties with an administrative base at St. Albans. Individual therapy £12 - £30. Weekend workshop £50 average. Offer bursaries and fee reductions to low income recipients. They offer Gestalt therapy and training.

Gestalt Studio
49 Croftdown Road
London NW5. (071) 485 2316.
Offer weekly beginners and advanced mixed groups, and beginners and advanced women's groups. Individual therapy, advanced events, including training and supervision events. Women's weekends, mixed weekends. Contact for brochure. £12-£30, depending on the therapist. Subsidised therapy for those in financial difficulties. They run a training in Gestalt Therapy. They offer Feminist Therapy, Gestalt Therapy.

Gestalt Therapy & Contribution Training
18 Granville Park
London SE13 7EA. (081) 852 4647.
They offer Gestalt Therapy and Contribution Training.

Gestalt Therapy in West London
36 Newburgh Road
Acton
London W3 6DQ. (081) 993 0868.
Established 1987. Centre for individual and couple therapy. Occasional small groups Individual sessions £20-£25. Concessions negotiable. They offer Couple Therapy, Gestalt Therapy.

Goldsmiths' College
Art Psychotherapy Unit
27 Albury St
London SE8 3PT. (081) 692 1424.
They offer a training in Art Therapy and Group Oriented Therapy.

Graigian Community
10 Lady Somerset Road
Kentish Town
London NW5 1UP. (071) 485

1646 (after 12 noon and before 6pm).
Beautiful house open to visitors on Sundays. Activities include 'Being in a Group' group (Sundays 4-6pm), art therapy, tarot and pottery tuition. Telephone or write before visiting. Members get 4 newsletters per year, access to regular Sunday group, access to art and pottery tuition, discounts on booklets and pottery, and are entitled to attend communal holidays in Wales after a year's membership. Members are expected to help support the society's environmental campaigning. No replies to letters without SAE. For groups: first visit make a contribution (e.g. milk, fruit juice or vegetarian biscuits); on second visit people are expected to become members for a year. Membership: £3 per annum (concessions), £5 per annum (waged). Couples (of any kind) £7 per annum. Communities, companies and societies £12 per annum.

Greater World Christian Spiritual Association
3 Conway Street
Fitzrovia
London W1P 5HA. (071) 436 7555.
Religious charity, seeking to spread the truths of Christian spiritualism and encourage the individual to develop his/her full potential as a spiritual being, achieving a true balance of mind/body/spirit. Give private consultations with recommended mediums. Lectures, bookshop, workshop and postal courses. They offer Hand Healing.

Green Wood College
'Parkside'
Ravenscourt Park W6 0UU.
(081) 741 5668.
They offer Aromatherapy, Massage, Reflexology, Relaxation Training, Stress Management, Shiatsu.

Group Relations Training Association
7 Stanley Rd
Oxford OX4 1QY. (0865) 724141.
They do an annual 5 day group relations training laboratory using the T group method. This residential includes food and accommodation. They also hold an annual conference, normally held over 4 days late

LIST OF CENTRES

September, early October. The conference gives the opportunity to join in a range of activities, including the latest in personal growth and therapeutic techniques. £300 (organisations), £200 (individual) for the group laboratory training workshop. £varies for the conference. They offer Group Oriented Therapy.

Guild of Aromatherapy Practitioners
59 Murray Road
London SW19.
They offer Aromatherapy.

Guild of Pastoral Psychology
5/36 Arterberry Road
London SW20 8AQ. (081) 946 3172.
Explores relationship between religion and depth psychology, particularly the work of Jung and his followers. No qualifications necessary for membership. Lectures, conferences. Library for members. Lecture pamphlets. Membership £16.50 for Londoners, £13 for ministers of religion and the retired. They offer Jungian Psychotherapy.

Gurdjieff Ouspensky School
New World
Box 1531
London NW3 6RW. (081) 786 7094.
Practical Fourth Way work for normal men and women in everyday life taught by word of mouth. Provides methods, tools and exercises for work to achieve higher states of consciousness and inner development. Strong emphasis on personal verification, understanding and efforts. Welcomes people from all backgrounds, nationalities and cultures who wish to work on themselves.

Haelen Centre
41 The Broadway
Crouch End
London N8. (081) 340 1518.
Clinic above wholefood shop. £15-£30 depending on practitioner ses-

sions between half an hour- one and a half hours. They offer Acupuncture, Herbalism, Homoeopathy, Massage, Osteopathy, Shiatsu.

Hahnemann College of Homoeopathy
243 The Broadway
Southhall
Middlesex
UB1 1NF. (081) 574 4281.
They offer Homoeopathy consultations and training.

Hahnemann College of Homoeopathy
342 Barking Road
Plaistow
London E13 8HI. (071) 476 7263.
Treatment by students of the college. They offer Homoeopathy.

Hakomi Institute
61 Grantham Rd
Chiswick
London W4 2RT. (081) 994 8544.
Teach Hakomi method, a body-mind therapy which emphasises gentleness and letting go. £85 for a weekend (including Friday evening). They offer Rolfing.

Hale Clinic
7 Park Crescent
Regents Park
London W1N 3HE. (071) 631 0156.
£vary. They offer Acupuncture, Alexander Technique, Chiropody, Chiropractic, Herbalism, Massage, Naturopathy, Osteopathy.

Hampstead Healing Centre
9 Cannon Place
London NW3 1EH. (071) 435 5432.
Ring for appointment. Established 10 years. Sliding scale for those who cannot afford a fixed fee. Offer a one year introduction to Humanistic Psychology at an evening class once a week. They offer Couple Therapy, Bach Flower Remedies, Hand Healing, Massage, Reflexology, Counselling.

Hampton Healing Centre
2a Belgrade Road
Hampton
Middlesex . (081) 979 6234.

McTimoney Chiropractic. Occasional workshops at the centre e.g. crystal healing, massage, preventative medicine. Some books available. From £16-30. Concessions. They offer Autogenic Training, Stress Management, Acupuncture, Chiropractic, Colonic Irrigation, Homoeopathy.

Hampton Holistic Centre for Homoeopath and Autogenic Training
12 Wolsey Road
Hampton Hill
Middlesex TW12 1QW. (081) 579 0068.
Established for 7 years. Appointments only. First consultation (1 1/2 - 2 hours) £45 including one item of homoeopathic medicine if needed. Follow up consultations £25-£30 including one item of homoeopathic medicine if needed. They offer Autogenic Training, Counselling.

Harry Edwards Spiritual Healing Sanctuary
Burrows Lea
Shere
Guildford
Surrey GU5 9QG. (048641) 2054.
Established in 1946, the Sanctuary covers 14 acres. Main work is distant or absent healing. Some books and cassettes available. No charge for services. They offer Hand Healing.

Hayes Hypnotherapy Centre
Suite 6
Grange Chambers
503 Uxbridge Road
Hayes, Middx UB4 8RL. (081) 561 5282.
By appointment only. No access. Free initial consultation, apply for fees. Concessions.

Healing Centre
Garden Flat
49 Cavenish St
London NW6 7XS.
They offer Hand Healing.

Healing Fields Practice
Garden Flat
65 Anson Road
London N7 OAS. (071) 607 1823.
Astrological birth charts and readings from a depth psychology perspective. Bach and Californian flower rem-

LIST OF CENTRES

edies. Can supply computerised psychological astrological analysis printout. £20 per session for bodywork. £60 for astrological birthchart and readings. Psychosynthesis £20. Flower remedies and colour healing £15. Up to 25% reduction for low incomes. They offer Astrological Psychotherapy, Biodynamic Massage, Bioenergetics, Bach Flower Remedies, Client-centered Therapy, Psychosynthesis, Massage, Colour Therapy.

Healing Shiatsu Education Centre
The Orchard
Lower Meascoed
Hereford HR2 0PH. (087) 387 207.
They offer a training in Shiatsu.

Healing Voice
C/O Gillian McGregor
Garden Flat, 9 Yonge Park
Highbury
London N4 3NU. (071) 607 5819.
Jill Purce has been inspired by the sonic yogas of India and Tibet, the use of mantra and shamanic use of sound and rhythm. Week long workshop, introductory weekends and one day 'Voice of Shamanism'. Workshops exploring sound for healing and transformation of consciousness using breathing. £45-£315. They offer Voice Therapy.

Healing Workshops
111 Queens Crescent
Chalk Farm
London NW5 4EY. (071) 482 4049.
Not a centre, but an organisation offering a variety of courses and one-to-one therapies. Guided visualisation, attitudinal healing and positive thought techniques.Courses include study groups based on the best-selling book, *You Can Heal Your Life* by Louise Hay. Venues vary, but one-to-one healing sessions and weekly healing circle take place in NW5. Also publishers and writers currently producing a range of books and audio tapes for mail order. Desk top publishing service available. Healing circle - entrance by donation. Individual sessions £23 (one and a half hours). Study groups £75 for 6 weeks. No concessions, but occasional bursaries at their discretion on some

courses. They offer Counselling, Hand Healing, Meditation.

Health Connection
7 Hereward Rd
London SW17 7EY. (081) 767 2935.
Eclectic approach includes humanistic therapy, gestalt, transpersonal psychology with an awareness of psychodynamic principles. £20-£27. Concessions available. They offer Psychotherapy.

Health Management
31 Rosslyn Hill
London NW3 5UJ. (071) 431 0760.
Established 1982. Courses and holidays. Private lessons also given. 6 week course £40, workshop £15-25. They offer Stress Management, Massage, Yoga, Meditation.

Healthy Living
67 Temple Road
Kew Gardens
Surrey TW9 2EB. (081) 948 1365.
They offer Aromatherapy, Acupuncture, Herbalism.

Herbs Hands Healing
2 Bridge Farm Cottage
Station Road
Pulham Market
Nr Diss Norfolk IP21 4SJ.
Pulham Market 8201.
They offer a training in Herbalism.

Herb Society
PO Box 599
London SW11 4RW. (071) 228 4417.
Disseminates information on herbs for all those interested. Members include professional growers, medical herbalists, beauticians, cooks and the merely curious. They receive quarterly Herbal Review and have use of the Society's library. Information on herb sources and local herb groups. Lectures for general public. Membership £12, £8 senior citizens, students and under 18s, £16 overseas. They offer Herbalism.

Heron Training Workshops
152 Park Street Lane
Park Street
St. Albans AL2 2AE. (0727) 72010.

Public courses held in hotels for both men and women. They also run Transactional Analysis in education for teachers and others working with young people. £125 per session. Individuals sponsoring themselves £35. Education programmes are £18 per day (weekends only). They offer Management, Transactional Analysis, Touch For Health, Kinesiotherapy.

Heruka Buddhist Centre
PO Box 84
London SW15 1JQ. (081) 788 7792
Founded in 1991 by Geshe Kelsang Gyatso Rinpoche to provide a facility in London where people can experience pure Buddhist view, meditation and action. The centre offers three special study programmes providing a structured approach to the study and practice of Mahayana Buddhism. Phone for enquiries about weekly meditation classes and occasional one day and weeked courses in central London.Evening courses £4. One day course £15. Weekends £25 approx.

Hidden Strengths
97 Warren Rd
Whitton
Middlesex TW2 7DG. (081) 755 0353.
Biodynamic psychotherapy workshops for women. Introductory days, weekend workshops and ongoing groups. Have been running groups for 4 years. £50 for a weekend workshop. Free initial consultation if interested in the groups. Concessions. They offer Feminist Therapy, Biodynamic Massage.

Highbury Centre
137 Grosvenor Avenue
Highbury
London N5 2NH. (071) 226 5805.
A small centre established for 6 years. Rooms to let to qualified therapists for groups and individual work. Also self-preservation work. Residential Alexander Technique courses run outside London. Individual sessions average around £10-20, weekend workshops £40-80. Concessions may be given by individual therapists. They offer Art Therapy, Counselling, Dreamwork, Psychosynthesis, Voice Therapy, Active Birth, Alexander

LIST OF CENTRES

Technique, Biodynamic Massage, Massage, Polarity Therapy.

Highgate Counselling Service
Tetherdown Halls
Tetherdown
Muswell Hill
London N10 1ND.

Hillside Practice
One Hillside
Highgate Road
Dartmouth Park
London NW5. (071) 482 3293.
The centre comprises three houses close together. Established 5 years. Overlooks Hampstead Heath. Receptionist available to answer phone calls mornings 9-1. Wheelchair access by prior arrangement. £vary depending on the practitioner. Concs. They offer Counselling, Couple Therapy, Gestalt Therapy, Jungian Psychotherapy, Primal Therapy, Biodynamic Massage, Homoeopathy, Shiatsu, Yoga.

Hocroft Clinic
3 Hocroft Road
West Hampstead
London NW2 2BN. (071) 435 9506.
First appointment one and a half hour, £25. Subsequent treatment sessions: 40 minutes, £18. They offer Naturopathy, Osteopathy.

Holistic Early Learning School
2 Amgerst Road
Ealing
London W 13 8ND. (081) 998 2732.

Holistic Health Consultancy
94 Grosvenor Road
London SW1V 3LF. (071) 834 3579.
Spagyrik practitioners. Established in 1983, the consulting room of this centre has a panoramic river view. Telephone consultations are offered to established patients, who can also order medicines mail order. Wheelchair access. First consultation (2 hours) £59.70 includes typed analysis, full explanation of findings, nutritional and naturopathic instructions and homoeopathic medication. Homoeopathic consultation £34 (one and a half hours inclusive of medica-

tion). Follow up £27 (1 hour). Herbal medications extra. Concessions available to pensioners and children. They offer Allergy Therapy, Bach Flower Remedies, Diet Therapy, Herbalism, Homoeopathy, Iridology, Naturopathy.

Holistic Yoga Centre
The Old Manor House
The Green
Hanslope, MK19 7LS. (0908) 510548.
The centre is a large house set in one acre ground at the edge of a small village with open countryside at back. Strictly by appointment only. The centre runs 4-5 enlightenment intensives a year. Established since 1981. Fully residential with a capacity for 24 people. Also provide correspondence course of spiritual exercises. Enlightenment Intensives: three day fully residential cost £95. Two week residential cost £295. Sessions for mind clearing and couple therapy cost £25 per hour. Concs. They run a training in Mind Clearing. They offer Couple Therapy, Enlightenment Intensive, Mind Clearing, Yoga.

Holwell Centre for Psychodrama and Sociodrama
East Down
Barnstaple
Devon EX31 3NZ. 0271 850 267/597.
Sociodrama, playback theatre, journal process and dream workshops. Some workshops in the Greater London area, but see 'Residential Workshops' for bulk of programme. Holwell is a farm dating back to 1244, with pond, lawns and a developing woodland. £120 per residential weekend, £315 per week. Concessions. They offer Psychodrama.

Homoeopathic Centre
55 Mattock Lane
West Ealing
London W13 9LA. (081) 998 2723.
Established 1983. Appointments only. First consultation (1 1/2 - 2 hours) £50 including one item of homoeopathic medicine if needed. Follow up consultations £30-£35 including one item of homoeopathic medicine if needed. They offer Autogenic Training,

Counselling, Bach Flower Remedies, Homoeopathy, Hypnotherapy.

Homoeopathic Development Foundation Ltd
73 Duke Street
London W1. (071) 629 3205.
Register of doctors practising Homoeopathy in London. They have a selection of books which are available on mail order free of charge. Donations are welcome as they are a charitable organization.

Homoeopathic Health Centre
342 Barking Road
Plaistow
London E13 8HL. (071) 476 7263.

Homoeopathic Health Clinic
29 Streatfield Road
Kenton
Harrow
Middlesex HA3 9BP. (081) 907 4885.
Well baby clinic, well women's clinic, special dermatological, asthmatic and bronchial clinic. Established for 10 years. Medically qualified doctor. Four room centre with easy access. Easy access to public transport. Parking facilities. They also offer telephone or postal consultation for patients at a long distance. Cervical smear tests are carried out by a woman doctor in a friendly environment with 24-36 hour results. Homoeopathic first aid seminars and self-help groups. Creche facilities and wheelchair access. Full medical consultation lasting 1 1/2 hours for £30 (£25 for children). Follow up sessions cost £18 (£15 for children). They offer Counselling, Homoeopathy, Diet Therapy.

Hong Tao Acupuncture and Natural Health Clinic
21 St Thomas Drive
Hatch End
Pinner
Middlesex HA5 4SX. (081) 421 2668.
Allergy testing. Consultation and first treatment £28, follow up £22. Concessions for Old Age Pensioners at

discretion of doctor. They offer Acupuncture, Herbalism.

House of the Goddess
33 Oldridge Road
London SW12 8PN. (081) 673
6370.
Contact, support, learning and celebration for the pagan community. For free contact list send SAE. Also counselling service, training courses (including initiation). Most important events are the Pagan Moon and Halloween. Most festivals & meetings cost between £1.50-£2.50. Counselling is £15 per hour session. Birth, death, wedding cost £25, funeral is free. They offer Paganism.

Human Potential Resource Group
Dept of Educational Studies
University of Surrey
Guildford
Surrey GU2 5XH. (0483)
509191.
Intensive Journal workshops, life work planning, exercises in expanding intelligence. Most workshops are held at the University of Surrey, some are in London. Broad range of courses, often at the weekend, so it's possible if you're a Londoner for you to commute. They run a number of short (one week) training courses in gestalt, NLP, counselling, group work, stress management and birth trauma issues. Approx £60 per weekend workshop. The short (one week) trainings cost approx £250.They run a training in Group Oriented Therapy. They offer Bioenergetics, Co-counselling, Counselling, Creativity Therapy, Encounter Therapy, Feminist Therapy, Group Oriented Therapy, Jungian Psychotherapy, Management, Neurolinguistic Programming, Stress Management.

Humanistic Psychology at LSE
Short Courses Office
Psychology Dept
London School of Economics
Houghton St, London WC2A
2AE. (071) 405 7686.
They offer a training in psychotherapy.

Hygela College of Colour Therapy
Brook House
Tetbury

Glos GL8 8NS. (045383) 2150.
Large 14 bedroomed house (29 rooms in all) standing in 4 acres with pond and stream, orchard and field. £95-50 residential weekend (nine and a half hours tuition with free hand-outs). They offer Colour Therapy consultations and training.

Hypnoanalysis Centre
The Hale Centre
7 Park Crescent
London W1.
The centre has a number of practitioners. Phone to make an appointment. Wheelchair access. First session £45. Subsequent sessions £40. Anti-smoking sessions £70. They offer Touch for Health (Kinesiology).

Hypnotherapy Training Centre
9 Avocet Mews
Plumstead
London SE28 0DA.
They run a training in Hypnotherapy.

Hypnotherapy/ Psychotherapy Practice
37 Orbain Road
Fulham
London SW6 7J2. (071) 385
1166.
Large therapy room. £15 on average per session. Concs. They offer Counselling.

I

IBISS
17 Castle Road
Isleworth
Middx TW7 6QR. (081) 560
5436/9347.
Converted physiotherapy gymnasium. First floor: warm, light and peaceful. £40 per class. £16 per half day. They offer Aromatherapy, Alexander Technique, Dance therapy, Yoga, Voice Therapy, Stress Management, Massage.

Identity Counselling Service
2 Warwick Crescent
London W2 6NE. (071) 289
6175.

Specialise in counselling for personal and relationship issues, and those confused about their sexual identity and orientation. Also offer training workshops for counsellors. No wheelchair access. Assessment session £25 (negotiable). Counselling sessions £16-£20. Limited number of sessions at reduced fees. Training workshops £20 per day. They offer Counselling.

Image Impact
15 Plane Tree House
Duchess of Bedford's Walk
London W8 7QT. (071) 937
7403.
Concerned with the impact colour makes on a person. Run workshops and individual consultations. They offer Colour Therapy.

Imprint
377 Wimbledon Park Road
London SW19 6PE. (081) 788
1500.
Based in the top floor of a private house with darkroom (photography), art and printing facilities. Fully equiped art studio. Established 1984. Appointment required. £25 for two hours of art therapy. £20-£30 for a psychotherapy session. They offer Art Therapy, Dreamwork, Jungian Psychotherapy.

Independent Register of Manipulative Therapists
32 Lodge Drive
Palmers Green
London N13 5JZ. (081) 886
3120.
Register of both osteopaths and neuro-muscular manipulators. They offer Osteopathy.

Inner Miracle Partnership
5 Galgate
Barnard Castle
Co Durham DL12 8EQ. (0833)
31236.
Run courses in *A Course In Miracles*. Mail order books, tapes and videos. Correspondence course. £20 for individual sessions, £45-£60 for weekend courses. They offer Psychotherapy.

Inner Track Learning
Forge House
Limes Road
Kemble
Glos. GL7 6AD. (0285) 770635.

LIST OF CENTRES

Courses in accelerating learning skills. The inner track method is derived from Suggestopedia, accelerated learning, neuro linguistic programming and Yoga. It also incorporates study skills developed by Tony Buzan. Its aim is to help you develop your full learning potential. Books and cassettes available. Weekend workshops £68. They offer Psychotherapy.

Insight
37 Spring Street
London W2 1JA. (071) 706 2021.
Personal development seminars which aim to be gentle, nurturing and give participants an experience of their own value. Has been operating in London for 11 years. Address given is a small office, but visitors are very welcome, however their personal development seminars are held at another venue. £300 per person for a six day course, but often special offers available for more than one person. Participants pay £75 registration fee before the course, then decide at the end of the course how much they would like to pay, using the £300 as a guideline.

Insight Care
24 Chapel Market
Islington
London N1 9EZ. (071) 278 1212/4610.
Patients generally see the senior practitioner and are prescribed homoeopathic treatment. Other therapies are used to enhance homoeopathic treatment. Open Mon-Sat 8am-5pm. Established for five years. Linked to the College of Opthalmic Somatology. £19 per consultation, exclusive of medications. Register. No concs. Wheelchair access. They offer Acupuncture, Homoeopathy, Iridology, Laser Therapy.

Institute For Arts In Therapy & Education
70 Cranwich Rd
London N16 5JD. (081) 809 5866.
The institute holds its courses at Regent's College, Regent's Park. £18-£28 for individual therapy, £10 for group work. They run a training in Art Therapy. They offer Art therapy,

Music therapy, Dance therapy, Drama and Sandplay.

Institute for Complementary Medicine
21 Portland Place
London W1N 3AF. (071) 636 9543.
Runs a referral service for the general public to complementary practitioners. Provides information on complementary medicine, campaigns and researches, and can give advice on trainings. Network of public information points around country run by people who are not practitioners (so that they can be independent). Library. Supporters' Club (£12 per year for membership) which meets and receives newsletter.

Institute for Optimum Nutrition
5 Jerden Place
Fulham
London SW6 1BE. (071) 385 7984.
ION was established in 1984. Educational, non-profit making organisation. Members can drop in a use library. Clinic and training. Register. Wheelchair access. Sell books, have space to hire, run annual conference and produce a quarterly magazine, *Optimum Nutrition*. £59 for consultation, including hair analysis. £39 for one-day workshop. They offer Diet Therapy consultations and training.

Institute for Social Inventions
20 Heber Road
London NW2 6AA. (081) 208 2853.
Promote social inventions (new and imaginative ideas and projects for improving the quality of life). Print a journal and a book called *The Encyclopedia of Social Inventions*.

Institute of Allergy Therapists
Ffynnonwen Natural Therapy Centre
Llangwyryfon
Aberystwyth
Dyfed SY23 4EY.
Register. They offer Allergy Therapy.

Institute of Biodynamic Psychology and Psychotherapy
23 High St

The Green, Ealing
London W5 5DA. (081) 567 6677.
They run a training in Biodynamic Massage and Biodynamic Psychotherapy.

Institute of Botanic Medicine
538 Forest Road
Walthamstow
London E17 4NB. (081) 520 3811.
£16 for consultation and remedies for two weeks. Concs £15. They offer Acupuncture, Naturopathy, Osteopathy.

Institute of Clinical Aromatherapy
22 Bromley Road
Catford
London SE6 2TP. (081) 690 2149.
Established 1970. Aromatherapy for the beauty therapist £217. Essential oils course £105.75. Diploma in Aromatherapy £522.88. (Prices include VAT). They run a training in Aromatherapy. They offer Aromatherapy, Reflexology.

Institute of Emotio-Somatic Therapy
52 Bishopthorpe Rd
London SE26 43PA. (081) 659 0021.
This mixing of osteopathy and psychotherapy is a combination of simple body technique and an electric counselling approach. 4 term course. £20 per session. They run a training in Complementary medicine. They offer Psychotherapy.

Institute of Family Therapy
43 New Cavendish St
Marylebone
London W1M 7RG. (071) 935 1651.
Charity formed in 1977. They offer a clinical service to families with a wide range of behavioural and relationship problems. These problems may include difficulties with young children and adolescents or they may relate to marriage, bereavement or the care of elderly parents.
They practice a systems framework of Family Therapy. Some work with couples and individuals. Conciliation service. They hire out training videos, hold day workshops and organise

conferences. Wheelchair access to some rooms. On a sliding scale depending on income. They offer Family Therapy consultations and training.

Institute of Group Analysis
1 Daleham Gardens
Swiss Cottage
London NW3 5BY. (071) 431
2693.
The institute is a teaching institution that has been responsible for the establishment of a widely recognised professional qualification in group analytic psychotherapy. The Group Analytic Society is concerned with the development of group analysis as a treatment, prophylaxis and science, its advancement through study, research and teaching and the provision of library service, lectures and publications. Associate Membership £55, full membership £77. Also holds workshops, Think Tanks, Symposia, Conversazione and large groups. Newsletter. They run a training in Group Oriented Therapy. They offer Group Oriented Therapy, Child psychotherapy, Family Therapy, Couple Therapy.

Institute of Holistic Massage
75 Dresden Road
London N19. (071) 263 4994 or (0483) 426293.
Individual treatment in massage and body awareness. Introductory and advanced courses. £25-£28. They offer Massage treatments and training.

Institute of Holistic Therapies
486 Fulham Road
London SW6 5NH. (081) 540 1743.
Relaxation and natural healing. £60 per weekend workshop. Full-time students and unemployed £50. They offer Alexander Technique, Iridology, Massage, Reflexology, Shiatsu, Touch For Health.

Institute of Psychosynthesis
The Barn
Nan Clarks Lane
Mill Hill
London NW7 4HH. (081) 959 2330.
Established 17 years, psychosynthesis psychotherapy for individuals, couples and groups. Group leaders will

offer workshops and seminars. Counselling service with interview procedure. Mail order books. Wheelchair access. Prices as arranged with individual therapists. Concessions. They offer Psychosynthesis and run a training in the subject.

Institute of Psychotherapy and Social Studies
18 Laurier Road
London NW5. (071) 284 4782.
Psychoanalytic and Humanistic psychotherapy practised here. Sliding scale; students provide low cost therapy. They run a training in Psychotherapy. They offer Psychoanalytic Therapy.

Institute of Pure Chiropractic
14 Park End Street
Oxford ONX 1HH. (0865) 246687.
They are a registered professional body for McTimoney Chiropractic. Send SAE for directory which lists practitioners througout the UK, but also in London. They offer Chiropractic.

Institute of Structural Bodywork
Hyatt Carlton Tower
C/O Roger Golten, The Peak
Cadogan Place
London SW1X 9PY. (071) 235 5411.
Established in 1988, this centre is an information service for body-mind therapies related to Dr Rolf's work, cranio-sacral therapy and Traeger work. They advise on ergonomic products and sell books and products on tensional integrity models and books by Buckmaster Fuller. The 'Peak' is an exclusive health club on top of one of London's most fashionable hotels where Roger Golten practises Hellerwork. ISB is a mailing address for information about structural bodywork in general. £40 - £60 per session depending on therapy and experience of therapist. Concs. They offer Astrological Psychotherapy, Aston Patterning, Hellerwork, Rebalancing, Rolfing.

Institute of Traditional Herbal Medicine and Aromatherapy
54a Gloucester Avenue

London NW1 8JD. (071) 272 7403.
They run a training in Aromatherapy. They offer Aromatherapy.

International Association of Colour Healers
33 St Leonards Court
East Sheen
London SW14 7NG.
They offer Colour Therapy.

International College of Oriental Medicine
Green Hedges House
Green Hedges Avenue
East Grinstead
West Sussex RH19 1DZ. (0342) 313107.
They offer a training in Acupuncture and Massage.

International Federation for Radionics
21 Portland Place
London W1N 3AF. (0425) 53677.
They offer Radionics.

International Federation of Aromatherapists
4 Eastmearn Road
West Dulwich
London SE21 8HA.
Professional body for Aromatherapists. Register and list of accredited courses - send SAE. Newsletter and insurance service to full members (qualified aromatherapists only). Membership also open to general public interested in the subject. They offer Aromatherapy.

International NLP Training
48 Ferme Park Rd
London N4 4ED. (081) 348 5949.
Eriksonian Hypnosis practised. They organise seminars on neuro-linguistic programming.
The centre is an office, the workshops take place at other locations. Average size of workshops is 50 persons. Associated centres in France, Belgium, Luxemburg and Germany. £95 for a two day introductory course including a fire walk! They offer Neuro-linguistic Programming.

International Order of Kabbalists
25 Circle Gardens

London SW19 3JX. (081) 542
3611.
Quarterly magazine, The Kabbalist,
£1.25 per copy plus 20p postage, or
£3.50 for a year's subscription, post
free. Send letter with SAE. Lodge
meetings once a month, and corresponding members work on a
monthly basis. Information on Kab-
balistic astrology available at the same
address. They offer Kabbalah.

International Primal
Association
79 Pembroke Road
London E17. (081) 521 4764.
Will refer you to primal integration
practitioners in the UK. £vary depending on the practitioner. They
offer Primal Integration.

International School of the
Golden Rosycross
(Lectorium Rosicrucianum)
45 Woodlands Road
Earlswood
Redhill
Surrey
Headquarters of Lectorium
Rosicrucianum .

International Society for
Krishna Consciousness
(ISKON)
10 Soho Street
London W1. (071) 437 3662.
Founded by Bhaktivendanta Swami
Prabhupada, ISKON adheres closely
to the Veda Scriptures, and chant the
Hare Krisha Mantra. Practice Bhakti
Yoga (the Yoga of devotion or love).
They are Vaishnavas or worshippers
of Vishnu, a Hindu deity. There's a
residential community at centre and
a vegetarian restaurant. They have a
college for Vedic studies in Herts,
'Bhaktivedanta Manor'. The monastic followers wear the traditional
saffron coloured robe and shaven
head of Indian holy men, and lay
followers wear white. They offer
Hinduism.

International Tai Chi
Chuan Association
The People's Hall
No 8 Oriental Arts Studio
91/97 Freston Road
Holland Park
London W11. (081) 229 2900.

International
Transactional Association
89 Muswell Hill Road
London N10.

Iris
13 Mornington Grove
London E3. 981 0480.
Takes photos.

Isis
33 Lorn Road
Stockwell
London SW9 0AB. (071) 733
7883.
Isis offers psychosynthesis workshops using the inspiration of myth,
story and imagination, as well as individual therapy sessions. They run a
programme of workshops for
women, and some mixed groups.
Subjects of workshops include 'The
Way of All Women', a personal journey weekend based on ancient initiation myth, 'The Goddesses Within'
exploring archetypal aspects of
women's identity, 'Creativity and
Sexuality', and a mixed weekend
'Families, Fibs and Fairytales'. Methods used include guided imagery,
artwork, drama, story, maskmaking
and participants sharing their own
experience. Cost: £58 for a weekend,
£20-26. They offer Psychosynthesis,
Feminist Therapy, Counselling.

Isis Centre for Holistic
Health
5 Clonmell Road
London N17 6SY. (081) 801
4406.
Practice established 1978, centre
opened 1983. Approx £18-25 depending on therapy. Donations for
spiritual healing. They offer Counselling, Psychotherapy, Acupuncture,
Cranial Osteopathy, Hand Healing,
Massage, Osteopathy.

Iyengar Yoga Institute
223a Randolph Avenue
London W9 1NL. (071) 624
3080.
The institute runs classes for children
and adults from beginners to teaching level. Remedial classes for people
with problems are also held. Students
can drop in any time. Daytime,
weekend and evening classes.
Numbers are small. Qualified teachers only. They also sell books, videos
and yoga mats. Information is available about classes round the country.

Yoga days, exhibitions, seminars and
lectures. Have details of qualified yoga
teachers countrywide. Typically £5.
Concs up to half price. They offer
yoga classes and training.

J

Jamyang Meditation
Centre
10 Finsbury Park Road
Finsbury
London N4 2JZ. (071) 359
1394.
Group following Gelug school of the
Tibetan Buddhist tradition. Resident
teachers are Geshe Namgyal
Wangchen (who is resident in the
UK) and Lama Thubten Zopa
Rinpoche (who visits). Run evening
and weekend groups on meditation
and Buddhist philosophy. Have
residential communities where
members live. Many other visiting
Lamas give teachings and initiations.
Occasional retreats in the UK. Gompa
(shrine room for meditation), bookshop, tea-room and library. Open for
drop-in visits every day except Tues
from 2pm. Regular pujas. Opening
times weekdays 2-9.30pm, closed
Friday; Sat and Sun 11-6pm. £4 (£2
concs) for evening session. £5-£30
for courses/workshops. They offer
Meditation.

Janice Ellicot School of
Reflexology
42 Alder Lodge
Stevenage Road
London SW6 6NP. (071) 386
9914.
They run a training in Reflexology.
They offer Reflexology.

Jeyrani Health Centre
4-6 Glebelands Avenue
South Woodford
London E18 2AL. (081) 530
1146.
Vega testing and courses for fertility,
gynaecological counselling. People
are more than welcome to drop in or
call for further information and an
informal chat. The centre has five
consulting rooms and a large reception area. Open six days a week, 9.30-
9 and out of hours appointments are

possible. Established for two and half years. General evenings are on Tuesdays 7-9. Blended essential oils are sold. Creche facilities on Tuesdays. Prices range from £3.50 for general classes to £150 for more specialised courses. Usual price is £50 for an initial consultation and £15 - £25 for a one hour therapy session. They run a training in Active Birth and Aromatherapy. They offer Gestalt Therapy, Stress Management, Acupuncture, Aromatherapy, Metamorphic Technique, Osteopathy, Polarity Therapy, Reflexology, Yoga.

John Seymour Associates
17 Boyce Drive
St Werburghs
Bristol BS2 9QX. (0272)
557827.
They offer a training in Neuro-linguistic Programming.

K

Karma Kagyu Cho Khor Ling
Unit 21F Perseverance Works
38 Kingsland Road
London E2. (071) 739 9430.
The Venerable Lama Chime Rinpoche is the director and teacher of this Tibetan Buddhist centre, and he gives some lectures here. Chanting and meditation are the practices here, and there are evening and weekend courses. They offer Buddhism, Meditation.

Kensington Consultation Centre
47 South Lambeth Rd
London SW8 1RH. (071) 793 0148.
They offer Counselling, Couple Therapy, Family Therapy.

Khalsa Institute
39b Fitzroy St
London W1P 5HR. (071) 388 4776.
Kundalini yoga. Also numerology practised. £30 per day workshop. They offer Yoga.

Ki Kai Shiatsu Centre
8 Willow Road

Hampstead
London NW3. (081) 368 9050.
Qi Gong and postural re-alignment (Sotai). Warm inviting workshop room overlooking Hampstead Heath. Classes are kept small (14) for maximum student-teacher contact. They offer a range of treatments, practice sessions and Qi Gong classes. There is also a flotation tank which can be used in conjunction with shiatsu treatments, to enhance the treatment process. Lending library on Chinese medicine/shiatsu related subjects. Weekend introductory classes cost £30. Average treatment price £20. Concs. They run a training in Shiatsu. They offer Flotation Tank Therapy, Shiatsu, Meditation, Martial Arts.

Kinesiology School
8 Railey Mews
Kentish Town
London NW5 2PA. (071) 482 0698.
Private room for individual sessions. Offer weekend workshops. £25-£35 per consultation. Concessions depending upon need. They offer Touch for Health (Kinesiology).

Kingston Natural Healing Centre
40 Eastbury Road
Kingston-Upon-Thames
Surrey . (081) 546 5793.
Range of holistic therapies. They offer Acupuncture, Alexander Technique, Aromatherapy, Bach Flower Remedies, Biodynamic Psychotherapy, Colour Therapy, Diet Therapy, Hand Healing, Iridology, Hypnotherapy, Homoeopathy, Herbalism, Massage, Osteopathy, Reflexology, Reiki, Shiatsu, Stress Management, Yoga.

Kushi Institute
188 Old St
London EC1V 9BP. (071) 251 4076.
Upstairs from the East-West centre macrobiotic restaurant, the Kushi institute runs courses on macrobiotic

cooking and nutrition. They offer Macrobiotics.

L

Lavender Hill Homoeopathic Centre
33 Illminster Gardens
London SW11 1PJ. (071) 978 4519.
Three practice rooms. Open Mon-Sat 9-7. £25-£40. Concessions negotiable with individual practitioners. They offer Homoeopathy, Acupuncture, Osteopathy, Aromatherapy.

Lever Clinic
25 Fyfield Road
Enfield
Middx EN1 3TT. (081) 366 0666.
Physiotherapy. £18-£27. They offer Acupuncture, Osteopathy.

Lever Clinic
10 Harley St
London W1. (071) 580 4280.
Physiotherapy and electrolysis. Five treatment rooms. Wheelchair access. £18 per session. They offer Acupuncture, Osteopathy.

Life Directions
9 Cork St
Mayfair
London W1X 1PD. (071) 439 3806.
Based in Cambridge, but some courses in London. Also in-house training for companies. Wheelchair access. Three day weekend workshop £75. Concessions. They offer Assertion Therapy, Management, Stress Management.

Life Training Centre
35a Chepstow Road
Notting Hill
London W2. (071) 727 0652.
Life Training: 5 sessions in small groups normally evenings, including audio tapes, occasional weekend format also available. Life Training Weekend: 35 hour intensive training in self-awareness, including sex exercises which can be used for personal development work in daily life. Follow up groups take the form of

self-led meetings once a week for support and continuation of the work of the courses. Training is available for teachers of the Self Esteem course. Advanced focus courses include: relationships, communication, sexuality, effective parenting. Self Esteem course £60 (including 5 session tapes). Life Training weekend £150. Advanced courses (2 day) £95. They offer Life Training.

Lifespace Associates
100 Gloucester Road
London SW7 4AU. (071) 584
8819.
Bodywork, eating disorders. Training in groupwork, individual and group therapy, weekend workshops, professional consultancy and training and non-managerial supervision. Summer workshop in Italy. Individual sessions £20-£25. Workshops £20-£23 (with reductions for a series). Concessions. They offer Client-centered Therapy, Gestalt Therapy, Transactional Analysis.

Lifespace Associates
100 Gloucester Road
London SW7 4AU. (071) 584
8819.
They offer Client-centered Therapy, Gestalt Therapy, Transactional Analysis.

Lifeworks
11 Southampton Road
London NW5. (071) 267 0269.
First session £30-£45, subsequent sessions £20-£25 for an hour. They offer Acupuncture, Aromatherapy, Colonic Irrigation, Hand Healing, Homoeopathy, Martial Arts, Massage, Naturopathy, Osteopathy, Reflexology, Reiki.

Lilly Stuart Resource Development Consultants
106 Heathwood Gardens
London SE7 8ER. (081) 854
3606.
Typically £85 per weekend workshop. They offer Transactional Analysis, Stress Management, Assertion Therapy.

Little Grove Education
Grove Lane
Chesham
Bucks HP5 3QL. (0494)
782720.

They offer Meditation, Feldenkrais, Voice Therapy.

Living Art Training
11 Stowe Road
Ravenscourt Park
London W12 8BQ. (081) 749
0874.
Personal and spiritual growth through painting and other creative work i.e. movement, chanting, music, meditation. Weekend workshops. Advance booking only. Living Art has been running for 15 years. £86 + VAT for weekend workshops. Approx £260 + VAT for a week in the country, fully residential, materials supplied. They run a training in Psychotherapy.

Living Colour
33 Lancaster Grove
Swiss Cottage
London NW3 4EX. (071) 794
1371.
Run courses on body consciousness and the effects of colour: colour counselling, colour reflection reading, body therapy. Individual therapy and courses from colour awareness to colour counselling. They perform colour analysis for clothes so that can find the colour that suits you best. £25-£65. Offer scholarships in genuine cases of need. They run a training in Colour Therapy. They offer Colour Therapy.

Living Qabalah
5 Hindmans Road
London SE22 9NF. (081) 693
9951.
Psychotherapy, teaching seminars in Qabalah, Tarot and Magick. Individual guidance and groupwork, public workshops that include dance, ritual, meditation, psychological exercises, visualisation etc. Public meetings in rented workshop spaces, individual work at centre. Run ongoing training in practical esoteric psychology including the qabalah and tarot. Reading Will Parfitt's books 'The Living Qabalah' and 'Walking Through Walls' gives a flavour of what's on offer. Also offer a one-off guidance of life purpose and the next step. Individual sessions £25 per hour session. Groups typically £60 for a weekend workshop. Negotiable concessions for those on low income.

They offer Psychosynthesis, Kabbalah.

London Association of Primal Psychotherapists
18A Laurier Road
Tufnel Park
London NW5 1SH. (071) 267
9616.
Primal therapy based on the work of Alice Miller and Arthur Janov. The centre has been established since 1986. They are five psychotherapists trained by Janov. Interviews on application. Therapy offered in German, French, Spanish, Italian and Norwegian. £32.50 per hour. Low cost therapy at £12 per hour available with training therapists. They run a training in Primal Therapy. They offer Primal Therapy.

London Buddhist Centre
51 Roman Road
Bethnal Green
London E2 0HU. (081) 981
1225.
Centre of the Friends of the Western Buddhist order, founded by the Venerable Sangharakshita, an Englishman who spent 20 years in India as a monk. Seek to synthesise elements from all Buddhist traditions. Day and evening classes, weekends in meditation and Buddhism. Own retreat centre in Suffolk, women's retreat centre in Shropshire and men's in Norfolk and Wales. The centre is a converted 19th century fire station, with two large meditation rooms, a bookshop and main reception room. The Cherry Orchard restaurant run by the Buddhists is next door. Weds introductory evening £5, £3 concs. Introductory Meditation course £60, £40 concs. Residential weekend retreat £60, £40 concs. all inclusive. Residential Mon-Fri retreat £150 all inclusive. They offer Buddhism, Meditation, Retreats.

London Centre for Clinical Hypnotherapy
Red Lion Square
London WC1. (071) 499 2813.
Individual consultations and workshops. Self improvement cassettes. £60 per session.

London Centre for Psychotherapy
19 Fitzjohn's Avenue
Swiss Cottage

London NW3 5JY. (071) 435
0873.
They run a training in Psychoanalytic
Therapy. They offer Psychoanalytic
Therapy.

London Centre for Yoga and Shiatsu Studies
49b Onslow Gardens
London N10 3JY. (081) 444
0103.
Chinese Tui Na, physiotherapy. £16-
£35. They run a training in Shiatsu
and Yoga. They offer Yoga, Shiatsu.

London Co-counselling Community
23 Bridge Avenue Mns
Bridge Av
London W6 9JB. (081) 748
1407.
You must do the training to become
a member. In London there are about
700 members. They produce a
newsletter which is now more a
journal on co-counselling. Various
workshops. Once you have completed the training it's free. They run
a training in Co-counselling. They
offer Co-counselling.

London College of Classical Homoeopathy
c/o Morley College
61 Westminster Bridge Road
London SE1 7HT. (071) 928
6199.
Offices and classrooms in Morley
College. Centrally located near Wa-
terloo and Lambeth North Tube Sta-
tions. Telephone or call for clinic
appointment. Fees by donation (are
applying for charity status). They run
a training in Homoeopathy. They offer
Homoeopathy.

London College of Crystal Healing
8 Albany Road
New Malden
Surrey . (071) 402 9576.
Mainly a training centre for crystal
healers, but with introductory day
seminars also. Crystal healing session £25 per hour. They run a training
in Crystal Therapy. They offer Crystal
Therapy.

London College of Massage
5-6 Newman Passage
London W1P 3PF. (071) 323
3574.

Established 1987 but moved recently.
Central London location. They also
visit businesses to provide relief for
aching muscles. £60-£80 approx per
weekend workshop. £220 approx for
a ten week beginner course. £35 upwards for individual sessions. They
run a training in Massage. They offer
Massage, Reflexology, Aromatherapy.

London College of Osteopathic Medicine
8-10 Boston Place
Marylebone
London NW1 6QH. (071) 262
5250.
Osteopathic association clinic, established 1927. Registered charity
providing treatment for those who
cannot afford usual private fees. Appointments always necessary. Payment by voluntary contribution.
Target cost price of first treatment
£10, follow up £8. They run a training
in Osteopathy. They offer Osteopathy.

London College of Shiatsu
1 Central Park Lodge
54-58 Bolsover St
London W1P 7HL. (071) 383
2619.
Central London location. Will see
people lunchtimes and after work in
addition to normal business hours.
Sell video and books on Shiatsu. £25
approx per treatment session. Concs
for OAP's and UB 40's. They run a
training in Shiatsu. They offer Shiatsu,
Acupuncture, Herbalism.

London College of Chinese Herbal Medicine and Acupuncture
129 Queens Crescent
London NW5 4HE. (071) 267
4561.
They offer a training in Acupuncture
and Herbalism.

London Group
BM Vixack
London WC1N 3XX.
A western mysteries group that offers
training in esoteric spiritual tradition
of the west. Courses by correspondence in the Qabalah and modern
mysteries. On completion there is the
opportunity to be considered for
initiation into a working group based

in South London. They offer Paganism, Kabbalah.

London Institute for the Study of Human Sexuality
Flat C
Langham Mansions
Earls Court Square
London SW5 9UH. (071) 373
0901.
Run weekend workshops, talks,
women's sexuality groups, AIDS
counselling courses, sex education
courses. They run a training in Sex
Therapy. They offer Couple Therapy,
Feminist Therapy, Sex Therapy.

London Kagyu Centre
Unit 21F Perseverance Works
38 Kingsland Road
London E2. (071) 609 8591.
Tibetan Buddhist group under the
direction of Lama Chime Rinpoche.
Meditation/puja Weds evening. They
offer Buddhism, Meditation.

London Lighthouse
111/117 Lancaster Road
London W11 1QT. (071) 792
1200.
Prominent in the field of counselling
AIDS patients, this organisation runs
training courses in counselling and
bereavement counselling. Residential and support centre. Day care,
home support, drop-in, cafe,
education and information. The
therapies are free. Three day non
residential course in bereavement
counselling £172.50 incl. VAT. They
offer Bereavement Counselling,
Counselling, Massage, Acupuncture,
Homoeopathy, Art Therapy, Music
therapy.

London Natural Health Clinic
Arnica House
170 Campden Hill Road
Notting Hill Gate
London W8 7AS. (071) 938
3788.
A friendly, relaxed and caring environment where practitioners co-operate to the benefit of the patient.
First visit £35, repeats £22. Concessions on request. They offer Acupuncture, Aromatherapy, Homoeopathy, Massage, Osteopathy, Counselling.

London School of Acupuncture and

Traditional Chinese Medicine

36 Featherstone St
London EC1Y 8QX. (071) 490 0513
The clinic offers treatment at reduced rates by final year students under supervision.They run a training in Acupuncture. They offer Acupuncture, Herbalism.

London School of Herbology and Aromatherapy

54a Gloucester Ave
London NW1 8JD.
They offer a training in Aromatherapy and Herbalism.

London School of Homoeopathy

57 Wise Lane
Mill Hill
London NW7 2RN. (0935) 224881.
They offer a training in Homoeopathy.

London School of Osteopathy

110 Lower Richmond Road
Richmond
London SW15 1LN. (081) 788 1991.
They offer a training in Osteopathy.

London Serene Reflection Meditation Group

23 Westbere Road
Cricklewood
London NW2. (071) 794 3109.
Private flat used on an occasional basis. They offer Buddhism, Meditation.

London Society for Ericksonian Psychotherapy and Hypnosis

1 Mill Lane
Stedham
Midhurst
West Sussex GU29 0RS. 083 081 5613.
Provides workshop education in Ericksonian psychotherapy for those with a qualification in one of the recognised helping professions (psychology, nursing, medicine, social work etc) and to full-time students

on courses leading to such a qualification.

London Sufi Centre

21 Lancaster Road
Notting Hill
London W11 1QL. (071) 229 1064.
The Centre was founded to offer genuine spiritual training for those interested in the Sufi path, and aims to be non-sectarian. Founded by Hazrat Inayar Khan. Present Head of Order Pir Vilayat Kahn who visits the UK. Holds classes on their teachings and on traditional Sufi practices including meditation, dance, prayers, breath and sound, visualisation etc. Healing course and service. Classes are for participating in and enable one to understand and experience the teachings on a deeper level. Individual retreats at the London Centre, group retreats (meditation, sacred dance, chanting, etc.) and residential UK Sufi Summer Camp, both at Hourne Farm, Essex. £3 per evening. They offer Meditation, Retreats, Sufism.

London Zen Society

10 Belmont Street
Camden
London NW1 8HH. (071) 485 9576.
Rinzai sect Zen group, offshoot of Ryutaku-Jai monastery in Mishima, Japan, whose abbot is Kyudo Nakagawa Roshi. Sitting every day: Monday-Friday 6-8pm, Weds 7-9pm and Thurs 6-8am. 7 day retreats at centre, day sessions. Basic instruction given to beginners. Resident monk at centre. No charge for classes. They offer Buddhism, Meditation, Retreats.

Lotus Healing Centre

129 Queens Crescent
London NW5. (071) 284 4614.
Multi-disciplinary alternative therapy centre with emphasis on preventative health care. £10-£30 per session. Concessions by arrangement with practitioner.They run a training in Complementary medicine. They offer Acupuncture, Herbalism, Aromatherapy, Ayurevedic Medicine, Counselling, Diet Therapy, Meditation, Osteopathy.

Lucis Trust

Suite 54
3 Whitehall Court
Victoria
London SW1 2EF. (071) 839 4512.
The Lucis trust administers a number of programmes: The Arcane School, a meditation school run by correspondence; Triangles, which is a global network of individuals from different spiritual paths who use prayer and meditation to spread goodwill in the world; World Goodwill, which publishes material presenting a global spiritual perspectives on the issues facing humanity; and Lucis Press which publishes Alice Bailey's books. Free lending library of esoteric books available in London. Meetings fortnightly in the Charing Cross Hotel. Meditation meetings at the time of the full moon, and lectures on healing, ecology, development, metaphysics etc at the time of the new moon .Bi-monthly journal, The Beacon, and quarterly, World Goodwill newsletter.Established by Alice A Bailey, an author and lecturer in the first half of this century who pioneered the idea of a New Age of global co-operation and wholeness. She wrote 24 books presenting an esoteric perspective on psychology, occult meditation and the evolution of humanity, which aim to help individuals be more effective in serving humanity and the Plan of Light and Love during what is seen as a time of transition into the Age of Aquarius. She founded the Lucis Trust as an international agency in the raising of human consciousness, and it now has consultative status with the United Nations.

M

Man To Man

17 Mackeson Road
London NW3 2LU. (071) 482 3588.
Evening and weekend personal growth groups for men. Admission to evening groups by interview only. Open to men of any sexual orientation. Individual and group work. Individual £11-£22 per session,

groupwork £10 per session They offer Men's Therapy, Rebirthing.

Marigold Treatment Centre
134 Montrose Avenue
Edgware
Middlesex HA8 0DR. (081) 959 5421.
Approx £25 per session plus remedies. They offer Herbalism.

Marigold Trust
PO Box 57
London WC1N 3NE. (071) 831 2962.
Registered charity providing Marigold therapy and homoeopathic chiropody. The trust furthers research into Marigold therapy and publishes the results for public benefit. It also provides training in homoeopathic podiatric medicine (chiropody). Concs. They offer Chiropody, Homoeopathy.

Martial Arts Commission
First Floor
Broadway House
15-16 Deptford Broadway
London SE8. (081) 691 8711.
Contact for details of approved martial arts clubs in London. They offer Martial Arts.

Mary Martin School of Reflexology
37 Standale Grove
Ruislip
Middlesex HA4 7UA. (0895) 635621.
They run a training in Reflexology. They offer Reflexology.

Maskarray
14 Mornington Grove
Bow
London E3 4NS. (071) 980 4534.
Runs workshops using masks. Emotional expression using drama and play to have fun and gain insight. They offer Psychotherapy.

McCarthy Westwood Consultants
25 Kite House
The Falklands
Grant Road
London SW11 2NJ. (071) 585 3445.
Management Courses in stress management and aromatherapy. They offer Stress Management, Aromatherapy.

Mehta Method of Therapeutic Head Massage
14 Stranraer Way
Freeling Street
Off Caledonian Road
London N1 0DR. (071) 609 3590.
A home practice where Indian head, neck and scalp massage which has been practiced in India for over 1,000 years is offered. Also offer weekend training courses in head massage. £12 for Indian head and shoulder massage, £20 for body massage and osteopathy. Weekend workshop £70. They offer Massage, Osteopathy.

Melissa Morant Centre
7 Heath Villas
The Vale Of Health
London NW3 1AW. (071) 435 8787.
Individual Shiatsu sessions as well as workshops. £36 per weekend workshop. They offer Homoeopathy, Shiatsu.

Mental Development Ltd
14 Ickburgh Road
London E5 8AD. (081) 806 5298.
Speed reading, memory training and sequential analysis. Large Victorian house close to Clapton station. £25 per session, £15 concs. They offer Biodynamic Massage, Biofeedback.

Meridians Clinic
40 Weymouth Street
London W1N 3LR. (071) 486 7494.
Physiotherapy, manipulative therapy. Established for 9 years, with three treatment rooms. Appointment only. Tea, chat and music on offer. All practitioners are registered or chartered. Initial session £30, £25 subsequent sessions. Concessions to dancers, OAP's and students. They offer Acupuncture.

Metamorphic Association
67 Ritherdon Road
Tooting
London SW17 8QE. (081) 672 5951.
Established for 7 years. Meeting/session room, office and display for books and other material. Mail order, sell books, cassettes and other products. Open day twice a month. Offer home visits for the disabled in the Greater London Area. Wheelchair access. Journal Metamorphosis 3 times a year, £1.50 each. £18 per 1 hour session. £50 for a 12 hour weekend workshop. Home visits cost of transport for practitioner and donations. They offer Metamorphic Technique.

Metanoia
13 North Common Road
Ealing Common
London W5. (081) 579 2505 .
Large house near Ealing Common. Also offer assessment and referral service for counselling and psychotherapy. £25-£45. Concessions to the unemployed. They run a training in Transactional Analysis and Gestalt Therapy. They offer Couple Therapy, Family Therapy, Gestalt Therapy, Transactional Analysis.

Micheline Arcier Aromatherapy
7 William Street
Knightsbridge
London SW1X 9HL. (071) 235 3545 .
Established 9 years. Mail order. From £20. They run a training in Aromatherapy. They offer Aromatherapy.

Mill Hill Health Care
3 Hankins Lane
Mill Hill
London NW7 3AA. (081) 959 1752.
Small centre (private house). Established 10 years, no drop-in. £12-£15. Concs. They offer Counselling, Radiathesia, Reflexology.

Minster Centre
55-57 Minster Road
Cricklewood
London NW2 3SH. (071) 435 9200.
Cover both traditional and humanistic psychotherapy. Work in groups and individual sessions. Also run professional programme specialist workshops for those in the helping professions. £varies for groups and weekends. Individual sessions £8 minimum. They run a training in Psychotherapy. They offer Assertion Therapy, Biosynthesis, Couple Therapy, Feminist Therapy, Gestalt Therapy, Group Oriented Therapy,

Psychodrama, Stress Management, Transactional Analysis.

Monkton Wyld Court
Nr. Charmouth
Bridport
Dorset DT6 6DQ. (0297) 60342.
They offer a place for a retreat, training and workshops.

Moving Line Counselling and Therapy
c/o 13 Oldfield Mews
London N6.
Londonwide counselling and therapy network using the methods and perspective of psychosynthesis. Individual sessions, couples, workshops. South-East/Croydon (081) 656 9209, East/Central (071) 790 8146, South-West/West (071) 733 7883, North/North West (081) 341 4413. £18-25 per session. They offer Counselling, Psychosynthesis.

Mu Sum Ba - Living Rhythm
93 Percy Road
London W12 9QH. (081) 743 7246.
Rhythm therapy in groups. Ring for details of workshops.
Influenced by the rituals of Africa, Brazil and India. Workshops explore rhythm as inter-relation of stillness, sound, and movement. Vocal rhythm, various ways of clapping, stepping and chanting, utilise the body as the personal musical instrument and facilitate to find and trust the inner source of rhythm. £60 for a weekend workshop, non residential. £95 residential. Introduction £20. They offer Music therapy.

Mushindokai
12 Finchley Park
North Finchley
London N12 9JN.
They offer Martial Arts, Buddhism.

Muswell Healing Arts
169 Avenue Mews
London N10 3NN. (081) 365 3545.

They offer Aromatherapy, Massage.

N

Nafsiyat Inter-Cultural Therapy Centre
278 Seven Sisters Road
Finsbury Park
London N4 2HY. (071) 263 4130.
Specialises in offering help to people from ethnic and cultural minorities. Runs workshops and seminars for people in the helping professions to enable them to work across other cultures, including the Diploma in Intercultural Therapy (run in association with University College, London). Also in-service training for organisations. Individual sessions free to Islington residents, otherwise sliding scale. Workshops usually £50 for two days. They offer Psychotherapy.

Napier Chiropractic Clinic
141 Golders Green Road
London NW11 8HG. (081) 458 3311.
Established 4 years. By appointment only. Two treatment rooms and two chiropractors, masseuse and chiropodist. Concs. Wheelchair access. Consultation £35, Chiropodist treatment £22. X-ray if necessary £40. Massage £25/hr. They offer Chiropody, Chiropractic, Massage.

Natale Institute London
18 Tregaron Avenue
Crouch End
London N8 9EY. 081 341 9032.
Offers personal development and experiential educational courses in self esteem, effective communication, channelling, mastering relationships and sexuality. London branch of The Natale Institute, which is an international organisation. Organise and promote individual therapists or lecturers. Wheelchair access for courses held in Kensington Town Hall. £160 for one weekend (two and a half days), £350 for 2 weekends plus three days. They offer Psychotherapy.

National College of Hypnosis & Psychotherapy
12 Cross Street

Nelson
Lancs BB9 7EN. (0282) 699378.
They offer a training in Hypnotherapy.

National Council and Register of Iridologists
80 Portland Road
Bournemouth BH9 1NQ.
Register of trained iridologists available with SAE. They offer Iridology.

National Federation of Spiritual Healers
Old Manor Farm Studio
Church Street
Sunbury-On-Thames
Middlesex TW16 6RG. (0932) 783164/5.
The head office of NFSH has been here for 12 years, looking after the needs of members and running a national referral register for those seeking a healer. Sell books and tapes, and publish 'Healing Review' quarterly (1, free to members). Courses and training in healing and its aspects. Approximately £110-£125 per training weekend. They offer Hand Healing.

National Institute of Medical Herbalists
9 Palace Gate
Exeter EX1 1JA. (0392) 426022.
Established in 1864, this is the oldest body of professional practitioners in the world. They have an annual conference for members. Maintain a register of qualified members, who must adhere to a code of ethics and practice. Members train on a four year course at School of Herbal Medicine in Sussex. Typically practitioners charge £15 - £20 plus remedies for initial consultation, £10 - £15 thereafter. They offer Herbalism.

National School of Hypnosis and Advanced Psychotherapy
28 Finsbury Park Road
London N4 2JX. (071) 359 6991.
They offer a training in Hypnotherapy.

Natural Death Centre
20 Heber Road
London NW2 6AA. (081) 208 2853.
The centre aims to improve the quality of dying; by helping people talk about death, encouraging people to prepare for dying well in advance and to help

the family take control of the dying from the big institutions. They offer Bereavement Counselling.

Natural Healing Centre
1A New Pond Parade
West End Road
Ruislip Gardens
Middlesex HA4 6LR. (0895)
675464.
This small centre has been established for eight years. £18 for initial consultation, £15 subsequent except acupuncture which is £25 for initial consultation, and psychotherapy and hypnotherapy which is £18 per session. They offer Counselling, Acupuncture, Allergy Therapy, Herbalism, Homoeopathy, Radionics, Reflexology.

Natural Healing Centre
165 Capel Rd
London E7 0JT. (081) 478 3942.
Beauty therapy and slimming clinic, Hellerwork, cranio-sacral therapy. Established in 1972, there are eleven therapists working at this centre. Books and products are sold. Wheelchair access. Creche facilities. Prices vary from £27-55. They offer Counselling, Acupuncture, Alexander Technique, Allergy Therapy, Aromatherapy, Chiropody, Homoeopathy, Laser Therapy, Magnetic Therapy, Massage, Osteopathy, Polarity Therapy, Reflexology.

Natural Health Clinic
286 Preston Road
Harrow
Middlesex HA3 0QA. (081) 908 4272.
This clinic has been established since 1984 and people can drop in. Small is beautiful. Mail order: vitamins, minerals, essential oils and homoeopathic medicines. Health food shop. Initial consultation £12 -£15 plus cost of medicines. Concs to unemployed. They offer Allergy Therapy, Diet Therapy, Homoeopathy, Shiatsu, Massage.

Natural Medicine Centre
87 Beckenham Lane
Shortlands
Bromley BR2 ODN. (081) 460 1117.
Biomobility offered. Two therapy rooms. 9-9pm Mon-Sat. Two steps for wheelchair. £16-35. Concs. They offer Gestalt Therapy, Acupuncture, Aromatherapy, Herbalism, Homoe-

opathy, Massage, Reflexology, Shiatsu.

Nature Cure Clinic
15 Oldbury Place
Marylebone
London W1M 3AL. (071) 935 6213.
Registered charity for those unable to afford private treatment. All patients see a qualified doctor on their first visit. Consultations by appointment only. Founded in 1928. Occasional lectures. Mailing list sent on request. Wheelchair access. £15 for first consultation. £7.50 for subsequent visits. Register of practitioners. Concs. They offer Acupuncture, Diet Therapy, Massage, Naturopathy, Osteopathy, Physiotherapy.

Naturecare
22 Oakdale Road
Streatham
London SW16. (081) 769 8232.
£25 per workshop. They offer Aromatherapy, Reflexology, Bach Flower Remedies.

Naturemed Partnership
Silver Birches
Private Road
Rodborough Common
Stroud, Gloucs GL5 5BT.
(045387) 3446.
Major centre in UK for Spagyrik therapy, also offer herbalism, AK, reflexology and Flyborg therapy. Register. Car parking facilities. Wheelchair access. £20 per session. They offer Complementary medicine.

Natureworks
16 Balderton Street
London W1. (071) 629 6183.
Types of massage available are: Eyerman technique, foot pressure massage, Indian head and neck massage, remedial massage. Also acuflex reflexology, fitness assessments, diet counselling, lifestyle management. Based in a dance centre, also dance and movement classes, body conditioning clinic (pilates). Alexander Institute also based in same building. Prices range from £15-35. Some therapists offer concessions by arrangement. They offer Counselling, Neuro-linguistic Programming, Relaxation Training, Stress Management, Acupuncture, Allergy Therapy, Aromatherapy, Colour Therapy, Hand Healing, Herbalism, Homoeopathy, Massage, Naturopathy, Os-

teopathy, Reflexology, Shiatsu, Qigong and Chinese physiotherapy. Also clinic for those coming off tranquillisers.

Neal's Yard Therapy Rooms
2 Neal's Yard
Covent Garden
London WC2 H9D. (071) 379 7662.
Psychic counselling and clairvoyancy. Established 1982. People can drop in for a chat, information, guidance on which therapy to choose. Toy box available for children. Information pack can be sent countrywide. Advice freely given even to non residents of South East. £20-40 for first consultation, from £15-25 for follow-ups. Concs. They offer Autogenic Training, Biofeedback, Sex Therapy, Acupuncture, Alexander Technique, Aromatherapy, Biodynamic Massage, Chiropractic, Colour Therapy, Cranial Osteopathy, Diet Therapy, Hand Healing, Herbalism, Iridology, Massage, Naturopathy, Osteopathy, Polarity Therapy, Reflexology, Shiatsu, Touch For Health.

New Cross Natural Therapy Centre
394 New Cross Road
London SE14. (081) 469 0858.
Next to New Cross tube. Limited access. Creche by arrangement. Limited parking. Established 1985. Mostly run by women. Women practitioner available for all but Shiatsu. Open weekends and evenings. The centre has the same rate for all of the therapies on offer. They offer Gestalt Therapy, Neuro-linguistic Programming, Psychoanalytic Therapy, Acupuncture, Alexander Technique, Cranial Osteopathy, Diet Therapy, Herbalism, Homoeopathy, Massage, Metamorphic Technique, Osteopathy, Polarity Therapy, Postural Integration, Reflexology, Reiki, Touch for Health (Kinesiology), Yoga.

New Life Lodge
60 Gloucester Road
Brownswood
London N4 2LN. (081) 800 3831.
Mid-life career counselling. They offer Biodynamic Massage, Massage.

Nichirin Shoshu of the United Kingdom
1 The Green
Richmond

Surrey. (081) 948 0381/2
Founded on the teaching of Nichiren Daishonin who lived in 13th century Japan. Main practice is mantra chanting. They offer Buddhism.

Nimatullahi Sufi Order
41 Chepstow Place
Notting Hill Gate
London W2 4TS. (071) 229 0769.
Centre of traditional Sufi order under the direction of the Master Dr Javad Hurbakush who is in residence. Order established in 700 A.D., London centre since 1976. Meditation takes place twice a week. Call or write for appointment. Books and journals about Sufism are available in English, French and Persian. Wheelchair access. Events free. Enquiries from seekers of Truth about their practice are welcome. They offer Sufism.

Nine Needles Health Care Centre
121 Sheen Road
Richmond upon Thames
Surrey TW9 1YJ. (081) 940 8892.
Established in the UK since 1987, appointments only Monday to Saturday. Practitioner trained in Japan, where he operated his own clinic for 7 years. Holds Japanese licences. First acupuncture session £30, thereafter £25. Shiatsu £25. Concessions to the elderly. They run a training in Acupuncture and Shiatsu. They offer Acupuncture, Shiatsu.

NLP Training Program
22 Upper Tooting Park
London
SW17 7SR. (081) 682 0733.
They offer a training in Neuro-linguistic Programming.

Nordoff-Robbins Music Therapy Centre
6 Queensdale Walk
London W11 4QQ.
Music therapy for children with special needs, normally one half-hour session per week. Established 1981 when 14 children attended weekly for their sessions. Now between 70-80 children come weekly, some in small groups. Two conferences annually. Discussions, illustrated with video material of the work are arranged for individuals and small groups. One parents meeting per

term. £confidential, according to parents means. They run a training in Music therapy. They offer Music therapy.

North London Centre for Group Therapy
138 Bramley Rd
Oakwood
Southgate
London N14 4HU. 440 1451.
Established 12 years. Referrals are usually made through a GP. Other professionals in related fields may also refer, and individuals seeking psychotherapy can contact the centre direct. Individuals, couples and families are offered an initial consultation at which the appropriate form of therapy is considered. They offer services to mental health professionals such as individual supervision, group supervision, consultations to professionals and staff groups and work discussion groups. Lunch time seminars and an annual group-analytic workshop (with residential facility). Group fees - £52 p.c.m. (one and half hour session per week). Concs. Other fees are available on request. They offer Couple Therapy, Family Therapy, Group Oriented Therapy and individual psychotherapy.

North London Counselling Practice
5 Turner Drive
London NW11 6TX. (081) 458 4036.
They are a group of trained counsellors and therapists, each working from home. Established four years. £20-£30 per session. Willing to negotiate price. They offer Counselling, Couple Therapy, Sex Therapy, Bereavement Counselling.

North London Counselling Service
28 Northolme Road
Highbury
London N5 2UU. (071) 359 2356.
A network of Psychosynthesis counsellors and therapists working in the North London area. Individuals, couples, courses and workshops for groups. No access. £15-£30 per hour for individual sessions. Concessions

based on a sliding scale. They offer Psychosynthesis, Couple Therapy.

Nutribiotics
35 Highview Avenue
Edgware
Middlesex HA8 9TX. (081) 958 7553.
Strictly by prior appointment. Established 1986. They offer Counselling, Bach Flower Remedies, Crystal Therapy, Diet Therapy, Herbalism, Homoeopathy.

Open Centre
188 Old Street
London EC1V 9BP. (081) 549 9583.
The UK's longest established independent growth centre. Run as a collective, with the staff sharing administration as well as their therapeutic skills. Runs wide range of workshops using different therapeutic approaches. On-going groups and weekend workshops. The centre is situated in a complex housing a bookshop (Genesis) and the East West Restaurant. Weekend workshops from £50. On going groups from £8 - £12 per evening. £20-£30 per individual session. They run a training in Postural Integration. They offer Bioenergetics, Encounter, Psychodrama, Transactional Analysis, Feldenkrais, Massage, Postural Integration, Pulsing, Primal Integration.

Open Gate
6 Goldney Road
Clifton
Bristol . (0272) 7345952.
Run a variety of workshops and residentials on shamanism. Courses on aspects of psychology and spirituality including Buddhism, dancing path workshops, myth, often with well known speakers and spiritual practitioners. They offer Creativity, Resonance Therapy, Retreats.

Order of Bards Ovates and Druids
260 Kew Road
Richmond

LIST OF CENTRES

Surrey
TW9 3EG.

Outreach Counselling
Sternberg Centre
80 East End Rd
London N3 2SY. (081) 346 2288.
They offer a training in Psychoanalytic Therapy.

P

Pace Personal Development
86 South Hill Park
London
NW3 2SN. (071) 794 0960.
They offer Neuro-linguistic Programming.

Pagan Link
c/o 4 Caznove Road
London N16 6BD. (071) 263 5966.
Pagan-Link meetings are held at the White Lion of Mortimer pub at Stroud Green Road, London N4, on alternate Thursday evenings. The meetings are friendly and informal and are open to people of all paths who are involved or simply interested in Paganism or the Occult and wish to exchange views and ideas. Contact Ray on the above number (eves) for details. They offer Paganism.

Paul Newham Voice Centre
11 Hanover Gardens
Upper Holly Walk
Leamington Spar
Warks CV32 4JW. (0926) 424080.
'The voice and the psychological make-up of an individual mutually influence each other. By developing the sound of the human voice through singing for health, the whole personality is influenced in a favourable manner. This is psychophonology, based upon the philosophy of C G Jung. It combines singing, massage and movement to liberate the voice from restriction and develop the whole person towards fruition'. Individual consultations and small groups. Singing lessons. Training in Voice Therapy. Programmes of weekend and one week courses in singing, voice and massage, voice and movement and psychophonology.
They offer Voice Therapy.

Pearl Healing Centre
37 Carew Road
Thornton Heath
Surrey CR7 7RF. (081) 689 1771.
£12 for healings, £15 for hypnotherapy. They offer Crystal Therapy, Colour Therapy, Hypnotherapy.

Pellin Centre
43 Killyon Road
Clapham
London SW8 2XS. (071) 622 0148.
Sessions £25-£30. Concs. Low cost therapy with trainees. They run a training in Gestalt Therapy. They offer Feminist Therapy, Gestalt Therapy, Couple Therapy and adolescent counselling.

Pellin Training Courses
15 Killyon Road
London SW8 2XS. (071) 720 4499.
Short courses, workshops and individual therapy. Typically £85 for a weekend workshop. Individual therapy £32.They run a training in Gestalt Therapy. They offer Gestalt Therapy.

Person-Centred Art Therapy Centre
17 Cranbourne Gardens
London NW11 0HN. (081) 455 8570.
Person-centred counselling, using art therapy and gestalt therapy when appropriate. Mainly one to one. Supervision. Individual plus group consultancy. House in residential area. £23 - £25 per hour. Workshops £30 per day per person in groups of 9. They run a training in Art Therapy. They offer Art Therapy, Gestalt Therapy.

Personal & Professional Development
19 Whittingstall Road
London SW6 4EA. (071) 736 4911.

Deal with organisations and the effectiveness of workers in their workplace.

Philadelphia Association
4 Marty's Yard
17 Hampstead High Street
London NW3 1PX. (071) 794 2652.
No therapy practised at the centre but:
1) Network of private psychotherapists working from own homes or practices. Some group therapy possible. 2)Low cost residential therapeutic community households. Started 1965. No drop-in. Monthly lectures. Individual therapy £10-£25 per session. The houses are according to local DSS board and lodging (not expensive).They run a training in Psychotherapy. They offer Existential Psychotherapy, Psychoanalytic Therapy.

Photo-Language Workshop
PO Box 1328
London NW6. (081) 961 6714.
Practise photo-langauge technique which involves subjects looking at photos and working with how the subjects construe the photos. £45 per one day workshop. They offer Psychotherapy.

Playspace
Short Course Unit
Polytechnic Of Central London
35 Marylebone Road
Marylebone
London NW1 5LS. (071) 486 5811 ext 465.
Runs a variety of part time courses in counselling and psychotherapy. Weekend workshop typically £38. They offer Art Therapy, Dreamwork, Group Oriented Therapy, Psychodrama, Voice Therapy, Dance therapy, Feldenkrais.

Playworld
2 Melrose Gardens
New Malden
Surrey . (081) 949 5498
Workshops and events around the theme of finding oneself: creativity, mask-making, movement and rhythm etc. Various venues in London. £12 per whole day workshop. Concessions. They offer Psychotherapy.

Polarity Therapy Association
11 The Lea

LIST OF CENTRES

*Allesley Park
Coventry W1H 7PH. (0203)
670847.*
List of qualified practitioners. They
offer Polarity Therapy.

Portobello Green Fitness Centre
*3-5 Thorpe Close
North Kensington
London W10 5XL. (081) 960
2221.*
£15-£25 per hour. They offer Acupuncture, Aromatherapy, Massage,
Homoeopathy, Reflexology, Shiatsu.

Primal Integration Programme
*36 Womersley Road
Crouch End
London N8 9AN. (081) 341
7226.*
Offer group and individual work in
primal integration, on both a long
and a short term basis; information
and occasional publications on primal
integration. Three practitioners. £60
per weekend group, £24 per hour
individual sessions. Concessions in
special cases. They offer Primal Integration.

Primrose Healing Centre
*9 St George's Mews
Primrose Hill
London NW1 8XE. (071) 586
0148.*
They offer Counselling, Rebirthing,
Stress Management, Voice Therapy,
Acupuncture, Alexander Technique,
Aromatherapy, Bach Flower Rem-
edies, Diet Therapy, Hand Healing,
Herbalism, Massage, Naturopathy,
Osteopathy, Polarity Therapy,
Reflexology, Reiki, Shiatsu.

Private Health Centre
*37 Green Street
Forest Gate
London E7 8DA. (081) 472
0170.*
Herbal teas, remedies and herbal
shampoos are also sold here. X-ray
department and pathology laboratory. Prices vary between £12- 35
depending on the practitioner and
the treatment. They offer Acupuncture, Chiropody, Homoeopathy,
Massage, Osteopathy, Reflexology.

Private Polyclinic
*142 Green Street
Forest Gate*

London E7. (081) 472 0170.
There is a health shop at the centre
where remedies, minerals, vitamins,
books, joint and back supports etc
are sold. Monthly talks for doctors
where local GP's are invited plus
specialist for consultants in orthodox
medicine, X-ray department, path.
lab. Wheelchair access. £16-23 initial
consultation, £12-18 thereafter. They
offer Acupuncture, Ayurvedic Medicine, Chiropody, Herbalism, Homoeopathy, Massage, Osteopathy,
Yoga.

Psychosynthesis and Education Trust
*48 Guildford Road
Stockwell
London SW8 2BU. (071) 633
8295.*
Run public programme of courses on
various topics from a psychosynthesis
perspective (e.g. dreams, woman's
identity, relationship with money,
body etc). Also ongoing interpersonal
groups, lectures. Course on
psychosynthesis and education, and
a young adults group for those between the ages of 15 and 20. Counselling service. Professional training.
Mail order books and publications.
Sliding scale for one to one counselling, public weekends £50.They run
a training in Psychosynthesis. They
offer Psychosynthesis.

Psychotherapy for Individuals, Couples & Groups
*101 The Avenue
London N10. (081) 365 3951.*
They belong to the Spectrum incest
intervention project, working with
survivors and perpetrators. Established eight years. Work in North and
South London. £25-£30 for individual
work. £30-£60 for couples work. £65
for weekends. Concs. Use various
approaches as appropriate such as
visualisation, family sculpting, sensitivity awareness. They offer Assertion
Therapy, Bereavement Counselling,
Gestalt Therapy.

Psychotherapy Workshops for Women
*97 Warren Road
Whitton
Middlesex . (081) 755 0353.*
Groups for women: ongoing, weekend workshops, individual sessions
in London and Brighton. Weekend

workshops £50 including Friday evenings. Concessions. They offer
Feminist Therapy, Biodynamic Massage.

Putney Natural Therapy Clinic
*11 Monserat Road
Putney
London SW15. (081) 789 2548.*
Small friendly centre. Professional and
confidential consultation. You can
drop in (best between 9.30-3) for
information. Leaflet available or ring
for advice. Occasional workshops.
Wheelchair access. Between £20-30
per session. Chiropody £13 a session.
Concs. They offer Acupuncture,
Aromatherapy, Chiropody, Diet
Therapy, Herbalism, Homoeopathy,
Massage, Naturopathy, Osteopathy,
Reflexology, Shiatsu.

R

Radiance Education Unlimited
*24 Duncan House
7 Fellows Road
London NW3 3LS. (071) 586
2980.*
Established in England for 6 years.
Introductory talks and seminars,
books and tapes. Register. Reiki Session £25, seminar £110. Concessions
available. They offer Reiki.

Radix
*90 Viceroy Close
Edgbaston
Birmingham B5 7UU. (021)
440 6129.*
Radix is a form of neo-Reichian
bodywork which aims to help students learn to increase awareness of
their emotions, and reduce blocking
of life energy as it flows through the
body. Occasional workshops in
London, and can refer you to local
London practitioners. They offer Psychotherapy.

Raphael Clinic
*211 Sumatra Road
West Hampstead
London NW6 1PF. (071) 794
0321.*

LIST OF CENTRES

Holistic healing centre. Also weekend courses including meditation, massage, dance, personal mythology, healing etc. Float room on the premises. Weekend courses £69 plus VAT. They offer Hand Healing, Massage, Meditation, Acupuncture, Aromatherapy, Biodynamic Psychotherapy, Colonic Irrigation, Cranial Osteopathy, Diet Therapy, Homoeopathy, Naturopathy, Osteopathy, Polarity Therapy, Reflexology, Shiatsu, Flotation Tank Therapy, Neuro-linguistic Programming.

Re-Vision
8 Chatsworth Road
London NW2 4BN. (081) 451
2165.
Re-Vision is a small organisation started in 1988 offering psychosynthesis training courses to practising counsellors, therapists and others in the caring professions who are wanting to widen their perspective of work. In addition, run self-development workshops in psychosynthesis, and some other therapies (e.g. gestalt, Jungian etc). Open evenings, network of therapists available for individual, couple or family therapy, supervision for professionals, in-service consultancy or training offered to organisations within the caring professions. They run a training in Psychosynthesis. They offer Psychosynthesis.

Rebirthing Centre
Flat B
2 Wandsworth Common West Side
Wandsworth
London SW18 2EL. (081) 870 9284.
Rebirthing, also dreamwork, the inner child, goal setting, balancing the masculine/feminine polarities. Phone to make an appointment for a free introductory talk. Established for five years. Register of practitioners kept. £40 for an individual session which can last for two hours. Concs.

Redwood Women's Training Association
Invergary
Kitlings Lane
Walton-on-the-Hill
Stafford
ST17 0LE. (0785) 662823.
Founded in 1980 by Anne Dickson, this is the administrative office for a network of approximately 135 train-

ers. Can help individuals, groups or organisations find trainer. Send £3 for one year's subscription to bi-annual programme. Concs. - some trainers offer a sliding scale. £varies.They run a training in Assertion Therapy. They offer Anti-smoking Therapy, Assertion Therapy, Feminist Therapy, Sex Therapy, Voice Therapy.

Reflexology Centre
8 Russell Court
London Lane
Bromley
Kent BR1 4HX. (081) 464 9401.
They offer a training in Reflexology.

Refuah Shelaymah Natural Health Centre
42c Braydon Road
London
N16 6QB. (081) 800 2200
Established 1987. This is a self-contained one-storey building with a consulting room for bodywork, small groups and colon hydrotherapy and a small consulting room for counselling and reflexology. Wheelchair accessible. Telephone advice line of the Natural Health Network. Creche facilities a possibility. First half hour consultation is free. Full fee £25 first session, £18 subsequently. Concessions down to £5 for some therapies. Colon hydrotherapy £36. Telephone counselling and advice free. First half hour assessment free. They offer Counselling, Colonic Irrigation, Diet Therapy, Herbalism, Osteopathy, Polarity Therapy, Shiatsu, Rebirthing, Chiropractic.

Register of Qualified Aromatherapists
54a Gloucester Avenue
London NW1 8JD. (071) 272 7403.
The register is a professional association. They offer membership to aromatherapists who have undergone a high level of training. They have a list of practitioners for public referral and supply a list of recognised trainings to prospective students. They offer Aromatherapy.

Register of Traditional Chinese Medicine
19 Trinity Road
London N2 8JJ. (081) 883 8431.
Professional association for acupuncturists whose training and practice embody techniques of di-

agnosis and treatment used in the People's Republic of China. Directory of Practitioners £1.50.

Reiki Centre
12b Steels Road
Chalk Farm
London NW3 4SE. (071) 586 3363.
Aston Patterning. They offer Astrological Psychotherapy, Aston Patterning, Reiki.

Resonance
17 Station Terrace
Great Linford
Milton Keynes
Bucks MK14 5AP. (0908) 605931.
Encounter Gestalt Therapy Group Oriented Therapy and courses on humanistic psychotherapy. This is not a drop-in centre. Located in large premises in annexe used exclusively for therapy which is also rented out to local therapists. Established 12 years in the UK. Telephone or write for appointments in individual psychotherapy. Programme available (send SAE). They do training groups and talks etc. for groups of people working together. Consultancy service available. Supervision for practising counsellors/therapists. Wheelchair access. £18-£20 per hour for individual sessions. £30-£40 per day for non residential groups. £8 per evening for ongoing encounter group. They offer Encounter Therapy, Gestalt Therapy, Client-centered Therapy and courses on humanistic psychotherapy.

Richmond Natural Health Centre
New Road
Ham Common
Richmond,
Surrey TW10 7HYH. (081) 332 1751/2.
Above address is not a business address. Calls only taken and therapist goes to the clients home. They offer Complementary medicine.

RIGPA Fellowship
330 Caledonian Road
London N1 1BB. (071) 700 0185.
Tibetan Buddhist group under the direction of Ven. Lama Sogyal Rinpoche who visits the centre and gives lectures and seminars and leads retreats in Britain, France and Ger-

299

many. Courses are led by the Lama and eminent teachers of different traditions on topics such as meditation, developing compassion, healing, care for the dying and Buddhist view and philosophy. Bookshop. Centre open for meetings and by appointment. £3-£5 evening class. Concessions. They offer Buddhism, Meditation, Retreats.

Rolfing Centre
85 Judd St
London WC1. (071) 388 6567
or (071) 834 1493.
They offer Rolfing.

Royal London Homoeopathic Hospital
Gt. Ormond St
Bloomsbury
London WC1. 837 3091x72.
NHS Hospital. They offer Homoeopathy.

S

Satyananda Yoga Centre
70 Thurleigh Road
Wandsworth
London SW12. (081) 673 4869.
Guru is Swami Satyananda Saraswati of who set up the Bihar School of Yoga in 1963 and has now gone into seclusion. Director is Swami Pragyamurti Saraswati who teaches at the centre, all over the UK, Eire and France, and organises the yearly visit to ashram in India. Practice through yoga and teach asanas (postures), breathing practices, relaxation, meditation and yogic cleansing practices. Classes, courses and seminars. Children's yoga classes. Concessions available. They offer Yoga, Hinduism, Meditation.

Sayer Clinic
Marble Arch
22 Seymour Street
London W1. 723 2725.
Sports and dance injury clinic, gynaecology clinic, physiotherapy. £30 chiropractic treatment. £17-£40 for other various treatments. Will reduce fees if necessary, but this is up to the individual therapist. They offer Acupuncture, Chiropody, Chiropractic,

Homoeopathy, Massage, Osteopathy, Reflexology.

Sayer Clinic Covent Garden
12/13 Henrietta Street
London WC2E 8LH. 497 2741.
See Sayer Clinic Marble Arch clinic for details.

Sayer Clinic Kensington
8 Sunningdale Gardens
Stratford Road
London W8 6PX. (071) 937 8978.
See Sayer Clinic Marble Arch for details.

School of Complementary Medicine
9 Sharpleshall Street
Primrose Hill
London NW1 8YN. (071) 586 1263.
Teaches people to think. Chinese Acupuncture, Shiatsu , Acupressure, M massage, reflexology, touch for health, kineosiotherapies, herbalism, bach, nutrition, psychosomatic medicine, counselling skills, TA techniques, NLP, Principles of CM. Chi Kung exercises., anatomy and physiology. One training course includes all of these. Three and half years. Part time starting in Feb. 60 weekends total in all. £140 per months for 44 months. Course in Complementary Medicine. It's a course to become a general practitioner in the field of Complementary Medicine. They run a training in Complementary Medicine. They offer Acupuncture, Reflexology, Herbalism, Shiatsu, Touch for Health (Kinesiology).

School of Electro-Crystal Therapy
117 Long Drive
South Ruislip
Middlesex HA4 0HL. (081) 841 1716.
Electro-crystal therapy only. Established for 9 years. Lectures throughout UK and abroad. Books. Wheelchair access. £15 per hour for treatments. Concessions available. They offer Crystal Therapy.

School of Herbal Medicine
Bucksteep Manor
Bodle Street Green
Hailsham

East Sussex BN27 4RJ. (0892) 30400.
They offer a training in Herbalism.

School of Meditation
158 Holland Park Avenue
London W11 4UH. (071) 603 6116.
Frequent public meetings. Ring office for details and they will send you a booklet. Public meetings are 60p. To learn the meditation it costs one week's wages, though they will look at each case individually and are likely to make concessions. They offer Meditation.

School of Psychotherapy and Counselling
Regents College
Inner Circle
Regents Park
London NW1 4NS. (071) 487 7406.
They run a training in Counselling.

School of T'ai-chi Ch'uan - Centre for Healing
5 Tavistock Place
St. Pancras
London WC1H 9HH. (081) 444 6445.
Intuitive foot massage, personal guidance, talks, workshops. Founded by Beverley Milne, director Ghislaine Picchio. Spiritual school providing complete studies for inner unfoldment. Lending library of books and cassettes. Sell monographs, lecture cassettes, study papers. Workshops and Lectures. £7.50 per T'ai Chi class minimum. £15 per hour private session. Some concessions available. They run a training in Martial Arts. They offer Hand Healing, Martial Arts, Meditation.

School of the Dancing Dragon
115 Manor Road
London N16 5PB. (071) 275 8002
Massage is based on a combination of Swedish and intuitive massage and energy balancing. It is taught as a dance-like form. £15 - £30 per massage session. They run a training in Massage and Hand Healing. They offer Counselling, Hand Healing, Massage.

Serpent Institute
18 Mark Mansions

Westville Rd
London W12 9PS. (081) 743 8124.
Psychotherapy for individuals and couples. Some talks and workshops. Sliding scale. They run a training in Psychotherapy. They offer Counselling, Feminist Therapy.

Servants of the Light
PO Box 205
St Helier
Jersey, Channel Islands

Shanti Sadan
29 Chepstow Villas
Notting Hill Gate
London W11 3DR. (071) 727 7846.
'Shanti Sadan' is Sanskrit for 'Temple of Inner Peace', and it was founded in 1933 by Dr Hari Prasad Shastri, who died in 1956. It is his teachings which are carried on by his followers. These are on the philosophy and practice of Adhyatma Yoga, the yoga of self-knowledge, as taught in the ancient Indian classical texts, the Upanishads and Bhagavhad Gita, and adapted to modern life. Lectures on Weds and Fris at 8pm during term time. Publish over 30 books on yoga and related subjects. Also lectures at other venues in central London. Public lectures and meditation courses are free - there is a voluntary collection. They offer Yoga, Hinduism, Meditation.

Sheila Revell Centre
49 Ellora Road
Streatham
London SW16 6JG. (081) 677 4685.
They offer Hypnotherapy and Psychoanalytic Therapy. £30 per session. Course of treatment works out cheaper. Relaxation tapes for sale. Training available in Self hypnosis.

Shiatsu College
20a Lower Goat Lane
Norwich NR2 1EL. (0603) 632555.
Established 1985. Beginners classes held in London. They run a training in Shiatsu. They offer Shiatsu.

Shiatsu Society
14 Oakdene Road
Redhill
Surrey RH1 6BT. (0737) 767896.
Register of practitioners. Network organisation for everyone interested in Shiatsu. Quarterly newsletter. They offer Shiatsu.

Shirley Goldstein
30 Gloucester Crescent
Camden Town
London
NW1. (071) 267 2552.
American essences diagnosis. Also sell massage tables and angel cards. Various courses. £28 per treatment. Courses from £385. They run a training in Massage. They offer Counselling, Aromatherapy, Bach Flower Remedies, Hand Healing, Massage, Polarity Therapy.

Shirley Price Aromatherapy
Wesley House
Stockwell Head
Hinckley LE10 1RD. (0455) 615466.
They offer a training in Aromatherapy.

Silver Birch Centre
29 Chambers Lane
London NW10 2RJ. (081) 459 3028.
A centre for alternative medicine, healing and self development. Small and friendly, run from a private house. Run talks given by residential and visiting therapists and therefore extend beyond the therapies offered at the centre. Sessions vary from one to one and half hours and cost £25. Initial acupuncture session (up to two hours) £30. Concessions according to need, income and situation. They offer Acupuncture, Aromatherapy, Astrological Psychotherapy, Bach Flower Remedies, Counselling, Feldenkrais, Herbalism, Hand Healing, Massage, Reflexology, Stress Management, Voice Therapy, Yoga.

Skills with People
15 Liberia Road
Islington
London N5 1JP. (071) 359 2370 or (081) 368 3605.
Specialises in providing in-company training, and a wide range of interpersonal skills training. £30 - £40 a day for workshops They offer Counselling, Creativity, Group Oriented Therapy, Stress Management.

Society of Analytical Psychology
1 Daleham Gardens
Swiss Cottage
London NW3 5BY. (071) 435 7696.
Register. They offer Jungian Psychotherapy and relevant training.

Society for Existential Analysis
Regents College
Inner Circle, Regents Park
London NW1 4NS. (071) 487 7556.
They offer a training in Existential Psychotherapy.

Sound Health
261 Grove Street
Deptford
London SE8 3PZ. (081) 691 7519.
Voice work and singing as a therapeutic process; counselling with a humanistic and psychodynamic approach. Workshops. Action profile assessment of decision style. No access. Individual sessions £30. Concessions occasionally. They offer Voice Therapy.

Sound Moves
10 Jasmine Grove
Anerley
London SE20 8JW. (081) 960 6612.
Inner creativity through sound and movement. £30 per workshop. They offer Voice Therapy.

South Camden Women's Centre
90 Cromer St
London WC1. (071) 837 8774.
Drop-in courses on health and women's issues. An advice centre which operates a natural health clinic that runs courses and workshops. Sliding scale £8-£18 for an individual session. They offer Assertion Therapy, Alexander Technique, Aromatherapy, Hand Healing, Herbalism, Homoeopathy, Shiatsu, Acupuncture.

South London Hypnotherapy
Oaklands House
29 Oaklands Road
Bromley
Kent. (081) 460 7578.
£20 smoking session. (£2 extra at evening and weekends.), £18 per session for lack of confidence, de-

LIST OF CENTRES

pression etc. Also do past life regression. They offer Hypnotherapy.

South London Natural Health Centre
7A Clapham Common South Side
Clapham Common
London SW4 7AA. (071) 720 8817.
Very large centre, reception open to personal visits 9-9 Mon-Fri, 9.30-5.30 Sats. 4 years old. 30-35 practitioners. Drop in any time to browse, plenty of information on everything at the centre and other interesting connected local events, workshops etc. Half hour consultations available for people to find out about what is available and which therapy might be appropriate for them. Mail order super blue green algae, books, audio tapes, Bach flower remedies, aromatherapy oils, food supplements, flotation tanks also available. No wheelchair access, but will carry people and chairs upstairs. £15-35 for a session.
£42 for an introductory series of three floats. They run a training in Massage. They offer Counselling, Flotation Tank Therapy, Acupuncture, Alexander Technique, Aromatherapy, Chiropractic, Colonic Irrigation, Colour Therapy, Cranial Osteopathy, Diet Therapy, Feldenkrais, Herbalism, Homoeopathy, Massage, Naturopathy, Osteopathy, Reflexology, Shiatsu, Touch for Health (Kinesiology), Yoga.

South London Network for Counselling and Psychotherapy
51 Clyde Road
Wallington
Surrey SM6 8PZ. (081) 647 7659.
A network of therapists working from home and the Pellin Centre. Pellin contribution training, a mixture of existential, gestalt and cognitive material psychotherapy. Individual £15-35, couples £20-£50, groups £100-£150 per ten sessions. Concs. They offer Existential Psychotherapy, Gestalt Therapy.

South London Psychotherapy Centre
6 Owen Walk
Sycamore Grove
Anerley
London SE20 8BY. 659 8486.

Spectrum
7 Endymion Road
London N4 1EE. (081) 341 2277.
Established for 13 years, Spectrum offer a humanistic, eclectic approach to psychotherapy. There are 17 rooms and 25 therapists are involved. Drop-in evenings and seminars. Run an incest project which has charitable status, a sexual abuse and dysfunction programme. Run a standing conference on incest. Wheelchair access. Individual sessions £20-46, workshops approximately £15 per session. Concessions. They run a training in Psychotherapy and Counselling. They offer Bioenergetics, Couple Therapy, Encounter, Feminist Therapy, Gestalt Therapy, Psychodrama, Sex Therapy, Homoeopathy.

Spiral
93 Percy Road
Shepherds Bush
London W12 9QH. (081) 743 7246.
Spiral aims to empower the individual by applying the ancient arts of Chi Kung and Tai Chi, using breathing and movement meditations. They also are intended to help you discover the source of your inner strength (Chi) and find ways to express and direct the unified power of body mind and spirit. These methods can help deal with stress and increase assertiveness. All women are welcome regardless of age or abilities. Day workshops, intensives and six to twelve week courses. Runs workshops on empowerment for women. £Neg. They offer Martial Arts, Assertion Therapy, Counselling, Stress Management.

Spiritualist Association of Great Britain
33 Belgrave Square
London SW1X 8QL. (071) 235 3351.
Seminars, workshops, lectures and demonstrations of clairvoyance. Individual sessions with mediums, which the SAGB state are 'to provide evidence of survival (after death) and NOT to predict the future'. £12 per day workshop (£10 members), individual sessions with mediums £19 per hour (£16 members). No charge for spiritual healing, but voluntary donations accepted from those who can afford it. They offer Hand Healing, Spiritualism.

Splashdown Birth Pools
17 Wellington Terrace
Harrow-on-the-Hill
Middlesex HA1 3EP. (081) 422 9308.
Free information, advice and workshops on water birth. Hire waterbirth pools which can be used at NHS hospitals or home and can be sent anywhere in the UK. Run regular workshops and show videos of underwater birth. Carry a small stock of books. Their service is run from home where their baby was born underwater on 20th Jan 1989. Give talks and demonstrations to the public and to midwives, not only at above address, but also in central London Pool hire is £175 for four weeks. Workshops £7.50. They offer Active Birth.

Sri Aurobindo Circle (Ashram)
8 Sherwood Avenue
Streatham Vale
London SW16 5EW. (081) 679 0854.
Follow teachings of Sri Aurobindo and the Mother, and now under the direction of Dri M P Pandit. Central belief is in evolution of consciousness, which is seen as divine at its core. Evenings, weekends, study circle, working groups, collective meditation. They offer Yoga, Hinduism, Meditation.

St James's Centre for Health and Healing
197 Piccadilly
London W1V 9LF. (071) 287 6711.
Psychotherapy, self-care, therapies and support groups. Cancer support. Individual sessions approximately £20 per hour. Concessions. Cancer support group free. Free clinics twice a month. They offer Art Therapy, Counselling, Relaxation Training, Stress Management, Acupuncture, Hand Healing, Herbalism, Osteopathy, Meditation.

St. Marylebone Healing and Counselling Centre
St. Marylebone Parish Church
17 Marylebone Road
London NW1 5LT. (071) 935 6374.

There is both a pastoral centre here and a medical centre. The pastoral centre was opened in 1987 and has a drop-in and referral system for counselling and befriending. It is situated in the restored crypt of St. Marylebone Church and has six counselling rooms, a small hall and a teaching room.

The medical centre is an NHS general practice which also provides osteopathy, acupuncture, massage, homoeopathy etc. for NHS patients registered with the practice. Sadly for those not living within the catchment area, this is only for locals. Let's hope however that this is the shape of things to come, and that more people will be able to be referred for complementary treatments on the premises by their GP. Free. Donation for counselling. They offer Counselling.

Stress Centre
60 Downside Road
Sutton
Surrey SM2 5HP. 642 7064.

Studio 8
10 Wycliffe Row
Totterdown
Bristol BS3 4RU. (0272)
713488.
Not so much therapeutic in orientation, more an exploration of creativity and imagination through art in weekend and residential format. See 'residential workshops' section. They offer Art Therapy.

Studio E
49 The Avenue
London NW6 7NR. (081) 459 5442.
Weekend workshops on myth, expression painting, inner dance etc. Tai chi weekly classes. Individual psychotherapy sessions. £30-42 per weekend. Concs. They offer Transpersonal therapy, Martial Arts, Meditation.

Subud Central London
50 Shirland Road
London W9 2JA. (071) 286 3137.

Sunnyholt Natural Health Centre
120 The Vale
London W3 7RQ. (081) 746 0499.
Centre for complementary medicine. Currently have 37 therapists working

at the centre. £varies with practitioner. They offer Biodynamic Psychotherapy, Aromatherapy, Acupuncture, Osteopathy, Naturopathy, Reflexology.

Sunra
26 Balham Hill
Clapham South
London SW12 9EB. (081) 675 9224.
From £3.20 per yoga class. Treatments from £20. Full membership of centre is £200 which gives unlimited use of sauna and jacuzzi. Classes and therapy do not require membership. Day membership for sauna and jacuzzi.They run a training in Massage. They offer Counselling, Mind Clearing, Rebirthing, Acupuncture, Aromatherapy, Homoeopathy, Martial Arts, Massage, Oriental and Chinese Medicine, Osteopathy, Reflexology, Shiatsu, Yoga, Meditation plus Tarot, compulsive eating therapy, sauna and jacuzzi (electron purified water).

Synthesis of Light Holidays (SOL)
112 Wood Vue
Spennymoor
Co Durham DL16 6RZ. (0388) 818151.
They offer a training in teaching Yoga as well as holidays.

Tavistock Clinic
120 Belsize Lane
Swiss Cottage
London NW3 5BA. (071) 435 7111.
Refer to brochure. They run a training in Family Therapy and Group Oriented Therapy and Psychoanalytic Therapy. They offer Family Therapy, Group Oriented Therapy, Kleinian Analysis, Psychoanalytic Therapy.

Teach Yourself Meditation
BCM ACT
London WC1N 3XX.

They offer Meditation.

Teilhard Centre
23 Kensington Square
London W8 5HN. (071) 937 5372.
A small educational charity, linked with others in Europe and the United States which share an interest in Teilhard de Chardin's evolutionary cosmology and its relation to the human future on earth. Small groups meet regularly, and annual weekend conference, annual lecture and occasional day conferences are held. Publish Teihard Review, Journal for Cosmic Convergence, three times yearly. Membership of £15 (unwaged £10) and they keep the costs of conferences etc. low. For small groups they ask for donations to cover costs.

Thames & Ganges Trading Co
94 Leonard Road
London SE20. (071) 631 4106.
Treatment with herbs (often Indian and Pakistan herbs). Appointment necessary. Open 5-8pm Mon, Tue, Wed and Sat. £vary. They offer Herbalism.

Theosophical Society
50 Gloucester Place
London W1H 3HJ. (071) 935 9261.
Public lectures on spirituality Vary from free lectures with collection to £5-£12 for day events. Cheaper for members and low waged.

Therapy Made Unique
21 Primrose Road
South Woodford
London E18 1DD. (081) 989 3510.
Aromatherapy for arthritic ailments and sports injuries. Specialists in homoeopathy for children's illnesses. Workshops on how to use Bach flower remedies, nutrition, and on the last Saturday of every month, pendulum dowsing to help maintain good health. £10-18 depending on status and treatment. Concessions for children and pensioners, £12 half massage, £18 reflexology and homoeopathy, £20 for full aromatherapy message. They offer Aromatherapy, Bach Flower Remedies, Diet Therapy, Homoeopathy, Reflexology.

Throssel Hole Priory
Carrshedd

Hexham
Northumberland NE47 8AL.
(0434) 345204.
Soto Zen Buddhist retreat centre and monastery in Northumberland affiliated with Shasta Abbey whose spiritual director/abbess is Rev. Master Jiyu-Kennett. Throssel Hole Priory is run by Rev. Master Daishin Morgan, one of her senior disciples, who lectures regularly there. Bookshop, tour of monastery, meditation instruction by appointment. Donation requested for all retreats. They offer Buddhism, Retreats.

Tibet Foundation
43 New Oxford Street
London WC1A 1BH. (071) 379 0634.
Registered charity aiming to increase understanding of Tibetan Buddhism and culture, including language and history. Information on Tibetan medicine. The Foundation runs seminars with Tibetan physicians who visit four times a year, with whom consultations are also available. Promotes Tibetan culture and events in the UK. £20 for initial consultation, £12 thereafter. Concs. They offer Tibetan Medicine.

Time to Unwind
20 Bevile House
Grays
Essex RM17 6RR. (0375) 376827.
Office address only. Workshops take place at different venues in London, individual sessions held at various locations around Grays in Essex. Massage which incorporates Swedish, intuitive and Shiatsu approaches. £35-£45 per one day workshop. They offer Massage.

Tisserand Institute
Linkline House
65 Church Road
Hove
East Sussex BN3 2BD. (0273) 206640.
Weekend courses. Introductory courses held at Kensington Park Hotel in London. £86 incl VAT per weekend. They run a training in Aromatherapy. They offer Aromatherapy.

Tobias School of Art
Coombe Hill Road
East Grinstead

Sussex RH19 4LZ. (0342) 313655.
The centre is on a rural campus with student accommodation. Summer courses (July/August). Weekend courses during school year. Lectures. They offer Art Therapy (plus relevant training) and Creativity Therapy.

Traditional Chinese Medicine Clinic
10 Sandown Way
Northolt
Middx UB5 4HY. (081) 743 0706.
Specialise in treating gynaecological problems and cancer patients that cannot be treated by orthodox medicine. Appointment only. Patients are seen by Dr Hsu who also tries to prevent the side effects of western drugs on cancer patients. Children's problems also treated. First visit £55, subsequent visits £35. Unemployed and low waged get up to 25% discount. They run a training in Acupuncture and Herbalism and offer Acupuncture, Diet Therapy and Herbalism treatments.

Transcendental Meditation
Freepost
London SW1P 4YY. (0800) 269303.
Centres countrywide. Three residential and seventy non-residential. One community. They offer Meditation.

Transcendental Meditation Baker Street Centre
24 Linhope Street
Marylebone
London NW1 6TH. (071) 402 3451.
Run courses on transcendental meditation. Free introductory presentations, phone for details. Cost of instruction is £180 per course fee. Concs. They offer Meditation.

Transcendental Meditation National Office
Mentmore Towers
Mentmore
Leighton Buzzard
LU7 0QH.
Can put you in touch with your local TM centre. They offer Meditation.

Trinity Hospice
30 Clapham North Side
London SW4 0RN. (071) 622 9481.

Has cared for those suffering from advanced cancer and other illnesses for the last 100 years. If you cannot get bereavement counselling from your present community then this hospice will see you for bereavement counselling free of charge. They offer Bereavement Counselling.

Tyers St. Centre
121 Tyers St
London SE11 5HS. (071) 820 0580.
Two therapy rooms, garden, reception, large meeting/seminar/workshop room, catering facilities in beautifully restored house. £10-£15. Concs by individual therapists. They offer Acupuncture, Aromatherapy, Herbalism, Homoeopathy, Massage, Yoga.

U

UK Training College of Hypnotherapy and Counselling
10 Alexander Street
Bayswater
London W2 5NT. (071) 221 1796.
They run a training in Hypnotherapy. They offer Counselling, Hypnotherapy, Assertion Therapy, Stress Management.

Universal Training
35 Tempo House
15 Falcon Road
London SW11 2PJ. (071) 351 7437.
Courses in personal development which include meditation, body language training, affirmations plus own brand of self exploration. Format for core course, Turning Points, is one weekend plus three evening. £250 plus VAT. They offer Psychotherapy.

Universitas Associates
5 Cedar Road
Sutton
Surrey SM2 5DA. (081) 643 4898.
A group of professionals who help people to discover their full potential and purpose in life. Individual consultation, training and seminars are

offered. £30–£60 per hour. They offer Stress Management, Hand Healing, Creativity, Art Therapy, Soul directed therapy and Soul directed astrology.

Welbeck Counselling Service

5 Clarkes Mews
Marylebone
London W1N 1RR. (071) 935 3073.
Humanistic counselling encompassing Rogerian, Egan, Gestalt and Transactional Analysis, as well as behavioural therapy and career counselling. Two consulting rooms. A number of the staff are chartered psychologists. Run open training events programme. Space to rent occasionally. Personal counselling £38, couples £45 including VAT. Career counselling only £75 per hour, stress management £65 per hour. They offer Counselling, Sex Therapy, Stress Management.

Wellspring Clinic

56 New King's Road
London SW6 4LF. (071) 736 3367.
Radionic hair analysis, vitamin assessments, detoxification programmes, skin treatments, energy medicine, herbal tonics. Established since 1987, 5 therapy rooms in a Victorian House. Sell vitamins, herbal remedies, skin care products. Colonics £40.25. Aromatherapy £30 for one and a half hours. Acupuncture £25. Hair analysis £34.50. Cellulite treatments £300 plus VAT for 6. Counselling £30 for 1 hour. They offer Counselling, Acupuncture, Aromatherapy, Chiropractic, Colonic Irrigation, Massage, Osteopathy, Radionics, Reflexology.

West London Buddhist Centre

7 Colville Houses
Talbot Road
Westbourne Park
London W11 1JB. (071) 727 0784.
A centre affiliated to the Friends of the Western Buddhist Order (see also London Buddhist Centre) founded by an Englishman, the Ven. Sangharakshita who spent 20 years in India studying Buddhism. Small centre which consists of two floors of a Georgian terrace staffed by volunteers. Evening classes, weekends, courses and retreats in Sussex and Suffolk. Residential communities (not at centre but nearby). Run wholefood shop, Friends Foods. Bookshop and practice rooms at centre, open for drop-in. Weekly drop in classes £3 per evening (£1.75 concessions). 5 week courses £30 (£20 concessions). Weekend retreats £35 (£25 concessions).They run a training in Massage. They offer Massage, Yoga, Buddhism, Meditation, Retreats.

West London School of Therapeutic Massage

42 Leinster Square
London W11 1DD. (071) 229 7411.
They run a training in Massage and Reflexology. They offer Aromatherapy, Massage, Massage, Reflexology, Shiatsu.

Westminster Natural Health Centre

43a Warwick Way
London SW1V 1QS. (071) 834 0861.
Open for drop-in information 9.30–4.30. Established in 1987, this natural health centre won the Journal of Alternative and Complementary Medicine's 'Practice of the Year' award in 1988 and 1989. There are 7 consulting rooms and 25 qualified practitioners who are also insured. Small reading room. Access: one set of stairs up to ground floor. Range £18–£30. Concessions. They offer Counselling, Acupuncture, Alexander Technique, Aromatherapy, Biodynamic Massage, Chiropractic, Herbalism, Massage, Naturopathy, Osteopathy, Reflexology, Shiatsu, Yoga.

Westminster Pastoral Foundation

23 Kensington Square
Kensington
London W8 5HN. (071) 937 6956.
A national organisation with headquarters at Kensington, affiliated centres in different parts of the country. Short courses on aspects of counselling and spirituality. Individual and group sessions. They run a training in Counselling and Group Oriented Therapy. They offer Bereavement Counselling, Counselling, Family Therapy.

White Eagle Lodge

9 St. Mary Abbots Place
Kensington High Street
London W8 6LS. (071) 603 7914.
Services of worship, healing, meditation and prayer for 'sending out the light'. Meetings at above address, also open for drop-in 2–5.30, Mon–Thurs. Bookshop, library, chapel for meditation. Two years service as an absent healer is required before training in contact healing. They offer Hand Healing, Yoga, Meditation.

Whole Brain Learning Ltd

266-268 Haydons Road
Wimbledon
London SW19 . (081) 543 3412.
Aims to increase intellectual performance. Provide books, cassettes and brain wave machines. They offer Psychotherapy.

Wholeness

26 Mulberry Way
South Woodford
London E18 1ED. (081) 530 8804.
This husband and wife team have been established for 3 years at this address. Mail order. Sell books and products. Wheelchair access. £25 for colonic irrigation, £20 for psychotherapy. Concessions available. They offer Neuro-linguistic Programming, Colonic Irrigation, Hypnotherapy.

Wholistic Health and Life Extension

290 Hanworth Road
Hampton
Middlesex TW12 3EP. (081) 979 7841.
Workshops on use of crystals and gems in healing. Also electronic gem therapy, dowsing and assemblance point shifting. £15–£30. Two day workshop £20–£60. They offer Crystal Therapy, Aromatherapy.

Wholistic Health Centre

1 Upland Road
South Croydon
Surrey CR2 6RD. (081) 681 8665.
The centre has been established since 1983 and is based on the holistic

LIST OF CENTRES

approach to health. Three quarters of an hour from Victoria station and it's a 'very dynamic' centre. They give talks, organise open days and participate in the local fairs. Sliding scale. A free fifteen minute 'chat' is available by appointment.
First diagnosis around £22. First treatment between £15 and £20. They offer Acupuncture, Aromatherapy, Bach Flower Remedies, Diet Therapy, Iridology, Laser Therapy, Macrobiotics, Osteopathy, Shiatsu.

Wild Goose Company
65 Roderick Road
London NW3 2NP. (071) 482 5502.
Provide a place in which people can experience energy work and other meditations. Most of the work is in groups; £2 per evening, £10 per day (apart from larger workshops). Videos and talks on energy work. They offer Massage, Meditation.

Will (Workshop Institute for Living Learning)
218 Randolph Avenue
London W9. (071) 328 8955.
They practise 'theme-centred interaction' which is a group dynamic method based on the belief that thought and feeling should not be separated and that every group member has equal rights. £40 per weekend workshop. They offer Group Oriented Therapy.

Wilson Associates
174 Franciscan Road
London SW17 8HH. (081) 767 6756.
Run 'Being Brilliant' course which aims to uncover inner talent and ability. 6 sessions of 90 minutes each £175. They offer Psychotherapy.

Wimbledon Clinic of Natural Medicine
1 Evelyn Road
Wimbledon
London SW19 8NU. (081) 540 3389.
EAV diagnosis, allergy testing and desensitisation, ozone therapy, bioenergetic medicine, sports injury clinic, psychotherapy. Large centre with up to date equipment for diagnosis and treatment, which has been established for 10 years. Open days, mail order water filters, equipment. Wheelchair access. From £10-50. They offer Counselling, Acupuncture,

Alexander Technique, Allergy Therapy, Aromatherapy, Colonic Irrigation, Laser Therapy, Massage, Osteopathy, Reflexology.

Women and Health
4 Carol St
London NW1 0HU. (071) 482 2786.
Women only health centre for all women who work or live in the borough of Camden. Student practitioners offer free treatment to women on low income. Most therapies £5-£15 (sliding scale). Classes £2-£2.50. They offer Counselling, Alexander Technique, Acupuncture, Aromatherapy, Herbalism, Homoeopathy, Massage, Osteopathy, Shiatsu, Reflexology.

Women Unlimited
79 Pathfield Road
London SW16 5PA. (081) 677 7503.
Consultancy work and group work offered to organisations who want their staff to get more out of their personal and working lives. Run a counselling skills course, covering listening and awareness techniques with opportunity for participants to work on their own personal development. £20-£30 for individual sessions, £70 for a two day course. They offer Assertion Therapy, Feminist Therapy, Stress Management.

Women's Natural Health Centre
1 Hillside
Highgate Road
London NW5 1QT. (071) 482 3293.
Run by a group of professionally qualified women offering alternative therapies to women and children. Mon-Fri 9-6. Established 1983. Appointment needed. For women and their children on a low income only. Access for wheelchairs limited though they can do home visits. £10 per session. They offer Counselling, Acupuncture, Hand Healing, Herbalism, Massage, Osteopathy, Reflexology.

Women's Therapy Centre
6 Manor Gardens
Holloway
London N7 6LA. (071) 263 6200.
Workshops and therapy given by women for women. Also workshops for black women, women with dis-

abilities, lesbians. Established for 14 years. Advice and information, referral to private therapy network. Sells books. The Women's Therapy Centre always needs volunteers, and is also currently looking for funding. Sliding scale for workshops and therapy. Very low fees available for unemployed. They run a training in Feminist Therapy. They offer Art Therapy, Assertion Therapy, Bioenergetics, Eating Problem Therapy, Feminist Therapy, Psychoanalytic Therapy, Sex Therapy, Stress Management, Massage.

Wood Street Clinic
133 Wood Street
Barnet
Herts
EN5 4BX. (081) 441 0231/449 7656.
Marriage guidance, psychotherapy, chiropody. Owned and run by Mr Mervyn D Cole. Consultation service for those unsure of which therapy to choose (for a fee). Appointments always needed. Established 1984. Prices vary with each type of therapy, but on average it is £16-£45 They offer Counselling, Acupuncture, Alexander Technique, Aromatherapy, Chiropractic, Herbalism, Homoeopathy, Massage, Osteopathy, Reflexology.

Working With Men
St. Giles Hospital
St Giles Road
London SE5 7RN. (071) 703 8780 & (081) 664 6196.
They offer Men's Therapy.

Workshops with a Difference
19 Fourth Cross Road
Twickenham
London TW2 5EL. (081) 894 5980.
Motivational workshops in groups and one to one work with individuals wishing to move into their vision through accessing their higher consciousness. Workshops take place in different venues -health clubs and centres mostly. One to one work in Twickenham or the client's own homes. Lending library of Lazaris material for clients and rental service for the general public. Wheelchair

306

access. Sample: 2 day workshop £75. They offer Psychotherapy.

Per week £210. Membership £10 per annum, £15 families. They offer Yoga.

Y

Z

Yoga Culture and Therapy Foundation
Flat G
22 Montague St
London WC1B 5BH. (081) 451 2783.
Yoga therapy is specifically aimed at curing disease, through postures, breathing, cleansing through exercises, diet, massage. Can put people in touch with yoga teachers. Yoga weekends. Will be starting a Yoga Therapy training course in 1991. Individual session costs vary depending on individual practitioners £20 per session average. They offer Yoga.

Yoga Dham
67 Pinner Park Ave
North Harrow
Middlesex HA2 6JY. (081) 428 6691/9402.
Individual and group yoga classes, also weekends. Unique yoga videos and audio cassettes sold. Large, clean premises. From £20-£42. Concessions to old age pensioners and students. They offer Yoga, Aromatherapy, Bach Flower Remedies, Reflexology.

Yoga for Health Foundation
Ickwell Bury
Ickwell Green
Nr Biggleswade
Bedfordshire SG18 9EF. (0767) 27271.
Massage and reflexology also available. Established 1978, this is a primarily residential, generally short stay (one/two weeks) centre. Day and overnight guests also welcome. Please notify in advance of day visits. Centre takes 25 guests residentially. Set in four acres of grounds. Books and tapes available by mail order. Special conferences and seminars during the year, as well as concerts. Family festival every August. Wheelchair access. Must be a member to stay. Per day (full board, yoga sessions and activities) £33. Weekends £59.50.

Ziva Belic Aromatherapy International School
20 Darwin Road
South Ealing
London W5 4BD. (081) 568 0415.
Established 6 years. Video available, aromatherapy and essential oils sold. Register. Model clients often required for trainees, so phone early mornings for this free treatment. Talks on aromatherapy given. £20 for individual sessions. They run a training in Aromatherapy. They offer Aromatherapy, Reflexology,

Index of Advertisers

About the publishers of this book
Brainwave: Serving Holistic Business

Brainwave

Who are we? Brainwave is a publisher and marketing specialist serving the Holistic health/New Age field. We serve publishers of books, audio and visual tapes, product suppliers and holistic health centres.

What do we do? Brainwave's activities cover two areas.

Resources include a comprehensive trade directory *The Brainwave Marketing Book*, essential for any business in the holistic health/New Age field. We also publish two other guides, *Holistic London* and *The Whole Person Catalogue* which aim to connect the interested public with holistic organisations. We can list your organisation, if appropriate for free in one or more of our guidebooks.

Services We offer a range of mailing lists, co-operative mailings and marketing packages.

What do we offer you? Affordable, quality marketing research, resources and services assisting holistic health/ New Age organisations to successfully reach this speciality market. Time saving research can save you years of information gathering, allowing you to easily make business connections. Think of us as your second marketing department which just happens to be in London.

> Mailing Lists
> Co-operative Mailings
> Marketing Packages
> Trade Directory (UK)
> Trade Directory (USA)
> Guidebooks (UK)

Mailing Lists

If you need to send your brochure/leaflet to individuals or organisations in the holistic health/ New Age field, we have a range of mailing lists on offer. Also, if you wish to mail out to particular organisations in this book we can supply the labels. Our laser printed address labels are high quality at a very affordable price.

Co-operative Mailings

We mail out on a regular basis to individuals and businesses in the holistic health/New Age field. If you wish to reach this specialist market we can include your brochure/leaflet in our mailings. This is a cost effective way to promote yourself. You simply supply the leaflets and we take care of the rest. We have regular mailouts to *retailers, holistic health centres* and *core advertisers* as well as extensive lists of the interested public.

Marketing Packages

We supply marketing packages. Each package enables you to easily reach your chosen target group. Each package contains a set of labels and a description of each organisation on the label. Simply read the information we supply on an organisation, and if they are someone you wish to reach, then stick the appropriate label on to the envelope containing your book/product/press release/brochure etc and post. Some packages we offer are *Reviewers Package, Press Release Package, Exhibitions Package, Core Advertisers Package, Publications Package, Submissions Package.* The *Reviewers Package* is handy for publishers, audio and visual producers, and product suppliers who wish to promote their new book, product etc. The *Press Release Package* is useful for anyone wishes to mail off their press release, (we supply details of specialist and national press). The *Exhibitions Package* consists of details of exhibitions so that you can plan ahead. The *Core Advertisers Package* consists of advertisers that advertise regularly in the MBS/New Age press; useful for those who wish to get advertising for their publication. The Submissions Package is for authors wishing to get their work published.

Trade Directory (UK)

We publish this book *The Brainwave Marketing Book,* the *only* business directory to the holistic health/ New Age field. Comprehensive and detailed listings which helps you make those essential business connections.

Trade Directory (USA)

Brainwave are agents for 'First Editions' a publishing company in the USA that produces a trade directory for the holistic health/New Age field. Our own trade directory is based on their excellent guide to the USA New Age marketplace. We have both volumes of this directory for sale.

Guidebooks

We publish two guidebooks aimed at the public who are interested in the holistic health/New Age field. *Holistic London,* now in it's third edition is packed with information on psychotherapy, alternative medicine and spiritual centres in the capital, as well as a list of resources including bookshops, products etc. It's an easy to use guidebook which has stood the test of time and is the only book of it's kind for London. *The Whole Person Catalogue* is new and is destined to be the definitive nationwide guide to this growing field.

(071) 733 7883 or (071) 978 9062
BCM Raft, London WC1N 3XX
serving holistic business